Linguistic Practic

Changing Condit

ENCOUNTERS

Series Editors: **Ana Deumert**, *University of Cape Town, South Africa*, **Zane Goebel**, *University of Queensland, Australia* and **Anna De Fina**, *Georgetown University, USA*

The Encounters series sets out to explore diversity in language from a theoretical and an applied perspective. So the focus is both on the linguistic encounters, inequalities and struggles that characterise post-modern societies and on the development, within sociocultural linguistics, of theoretical instruments to explain them. The series welcomes work dealing with such topics as heterogeneity, mixing, creolization, bricolage, crossover phenomena, polylingual and polycultural practices. Another high-priority area of study is the investigation of processes through which linguistic resources are negotiated, appropriated and controlled, and the mechanisms leading to the creation and maintenance of sociocultural differences. The series welcomes ethnographically oriented work in which contexts of communication are investigated rather than assumed, as well as research that shows a clear commitment to close analysis of local meaning making processes and the semiotic organisation of texts.

All books in this series are externally peer-reviewed.

Full details of all the books in this series and of all our other publications can be found on http://www.multilingual-matters.com, or by writing to Multilingual Matters, St Nicholas House, 31–34 High Street, Bristol BS1 2AW, UK.

ENCOUNTERS: 21

Linguistic Practice in Changing Conditions

Ben Rampton

with Constadina Charalambous, Panayiota Charalambous, Melanie Cooke, Louise Eley, Roxy Harris, Sam Holmes, Kamran Khan, Janet Maybin and Celia Roberts

MULTILINGUAL MATTERS
Bristol • Blue Ridge Summit

DOI https://doi.org/10.21832/RAMPTO9998
Library of Congress Cataloging in Publication Data
A catalog record for this book is available from the Library of Congress.
Names: Rampton, Ben, author.
Title: Linguistic Practice in Changing Conditions/Ben Rampton.
Description: Bristol, UK; Blue Ridge Summit: Multilingual Matters, 2021. | Series: Encounters: 21 | Includes bibliographical references and index. | Summary: "This book draws on 10 years of collaborative sociolinguistic work on the changing conditions of language use. It begins with guiding principles, shifts to empirically driven arguments in urban sociolinguistics, and concludes with studies of (in)securitised communication addressed to challenges ahead"— Provided by publisher.
Identifiers: LCCN 2021027804 (print) | LCCN 2021027805 (ebook) | ISBN 9781788929981 (paperback) | ISBN 9781788929998 (hardback) | ISBN 9781800410008 (pdf) | ISBN 9781800410015 (epub)
Subjects: LCSH: Sociolinguistics. | Anthropological linguistics.
Classification: LCC P40 .R355 2021 (print) | LCC P40 (ebook) | DDC 306.44—dc23 LC record available at https://lccn.loc.gov/2021027804
LC ebook record available at https://lccn.loc.gov/2021027805

British Library Cataloguing in Publication Data
A catalogue entry for this book is available from the British Library.

ISBN-13: 978-1-78892-999-8 (hbk)
ISBN-13: 978-1-78892-998-1 (pbk)

Multilingual Matters
UK: St Nicholas House, 31–34 High Street, Bristol BS1 2AW, UK.
USA: NBN, Blue Ridge Summit, PA, USA.

Website: www.multilingual-matters.com
Twitter: Multi_Ling_Mat
Facebook: https://www.facebook.com/multilingualmatters
Blog: www.channelviewpublications.wordpress.com

The policy of Multilingual Matters/Channel View Publications is to use papers that are natural, renewable and recyclable products, made from wood grown in sustainable forests. In the manufacturing process of our books, and to further support our policy, preference is given to printers that have FSC and PEFC Chain of Custody certification. The FSC and/or PEFC logos will appear on those books where full certification has been granted to the printer concerned.

Typeset by Nova Techset Private Limited, Bengaluru and Chennai, India.
Printed and bound in the UK by Short Run Press Ltd.

To my two colleagues, friends and teachers
Jan Blommaert and Roxy Harris

Contents

Acknowledgements

Although there are adjustments and quite substantial revisions in some chapters, most of the material in this book has been published between 2009 and the present, and I am grateful to the publishers for permission to reuse it:

- Chapter 2 was published as 'Interactional sociolinguistics' in K. Tusting (ed.) (2020) *The Routledge Handbook of Linguistic Ethnography* (pp. 13–27). London: Routledge.
- Chapter 3 was published as 'Theory and method in linguistic ethnography' in J. Snell, S. Shaw and F. Copland (eds) (2015) *Linguistic Ethnography: Interdisciplinary Explorations* (pp. 14–50). Palgrave Advances. Houndmills: Palgrave Macmillan.
- Chapter 4 was published as 'Sociolinguistic citizenship' in *Journal of Social Science Education* (2018) 17 (4).
- Chapter 5 was published as 'Ethnicities without guarantees: An empirical approach' in M. Wetherell (ed.) (2009) *Identity in the 21st Century: New Trends in Changing Times* (pp. 95–119). Basingstoke: Palgrave Macmillan.
- Chapter 6 was published as 'Style contrasts, migration and social class' in *Journal of Pragmatics* (Elsevier) (2011) 43, 1236–1250.
- Chapter 7 was published as 'From "multi-ethnic adolescent heteroglossia" to contemporary urban vernaculars' in *Language & Communication* (Elsevier) (2011) 31, 276–294.
- Chapter 8 was published as 'Styling in a language learned later in life' in *Modern Language Journal* (2013) 97 (2), 360–382.
- Chapter 9 was published as 'Security and language policy' in J. Tollefson and M. Perez-Milans (eds) (2018) *Oxford Handbook of Language Policy and Planning* (pp. 633–653). Oxford: Oxford University Press.
- Chapter 10 was published as 'Crossing of a different kind' in *Language in Society* (Cambridge University Press) (2019) 48 (5), 629–655.

- Chapter 11 was published as 'Everyday surveillance, Goffman, and unfocused interaction' in *Surveillance and Society* (2020) 18 (2), 119–215.
- The Afterword was published as 'Jan Blommaert and the use of socio-linguistics: Critical, political, personal' in *Language in Society* (2021) 50 (3) (Cambridge University Press).

I would also like to record my thanks to the funding bodies that have supported a lot of the research on which these chapters are based: The Leverhulme Trust (RPG-2012-477; RPG-2015-279); The Economic & Social Research Council (R-000-23-6602; RES-035-25-0003; RES-062-23-0604); The British Academy (SG160630).

The book owes a great deal to the people with whom it has been my pleasure and privilege to work as co-authors and collaborators: Constadina Charalambous, Panayiota Charalambous, Melanie Cooke, Louise Eley, Roxy Harris, Sam Holmes, Kamran Khan, Janet Maybin and Celia Roberts; Jeff Bezemer, Didier Bigo, Jan Blommaert, Dermot Bryers, Zannie Bock, Alexandra Georgakopoulou, Carey Jewitt, Adam Lefstein, Constant Leung, Emma Mc Cluskey, Miguel Pérez Milans, Lavanya Sankaran, Devyani Sharma, Lauren Small, Julia Snell, Chris Stroud, Becky Winstanley. Generated over more than a decade, the writing of this book hasn't been particularly intense or reclusive, and this magnifies beyond description my debt to Amelia's companionship.

Transcription Conventions

Fonts Used to Represent Specific Speech Styles

(for further uses of fonts to represent different speech styles, see the keys in specific chapters)

text	speech with more distinctly Creole pronunciation
text	speech with more distinctly Punjabi pronunciation
TEXT	speech with more distinctly RP/standard pronunciation
text	speech with more distinctly vernacular London pronunciation
`text`	speech which is less marked as distinctively Creole, Punjabi, RP or vernacular London (`Courier New`)

Segmental Phonology

[ ]	IPA phonetic transcription

Prosody

\text	low fall
/text	low rise
\text	high fall
/text	high rise
˅text	fall rise
^text	rise fall
ˈtext	high stress
ˈˈtext	very high stress
ˌtext	low stress
ˌˌtext	very low stress

Conversational features

(.)	pause of less than a second
(1.5)	approximate length of pause in seconds
[[	overlapping turns
TEXT	capitals indicate loudness
>text<	more rapid speech
°text°	quietly spoken
.hh	in-breath
"text"	direct reported speech
( )	speech inaudible
(text)	speech hard to discern, analyst's guess
((text:))	'stage directions'

1 Introduction: Linguistic Practice in Changing Conditions

This book belongs to a tradition of research that examines social change through the prism of everyday communicative practice. It is anchored in the foundational work of John Gumperz and Dell Hymes in the 1970s and 1980s. It discusses the relevance of this tradition in a range of practical spheres (especially but not only education), and it elaborates the tradition in interdisciplinary encounters that focus both on well-established and on more recent issues: migration, race/ethnicity and social class, as well as citizenship, conviviality, surveillance and insecurity.

The discussion is carried forward in a collection of sociolinguistic papers that address:

(a) the development of theory and methodology in a space between linguistic anthropology and applied linguistics, combining frameworks from the former with the practical goals of the latter, holding to an ethnographic epistemology throughout (Part 1; Afterword);
(b) informal linguistic practices in multi-ethnic urban settings, reflecting on their significance and their development in Britain over nearly half a century (Part 2);
(c) growing fear and (in)securitisation in everyday life, exploring some of the implications for the theory and practice of sociolinguistics (Part 3).

Most of the book involves the interplay of theory, method and empirical data conventional in research studies. But universities are social institutions, and as well as doing research, academics teach students, collaborate with colleagues, organise activities and networks and interact with ordinary people. These experiences also shape their sense of the value, purpose and direction of the research they undertake, thinking beyond questions of coherence and rigour (essential though these remain). There are several ways in which this is reflected in what follows. Traditionally in research, the normative ('should') element is fairly muted in theories and findings themselves, and wider outcomes are often hard to observe. But especially in Part 1, there is discussion of policies, intervention strategies and training courses that seek to change or influence specific groups and institutions in particular ways. Indeed theories too can have potential consequences beyond the specialised university niches in which they are initially credentialed, directing attention to hitherto neglected processes, challenging the hegemony of particular styles of thought and action and arguing for others. And this is certainly true in the programme of research established by Gumperz and Hymes, with which the book aligns.

The principles, procedures and potentials of this programme are explored in **Part 1: Sociolinguistic Frameworks Tuned to Social Change**, and my discussion in this section gradually widens in scope, shifting in emphasis from the intra- to the interdisciplinary and then to the applied.

Chapter 2 discusses *Interactional Sociolinguistics* (IS) and, after sketching Gumperz and Hymes' early efforts to build a general theory of language and society, it describes how Gumperz developed methods of analysis that reveal 'how linguistic signs interact with social knowledge in discourse', leading from there to a 'dynamic view of social environments where history, economic forces and interactive processes ... combine to create or to eliminate social distinctions' (Gumperz, 1982: 29). In the social sciences more generally, 'practice theory' has been hugely influential and has been characterised as a '*broad and capacious ... general theory* of the production of social subjects through practice, and the production of the world itself through practice' (Ortner, 2006: 16, emphasis added). But Gumperz stands out for developing a set of concepts and procedures that take us very close to the details of these production processes as they occur and, as well as discussing how Gumperz's own work has been updated in, for example, studies of asylum procedures, the chapter points to surveillance and online/offline interaction as priorities for contemporary IS research.

The chapter on interactional sociolinguistics sets the key for the whole book, but it is mainly concerned with the positioning of IS in the heartlands of research on language and society. Chapter 3, on *Linguistic Ethnography* (co-authored with Janet Maybin & Celia Roberts), broadens the frame of reference, focuses more on Hymes, and locates the Hymes/Gumperz tradition in interdisciplinary space. It explores the ways in which this tradition has been taken up and reformulated in Europe since 2000, pointing to ways in which relatively recent historical changes have influenced the relationship between ethnography and linguistics, strengthening ethnography's epistemological status and heightening the analytic relevance of linguistics. To illustrate the interdisciplinary resonance of their combination, it describes a training programme in linguistic ethnography designed for doctoral social scientists from a plurality of academic backgrounds, and then addresses the complexities that emerge in work with education and health professionals, designed to improve institutional practice.

Linguistic ethnography often has to negotiate its stance, shifting between 'is' and 'ought'. In Chapter 4, on *Sociolinguistic Citizenship* (co-authored with Melanie Cooke & Sam Holmes), normative considerations move centre stage in a discussion of the politics and practices of language education. Here Hymes' conception of ethnography as a 'democratic science' is integrated with the notion of linguistic citizenship (LC) developed by Christopher Stroud and colleagues. LC itself articulates a commitment to democratic participation, to voice, to the heterogeneity of linguistic resources and to the political value of sociolinguistic understanding. As well as addressing some of the criticisms of the LC idea (utopianism, self-declared marginality), the chapter considers the scope for promoting LC beyond Southern Africa, where it was conceived. The chapter looks at some recent not-for-profit initiatives aligned with the values of LC in England, identifies problems of sustainability and points to the ways in which universities can help to keep them going.

Sociolinguistic terrain well suited to the notion of LC becomes the central focus in **Part 2** of the book: **Ethnicity, Race and Class in Micro-practices of Differentiation and Alignment**. This follows Gumperz in the quest for a 'dynamic view of social environments where history, economic forces and interactive processes ... combine to create or to eliminate social distinctions' (Gumperz, 1982: 29), and it draws together a series of empirical studies of urban speech in and around London spanning approximately 25 years. It gravitates towards the fine grain of talk and interaction, but in doing so it always attends to the formative role played by longer, wider processes and structures (sometimes supplementing the analysis with quantitative methods from variationist sociolinguistics). Throughout, it repeatedly returns to the question: What does this kind of micro-analysis actually add to our understanding?

It is this question that opens the first paper in Part 2 – Chapter 5, *Ethnicities without Guarantees*, co-authored with Roxy Harris. This chapter involves a careful examination of the ways in which race and ethnicity are noted or evoked in ordinary encounters, and it points to a nuanced and potentially very consequential dynamics of differentiation that is easy to miss in broad-brush discussions of racism, subordination and exclusion framed in terms of clearly demarcated groups. Major commentators like Stuart Hall and Paul Gilroy have emphasised the wider significance of the hybrid cultures emerging in multi-ethnic urban environments, but sociolinguistics helps us to explore the complexities of this empirically.

This is taken further in Chapter 6, *Style Contrasts, Migration and Social Class*, which focuses more fully on vernacular speech practices themselves (rather than comparing them with established ideological discourses). It reviews two earlier studies of crossing and stylisation, practices that involve the relatively self-conscious use of languages and speech styles that lie outside the speaker's normal repertoire (Rampton, 1995/2018, 2006). In doing so, the chapter highlights the grounded creativity with which adolescent peer groups use different voices to problematise and interpret particular aspects of their sociohistorical environment, materialising different sociopolitical concerns and strategic responses. In one case, exaggerated performances of posh and Cockney denaturalise the pervasive cultural hierarchy associated with social class. In the other, Creole and Asian English are used to make ethnic difference familiar, orderly and enjoyable despite the racism elsewhere.

The fact that sociohistorical structures and processes like class and migration show up in the performance of different voices produced spontaneously in the quick of daily activity shows how a sensitivity to large-scale processes reaches deep into the practical consciousness of individuals. Chapter 7, *From 'Youth Language' to Contemporary Urban Vernaculars*, takes this further. It argues that the kind of low-key verbal art evidenced in Chapter 6 is integrally linked to the more unselfconscious styles identified in many studies of contemporary speech in multi-ethnic Western European cities. And as well as being attested in research dating from the 1980s to the late 2000s, the *durability* of this type of vernacular sensibility is evidenced in the case study of a successful middle-aged businessman, who still shifts into this style when talking to his oldest friends from school.

Located in exactly the same time and place as Chapter 7, the case study in Chapter 8, *Styling in a Language Learnt Later in Life*, brings in another very significant figure of the urban linguascape, the migrant adult second (or additional) language learner. As before, two axes of social differentiation stand out in the English speech styles of the focal research participant: first, a local versus immigrant distinction, produced by migration and movement between Britain and the Indian subcontinent and, second, the high/low binary associated with British social class. So even though the focal participant only started to speak the language relatively recently, he displayed a practical sensitivity to key dimensions of local English sociolinguistic structure. To produce this account, the analysis combines the Gumperzian framework (elaborated by Silverstein and others) with quantitative findings generated by Devyani Sharma and Lavanyi Sankaran, and it tries to steer a path between, on the one hand, the romantic celebration of difference traditionally found in sociolinguistics and, on the other, the attention to deficiency and remedial need characteristic of second language research. Instead, the chapter aims for a description of first-generation migrants that takes us closer to their embedded complexity as parents, siblings, aunts and uncles, friends and workmates, who also make an agentive contribution to local sociolinguistic processes.

Much of the unity of the four studies in Part 2 lies in the layered analytical framework they employ, in their focus on stylistic practice, and in the processes of empirical comparison developed within and across these chapters (established and explicit ideologies versus emergent and enacted ones in Chapter 5; stylisations of class versus ethnicity in Chapter 6; adolescents in the 1980s versus adults in the 2000s in Chapter 7; L2 versus L1 speakers of English in Chapter 8). In addition, of course, these papers share much the same geohistorical backdrop – urban England, reflected in data collected between 1985 and 2009. So, in combination, they present a series of urban English scenes in which linguistic practice projects liveable worlds at the intersection of class, migration and diaspora. Tensions and difficulties certainly also play a constitutive role, but overall, these four chapters spotlight complex practices of conviviality which are also an important element in contemporary urban life in other places.

At the same time, Part 2 is clearly selective in its focus, and it makes no claim to being a comprehensive survey or chronicle of urban sociolinguistic practice since the 1980s. In fact, since the start of the millennium, people and environments like those studied in Part 2 have become the target of government suspicion, positioned within growing political emphasis on existential threats to the nation-state. These processes of (in)securitisation also call for closer sociolinguistic scrutiny, and **Part 3** of the book, **Everyday (In)securitisation**, draws on an interdisciplinary dialogue with critical security studies (CSS), exploring the challenges and the contributions, both theoretical and empirical, that emerge in this encounter.

Chapter 9, *Sociolinguistics and Everyday (In)securitisation* (co-written with Constadina Charalambous, Panayiota Charalambous and Kamran Khan), describes how CSS reconceptualises traditional concepts like 'the state', 'security' and 'borders' as ongoing practices. So instead of seeing it as the condition of being safe from external threats, security is viewed as 'a practice of making "enemy" and "fear" the integrative, energetic principle of politics, displacing the democratic principles of freedom and justice' (Huysmans, 2014: 3). At the same time, the term '(in)securitisation' emphasises the fact that the effects of these practices are both unstable and relational: security to one person is insecurity to another, and this may change with the situation, sometimes quite quickly. As well as pointing to gaps in sociolinguistics, the relevance of all this is illustrated in an account of how security policies and discourses have been normalising new kinds of racism in Britain, redefining the responsibilities of professionals, working through into new forms of monitoring, and re-specifying the goals for language education, even though these processes are neither uncontested nor especially coherent. After that, the chapter turns to Cyprus, a setting profoundly affected by violent conflict, where reconciliation initiatives have led to the introduction of lessons in the language of the traditional enemy, Turkish. Here, the chapter outlines the ways in which assumptions about intercultural language education formulated in peace and stability are up-ended in post-conflict environments, and this is illustrated with a report on Greek-speaking adolescents learning Turkish at secondary school.

Chapter 10, *Crossing of a Different Kind* (co-authored with Constadina Charalambous and Panayiota Charalambous), extends the discussion of Greek-Cypriot adolescents learning Turkish. In order to capture the ways in which students actually manage to do so, it refurbishes the sociolinguistic concept of language crossing. Hitherto in sociolinguistics, crossing practices have been extensively analysed in multi-ethnic, multilingual urban settings of the kind described in Part 2, most often in recreational settings and popular culture. But in the Turkish language lessons in Cyprus, crossing is shaped by the constraints and affordances of schooling, and intergenerational links also count as much as or more than peer group relations. Overall, our analysis extends the significance of the concept of crossing by pointing to its authorised occurrence in *official* sites struggling with a legacy of violent division, and it contributes to growing interest in the low-key peacebuilding activity of ordinary people in Peace & Conflict Studies.

Chapter 11, *Goffman and the Everyday Experience of Surveillance* (co-authored with Louise Eley), shifts back to everyday urban life where, both in sociolinguistics and in Surveillance Studies, there is a dearth of fine-grained interactional research on what it means to be surveilled. But there is a powerful starting point in Goffman's account of 'unfocused interaction', in which people maintain a 'side-of-the-eye', 'half-an-ear' awareness of the people, objects and events in the space around them. This is used to explore three scenes of everyday surveillance: a woman walking down a city street, two men putting up street stickers (a civil offence), and passengers being scanned at an airport (all in Germany). The chapter shows how different senses of potential threat and illegality enter the experience of surveillance, building a rudimentary model of surveillance experiences, connecting its analysis to the (in)securitisation of minorities and migrants, and arguing that in its emphasis on mutual monitoring, Goffman's account is better adapted to contemporary surveillance than Foucault's famous panopticon.

Capitalising on the knowledge and fieldwork of my collaborators, the geographical sites covered in Part 3 are more varied than in Part 2. Goffman is also a more significant influence, and in Chapter 11 the analysis extends beyond language and speech to embodied interaction. But both are entirely compatible with IS. And although these three chapters are distinctive in their shared concern with (in)securitisation's implications for sociolinguistics in general and situated micro-analysis in particular, the discussion moves, as before, between analytical and normative perspectives, considering cross-disciplinary links and practical applications as well.

Half of the chapters in this book are co-authored, formulated within multi-stranded working relationships that in some cases reach back 25 years. Over this period, my work has also been profoundly influenced by Jan Blommaert, founder and co-editor of the *Encounters* series, who died just after the book was completed. As well as being an extraordinary person and a brilliant scholar, Jan was a really powerful exponent of the sociolinguistic programme articulated by Hymes and Gumperz. He developed the programme with new perspectives, new concepts and empirical topics, and extended its interdisciplinarity and political relevance. A reflexive ethnographer to the core, he was also very influential as a source of critique and innovation in the organisation of contemporary academic life. So the book closes with my tribute to Jan, also drawing on the words of others to celebrate his work and to evidence his extraordinary contribution.

The book's chapters were written over a period of about 10 years (2009–2020) and, as well as appearing in journals and edited collections, earlier versions of most of them can be found in Working Papers in Urban Language & Literacies.[1] References to the literature have not been comprehensively updated (especially in Part 2), and there is variation in the interdisciplinary links pursued in Parts 2 and 3 (sociology and cultural studies in the former; International Relations, Critical Security and Surveillance Studies in the latter). There are also shifts in the granularity of the analyses, and the labels used to classify my approach vary in degrees of specificity, very loosely in line with the imagined audience ('interactional sociolinguistics' for other linguists, 'linguistic ethnography' for other kinds of social scientist and just 'sociolinguistics' for non-academics).[2] But all of the papers have been adapted to bring out the links and progression across them, and to try to ensure that the whole amounts to more than just the sum of the parts. Potentially at least, the work's embedding within energetic collaborations increases its resonance, and while some papers look back to earlier research, others point in directions where there is still a lot to do.[3]

All in all, the book seeks to identify relatively new issues requiring a lot more sociolinguistic work, and to propose revisions for concepts and perspectives that are well established. Whatever the changes ahead, communication is fundamental to social life, and my hope overall is that this text can be read as further testimony to the relevance and adaptability of the modes of engagement and enquiry formulated by Gumperz and Hymes, and of course Goffman as well.

Notes

(1) See https://kcl.academia.edu/WorkingPapersinUrbanLanguageLiteracies.

(2) There is also variation in my capitalisation of disciplines and (sub-)disciplinary schools, broadly reflecting my familiarity with and distance from them in the academic field. For the most part, I use lower case for the approaches I am most familiar and/or identify with ('sociolinguistics', 'linguistic ethnography', 'interactional sociolinguistics', 'conversation analysis') as well as with names that are part of common parlance ('sociology', 'anthropology'). Upper case is generally reserved for traditions that I am less closely involved with and/or are less commonly cited in sociolinguistics ('Critical Security Studies', 'International Relations').

(3) These have been based around courses and projects at the Centre for Language Discourse & Communication at King's College London, as well as: the Linguistic Ethnography Forum, 2000– (http://lingethnog.org); the International Consortium on Language & Superdiversity 2010–2017 (www.incolas.eu); the Ethnography, Language & Communication Summer School, 2008–; the Language, (In)security & Everyday Practice Lab 2016 (www.kcl.ac.uk/liep); and the Hub for Education & Linguistic Diversity, 2018– (www.kcl.ac.uk/held).

Part 1

Sociolinguistic Frameworks Tuned to Social Change

2 Interactional Sociolinguistics[1]

2.1 Introduction

Interactional sociolinguistics (IS) developed as the expression of John Gumperz' approach to research, and it most typically focuses on face-to-face interactions in which there are significant differences in the participants' sociolinguistic resources and/or institutional power. IS has a broad methodological base, with deep roots in ethnography, dialectology, pragmatics, and Goffmanian and conversation analysis, and it generally seeks as rich a dataset on naturally occurring interaction as it can get. Data collection involves the audio- and/or video-recording of situated interaction from particular events, people and groups, supplemented by as much participant observation and retrospective commentary from local participants as possible, and analysis moves across a wide range of levels of organisation, from the phonetic to the institutional and the societal. Overall, IS constitutes quite a comprehensive framework for engaging with the empirical specifics required for any social science aligning with practice theory (Ortner, 2006) and, more particularly, it is a central pillar within linguistic ethnography, encouraging researchers to 'roll up [their] linguistic sleeves and drill down to the detail of social problems' (Auer & Roberts, 2011b: 381), making optimum use of the sensitising frameworks available in the (sub-)disciplines focusing on language.

With Dell Hymes, Gumperz was also a foundational figure in contemporary sociolinguistics and linguistic anthropology more generally, but while 'Hymes outlined the broad goals of sociolinguistics research, Gumperz concentrated on concrete evidence of sociolinguistic methodology in action' (Sarangi, 2011: 377). Where Hymes produced new maps for the relationship between linguistics and anthropology in programmatic manifestos that stressed practical and political relevance to contemporary social life, Gumperz developed and tested the analytic resources emerging across this newly constituted field, putting them to work in empirical demonstrations of the connection between 'small-scale interactions' and 'large-scale sociological effects' (Jacquemet, 2011: 475), providing a 'dynamic view of social environments where history, economic forces and interactive processes ... combine to create or to eliminate social distinctions' (Gumperz, 1982: 29). And while Hymes' vision of ethnography as a 'democratic science' has provided linguistic ethnography in the UK and Europe with an especially powerful warrant for engagement beyond the academy (Blommaert, 2009c; Chapter 3, this volume), Gumperz theorised and deployed a synthesis of (potentially divergent) perspectives that stands as a touchstone for 'anti-structuralist rigour' in the multi-layered analysis of situated practice (Auer & Roberts, 2011b: 382; Section 2.3, this volume).

2.2 Origins

Building on links formed in the 1960s, Gumperz and Hymes' seminal 1972 collection, *Directions in Sociolinguistics: The Ethnography of Communication*, articulated several concerns central to interactional sociolinguistics (as well as containing an exemplary early IS study in Blom & Gumperz, 1972). First, there was the search for a theory capable of treating language as integral to social and cultural process, as well as the need to develop methods and technical concepts suited to describing this. Hymes (1972b: 38) referred to 'a basic science that does not yet exist', and Gumperz and Hymes (1972: vi–vii) suggested that '[r]ecent publications ... have, so far, not been integrated into any general theory of language and society'. Second, this was infused by a commitment to making language analysis count in a period of major political upheaval – decolonisation, civil rights, the quest for fairness in education (Hymes, 1972b: 38, 53). Third, in order to build adequate models of the interaction of language and social life, 'there must be ... an approach [to description] that partly links, but partly cuts across, partly builds between ... the disciplines' (Hymes, 1972b: 41). Indeed, the collection brought contributors together from very different backgrounds in linguistics, anthropology, sociology and psychology, and Hymes subsequently reflected, '[a]n important attraction in the early years of sociolinguistics was that a number of individuals, interested in [language] use, were marginal to their official affiliations' (Hymes, 1997: 125).

But this changed as the study of language and society expanded in the period that followed, and several of the perspectives represented in the 1972 volume consolidated themselves as separate sub-disciplines – for example, conversation analysis (Sacks and Schegloff), variationist sociolinguistics (Labov), the sociology of language (Fishman) (cf. Bucholtz & Hall, 2008; Duranti, 2009). As editor of *Language in Society* from its inception in 1972 until 1994, Hymes certainly stayed in touch with this diversification, promoting cross-fertilisation, and in 1982, Gumperz established a book series, *Studies in Interactional Sociolinguistics* (subsequently co-edited with Paul Drew, Marjorie Goodwin and Deborah Schiffrin) for research on the social dynamics of talk in everyday and institutional settings (clinics, schools, workplaces, courtrooms, news interviews, focus groups). But if one looks across the range of scholars and approaches represented in Gumperz' series – for example, Tannen, Schiffrin, De Fina, Culpepper, Myers, Couper-Kuhlen, Selting, Heritage, Stivers, Sidnell, Jacquemet; discourse analysis, pragmatics, interactional linguistics, conversation analysis, linguistic anthropology – IS seems like a relatively loose grouping of mutually intelligible perspectives, rather than a tight alignment. Gumperz himself, however, persisted in the quest for 'a general theory of verbal communication which integrates what we know about grammar, culture and interactive conventions into a single overall framework of concepts and analytic procedures' (Gumperz, 1982: 7), and we can see what this looked like in the next section.

2.3 Approach to Analysis

The 'general theory of verbal communication' associated with interactional sociolinguistics builds on one of Gumperz and Hymes' crucial early insights, which was 'to take the speech event as the unit of analysis rather than community-wide linguistic and cultural norms, to see that culture did not stand outside talk but was constituted in and through situated speaking practices' (Auer & Roberts, 2011b: 385; Gumperz & Cook-Gumperz, 2008: 536). The theory brings together several major sets of resources: *linguistics and discourse analysis*, which provide a provisional view of the communicative affordances of the linguistic resources that participants draw on in situated communication; *Goffmanian* and *conversation analysis*, which illuminate the ongoing, sequential construction of 'local architectures of intersubjectivity' (Heritage, 1997), the rituals and moral accountabilities permeating the use of semiotic forms and strategies, and the shifting spatio-temporal distribution of attention and involvement in situations of physical co-presence; and *ethnography*, which provides a sense of the stability, status and resonance that linguistic forms, rhetorical strategies and semiotic materials have in different social networks beyond the encounter-on-hand, an idea of how and where an encounter fits into longer and broader biographies, institutions and histories, and a sense of the cultural and personal perspectives/experiences that participants bring to interactions, and take from them. Finally, with these elements in place – very loosely, 'grammar, culture and interactive conventions' – Gumperz adds the vital notions of conversational '*inferencing*' and '*contextualisation*' (see, for example, Gumperz, 1996: 378–381).[2]

'Inferencing' refers to the interpretive work that people perform in trying to reconcile the material that they encounter in any given situation with their prior understanding. It refers to the normally effortless sense-making that occurs when people work out the significance of a word, an utterance, an action or an object by matching it against their past experience, against their expectations of what's coming up, their perceptions of the material setting and so forth. The term 'contextualisation cue' is complementary, although it shifts the focus from receptive sense-making to speech production. When someone formulates an utterance, it is more than just the semantic proposition that they construct. They also produce a whole host of small vocal signs that evoke, for example, a certain of level of formality (shifting to a more prestigious accent, selecting the word 'request' rather than 'ask'), that point to the presence of bystanders (talking quietly), etc., and this non-stop process of contextualisation may either reassure their listener that they are operating with a broadly shared understanding of the situation, or it can nudge the recipient's inferences in another direction. A lot of this processing is relatively tacit, with participants constantly engaged in low-key monitoring of how all the details of verbal communication fit with their grasp of the propositions being expressed, with their sense of the speaker's intent, with their understanding of the activity they are engaged in and how it should proceed, etc. But it only takes a slight deviation from the habitual, a small move beyond expected patterns of variation in the way in which somebody speaks or acts, to send recipients into inferential overdrive, wondering what's going on when a sound, a word, a grammatical pattern, a discourse move or bodily gesture doesn't quite match: Should I ignore or respond to this? Is it a joke or serious? What ties these apparently unconnected ideas together? Is the speaker still wearing their institutional hat, or are they now suddenly claiming solidarity with a particular group?

This theorisation has major implications for our understanding of 'context'. As noted above, word denotation, the formal structures of grammar and the propositional meaning of sentences still count, but they lose their traditional supremacy in linguistic study, and instead become just one among a large array of semiotic resources available for the local production and interpretation of meaning (cf. Hanks, 1996; Verschueren, 1999). Language is regarded as pervasively indexical, continuously pointing to persons, practices, settings, objects and ideas that never get explicitly expressed and, in what Erickson (2011: 399) calls a 'Copernican shift in perspective within sociolinguistics', context stops being the relatively static, external and determining reference point traditionally added to language analysis as something of an afterthought – what Drew and Heritage (1992: 19) call the 'bucket' theory of context. Instead, it is seen as dynamic, interactively accomplished and intrinsic to communication.

So context is an understanding of the social world activated in the midst of things, an understanding of the social world that is interactionally ratified or undermined from one moment to the next as the participants in an encounter respond to one another. At the same time, however, when people engage with one another, there is considerable scope for social difference in the norms and expectations that individuals orient to, as well as in the kinds of thing they notice as discrepant, and there can also be a great range in the inferences that they bring to bear ('good' or 'bad', 'right' or 'wrong', 'art' or 'error', 'call it out' or 'let it pass', 'typical of this or that'). The normative expectations and explanatory accounts activated like this in the interactional present seldom come from nowhere. Instead, they instantiate discourses that the participants have picked up through prior involvement in sociocommunicative networks that can range in scale from intimate relationships and friendship groups to national education systems and global media – 'what we perceive and retain in our mind is a function of our culturally determined predisposition to perceive and assimilate' (Gumperz, 1982: 12). In this way, the notions of inferencing and contextualisation offer us a way of seeing how long-term experience and more widely circulating ideologies infuse the quick of activity in the here-and-now, introducing the force of social expectation (aka 'structure') without overlooking the participants' skilled agency (cf. Blommaert & Rampton, 2011a: 11).

From very early on, Gumperz contested the view that language merely reflected more basic social forces. He insisted that 'the relationship of ... social factors to speech form is quite different from what the sociologist means by correlation among variables' (Gumperz & Hernández-Chavez, 1972: 98), and he proposed 'an important break with previous approaches to social structure and to language and society. Behavioural regularities are no longer regarded as reflections of independently measurable social norms; on the contrary, these norms are themselves seen as communicative behaviour' (Blom & Gumperz, 1972: 432). In this way, his theory of communication aligns with constructionist theories of social practice, connecting, for example, with Giddens' conception of practice as the 'production and reproduction of society ... as a skilled [but by no means wholly conscious] performance on the part of its members' (Giddens, 1976: 160). Practice theories have become influential right across social science (Bourdieu, 1977; Ortner, 2006), and Gumperz' theorisation positions sociolinguistics as an exceptional interdisciplinary resource for 'yield[ing distinctive] insights into the workings of social process' (Gumperz, 1982: 4, 7).

Once positioned like this in a larger interdisciplinary field of social science, however, IS faces a question raised by John Twitchin in a 1979 interview with Gumperz, a question that is likely to resonate with researchers who take a macro-scopic approach to social processes and/or lack the time to learn linguistics. Twitchin commented:

> Now all these points you've made about the details of the way language is used are very interesting, but in terms of race relations and achieving a successful multi-racial society, isn't it all an extremely marginal consideration? I mean, isn't this matter of language really unimportant, compared with the fundamental problems of racial discrimination and the social and economic disadvantages of black and other ethnic minorities in Britain? (Gumperz, 1979/1990: 51)

Gumperz responded:

> there's no denying that politics and economic conditions are extremely important in race relations, and that ultimately redressing the balance of discrimination is a matter of power. But communication *is* power.

And to persuade non-linguists of this,

> there is no need for real technical analysis ... we need to use a tape recorder [for] a sort of action replay like our TV newscasters do when they use a slow-down mechanism to show us the details of a particular piece of play in football. (Gumperz, 1979/1990: 52)

The BBC's intercultural communication training video *Crosstalk* illustrates this, and it was designed to help public service and other workers 'to learn and practise awareness immediately' (Gumperz *et al.*, 1979). But much more generally, the slow and intensive analysis of selected strips of audio- or video-recordings of situated interaction, following its moment-by-moment unfolding, is central to IS, both as a resource for communication with non-academics and researchers from other disciplines, and as a fundamental discovery procedure (Erickson, 2011: 397; see below and Sections 3.3 and 3.4, this volume).

In Gumperzian IS, issues of relatively widespread concern to social scientists, politicians and/or the public – for example, race discrimination, class stratification, gender relations – are a vital point of departure (Gumperz & Cook-Gumperz, 2008: 537–538), but they are addressed by micro-analysing recorded interactions in ways that avoid the overgeneralisation and essentialism to which other research methods (interviews, surveys) are often vulnerable. Dwelling on recordings and transcripts of people interacting in particular activities – being interviewed for a job, sitting in class, having a meal, hanging around with friends, talking about recent events, work, food, music and so forth – you soon realise that local, institutional, activity- and discourse-specific identities[3] may be a lot more compelling for the participants than, for example, their Anglo, Pakistani or African Caribbean family backgrounds, and that when ethnicity does become an issue, this happens in all sorts of different ways – deconstructive, respectful, racist, some quite spectacular and others hardly noticed. This procedure also offers a validity check on notions like 'contradiction' or 'ambivalence', which in more macro studies sometimes seem more like analyst attributions than participant experiences. Within any single episode, there is usually a lot of information on the specifics of the situation, and so if you are interested in political analysis, you can look at a particular act as a micro-political intervention in particular social relations there-and-then (see, for example, Sections 6.2 and 6.3, this volume).

Given its commitment to interdisciplinarity, this isn't a claim that IS micro-analysis should take precedence over all other types of research on culture and society. But it certainly finds a parallel in Foucault's notion of 'eventalisation'[4] – 'analysing an event according to the multiple processes that constitute it', 'proceed[ing] by progressive, necessarily incomplete saturation', fighting the 'temptation to invoke a historical constant, an immediate anthropological trait, or an obviousness that imposes itself uniformly on all', 'show[ing] that things "weren't as necessary as all that" ... in what subsequently counts as being self-evident', that there is actually 'a plethora of intelligibilities, a deficit of necessities' (Foucault, 1980/2003: 249–250). Working in this way, it can be hard to produce findings with eye-catching elegance. But overall, the IS micro-analysis of recordings of situated activity helps to push the processes associated with ethnicity, gender, generation, class, etc. *into perspective*, documenting their intricacy, distribution and significance in ordinary lives beyond the headline representations in politics and the media (see Chapter 5, this volume).

Carrying the comparison with Foucault one step further, Gumperzian IS can also be read as a counter-hegemonic critique of disciplinary knowledge/power regimes, focusing on the influential reifications involved in linguistic modelling (Foucault, 1977; Rampton, 2016). So Gumperz and Cook-Gumperz argue that 'the structuralist view of grammar ... feeds into monoglot ideologies of language standardisation ... and ... have led to unrealistic, self-defeating and potentially oppressive language and educational policies' (Gumperz & Cook-Gumperz, 2005: 271). In fact the conceptual distinctions at the core of Gumperz' work imply a similar critique. Gumperz emphasises the distinction between (a) contextualisation cues and (b) the propositional meaning formulated with syntax, lexis and semantics,[5] codified in linguistics, preserved in writing, and taught and assessed at school, and in doing so he also criticises institutions operating in ethnically diverse environments for relying too heavily on the aspects of meaning that seem to be stabilised in lexico-grammar (≈ b). These institutions overlook the crucial contribution of less standardised sources of meaning (contextualisation cues), and give poor ratings to minority speakers as a result, not because institutional representatives are socially prejudiced against specific groups, but because their habits of interpretation are skewed by their literacy and education, whether these interpretations are focused on code-switching at school or cross-cultural English in job interviews (Gumperz, 1982; Gumperz & Hernández-Chavez, 1972; also Rampton, 1995/2018: Ch. 13). At this point, we can draw in Scott's (somewhat Foucauldian) 1998 book, *Seeing Like a State*, which describes

> the modernist 'state's attempt to make society legible, to arrange the population in ways that simplified the classic state functions of taxation, conscription, and prevention of rebellion ... [through] processes as disparate as the creation of permanent last names, the standardisation of weights and measures, the establishment of ... surveys [for taxation] and population registers, the invention of freehold tenure, the standardisation of language and legal discourse. (Scott, 1998: 2)

In this context, Gumperz' work can be read as a critical response to institutionalised models promoting the linguistic legibility of populations, as a reassertion of the importance of the 'complex, illegible and local' (Scott, 1998: 2), and as the development of an analytic apparatus for demonstrating the limitations of prevailing institutional ideologies of language, encouraging us to 'listen in a new way' (cf. McDermott, 1988).

2.4 IS, Linguistic Anthropology and Conversation Analysis

But if Gumperz' approach resonates so well with current perspectives in social science, why isn't the term 'interactional sociolinguistics' much more widely used in ongoing work on language, culture and society? Is it now just merely an 'antecedent', with very little contemporary bite? In fact in the US, one-half of the phrase – the term 'sociolinguistics' – is now generally associated with the quantitative variationist tradition, which still holds to the correlational perspective that Gumperz explicitly repudiated (Bucholtz & Hall, 2008: 402; Duranti, 2009: 2). To win space for the continuing vitality of a broad perspective of the kind that Gumperz sought, Bucholtz and Hall speak of 'sociocultural linguistics' (e.g. 2008) and, in a similar vein, British and European scholars are now more likely to refer to 'linguistic ethnography' (Chapter 3, this volume).

A clue to the answer lies in the broad range of approaches covered in the *Studies in Interactional Sociolinguistics* series noted above, which effectively position IS as an 'umbrella', now almost more an 'ontology', more a foundational account of the qualities and processes underlying communication, than a 'substantive theory' with claims that are designed as open to empirical refutation.[6] Gumperz certainly was an empirical researcher, also seriously committed to improving methods for analysing interaction (inter alia developing his own system of transcription; Gumperz & Berenz, 1993). But he combined empirical work with a deep and sympathetic engagement with the schools and literatures that went their separate ways after 1972, developing substantive theories about different aspects of communication. Out of this, he developed a deeper theoretical synthesis capable of accommodating many of the advances made in different (sub-)disciplinary traditions, while also suggesting how they could be brought back together.

Although it is now seldom cited as a distinctive approach there, Gumperzian IS fits most easily into contemporary linguistic anthropology (LA), itself quite a broad church (e.g. Duranti, 2009; Gumperz, 1996). The effort to develop a 'closer understanding of how linguistic signs interact with social knowledge in discourse' (Gumperz, 1982: 29) predates Silverstein's influential formulation of the 'total linguistic fact', which argues that 'the datum for a science of language, is irreducibly dialectic in nature ... an unstable mutual interaction of meaningful sign forms, contextualised to situations of interested human use and mediated by the fact of cultural ideology' (Silverstein, 1985: 220; also Hanks, 1996: 230).[7] At the same time, however, even though he undoubtedly appreciated it, Gumperz did not himself participate in, for example, the elaborate theorisation of semiotic systems that has flourished in LA (e.g. Agha, 2007). Where others have explored in detail the subtle differences between indexes, icons, interpretants and so forth, Gumperz' theorisation of 'contextualisation' and 'inferencing' is less differentiating. The account is well tuned to the dynamic parameters within which sense-making occurs, but it holds back from the simplifying abstraction that the modelling of systems necessarily entails and, instead, it leaves semiotic processes closely embedded in the contingencies of situated here-and-now interaction between socially located individuals, where both the effectivity and ambivalence of signs emerge.

This lack of formalisation also distinguishes Gumperzian IS from conversation analysis. CA and IS share a commitment to the slow and intensive analysis of recordings of natural interaction, but whereas IS examines the dialectic between linguistic signs and social knowledge in discourse, 'the goal in CA is to identify structures that underlie social interaction' (Stivers & Sidnell, 2013: 2). CA researchers are certainly very well aware of the uniqueness of each episode they analyse, but they respond to this by zooming in on the designs, actions and sequences that give it predictable structure. Of course, there is much more to the interpretive process in conversation than CA can reach through this prioritisation of structure (Auer & Roberts, 2011: 385b; Blommaert, 2001), and it differs from IS in other ways as well: CA has often taken cooperative conversational involvement for granted, focusing on sociolinguistically homogeneous settings (Gumperz, 1982: 4), and it attaches little significance to the metalinguistic commentary on interaction provided by participants. Nevertheless, CA research is very well represented in *Studies in Interactional Sociolinguistics*, and it has generated a set of rigorous procedures and descriptions that no-one investigating interaction can really dispense with (cf. Duranti, 1997: Ch. 8), even though they might want to say they were 'using' rather than 'doing' CA. Ethnography plays a substantial part in workplace CA (Mondada, 2013: 37), and at the interface of CA and LA, Clemente (2013: 696–698) identifies studies which actually look very similar to Gumperz' 'dynamic view of social environments where history, economic forces and interactive processes … combine to create or to eliminate social distinctions' (Gumperz, 1982: 29) – M.H. Goodwin's *The Hidden Life of Girls: Games of Stance, Status and Exclusion*, and Moerman's 'contexted conversation analysis', 'directed toward discovering which of the many culturally available distinctions are active and relevant to the situation, how these distinctions are brought to bear, and what they consist of' (Moerman, 1988: 70).

Part of the viability of Gumperz' 'general theory of communication' no doubt derives from his position as founding figure, sowing the seeds and/or supporting the growth of subsequent developments. But it is sometimes harder for less senior scholars to promote integrative approaches like IS, and Bucholtz and Hall (2008: 405), for example, reported being 'confronted [with] a wide range of responses to our efforts to bring together perspectives from multiple areas of inquiry, from "That's not linguistics (or anthropology or …)" to "Linguistics (or anthropology or …) has already done that!"'.[8] This raises two questions.

First, with reactions like these, why persevere? The answer is unsurprising: to engage with pressing real-world issues, recognising that 'problems lead where they will and that relevance commonly leads across disciplinary boundaries' (Gumperz & Cook-Gumperz, 2008: 533, 537–538; Hymes,

1969: 44; also Sapir, 1929/1949: 166). So Bucholtz and Hall say their approach 'coheres less around a set of theories, methods, or topics than a concern with a general question: how does the empirical study of language illuminate social and cultural processes?' (2008: 405; Duranti, 2003: 332–333). In linguistic ethnography, concepts and methods developed in fields like LA are viewed as valuable both for other disciplines such as sociology, psychology or management studies, and for engagement with professionals such as teachers, doctors and social workers (see Chapter 3, this volume). Across endeavours like these, the frameworks and substantive theories developed in fields like CA and LA play an absolutely vital role, but as in ethnography more generally, they provide an array of sensitising rather than definitive constructs, 'suggest[ing] directions along which to look' rather than 'prescriptions of what to see' (Blumer, 1969: 148).

Second, how do you actually teach the kind of synthesis that IS involves? Traditions like CA and variationist sociolinguistics have clearly defined theories and procedures that make them quite easy to learn *ab initio*, but in IS it can take quite a lot of experience to appreciate the span of sub-disciplinary perspectives potentially available/relevant, and to figure out how micro-analysis can speak to issues of wider concern in the social settings in focus. So to embark on the IS mission – to try to ensure that academic and political generalisations about social life are accountable to the kinds of small-scale everyday activity that we can observe, record and transcribe – apprentices either only begin once they have received a fairly thorough all-round training in linguistics (phonetics, pragmatics, functional grammar, CA, etc.). Or they start with substantial experience of a particular domain – working as professionals in health, education, etc., or researching them in another discipline – and they gradually pick up the IS ingredients piecemeal, drawn by their relevance to particular aspects of the larger problem they are addressing. But either way, data sessions again play a central role, immersing students in a recording and its accompanying transcript: running with their interests and interpretations while at the same time pointing to the insights afforded by the new perspectives; pushing them to make their claims accountable to evidence, with an eye on the perils of under- and over-interpretation (cf. Erickson, 1986). The format partly resembles the traditional CA data session – there are the insistent questions like 'why this now?', 'what next?', etc. (ten Have, 1999). But instead of prioritising a drilling down into the sequential machinery of interaction, these sessions also work outwards to larger scale institutional and societal processes, reflecting for example on the data's implications for the next steps in ethnographic fieldwork (see also Scollon & Scollon, 2007: 615, 619; see Section 3.4 for further discussion).

As well as playing a key role in IS training, data sessions with research informants – eliciting retrospective commentary on excerpts of recorded data in which the informants participated – can be a vital part of data collection in actual research projects (Erickson & Shultz, 1982: 56–63; Rampton, 1995/2018: 333–334). They allow the researcher to find out more about, for example, the background and typicality of particular episodes, to tap into local language ideologies and to address informants' concerns and gain trust. Post-project, they can be a valuable resource for feedback, providing opportunities to examine and debate policies and practices with research informants and their colleagues. And for IS research, they are also central to more extensive practical interventions outside the academy.

2.5 Practical Interventions beyond the Academy

So far, I have characterised Gumperzian IS as a critical programme founded in a deep regard for the consequential subtleties of interaction. In line with this, its practical intervention strategy seeks relatively low key, partial and specific transformations, compatible in fact with the approach outlined by Foucault: 'analyzing and reflecting on limits' in order to open 'the possibility of no longer being, doing, or thinking what we are, do, or think', 'practical critique that takes the form of a possible crossing-over', 'grasp[ing] the points where change is possible and desirable' (Foucault, 1984/2003: 23, 2003: 53–54; Rose, 1999: 282–284). So when Gumperz and colleagues tackled race discrimination in institutional encounters using the 'tape recorder' and 'action replay[s]' in their 1979 *Crosstalk* programme, they sought to facilitate a rethinking that engaged with the complex lived relationship between situated actions and their longer term influences and effects. Watching fairly familiar institutional interactions like a lesson or a job interview encourages professionals to bring their own first-hand experience into the frame, along with their sensitivity, interest or affection for clients as individuals, while at the same time, micro-analysis shows that actions are *jointly* produced among participants, that what people say and do is minutely synchronised with the feedback they are receiving from interlocutors differentially tuned to the institutional requirements. Once the co-constructedness of activity is made visible, it is much harder just to blame individuals, and discussion can turn to the constraints and affordances of the systems in play. As outlined in more detail in Section 3.5, there can be challenges and tensions around what counts as analysable and whether and how that matters, and these playback data sessions are also places where relationships can be renegotiated, with institutional and professional knowledge trumping the researcher's interpretations. Still, this IS approach to intervention is consistent with the Foucauldian perspective of Nikolas Rose, who notes, for example, that:

> [t]he notion of resistance, at least as it has conventionally functioned with the analyses of self-proclaimed radicals, is too simple and flattening ... [Instead,] one [s]hould examine the [much smaller] ways in which creativity arises out of the situation of human beings engaged in particular relations of force and meaning, and what is made out of the possibilities of that location. (Rose, 1999: 279; see also Harris & Lefstein *et al.*, 2011; Lefstein & Snell, 2014: Ch. 12)

2.6 More Recent Contributions and Research Areas

Much of my account so far has looked back to Gumperz' work in the 1970s, 1980s and 1990s. What about more recent IS research? This question is rather hard to answer in view of the general lack of boundary policing around IS, its interdisciplinary openness and its relationships with adjacent fields – foundational but low profile in LA, engaged but not identified with CA. A summary of the work published in *Studies in Interactional Sociolinguistics* could lead in different directions, and indeed, although IS is usually qualitative, it can also be combined with variationist sociolinguistics and other forms of quantification (Bucholtz, 2011; Cutler, 1999; Erickson & Shultz, 1982; Gumperz & Cook-Gumperz, 2008: 535; see Section 6.2 and Chapter 8, this volume). But for the sake of convenience, we can take two topics that were central in Gumperz' own work – code-switching and intercultural communication in institutional settings – and briefly consider the ways in which these topics have been treated more recently, expanding into a sociolinguistics of globalisation (Blommaert, 2010a; Jacquemet, 2005b).

Gumperz' research on code-switching focused on people alternating between languages that were well established in their own repertoires (e.g. Auer, 1988; Blom & Gumperz, 1972; Gumperz, 1982; Gumperz & Hernández-Chavez, 1972). But since the 1990s there has been a good deal of work on language crossing and stylisation – the former refers to the (potentially) transgressive use of other-ethnic varieties in settings where ethnic boundaries are quite sharply drawn, while the latter also involves the use of styles beyond one's normal repertoire but raises fewer questions of legitimacy for the participants (Bucholtz, 1999b; Cutler, 1999; Hewitt, 1986; Jaspers, 2005; Rampton, 1995/2018; for a review, see Rampton & Charalambous, 2012). This research shows people using different speech styles to denaturalise social category membership, variously challenging, shifting or reaffirming ascribed and established social identities and community affiliations, and the focus has extended beyond ethnicity to gender, social class, generation and their intersections (e.g. Barrett, 1997; Clark, 2010; Coupland, 2009; Hall, 1995; Jaspers, 2005; Malai Madsen, 2015; Rampton, 2006; see Chapters 6, 7 and 8, this volume). As an 'observer of recent history', Gumperz suggested in 1982 that 'individuals are freer to alter their social personae with the circumstances', and he explicitly questioned 'the assumption that speech communities, defined as functionally integrated social systems with shared norms of evaluation, can [still] actually be isolated' (Gumperz, 1982: 26). He also replaced speech community with social network as a framework for understanding the distribution of linguistic practices (Gumperz, 1982: Ch. 3; also Blom & Gumperz, 1972). So IS was been conceptually very well positioned to engage with the shift from a multiculturalism of communities framed within the nation-state to the globalised superdiversity experienced in many countries (Arnaut *et al.*, 2016; Auer & Roberts, 2011b: 390).

Gumperz also carried out a good deal of work on intercultural communication, focusing on interaction between bureaucratic 'gatekeepers' – managers, personnel officers, social workers, etc. – and people who had migrated for reasons of employment (see also Bremer *et al.*, 1996). But in response to massively increased population displacement since the 1990s, there is now a substantial body of work examining the encounter between state officials and asylum seekers and refugees (e.g. Blommaert, 2001, 2009b; Maryns, 2006). In this work, there is a more extensive focus on the discursive technologies through which gatekeeping operates (Jacquemet, 2011: 478). Gumperz and colleagues examined the affordances and constraints of the interview as an institutional genre (e.g. Gumperz *et al.*, 1979; Roberts, 2016), but research on asylum procedures has brought writing and the trajectory of documents much more fully into the account, examining the shaping influence of bureaucratic protocols and the ways in which talk gets entextualised and reports get transmitted and recontextualised through the application assessment system (Bauman & Briggs, 1990; Blommaert, 2001, 2009b; Maryns, 2006; see Section 3.3, this volume). The multilingualism and the language ideologies in these encounters are also more elaborate. Where Gumperz examined unmediated interaction between minority and majority speakers in the dominant language (English), asylum interviews often involve interpreters and/or a lingua franca (Jacquemet, 2005a, 2011; Maryns, 2006). And whereas Gumperz targeted a common-sense belief in the communicative effectiveness of lexico-grammatical propositions, when officials use language analysis for the determination of origin (LADO) they refer to outdated and/or irrelevant sociolinguistic survey data to determine the veracity of the narratives with which asylum applicants present their cases (Blommaert, 2009b; Maryns, 2006; Spotti, 2016).

With work of this kind, claims to interdisciplinary relevance have also been strengthened over the last 10–20 years by a more explicit interest in connecting the intensive analysis of specific interactional episodes to the work of major theorists in the humanities and social sciences like Bakhtin, Bourdieu, Foucault and Williams (e.g. Blommaert, 2005; Borba, 2015; Coupland *et al.*, 2001; Duchêne *et al.*, 2013; Erickson, 2004; Jacquemet, 2005b, 2011; Pérez-Milans, 2013; Rampton, 1995/2018, 2006: 10.3.4, 2016). In fact, as the next section suggests, the work of social theorists like these (and those they have influenced) is likely to remain a vital interdisciplinary reference point for future work.

2.7 New Directions

Social issues have played a central role in the development of IS, and because of this, a discussion of future directions needs to reckon with contemporary social change. Even if we only take the topics of code-switching and institutional communication as points of departure, it is clear that new challenges are opening up, as Jacquemet indicates:

> an increasing number of settings (from living rooms to hospital operating rooms or political meetings) [are] experiencing a translocal multilingualism interacting with the electronic technologies of contemporary communication. The world is now full of locales where speakers use a mixture of languages in interacting with friends and co-workers, reading English and other 'global' languages on their computer screens, watch local, regional, or global broadcasts, and listen to pop music in various languages. Most of the times, they do so simultaneously. (Jacquemet, 2005b: 266)

According to sociologists, mobile phones partially dissolve 'distinctions between presence and absence, attention and inattention ... as phone calls are answered, text messages are sent' (Larsen *et al.*, 2008: 650), and 'the scarce resource is attention, not information' (Wellman, 2001: 236). This is targeted in the 'attention economy', where 'the interest of consumers needs to be caught as eyeballs migrate from television to tablet to mobile phone to laptop' (van Dijck, 2013a: 122). In the words of a best-selling manual, '[h]abit-forming technology is already here, and it is being used to mould our lives ... [This can] unleash the tremendous new powers innovators and entrepreneurs have to influence the everyday lives of billions of people' (Eyal, 2014: 8, 9). And new forms of online digital sociality are developing, in which '[a]lgorithms, protocols, and defaults profoundly shape the cultural experience of people active on social media platforms ... Online sociality has increasingly become a coproduction of humans and machines ... . [and] a platform [like Facebook, YouTube or Wikipedia] ... shapes the performance of social acts instead of merely facilitating them' (van Dijck, 2013a).

With these developments, there are also new forms of social control. According to Deleuze, boundaries and enclosures of all kinds – hospitals, factories, schools, families – are giving way to the flows of people, objects and information associated with neoliberal marketisation, and 'ultrarapid forms of free-floating control [are replacing] the old disciplines operating in the time frame of a closed system' (Deleuze, 1992: 4). These new forms involve digital surveillance, which now plays a major role in the processes that constitute the population as consumers and seduce them into the market economy, 'constructing and monitoring consumption' (Bauman & Lyon, 2013: 16, 121ff.; Haggerty & Ericson, 2000: 615; van Dijck, 2013a). At the same time, many see a 'dual society' developing, where 'a hyper-competitive, fully networked zone coexists with a marginal sector of excluded low-achievers' (Fraser, 2003: 169). For marginalised asylum seekers, immigrants and ethnic minorities, there is a proliferating transnational 'archipelago' of security experts – police, intelligence, military, immigration control, private companies, specialist lawyers and academics – whose job is to watch out for exceptional risks and potential enemies among these groups, attending to them in ways that are often licensed to exceed the usual democratic accountabilities (Bigo, 2002, 2006; Khan, 2014; see Chapters 9 and 11, this volume).

These are not all-or-nothing developments, and they themselves require a lot more sociological investigation. But there is a strong communicative and interactional dimension in these shifts, and to capture this, many scholars refer to Foucault's notion of governmentality, which involves 'small-scale techniques of coordination [widely diffused throughout society] [which] organise relations on the "capillary" level ... organising individuals, arraying bodies in space and time, coordinating their forces, transmitting power among them ... ground-level social relations [ordered] according to expertly designed logics of control' (Foucault, 1978/2003: 229–245; Fraser, 2003: 162). To study governmentality, says Rose, one should 'try to track force relations at the molecular level, as they flow through a multitude of human technologies, in all the practices, arenas and spaces where programmes for the administration of others intersect with techniques for the administration of ourselves' (Rose, 1999: 5). Gumperzian analysis can make a powerful empirical contribution to this, and it is worth briefly sketching the kinds of area that IS could engage with, even though IS will undoubtedly need further development to do so (cf. Jacquemet, 2011; Jones, 2015; Rampton, 2016).

Gumperz' work on code-switching managed to put real-time attentional tracking, cognitive inferencing, shifts in interactional footing and cultural repositioning all together in a single analysis, and this provides a good base for addressing the sociocommunicative practices (and sensibilities) developing in the everyday use of digital technologies. Of course, the code-switching framework needs to be expanded beyond just styles and languages to different media, but this isn't difficult and Ron Scollon, for example, offers tools for analysing multitasking, where 'keep[ing] open several competing sites of [media] engagement' simultaneously is 'the normal attention pattern' (Scollon, 1998: 256; also Schegloff, 2002).

At the same time, although the analysis of real-time processing in the here-and-now is vital, it is never enough in Gumperzian analysis. Beyond the understandings articulated by co-present individuals, there are historically shaped and potentially discrepant communicative sensibilities operating unnoticed in the background. Gumperz looked at this in the interaction between majority and minority ethnic groups, and at least in part, he attributed misunderstandings to hidden differences in their cultural and linguistic socialisation. But as van Dijck (2013a: 29) indicated with a call to 'make the hidden layer visible', there are often very influential 'communicative styles' in online Web 2.0 environments which, far from disadvantaging their carriers, are logics of control expertly designed to generate profit.

Gumperz' concern about the superficiality with which institutions construe and assess individuals also gains extra edge when Haggerty and Ericson refer to the profiles constructed through digital surveillance:

> Rather than being accurate or inaccurate portrayals of real individuals, [these profiles [aka 'data doubles']] are a form of pragmatics: differentiated according to how useful they are in allowing institutions to make discriminations among populations … [S]urveillance is often a mile wide but only an inch deep … Instead, knowledge of the population is now manifest in discrete bits of information which break the individual down into flows for purposes of management, profit and entertainment. (Haggerty & Ericson, 2000: 614, 618, 619)

At the opposite end of the surveillance process, IS studies of interactional conduct tuned to the 'eavesdropper' in Goffman's (1981) participation frameworks could investigate the experience of surveillance which, according to Ball, 'has not yet been addressed in any detail' (Ball, 2009: 640; see Chapter 11, this volume). Likewise, data sessions focused on the ways in which people actually experience – use, enjoy and depend on – digital technologies in their everyday practice, could probe Ball's suggestion that although 'individuals sometimes appear to do little to counter surveillance[, that] does not mean that surveillance means nothing to them' (Ball, 2009: 641).

If IS researchers are to engage fully with new sociocommunicative practices and forms of control like these, they will need to collaborate with computational specialists to tackle, inter alia, the codes, algorithms and protocols that translate human bodies, movement and communication into digital information, and they will also face the practical problem of getting access to the 'scattered centres of calculation' where all the data gets processed (Haggerty & Ericson, 2000: 613). But short of this, there is still a great deal to learn about the manner and extent to which new technologies are (or are not) changing the institutional regimes and participant practices in offices, clinics and schools (on the latter, see Georgakopoulou, 2014; Lytra, 2014; Rampton, 2016: § 5). Foucault's governmentality is a major reference point for social scientists trying to make sense of these developments, and offering interactional sociolinguistics such a clear point of connection, this is important new territory for IS to continue its interdisciplinary endeavour in.

In what follows, Chapters 6, 7 and 8 illustrate interactional sociolinguistics most clearly, insofar as they analyse the details of linguistic structure in interactional discourse and tie all this to large-scale sociohistorical processes (class, migration and ethnicity). But interactional sociolinguistics also feeds into a broader, more encompassing current of contemporary ethnographic work on communication, drawn together by a commitment to interdisciplinary relevance and the practical applications of research. This is 'linguistic ethnography', a tradition that has taken shape in the UK and Europe over the last 20 years or so.[9] Gumperz is obviously influential here as well, but there is a more comprehensive reference guide in Dell Hymes' foundational writings on ethnography, and all this is the focus of the next chapter.

Notes

(1) I am very grateful to Celia Roberts (who introduced me to interactional sociolinguistics) and to Jan Blommaert for some very helpful feedback on the arguments here.

(2) For further details, see, for example, Gumperz, 1999, Rampton, 2006: Ch. 10, 2007a, 2009b.

(3) Neighbour, pupil, trouble-maker, goal-keeper, card-dealer, joke-teller, bore, etc., etc. – see, for example, Zimmerman, 1998 on 'transportable', 'situated' and 'discourse' identities.

(4) I am grateful to Kamran Khan for pointing out this connection.
(5) More recent work rejects this distinction, insisting that in language use, propositional meaning is itself always indexical as well (cf. Agha, 2007: Ch. 1). So Gumperz' distinction between indexical and literal meaning is too sharply drawn, and maybe this not only reflects his partial susceptibility to institutional language ideologies prioritising the latter, but also the strength of his opposition to them.
(6) 'The ontological element of scientific theory can be understood as a series of internally consistent insights into the trans-historical *potentials* of the phenomena that constitute a domain of inquiry, ie the fundamental processes and properties that may be activated or realised in numerous different ways on different occasions ... [T]he development of substantive theories is required to determine how these processes and properties operate and appear in any given context, and these theories are subject to empirical refutation ... [A]n acceptable ontology of potentials may be sufficiently flexible to allow for the development of a variety of different substantive theories addressed to the same subject-matter ...' (Cohen, 1987: 279; Rampton, 2001a).
(7) Comparably, the early distinction between 'metaphorical' and 'situational' code-switching (Blom & Gumperz, 1972) speaks to what Silverstein subsequently differentiated as 'presupposing' and 'creative' indexical signs (Collins, 2011: 412; Rampton, 1998: 302ff.; Silverstein, 1976).
(8) My own work has faced similar censure – see the discussion of Koole (2007) in Section 3.4 below.
(9) In fact a version of the present chapter appeared in the section on 'Antecedents, related areas and key concepts' in the *Routledge Handbook of Linguistic Ethnography*, edited by Karin Tusting (2020b).

3 Linguistic Ethnography

(co-authored with Janet Maybin and Celia Roberts)

3.1 Introduction

Since 2000, quite a substantial body of work has emerged in Britain and Europe describing itself as 'linguistic ethnography' (LE). In contrast to the situation in North America, the sub-discipline of linguistic *anthropology* has very little institutional presence here (Rampton, 2007b: 586), but in 2000 a group of researchers at the annual conference of the British Association for Applied Linguistics (BAAL) agreed to interact more closely under a broadly ethnographic umbrella, looking for links across the different traditions with which they were most closely associated: Gumperzian Interactional Sociolinguistics (e.g. Gumperz *et al.*, 1979; Rampton, 1995/2018: Ch. 2; Roberts *et al.*, 1992); New Literacy Studies, in the tradition of Heath (1983) and Street (1984) (e.g. Barton, 1994; Barton *et al.*, 2000); Critical Discourse Analysis (e.g. Fairclough, 1989, 1992); neo-Vygotskian research on language and cognitive development (Maybin, 2006; Mercer, 1995; Vygotsky, 1978); and interpretive applied linguistics for language teaching (AL for LT), associated with scholars such as Widdowson (1984), Brumfit (1984) and Strevens (1977) (Rampton, 2007b: 586–589).

The ensuing collaboration involved seminars, position papers, training courses and publications, as well as the initiation of BAAL's first Special Interest Group, and the currency of the term 'linguistic ethnography' has steadily increased, from two citations on Google Scholar in 2000 to well over 350 during 2017 (see Tusting, 2020a: 1–2). A first conference was organised in 2008, and it developed into the biennial *Explorations in Ethnography, Language & Communication* (held in Copenhagen, Stockholm and Oslo as well as different locations in Britain). There is now a *Routledge Handbook of Linguistic Ethnography* (2020b, edited by Tusting), and something of the tenor of this work can be glimpsed in the first collection of explicitly LE papers, published in 2015 as *Linguistic Ethnography: Interdisciplinary Explorations*, edited by Snell, Shaw and Copland. Rather than concentrating on ethno-cultural groups and communities, the chapters in the collection focus overwhelmingly on institutions and professions; about half of the 20 contributors came into research with extensive first-hand personal experience as professionals in the sites they investigate (especially in education and health); and all of the studies are based in the countries where the authors live, for the most part working in their first languages.

The chapter that follows provides a fuller account of the assumptions, values, frameworks and techniques that underpin LE. In keeping with the dynamic that has animated LE, the account is grounded in a series of historical, institutional and/or methodological encounters, looking at the questions and possibilities that these interactions generate. So we consider the relationships between:

- linguistics and ethnography;
- elements interacting in the communicative process;
- linguistic ethnography and researchers from different disciplines;
- linguistic ethnography and non-academic professionals.

The next section looks at what is involved in the combination of linguistics with ethnography, and at some relatively recent historical changes that have influenced their relationship, strengthening the epistemological status of ethnography and sharpening the analytic relevance of linguistics. Turning to the communication process, Section 3.3 dwells on the theoretical debt to linguistic anthropology and points to fundamental concepts that are certainly compatible with interactional sociolinguistics but now extend beyond the analytic repertoire that Gumperz developed (see Chapter 2 above). After this discussion of disciplinary and theoretical issues, the chapter then turns to practical experiences of promoting linguistic ethnography in a discussion of LE's interdisciplinary potential and the scope it offers for engaging with non-academic professionals. Section 3.4 reviews a long-running LE training programme for social scientists that has taught linguistic and discourse analytic tools embedded in an ethnographic epistemology, emphasising heightened methodological reflexivity as the only way of responding to the inevitably very diverse ways in which LE gets appropriated. Section 3.5 then explores more of this diversity, describing LE's encounter with the knowledge and experience of non-academic professionals in two ways. The challenges facing educators who take up LE research are discussed first, followed by an account of the interaction between well-established linguistic ethnographers and health professionals in collaborative projects designed to improve institutional practice.

We can begin with a discussion of the relations between ethnography and linguistics.

3.2 Ethnography, Linguistics and Linguistic Ethnography

To examine the dynamic relationship between linguistics and ethnography, there are at least three questions: Exactly how do we define these two perspectives? What kinds of potential emerge when they are put together? And what is the recent history of their combination? We can take each of these questions in turn.

There has always been disagreement across the social sciences about what exactly counts as ethnography, but from our perspective, the constitutive features are:

(a) *Regard for local rationalities in an interplay between 'strangeness' and 'familiarity'*: Ethnography typically looks for the meaning and rationality in practices that seem strange from afar or at first. It tries to enter the informants' life-world and to abstract (some of) its structuring features, and this entails a process of continuing alternation between involvement in local activity on the one hand and, on the other, an orientation to external audiences and frameworks beyond (cf. Todorov, 1988, on making the strange familiar and the familiar strange). Ethnography tries to comprehend both the tacit and the articulated understandings of the participants in whatever processes and activities are being studied, and it tries to do justice to these understandings in its reports to outsiders.
(b) *Anti-ethnocentricity and relevance*: Ethnography normally questions the oversimplifications in influential discourse, and interrogates prevailing definitions.
(c) *Cultural ecologies*: Ethnography focuses on a number of different levels/dimensions of sociocultural organisation/process at the same time, and it assumes that the meaning and significance of a form or practice involves an interaction between these (and other) levels/dimensions.
(d) *Systems and particularity:* Ethnography looks for patterns and systematicity in situated everyday practice, but it recognises that hasty comparison across cases can blind you to the contingent moments and the complex cultural and semiotic ecologies that give any phenomenon its meaning (see [c]). Ethnography seeks to produce theoretically 'telling' (rather than typical) cases, using 'the particular circumstances surrounding a case … to make previously obscure theoretical relationships suddenly apparent' (Mitchell, 1984: 239), and it demands our attention for the 'delicacy of its distinctions [rather than] the sweep of its abstractions' (Geertz, 1973: 25).
(e) *Sensitising concepts, openness to data, and worries about idealisation*: Ethnographic analysis works with 'sensitising' concepts

'suggest[ing] directions along which to look' rather than with 'definitive' constructs 'provid[ing] prescriptions of what to see' (Blumer, 1969: 148). Questions may change during the course of an enquiry, and the dialectic between theory, interpretation and data is sustained throughout (Hymes, 1978/1996: 10ff.). Although it recognises that selectivity and idealisation are intrinsic to data, ethnographic analysis tries to stay alert to the potential consequentiality of what gets left out.

(f) *Reflexivity and participation*: Ethnography recognises the ineradicable role that the researcher's personal subjectivity plays throughout the research process. It looks to systematic field strategies and to accountable analytic procedures to constrain self-indulgent idiosyncrasy, and it expects researchers to face up to the partiality of their interpretations (Hymes, 1978/1996: 13). But the researcher's own cultural and interpretive capacities are crucial in making sense of the complex intricacies of situated everyday activity among the people and events being studied, and tuning into these takes time and close involvement.

(g) *The irreducibility of experience*: Ethnography's commitment to particularity and participation ([d] and [f]) combines with its concerns about idealisation ([e]) to produce a strong sense of what is unique and 'once-only' in situated acts and interactions (see Willis & Trondman, 2000, on 'this-ness'). Ethnographic writing is often tempered by a sense of the limitations of available forms of representation, and it recognises that there is an important element in actions and events that eludes analysis and can only be intimated or aesthetically evoked (Hymes, 1978/1996: 12, 118).

Linguistics is also a highly contested field. There are a number of very robust linguistic sub-disciplines that treat language as an autonomous system, separating it from the social contexts in which it is used, and there are also varied, large and long traditions of research that have addressed language, culture and society together, using both linguistics and ethnography. But whatever their views on which aspects of language are worth studying, cursory inspection of any textbook or reference work (e.g. Crystal, 2010) shows that among linguists, as well as among many linguistically oriented discourse analysts, it is widely accepted that:

- language is universal among humans, at the same time as changing over time and varying across social groups (of different sizes, durations and locations);
- it is possible to isolate and abstract structural patterns in the ways in which people communicate, and many of these patterns are relatively stable, recurrent and socially shared (to different degrees);

- there is a wide range of quite well-established procedures for isolating and identifying these structures;
- the description and analysis of these patterns benefit from the use of technical vocabularies; and
- although there is certainly much more involved in human communication, these technical vocabularies can make a valuable contribution to our understanding of the highly intricate processes involved when people talk, sign, read, write or otherwise communicate.

When the tenets of linguistics and ethnography are set together like this, substantial differences stand out, in both method and aspiration. In linguistics, the empirical procedures – the elicitation techniques, the processes of idealisation and data preparation and the rules of evidence – are relatively standardised and they are often taken more or less for granted, at least within particular schools and paradigms. The social and personal processes that have brought the researcher to the level of understanding where s/he could start to formulate linguistic rules are seen as relatively insignificant. In contrast, in ethnography, participant-observation plays a major role, and the processes involved in learning and adjusting to different cultural practices are themselves regarded as potentially consequential for the analysis. The researcher's presence/prominence in the field defies standardisation and it introduces a range of contingencies and partialities that really need to be addressed and reported.

The differences between linguistics and ethnography also often extend to the goals of research. Linguistics usually seeks to generalise about language structure and use, and typically only looks beyond what is actually said/signed/written when implied meaning is highly conventionalised (as in, for example, 'presupposition' and 'implicature'). In contrast, ethnography dwells longer on situated particularities, and this difference between them shows up in their finished products. Ethnographies involve rhetorical forms, such as vignettes and narratives (Hymes, 1996: 12–13), that are designed to provide the reader with some apprehension of the fullness and irreducibility of the 'lived stuff' from which the analyst has abstracted structure. Grammars normally don't.

Plainly, LE is founded in the view that the differences between linguistics and ethnography certainly do *not* amount to incompatibility, and among LE practitioners there is a broad consensus that:

(i) the contexts for communication should be investigated rather than assumed. Meaning takes shape within specific social relations, interactional histories and institutional regimes, produced and construed by agents with expectations and repertoires that have to be grasped ethnographically;

(ii) analysis of the internal organisation of verbal (and other kinds of semiotic) data is essential to understanding its significance and position in the world. Meaning is far more than just the 'expression of ideas', and biography, identifications, stance and nuance are extensively signalled in the linguistic and textual fine-grain.

This formulation can of course cover a much larger and older body of scholarship on language and culture – Hymes, for example, sketched much the same ground in his call for 'social inquiry that does not abstract from verbal particulars, and a linguistic enquiry that connects verbal particulars ... with social activities and relationships' (Hymes, 1975/1996: 87). It also allows differences in emphasis, so that in some research:

- ethnography serves as a way of enriching a fundamentally linguistic project, as in, for example, Eckert's research on language change (2000) or Levinson's cultural model of cognition (1996),

while in other work,

- linguistics can be a way of helping researchers with a range of different backgrounds to reach deeper into the ethnographic description of social or institutional processes (cf. Hymes, 1996: 8; Sapir, 1929/1949: 166).

But whichever way the balance tilts, a number of processes have added impetus to the integration of linguistics and ethnography in recent years, and it is worth describing these in more detail.

Although the history of their relationship reaches back much further, Gumperz and Hymes' seminal 1972 edited collection, *Directions in Sociolinguistics: The Ethnography of Communication*, provides a useful reference point from which to sketch these recent developments. The volume brought contributors together from very different backgrounds in linguistics, anthropology, sociology and psychology, and Hymes' first chapter explained that '[i]n order to develop models, or theories, of the interaction of language and social life, there must be ... an approach [to description] that partly links, but partly cuts across, partly builds between ... the disciplines' (Hymes, 1972b: 41). Some of the chapters used sociocultural methods to enhance the analysis of linguistic structure (e.g. Labov), and others drew linguistics into the examination of principally cultural questions (e.g. Bernstein). But since then, much has changed, both in the organisation of academic knowledge and in real-world experience, and there have been at least three major shifts that have affected the linguistics/ethnography relationship.

First, in the humanities and social sciences, the development of post-structuralism has weakened the authority of formal structural linguistics as an epistemological reference point. During the post-war heyday of structuralism, there was widespread anxiety that the humanities and social sciences were 'pre-scientific' (Hymes, 1983: 196), and linguistics was held up as a model for the scientific study of culture as an integrated system – indeed, suggests Hymes, the intensity of US anthropologists' interest in linguistics as a key to the organisation of culture was matched by linguists' lack of regard for ethnography. But since the 1970s there has been a decline in the cross-disciplinary significance of formal linguistics as a model of knowledge production. With the emergence of post-structuralism, a burgeoning interest in agency, fragmentation and contingency has weakened the linguists' traditional assumption that system and coherence were there in their data, just waiting to be discovered. Linguists' claims to the scientific status of their knowledge have also been relativised by growth in the belief that knowledges are situated and plural, and indeed it is now quite commonly felt that the natural sciences have themselves been worryingly 'pre-social', with ethnography and other forms of contextual study being invoked as necessary correctives (Gibbons *et al.*, 1994: 99).

Second, the critique associated with post-structuralism has of course entailed much more than just dislodging linguistics from its former pre-eminence. Received notions like 'society', 'nation', 'community', 'gender' and 'ethnicity' have also been the subject of extensive reassessment, so that now, rather than being seen as natural and unchangeable entities or identities, the default position in a great deal of social science is that these are social constructions, produced in discourse and ideology (see, for example, Anderson, 1983; Foucault, 1972). In addition, beyond the academy, established categories in social analysis and policy have been profoundly challenged by the material, real-world changes associated with globalisation, with massively increased population mobility and rapid developments in communication technology (Blommaert & Rampton, 2011a; Platt, 2008; Vertovec, 2007). The implications of these changes for empirical research are at least twofold:

(i) ethnography becomes an invaluable resource. One of ethnography's key characteristics is its commitment to taking a long hard look at empirical processes that make no sense within established frameworks, and if we are experiencing a period where traditional frameworks look a lot less well established than they used to, then ethnography is one important option to turn to. But, at the same time,

(ii) if we relax the strictures of formalist theory and draw instead on its power as a resource for describing the patterns in communication, linguistics comes to the fore as a vital ingredient in the development of empirical analyses tuned to the contemporary material and philosophical environment. With post-structuralist critiques of essentialism firmly in place, it is now conceptually rather hard to justify any project that sets out to analyse particular peoples, groups and communities. Rather, the challenge is to understand how these group identities get constructed in culture, discourse and ideology, and how humans come to inhabit these social categories in ways that are both similar and different. So instead of, for example, setting out to study the Roma in Hungary, the aim should be to analyse how 'Roma' circulates as a representation in Hungarian discourse, how it settles on particular humans, how it comes to channel and constrain their activity and material position (cf. Tremlett, 2007; see also Moerman, 1974: 62). Once we make these commitments, linguistics becomes highly relevant. Categories and identities get circulated, taken up and reproduced in textual representations and communicative encounters. So if we want to understand the social and cultural construction of identities, persons and groups, linguistics can help us take a serious look at the discursive processes.

Third, at least in the UK, the social sciences have seen a substantial shift in the dynamics of interdisciplinary knowledge production itself, moving from what researchers have termed 'Mode 1 interdisciplinarity' to 'Mode 2' (Gibbons *et al.*, 1994). In Mode 1 interdisciplinarity, focal problems are identified within a particular (sub-)discipline, and there is cross-referencing to other paradigms or lines of research in order to get past a bottleneck that researchers have reached using only the concepts and methods available within their own discipline. The rationales for cross-referencing, and the parameters of what to include and leave out, are set fairly clearly, and there is a well-defined sense of exactly what kinds of methodological borrowing and combination are in order. In contrast, in 'Mode 2' interdisciplinarity, 'real-world' issues of social, technical and/or policy relevance provide the starting point; there may be non-academic stakeholders involved throughout, and it is the multi-dimensional complexity of the problem that motivates the mixing. Quite a high tolerance for ambiguity is required, and it is important not to commit too quickly to the specification of the key methods and dimensions of analysis. In the 1972 Gumperz and Hymes collection, there was a strong awareness of real-world issues (e.g. Gumperz & Hymes, 1972: 10, 13, 38, 53), but the interdisciplinary project was itself formulated in principally Mode 1 terms: linguistics was thought to have reached a cul-de-sac; there was a considerable discussion of methods for future work (e.g. Gumperz & Hymes, 1972: 23ff., 36); and the goal was to create 'a basic science that does not yet exist' (Hymes, 1972b: 38). In contrast, over the last two or three decades in the UK and elsewhere, the research and higher education funding councils have increased the emphasis on interdisciplinary work that takes real-world problems as a starting point, that involves collaboration with stakeholders and that reckons explicitly with impacts beyond the academy. The upshot is that in, for example, a study by Abreu *et al.* in 2009, 60% of British social scientists were reported working with public sector partners, 45% with the third sector, 45% with both, and around 40% with the private sector (*Times Higher Education*, 25 June 2009). This shift towards interdisciplinary research involving non-academic impacts and collaboration looks increasingly well embedded (Bernstein, 1996: 68; Gibbons *et al.*, 1994; Strathern, 2000), and if ethnography is characterised by a commitment to dialogue and to adaptive sensitivity to feedback from different audiences (e.g. Hymes, 1996: 7), then Mode 2 interdisciplinarity may be especially compatible with an ethnographic sensibility.

These three shifts – the philosophical shifts associated with post-structuralism, the real-world changes effected by globalisation, and the emphasis on Mode 2 interdisciplinarity in research funding policy – impact on ethnography's status in the relationship with linguistics. Before, ethnography could simply be seen as an additional method of data collection, supplementing the otherwise standard procedures of elicitation and analysis in linguistic science. But as we become more conscious of the social and historical particularity of knowledge, ethnography gains foundational weight as a way of seeing, building on dialogue and on a reflexive recognition of the researcher's own positioning. Instead, it is linguistics that becomes the operational resource, prized for its capacity to spotlight even the very smallest moves in the practical negotiation of social relations, but no longer revered as the path from interpretation to objective science. At the same time, perhaps somewhat paradoxically, this decline in the epistemological authority of linguistics opens the door to fuller interdisciplinary engagement, increasing the scope for combining its powerful techniques and findings on communication with the pursuit of issues and agendas formed elsewhere. This is something that Duranti reports in a historical survey of linguistic anthropology in the US:

> In contrast to earlier generations ... students today typically ask 'What can the study of language contribute to the understanding of this particular social/cultural phenomenon (e.g. identity formation, globalisation, nationalism)?' ... for many young scholars today linguistic anthropology is a tool for studying what is *already* being studied by scholars in other fields, for instance, race and racism. (Duranti, 2003: 332–333)

Duranti's characterisation is compatible with a great deal of the work in LE in Britain and Europe, and this perspective also seems to be growing more influential in sociolinguistics more generally. In their introduction to the second edition of *The New Sociolinguistics Reader* (2009), Coupland and Jaworski see contemporary sociolinguistics as 'a broad and vibrant interdisciplinary project working *across* the different disciplines that were its origins [sociology, linguistics, social psychology, interactional sociolinguistics, discourse analysis]', and of the papers they include in the collection, 'a clear majority ... favour more open-ended, observational research methods and smaller-scale data ... This is the *ethnographic* research design that has considerable momentum in ... Sociolinguistics' (Coupland & Jaworski, 2009: 19, emphasis in original).

So far, then, we have offered an outline of the fundamental characteristics of ethnography and linguistics, and described recent processes that have given momentum to their combination in LE. Gumperz and Hymes' 1972 volume featured as the starting point for our historical comments, and in fact it also serves as an excellent point of departure for the next section of this chapter, in which we review some key concepts for LE, focusing on the elements interacting in communication.

3.3 Describing the Elements Interacting in Communication

In the preface to their 1972 collection, Gumperz and Hymes took the view that the 'ready currency of the term *sociolinguistics* ... does not reflect fundamental agreement on common problems, sources of data, or methods of analysis ... [R]ecent publications ... have, so far, not been integrated into any general theory of language and society' (Gumperz & Hymes, 1972: vi–vii). A number of the scholars assembled in that collection subsequently developed relatively independent schools and traditions of their own (see Section 2.2 above), but a core remained within linguistic anthropology, where a very substantial programme of sub-disciplinary consolidation and refinement emerged, especially in North America (cf. Duranti, 2003). Following in Gumperz and Hymes' path, scholars such as Ochs, Silverstein, Bauman, the Goodwins, Hanks, Briggs, Blommaert and Agha have produced a remarkably coherent vocabulary, which is not only congruent with ethnography but is also capable of producing detailed descriptions of the processes that are of central concern to theories of social practice, with practice understood as the 'production and reproduction of society ... as a skilled [but by no means wholly conscious] performance on the part of its members' (Giddens, 1976: 160; Bourdieu, 1977; Ortner, 2006).

Blommaert provides an encapsulation of the perspective, tracing it back once again to Gumperz and Hymes. In sociolinguistics, he says, there is

> a very long tradition in which language, along with other social and cultural features of people, was primarily imagined relatively fixed in time and space ... Gumperz and Hymes (1972: 15), however ... destabilized these assumptions, ... they defined social and linguistic features not as separate-but-connected, but as *dialectic*, i.e. co-constructive and, hence, *dynamic*. (Blommaert, 2012: 11–12, emphasis in original)

This emphasis on the dynamic co-construction of social order and linguistic meaning can be found in Gumperz' call for 'closer understanding of how linguistic signs *interact* with social knowledge in discourse' (Gumperz, 1982: 29, emphasis added), and as already noted in Chapter 2 and discussed in more empirical detail in Chapter 8, it also matches Silverstein's succinct formulation of the 'total linguistic fact': '[t]he total linguistic fact, the datum for a science of language is irreducibly dialectic in nature. It is an unstable mutual interaction of meaningful sign forms, contextualised to situations of interested human use and mediated by the fact of cultural ideology' (Silverstein, 1985: 220; see also Hanks, 1996: 230). Crucially, this contrasts sharply with structuralist linguistics, in which the formal properties of language are treated independently of their use (as in Saussure's prioritisation of 'langue' over 'parole' and Chomsky's insistence on 'competence' not 'performance'). But there is little surrender in analytic precision, and a flourishing linguistic anthropological literature has done much to achieve another of the goals outlined in 1972: 'to explain the meaning of language in human life ... and not in the abstract, not in the superficial phrases one may encounter in essays and textbooks, but in the concrete, in actual human lives' (Hymes, 1972b: 41).

So what are the central concepts and perspectives in the 'general theory of language and society' that has now emerged? Fuller exposition of a much wider range of ideas can be found in textbooks such as Duranti (1997), Blommaert (2005), Agha (2007) or Ahearn (2012), but to give an indication of the scope and tenor of this apparatus, it is worth outlining three sets of concepts, which in turn illustrate or engage with:

- dynamic contingency, reckoning with human agency and interpretation – the concepts of inferencing, indexicality and reflexivity;
- convention, structure and the building blocks of institutions, pointing to patterns and expectations of regularity ingrained in our practical consciousness and everyday activity – the notions of genre and register; and

- histories, outcomes and material processes beyond, before and after specific communicative encounters, expanding the spatio-temporal horizons of empirical description – multimodality, textual trajectories and contextual processes of different scales.

'*Inferencing*' is a concept that Gumperz emphasised, and it refers to the interpretive work that people perform in trying to reconcile the stuff that they encounter in any given situation with their expectations, prior understandings and so forth (see Section 2.3 for a fuller discussion). When turning from receptive sense-making to speech production, Gumperz spoke of 'contextualisation cues', but contemporary linguistic anthropologists generally use the term '*indexicality*' to refer to the fact that signs are always taken as pointing beyond themselves, to something else in the past, the future or the surrounding environment. So when a word, phrase or sentence is used in communication, it is always taken as a lot more than just its dictionary definition or literal meaning, important though these are. In addition, it will be assessed for, for example, its fit to the visible location, its stylistic elegance, its consistency with the speaker's usual ways of talking, etc. This process of assessment, calibrating the words you hear with your sense of the (dynamically evolving) situation, is referred to as 'meta-pragmatic' *reflexivity*, and it is a feature of speaking as well as listening. A lot of this processing is relatively tacit, with participants constantly engaged in low-key monitoring of how all the details of verbal communication fit with their grasp of the propositions being expressed, with their sense of the speaker's intent, with their understanding of the activity they are in and how it should proceed, etc. But in E.M. Forster's (1924/1973: 267) formulation, '[a] pause in the wrong place, an intonation misunderstood, and a whole conversation [can go] awry'.

With inferencing, indexicality and reflexivity, analytic attention leans towards agency in the ceaseless interplay of agency and structure, even though normative expectations and their social currency and origins follow very closely in the account. With *genre*, the balance tilts towards stability, structure and convention, although here too there is an inextricable role for both agentive action and unpredictable contingency.

In the tradition associated with Bakhtin (1953/1986; Bauman, 2001; Hanks, 1987), a genre is a distinct set of conventionalised expectations about a recognisable type of activity that is also often named – for instance, an argument, a sales transaction, a committee meeting, a game of poker, reading the newspaper. These expectations include a sense of the goals and possible tasks on hand, the roles and relationships typically involved, the ways in which the activity is organised and the kinds of resource suited to carrying it out. Genres help us construe what is happening in interaction and to work out the direction of activity from one moment to the next, and they channel the kind of inferences we make (e.g. laughing or being alarmed by some drastic report, depending on whether or not it is told as a joke): 'Genres guide us through the social world of communication: they allow us to distinguish between very different communicative events, create expectations for each of them, and adjust our communicative behaviour accordingly' (Blommaert, n.d.; Gumperz, 1972: 16–18).

In their potential for stability, genres are one of the building blocks of institutions – think of lessons, detentions and assemblies in a school, or consultations and ward rounds in a hospital. While genres provide the larger bearings that orient our moment-to-moment micro-scale actions on the one hand, they also constitute some of the smallest units in the structural organisation of large-scale institutions on the other. Indeed Bakhtin (1986: 65) saw genres as 'the drive belts from the history of society to the history of language'. But the stability of genres is only ever temporary: '[a] genre ... [cannot] be viewed as a finished product unto itself, but remain[s] partial and transitional ... Because they are at least partly created in their enactment, ... genres are schematic and incomplete resources on which speakers necessarily improvise in practice' (Hanks, 1987: 681, 687). Genres have to be 'accomplished' or 'brought off' in interaction, and participants have to keep checking that they're all tuning to the same stage in the activity, giving and noting indexical signs that, for example, an event should now be moving to a close. There is plenty of scope for failures in generic coordination, and for the participants to be judged as socially insensitive, awkward or incompetent (or maybe just as the unlucky victims of disruptive intrusions from outside). Knowledge and expertise in different genres is of course very unevenly spread among individuals and across social groups, and properly genred performance is a central concern in socialisation throughout the lifespan, whether this involves learning to 'behave nicely at the dinner table' or to 'write a history essay'. As encapsulated visions of the social world tuned to practical action in recurrent situations, projecting particular kinds of conduct and relationship, promising the participants with particular types of personhood, genres are crucial to social reproduction, and they can become the focus of intense struggle as people and institutions try to fix or change their own and others' practice or potential (as can be seen, for example, in repeated UK government attempts to reformat classroom pedagogy and interaction; Rampton & Harris, 2010). But because there is no 'timeless closure' or 'unlimited replication' intrinsic to any genre (Bauman, 2001: 81), a great deal of ideological work (in the form of training, publicity, penalties, consultant advice etc. etc.) is often needed if the preferred genres are to remain steadily in place.

With '*register*' (or 'style'), we move from the conventionalisation of situations and the arrangements for communicative interaction in genre to relatively stable patterning among signs in the flow of speech and discourse (Agha, 2007; Auer, 2007b; Eckert, 2008; Gumperz & Hymes, 1972: 21; Chapters 7 and 8, this volume). Among other things, register covers accent and dialect, which are very commonly seen as reflections of social structure, marking differences in ethnicity, class, region, generation and/or gender. Conceptually, register is quite close to the well-established sociolinguistic notion of 'variety', but whereas sociolinguistics has traditionally treated the relationship between varieties and social structure as a 'separate-but-connected' correlation, the linguistic anthropological notion of register or style is once again aligned with the interaction of form, ideology and situated action identified in Silverstein's total linguistic fact.

Registers are distinctive sets of linguistic and other semiotic signs that get indexically associated with different types of person, group, activity or situation (they can also contribute to the differentiation of genres). The typification process that is crucial to the recognition of a register involves inferring, for example, that someone is from the north of England because of the way they pronounce 'bath' and 'one', that they've had an expensive private education when they say 'yaaa' rather than 'yeh' or 'yes', or that they've got a medical background because of the words they use to talk about bodies. Of course this linkage depends on our perceptions of stratified and segmented social space, which are themselves an aspect of ideology (Bourdieu, 1991; Irvine, 2001: 23–24). So whenever we make a spontaneous link between a speech sound and a social type, ideology is once again integral to locally situated sense-making, often with subsequent interactional effects (maybe increasing the participants' rapport, or alternatively undermining their self-confidence). The 'language ideological' practices that forge or reproduce these links between ways of speaking and social types can vary a great deal in their scale, explicitness and intensity, ranging from curriculum instruction and mass-mediated impersonations to fleeting self-corrections in conversations face-to-face. And register is often a resource for agentive action, as when, for example, pupils in a working-class urban school respond to being patronised by their teacher with a very exaggerated upper-class accent, even though they hardly ever refer to social class explicitly (Section 6.2, this volume). More generally, though, register draws our attention to the fact that in the stream of linguistic expression that people produce together, they are continuously vulnerable to a reflexive process of low-key socio-ideological observation and coding, in ways that are far more enacted than declared (cf. G.B. Shaw's '[i]t is impossible for an Englishman to open his mouth without making some other Englishman hate or despise him' (Shaw, 1916: Preface)).

When other social scientists read sociolinguistic accounts of interactional practice, they are sometimes struck by the agility and speed with which participants adjust or shift their stance, position or self-projection, and this sometimes leads to talk of identities being 'multiple, fluid and ambiguous'. There is at least some justification for this if these accounts of interactional positioning are compared with static demographic identity ascriptions of the kind often used in studies that treat language and society as separate-but-connected and, plainly, the production, interpretation and reflexive monitoring are all agentive processes. But communication entails close and continual attunement among the participants, calibrating what is produced with the range of patterns one has hitherto come to expect, and there is often considerable socio-ideological investment in these expectations. This was clear in the discussion of genre and register, referring to the patterns of expectation for, respectively, the arrangements of activity and the stream of signs, and the proprieties regimenting communicative conduct reach much further. Yes, the normative expectations orienting our interaction certainly do shift as we move from one scene to another in our daily routine, and the opportunities for individual innovation can certainly be greater in some than in others. But there are pressures and constraints all the same, reaching right down into the way in which we formulate the smallest pieces of language. Rather than exemplifying the inherent fluidity of identity production, creativity is more aptly seen as the fleeting exploitation of what Erickson (2001) calls 'wiggle-room' – just a little bit of space for innovation within what is otherwise experienced as the compelling weight of social expectation.

It should be clear by now that although the perspective we are outlining offers an exceptionally sharp view of activity 'on-line' as it unfolds in the present, it also implies longer temporalities. As noted earlier, Gumperz and Hymes' early research programme centred on the 'speech event', but an expansion in the spatio-temporal horizons of theory and analysis has been one of the most important developments since Gumperz and Hymes (1972).

Following scholars like Goffman and the Goodwins, there has been systematic attention paid to non-linguistic sign systems and to the fact that communication is always *multimodal*, with bodies, places and visual perception playing a major part (see Chapter 11, this volume). As C. Goodwin (2000: 1517) explains, 'the [human] body [is] an unfolding locus for the display of meaning and action', and eye gaze, hand gestures, head movement and the posture, movement and positioning of bodies all contribute to this. Obviously, these are themselves affected by material objects and the natural and built environment – compare the scope for expression in a cinema and a dinner table or a park bench – and although the material substance and surround is often treated as irrelevant (as when, for example, the readers of this chapter take the font and paper quality for granted), there are innumerable occasions when our level of attention to it increases (referring to objects, changing location, getting dressed, cleaning, clearing away). In addition, even though we are often only dimly aware of them (if that!), much of our material environment bears the traces of past designs, efforts and resource expenditures (Blommaert, 2012).

When the relative durability of physical matter is combined with our capacity to inscribe it with meaning, individual events are positioned within much longer spans of time. The production and interpretation of meaning in the here-and-now becomes just one stage in the mobility of signs and texts, and participants are seen as themselves actively orienting backwards and forwards to the *trajectories* through which their semiotic products travel (Briggs, 2005). Whereas event-centred sociolinguistics had earlier focused on the local use-value of a particular communicative sign or practice, studying its effect within a given encounter, the 'exchange value' of a sign, text or semiotic object now enters the reckoning, and '*en*textualisation' and '*re*contextualisation' become key terms, addressing (a) the (potentially multiple) people and processes involved in the design or selection of textual 'projectiles' which have some hope of travelling into subsequent settings, and (b) the alteration and revaluation of semiotic objects as they are subsequently taken up in different settings (Agha & Wortham, 2005; Bauman & Briggs, 1990; Silverstein & Urban, 1996).

Interest in the projection and circulation of texts and signs across different events and settings invites comparative analysis of the scale of the networks, media, materials and processes in which these signs travel – their spatial scope, temporal durability and social reach (Blommaert, 2008, 2010a; Pennycook, 2007; Scollon & Scollon, 2004). Section 2.3 discussed the shift away from context-as-'bucket' to context-as-process, but this itself now needs to be conceptualised as layered and *multi-scalar* (Blommaert, 2010a; Cicourel, 1992; Hymes, 1972b: 53). The contexts in which people communicate are partly local and emergent, continuously readjusted to the contingencies of action unfolding from one moment to the next, but they are also infused with information, resources, expectations and experiences that originate in, circulate through and/or are destined for networks, media and processes that can be very different in their reach and duration. This is vividly illustrated in Tusting's account of a few minutes in the work of a nursery nurse in an Early Years Centre, attending to small children while also trying to fill in a form she has been given for recording her observations of individuals:

> [t]he process of writing the observation integrates the immediate activities in the room into broader social systems, and to systems at longer timescales. These broader and longer-term systems include (among others) the interpersonal relationships in the room; the Early Years Centre and its planning procedures; Thea's lifespan, career and training; and government policy and inspection. Each of these is associated with different goals and plays out at different timescales. This is an example of a situated activity which locally produces and reproduces broader social orders. (Tusting, 2010: 85)

Gumperz emphasised the importance of embedding interactional encounters within broader spatio-temporal processes when he called for a 'dynamic view of social environments where history, economic forces and interactive processes ... combine to create or to eliminate social distinctions' (Gumperz, 1982: 29). Notions like multimodality, textual trajectory and multi-scalar context increase our capacity to provide this. Admittedly, the job of describing the processes at play in any layered notion of context is challenging, requiring engagement with, if not expertise in, not just linguistics but potentially also history, economics, sociology, cultural studies, international relations and so forth. But it is worth reflecting on the account of ideology that this apparatus can bring to interdisciplinary research. In a great deal of policy and interview discourse analysis, ideology gets treated only as sets of explicitly articulated statements, but compare this with our portrait of tacit power emerging from ideology's links to inference and indexicality, or of ideological investment and struggle over genres and registers, both of them potentially inscribed in practical consciousness. Equally, if we take up the notion of textual trajectories and study what actually gets entextualised and what subsequently succeeds in carrying forward – or even translates into higher scale processes – then we can bring considerable empirical precision to political notions of 'hearability' and 'voice' (Blommaert, 2005; Briggs, 1997; Hymes, 1996; Mehan, 1996; Section 4.3, this volume). In short, the apparatus developed in linguistic anthropology allows us to trace the palpable mundane reality of widespread societal ideologies through close scrutiny of situated discourse processes, and there is a good case for saying that this layered, multi-scalar and empirically grounded understanding of ideology is one of the most sophisticated in current social science (Blommaert & Rampton, 2011a: 13).

So that is a glimpse of the *instrumentarium* of contemporary linguistic anthropology, and it immediately gives rise to a question about the disciplinary positioning of linguistic *ethnography*: if linguistic anthropology is such a rich resource for the theory and description of communication in contemporary conditions, how come this chapter refers to linguistic ethnography, not anthropology, in its title? There are two reasons. First, for the most part, the researchers aligning with LE do not hold degrees in anthropology. Second, like Hymes, Gumperz and many others, they hold the conviction that the perspectives and concepts described here have potential relevance that reaches much further than anthropology – relevance both for other disciplines such as sociology, psychology, health or management studies, and for engagement with professionals such as teachers, doctors and social workers. This relevance is addressed in the next two sections.

3.4 Linguistic Ethnography in Interdisciplinary Training

The previous section outlined some central concepts developed in linguistic anthropology, and argued for the distinctiveness of their contribution to contemporary debates about social process. Words like 'contingent', 'fluid' and 'unstable' are now frequently repeated in the social sciences, and there is widespread recognition that in order to grasp the new complexities of the contemporary period, the vocabularies of empirical analysis need to be extensively refurbished. We have proposed that the analytic vocabulary of linguistic anthropology provides a robust set of resources with which to address this challenge, and it is worth now showing that this claim to *interdisciplinary* relevance is not just an empty boast.

To do so, it is worth describing a research training programme that has been running for doctoral and post-doctoral researchers across the social sciences since 2007, originally funded by the UK Economic and Social Research Council (the tutors have been Jeff Bezemer, Jan Blommaert, Carey Jewitt, Adam Lefstein, Ben Rampton (director), Celia Roberts and Julia Snell). The programme is entitled *Ethnography, Language & Communication* (ELC). It is targeted at researchers facing the challenge of analysing the data they have collected – it is advertised with the headlines *'Is "qualitative data analysis" too vague for you? Are you wondering how to do justice to your data?'*. It has consisted of intensive two- to five-day summer schools, master classes (with distinguished US researchers such as Elinor Ochs and Ray McDermott), data sessions and day workshops variously thematising education, asylum, health and new media; and in, for example, the period 2007–2010, there were 650–700 participants in the programme, coming from, inter alia, applied and sociolinguistics, health, education, management, psychology, sociology and anthropology. The participants have generally responded to the programme very positively in their formal evaluations of it, and our belief in the cross-disciplinary resonance of concepts from linguistic anthropology has been considerably strengthened by our own first-hand experience of the teaching. Indeed, within this general context of interdisciplinary interaction, it is worth dwelling longer on the programme: (i) because it offers illumination of our approach to enriching ethnography with linguistics; (ii) because we have found a form of teaching that seems to avoid reification, even though pedagogic simplification often threatens to extinguish the kinds of interactive dynamism that we are identifying at the heart of LE; and (iii) because this will allow us to address some of the criticisms of LE as an interdisciplinary endeavour.

In the ELC programme curriculum, we capitalise on ethnography's wide dispersion across the social sciences by assuming that the participants already know about it, and our teaching focuses on the analytic resources offered by sociolinguistics and linguistic anthropology. There are no sessions on ethnographic interviewing or participant observation, and instead we get students to engage with authors or traditions like Goffman, Gumperz, conversation analysis, Goodwin and Goodwin, Briggs and Mehan. This points to a pattern of hybridisation that is likely to occur much more widely in LE. Although we see the LE enterprise as fundamentally ethnographic in character, bringing the ethnographic priorities and perspectives sketched in Section 3.2 (a)–(g) to bear on a range of different topics, it is the linguistics that makes our own contribution really distinctive. What our programme offers students are analytic tools from linguistics and discourse analysis embedded in an ethnographic epistemology (cf. Section 3.2 above; Blommaert, 2007). This means that the apparatus of linguistics and discourse analysis are treated as a set of 'sensitising' concepts, and these have to be applied with reflexive understanding of the researcher's own participation in the circulation of power/knowledge. Once the linguistic apparatus is epistemologically repositioned like this – repositioned as just the extension of ethnography into intricate zones of culture and society that might otherwise be missed – then linguistics offers a very rich and empirically robust collection of frameworks and procedures for exploring the details of social life, also providing a very full range of highly suggestive – but not binding! – proposals about how they pattern together.

So how do we teach linguistics as a set of sensitising concepts? Indeed, how do we prevent students from forgetting the dialectical dynamism encapsulated in the 'total linguistic fact'? There are two steps.

First, focusing on what we have categorised as 'micro', 'genre', 'multimodal' and 'transcontextual' analysis, we provide an accessible distillation of key frameworks and methods, extracting ideas like 'adjacency' and 'entextualisation' from the intellectual traditions in which they gather so much (doctrinal) weight and authority. We acknowledge that of course sub-disciplinary disputes between, say, critical discourse analysis and conversation analysis, do matter, but we tell course participants that these are for later, once they have decided that these analytic perspectives are really worth pursuing. Instead, in regular stocktaking discussions, we push students to be realistic and reflexive in their appropriation of what we are offering, getting them to consider, for example, 'What are the limitations of linguistic ethnography?' or 'Could I successfully defend this approach in my viva examination or a job talk?'

Second – and this is also particularly important for students who already have some background in linguistics – we put the apparatus to use in data sessions (see Chapter 2, this volume), quite often working on data that the course participants have provided themselves. In each roughly two-hour session, we immerse the students in a recording and its accompanying transcript, running with their interests and interpretations while at the same time pointing to the insights afforded by the new perspectives, and pushing them to make their claims accountable to evidence, with an eye on the perils of under- and over-interpretation (cf. Erickson, 1986). The format partly resembles the traditional data session in conversation analysis – there is emphasis on the aesthetic of 'slowness' and 'smallness' (Silverman, 1998), and there are the insistent questions like 'why this now?', 'what next?', etc. (ten Have, 1999). But instead of prioritising a drilling down into the sequential machinery of interaction, we also work outwards to larger scale processes, reflecting for example on the data's implications for the next steps in ethnographic fieldwork (see also Scollon & Scollon, 2007: 615, 619). In some ways, the data in these sessions function in a similar way to the vignette in anthropology, where there is always more going on than the analysis discloses. The sessions generate a huge surplus to what any researcher can actually use in their argument, but there is also a much clearer sense of what is going on, and what you can and really cannot say about the episode in focus. By the end, participants' initial ideas often look either crude or just plain wrong, and there is a much sharper idea of which aspects of the interaction are amenable to plausible interpretation, as well as a much stronger sense of the dimensions that remain opaque, even though intriguing.

These sessions are highly accessible to people with different disciplinary backgrounds, involving interpretative processes that draw both on their ordinary sense-making capacities as language users, and on their biographical experience, including their knowledge of the sites where the data come from and their sense of the relevant life worlds. But beyond the enjoyment of the sessions themselves, what can they get out of them?

For many participants, the process of slow, intensive analysis is itself a revelation, disclosing vivid empirical details in the processes of social construction that they had hitherto had little or no conception of. As this ontological re-gearing takes effect, students become clearer about the potential relevance to their own projects of the apparatus we are offering. Of course there are sure to be some people who decide not to make any further use of these tools, but our hope is that their intensive exposure to the tangible, on-line moment-to-moment co-production of social relations has at least put them in a different position intellectually. Even if they revert to the content analysis of fieldnotes or interview transcripts as their main analytic strategy, we still hope that they retain some residual sense of what they are glossing over. To encourage a degree of more active adoption, we do tell the participants that if there is a small stretch of interaction that forms the crux of an argument that they want to develop, then it is worth double-checking with the concepts and procedures learnt in the data sessions, using them as a safety measure to ensure that they have not jumped the gun in their first interpretations. More than that, data-session procedures can help to work up a thesis chapter with data they had initially viewed as poor, insufficient and destined for the bin. And then at the highest level of interdisciplinary engagement, our aim is to provide the participants with the resources for varying the magnification in their analyses, moving flexibly across processes of different scales in line with the development of their arguments and questions. There is no retreat from larger generalisation about contemporary society in LE, and plainly, participants with non-linguistic backgrounds bring a range of sophisticated vocabularies that are very well tuned to the description of historical, political, institutional and other processes. But our overall commitment is to making both academic and political generalisations about social life accountable to the kinds of small-scale everyday activity that we can observe, record and transcribe, and data sessions represent a first arena in which to explore the analytic practices that this entails.

As we have said, when one alters the magnification and shifts from one process to another in a layered and multi-scalar view of context, it is necessary to draw on different sets of analytic resources, reading different literatures. This is very well accepted in ethnography (cf. e.g. Burawoy, 1998; Hammersley, 2007: 694; Scollon & Scollon, 2007: 617), but the mixing of perspectives is obviously not straightforward, and it can often give rise to some discomfort. Bricolage and eclecticism can sometimes amount to 'factitious amalgamation of dissimilar ideas or theses that look compatible only insofar as they are not clearly conceived' (Angenot, 1984: 159, cited in Hammersley, 1999: 577). Indeed, we ourselves have been scolded for failing to realise that, for example, 'post-structuralist theory ... sociolinguistic quantitative empirical studies, [and] qualitative conversation analytical work ... are not of the same epistemological status, and therefore they cannot be added up to a single argument' (Koole, 2007, reviewing Rampton, 2006). But the point is that paradigms do not have to be swallowed whole. Sociolinguistic quantitative studies and conversation analysis *can* be mixed if one is careful and willing to separate findings and methods from the explanations and interpretations with which they are conventionally packaged. So it is, for example, perfectly possible to work with the fact that there are systematic quantitative differences in the extent to which speakers use particular sounds in particular settings, *without* having to buy into the idea that these are produced by variations in 'attention to speech' (cf. Labov, 1972; see Chapters 6 and 8, this volume). Similarly, it is easy to make very productive use of CA findings on the sequential organisation of talk *without* refusing to consider the participants' ideological interpretations (Schegloff, 1999; Wetherell, 1998).

In fact this denaturalisation of paradigms is hard to avoid in interdisciplinary dialogues of the kind instantiated in our training programme, and it generates a methodological reflexivity that has to be embraced. In interdisciplinary regions oriented to real-world problems – 'Mode 2' discussed in Section 3.2 above – definitions and assumptions are repeatedly relativised and there is 'a continuous process of negotiating authority and relevance' (Roberts & Sarangi, 1999: 475). There is incessant pressure to account for the particularity of the angles and occlusions that different methods and approaches entail, and one is forced back to fundamentals in order to try to work out how different things fit together. In the ELC programme, there has been no question of trying to establish the kind of orthodoxies one might expect in singular disciplines like anthropology and linguistics. As a programme team based outside the institutions and disciplines where individual participants are doing their research, we have had no control over what our short course graduates eventually do with the training we provide: we have not been able to impose any uniformity in the theoretical questions driving them; and since there are no assessed assignments and they soon return home to the diverse disciplinary departments where their PhDs are examined, we have made no attempt to standardise criteria and monitor the adequacy of their data analyses (Rampton, 2007b: 594–595; contrast Hymes, 1972: 52). Indeed, the training itself could be characterised, albeit a little flippantly, as (a) 'coming together', (b) 'getting down to basics' in the sessions, and then afterwards, (c) 'anything goes'. Heightened methodological reflexivity is the only option here, tuned to the task with encouragement from Hymes (1969: 44–45): '[p]roductive scholars know that problems lead where they will and that relevance commonly leads across disciplinary boundaries'.

Some similar issues emerge in LE's encounter with non-academic professions, although here it is also likely to face a range of doubts and resistances that are firmly grounded in specific institutions.

3.5 Linguistic Ethnography and Non-academic Professions

Carrying across the Atlantic, US linguistic anthropology was welcomed within a very active tradition of applied linguistics in Britain (Section 3.1), and this commitment to practical intervention in real-world processes has gathered momentum with the development of Mode 2 interdisciplinarity. So this section looks at LE's encounter with non-academic professionals from two perspectives. First, it considers the shifts in orientation involved when, in an experience of re-socialisation, people with backgrounds in education become LE researchers. Second, it discusses what LE looks like when, in contexts of collaborative research, it encounters the very well established perspectives of professionals in health.

In *research in educational settings*, the stimulus for engaging with LE often starts from an educator's professional experience and practice. But the questions they subsequently explore as linguistic ethnographers often require some substantial shifts – from a teaching, advisory or educational management role to that of researcher, or from a professional school gaze to the ethnographic scrutiny of phenomena and their meaning between, around and cross-cutting official activity (e.g. Maybin, 2006). These shifts entail radical changes in the perception of what is happening in the classroom and how it is significant, and educationalists can face quite formidable ontological and epistemological challenges in achieving this: 'it takes a tremendous effort of will and imagination to stop seeing only the things that are conventionally "there" to be seen ... [I]t is like pulling teeth to get [researchers] to see or write anything beyond what "everyone" knows' (Becker, 1971: 10). The authoritative, knowledge-full professional who is responsible for guiding students through a particular curriculum has to become a novice researcher, striving to immerse her/himself in 'the moment to moment interactional implementation of locally instantiated social organisation' (Cicourel, 1993: 89).

This contrast between educational and ethnographic perspectives stands out especially clearly when language and literacy are in focus. In schools in England, for instance, English language in the National Curriculum is largely codified through rather formal descriptions of grammar and genre. Terms like 'context', 'speaker', 'listener', 'meaning' and 'function' are relatively fixed concepts in the analysis and evaluation of speech and writing. Students' individual progress is measured against specified language targets, and their results are treated as indicators of the success of teaching and learning, on which teaching careers and school survival depend. This is in stark contrast to LE, which emphasises the complexity of contextualisation, the dynamics of dialogue, the multi-scalar implications of language functions and the contingency and ideological saturation of meaning. So researchers moving from language education to LE have to engage with at least three kinds of epistemological shift. First, they need to move from an educational view of language and literacy as skills and competencies to a more anthropological focus on how language is used as part of social practice, deeply connected with relationships, identity, power and cultural values. Second, there is a shift from seeing language as produced by individuals, reflecting their knowledge and competence, to focusing on language as produced between people, providing a site for their exploration and negotiation of knowledge and positioning. And third, there is a shift from treating language as a coherent product, a system that needs to be learnt, to studying it as part of a dynamic ideological communicative process emerging in everyday life and experience. In terms of fieldwork practice, these moves also often entail a shift of empirical gaze, looking beyond students' spoken language and literacy in official classroom activities, to collecting data from different sites across the school, investigating the meaning and significance of their different language practices for the individuals themselves. And data are no longer analysed in terms of how they speak to an educational framework of skills, competencies and improvement – instead they are examined in terms of emergent meanings and significance for participants' (different) perspectives, generating a far richer understanding of context and contingency.

In reality, of course, there is a good deal of variation in how far people travel along the route from education into LE (see Green & Bloome, 1997; Lefstein & Snell, 2014), and hybridisation also occurs the other way when well-established and experienced LE researchers work with professionals side by side (see Hymes, 1980a; and Van der Aa & Blommaert, 2011, on ethnographic monitoring). Indeed, collaboration is by no means simple, as can be seen if we now turn to LE work on *health communication.*

In research on health communication, there are some people with medical training who develop expertise in LE in order to address issues that concern them professionally (e.g. Swinglehurst, 2015), but most of the research has been driven by academic social scientists without health backgrounds. Instead of involving the process of de-familiarisation described in the educational case above, the initial challenge bears a closer resemblance to the classic anthropological task of becoming familiar with the strange (Bezemer, 2015). But the work does not end there: when researchers take on advisory and consultancy roles, they also have to show the professionals that their own perspective has practical relevance in a process that involves problematising the issues rather than attempting easy solutions (Roberts *et al.*, 2000). This requires perspectival shifts – and can generate resistances – that can be quite considerable.

First, language is not generally an object of gaze within the health professions, except in its narrowest, deficit formulation as 'poor language'. When communication is addressed as 'communication skills', this is done normatively, using social psychological terms or prescriptive nostrums like 'use open questions'. So there is a substantial distance between this position, where language is treated as a transparent medium for referring and for achieving actions, and the linguistic ethnographic view of situated language practices playing a major role in constructing healthcare and shaping the medical (Candlin & Candlin, 2003; Freeman & Heller, 1987). There are also substantial differences in approaches to research, and the move to joint problematisation requires the professionals to abandon the stance of a research consumer, shifting into a more collaborative relationship (Roberts & Sarangi, 2003). Alongside the positivist and statistical perspectives rated most highly within medicine, medical professionals need to make space for findings that derive from long periods in the field and from the slow and protracted examination of what initially looks small and banal, eventually coming to integrate these with wider ideologies and processes.

The kinds of process involved can be illustrated by referring to Roberts' work with the Royal College of General Practitioners (work strongly influenced by Gumperz and interactional sociolinguistics). In an involvement that proved long term, Roberts was first approached in the 1990s and then invited in again 15 years later, with a request to investigate the selection processes that the RCGP used to license family doctors in the UK, in order to see whether they involved practices that might account for a persistent gap in the success rates of white British candidates and candidates from migrant or ethnic minority backgrounds (Roberts *et al.*, 2000). The mix of health, 'race' and exclusion is a potent one, made more complex and political by (sometimes productive) tensions around credibility and authority. During the project, there were debates around what counted as language, about the extent to which language and cultural processes were wired together and about where indeed 'language' actually was in the simulated consultations that were the centrepiece of the licensing exam. Much of this debate focused on the way in which candidates were rated for 'data gathering', 'clinical management' and 'interpersonal skills'. While the professionals treated these as unproblematic categories, Roberts sought to analyse the encounters more holistically and to draw out the taken-for-granted assumptions about language use and linguistic competence that permeated the exam.

Another central debate focused on the ways of thinking that governed the design and implementation of the examination. The RCGP evaluated the exam within a definition of reliability and validity, which among other things excluded consideration of the effect on candidate behaviour of *simulation* itself in the mock consultations conducted in the exam, as well as of the degree of linguistic and cultural diversity within the population of patients they would be serving as GPs. RCGP colleagues could recognise and approve of the science in the linguistic analysis, the detailed transcripts and the effort to seek patterns across relatively large amounts of data, but there were some tensions when: (i) researchers tried to link the linguistic detail to the wider issues of exam validity; (ii) they used small and highly detailed examples to make telling points rather than persuading through numbers (also Bezemer, 2015); and (iii) they introduced new classificatory systems which focused on how local inferencing processes combined broad normative judgements (e.g. 'the candidate was clunky') with the evaluation of micro-linguistic features that operated below the level of conscious awareness. Within the RCGP's regime of thought, it was generally very hard to understand the perspective of linguistic ethnography/interactional sociolinguistics, and if the researchers were not actually regarded as mad or bad, it was easy to see them as just sad, spending so much time on what looked irrelevant to the professionals, either all too obvious or really rather meaningless (Foucault, 1971: 12–16). With the researcher acting both as ethnographer and as critical consultant, there was also considerable scope for suspicion. In the examination centre, the associate researcher on the project initially referred to the spaces where she was not permitted to go as 'sacred places' – as areas where she needed to go as a researcher working in partnership with the RCGP, but was not seen as 'one of us'.

The researchers also found that the interpretations, findings and conclusions produced in reports and papers often seemed overly tentative and open when compared with the styles of research communication that medical professionals are used to. Over the course of Roberts' relationship with the RCGP, which involved a good deal of data collection and analysis working across several scales, there was a lot of productive discussion about how categorical a particular stance or interpretation ought to be, and whether it is possible to acknowledge multiple interpretations. What may seem to be a healthy and realistic interpretive plurality in LE may look like 'dormouse valour' to professionals, and in the end, a consensus on new ways of looking at institutional and professional problems – in this case, a new analytic language for talking about the oral examination – can itself require both professionals *and* researchers to embrace impurity, seeking productive compromises.

Certainly, it is important to acknowledge the complexity of interaction and its relationship to broader themes such as assessment, standards and fairness, but there are limits to how far one could expect any professional institution to embrace the dynamic contingency involved in something like the total linguistic fact. In purely academic terms, correlational approaches to communication that treat the ingredients as only separate-but-connected clearly lead to an impoverished understanding of meaning-making in human interaction. But if language is to be used in any kind of institutional measurement or assessment, a stabilised system has to be established in which some dimensions of communication are given priority over others. For linguistic ethnographers who seek to engage with these institutional regimes practically, there is no question of standing outside the ideological processes that this fixing entails. Instead, the task is to try to understand them as fully as possible, to appreciate reflexively the strengths and limits of their own position and to nudge the standardisation process in directions that seem more defensible (see also Section 4.3).

This health communication case also throws light on joint data sessions and the different kinds of understanding they make possible among professionals and LE/IS researchers (see Section 2.5). Engaging professionals in data sessions focused on interactions relevant to their work interests can either serve as part of the ethnographic data-collection process itself (Lefstein & Snell, 2011, 2014), or as a post-research activity, providing opportunities to examine and debate professional policies and practices with research informants and their colleagues (Bezemer, 2015; Bloor, 1997: 320–321). Responses to these data may be anywhere on the spectrum, from ad hoc and immediate reactions to a specific incident, to feedback in formal group sessions where data illustrate the researcher's likely findings, and there are traps and affordances in the process of joint analysis that relate to stance, to values and to purposes.

The encounter between the ethnographer, professionals and the data can spark the renegotiation of subject positions around authority, credibility, trust, status and expertise. Exposing professionals to video-recordings of their own practice can have quite wide organisational ramifications, independent of the researcher's perspective (Iedema & Carroll, 2011), while in Mey's (1987) disturbing metaphor, the researcher may him/herself be seen as 'the poet' handing out knowledge to 'the peasants', since the researcher's justification for these joint sessions resides in claims to expertise that prioritise their own ways of looking and knowing over the practical knowledge of the professional group. There can be tensions around what counts as analysable and whether and how that matters, and data sessions are also places where learner/teacher relationships can be renegotiated, with institutional and professional knowledge trumping the researcher's interpretations, producing new and more ecologically valid analysis (Cicourel, 2007). In the discussion of the interdisciplinary training courses in Section 3.4, the data sessions had a principally pedagogic function, but in the interaction with professionals, they can serve a much wider range of purposes. Some of these relate to knowledge and understanding: using data sessions to persuade, to discover about the insiders' perspective, to demonstrate new ways of seeing, to see language as a topic in itself (and not just take it for granted), to move through the micro to more macro processes. But data sessions also play an important part in the management of field relations: gaining trust and access to opportunities for more 'lurking and soaking', satisfying curiosity, justifying the time that informants have had to give to the project and appeasing their concerns. On matters such as these can depend the outcomes of research, their authority, credibility and usefulness.

3.6 Conclusion

When Hymes started theorising the relationship between linguistics and ethnography, he inserted it into the larger project of bringing anthropology 'back home', turning away from the 'study of people not ourselves', 'of coloured people by whites', back to the analysis of educational and other institutional processes in the US (Hymes, 1969; 1996: 4, Ch. 3). He went on to sketch out a 'vision' of ethnography disseminated through society at large. At one pole, he suggested, there would be people who had been professionally trained in ethnography, and at the other pole there would be the general population, respected for their intricate and subtle knowledge of the worlds they lived in. In between, there would be people who could 'combine some disciplined understanding of ethnographic inquiry with the pursuit of their vocation' (Hymes, 1980: 99). Hymes wanted to make the middle group as extensive as possible, arguing that 'of all forms of scientific knowledge, ethnography is the most open, the most compatible with a democratic way of life, the least likely to produce a world in which experts control knowledge at the expense of those who are studied' (Hymes, 1980a: 105). But in his view at the time, it was the professional ethnographers who would provide the launching pad for this. Since then, significant parts of this programme have carried across the Atlantic, but in doing so, it has taken root in terrain where anthropological ethnographers interested in language have been relatively scarce. In the absence of a UK linguistic anthropology ready and able to train students *ab initio* and to operate as a community of practice where novices could develop skills in language-and-culture analysis, Hymes' programme has been embraced by a mixture of his middle group and non-anthropologists doing research in applied and sociolinguistics.

Many of these researchers have had to find out for themselves how to work ethnography into their existing interests in language, and their background and position have turned the emerging mixture into a way of getting analytic distance on practices and processes quite close at hand. Judged by the textual standards expected in traditional academic work, the written products of interdisciplinary and collaborative linguistic ethnography undertaken with professionals in education, health, law, etc. can sometimes look awkward or relatively low key, conceptually and/or methodologically. But all of this meshes with a much broader shift in the organisation of academic knowledge production, away from mono-disciplines with clear boundaries towards regions where different disciplines overlap, drawn into interaction through their attention to practical problems in the world beyond the academy (Bernstein, 1996: 68; Gibbons *et al.*, 1994; Strathern, 2000). Way back in the late 1960s, Hymes noted, somewhat poetically, that anthropology 'had sequestered much of its strength on departmental hilltops', but that it was 'nevertheless responding to the challenge of its time, creatively, in many ways, and moving out onto the ... plain defined by [broader human] interests' (Hymes, 1969: 6–7, 55). Linguistic ethnography is one of the ways in which this larger endeavour has continued.

The next chapter carries the discussion of this project into language policy and the politics of language, connecting Hymes' (1980b: 89) vision of ethnography as 'a gain for a democratic way of life' to the theorisation of linguistic citizenship in Southern Africa, exploring their implications for education in a country like England.

4 Sociolinguistic Citizenship

(co-authored with Melanie Cooke and Sam Holmes)

4.1 Introduction

In a 2010 Institute of Public Policy Research report, '*You Can't Put Me in a Box*', Fanshawe and Sriskandarajah call for a shift in British policy discourse: '[w]e need a new way of talking about diversity in the UK. Overzealous pursuit of crude equalities measures ... ha[s] created a lot of awkwardness ... when talking about identity, diversity and equality ... . The tick-box approach to identity seems to be missing out on growing numbers of people who fall outside or across standard classifications' (Fanshawe & Sriskandarajah, 2011: 33–34, 5). This is also a problem for how we talk about language in policy and politics, and to try to find an alternative, this chapter explores Christopher Stroud's notion of 'linguistic citizenship'.

Linguistic citizenship (LC) is 'an attempt at a comprehensive *political* stance on language' (Stroud, 2008: 45), and its central argument is that a subtle understanding of how language positions people in society can and should enhance democratic participation. Stroud's conception of linguistic citizenship is outlined in Section 4.2 below, and Section 4.3 then shows how this can be strengthened by its connections to the sociolinguistic traditions established by Hymes and Gumperz (e.g. Gumperz, 1982; Hymes, 1975/1996: 63–106), overcoming a number of challenging questions: Do the arguments for linguistic citizenship ditch Linguistic Human Rights too quickly? Is linguistic citizenship too small-scale? Is it too oppositional? Is it romantically utopian when it talks about social transformation? After that, the discussion shifts from South Africa, where the idea of LC was formulated, to England, where contemporary state discourses linking language to citizenship are very inhospitable – to the extent, indeed, that in the British context, Stroud's linguistic citizenship needs to be renamed '*socio*linguistic citizenship', both to emphasise its sociolinguistic pedigree and to distinguish it from national state discourses (Section 4.4). Even so, there are small-scale educational initiatives that seek to cultivate linguistic repertoires and practices with the variety and mixing recognised in LC, and we describe two recent examples (Section 4.5). After that, we look back briefly at language education in England from the 1960s to the late 1980s, suggesting that even though current conditions are inauspicious, there is no intrinsic incompatibility between sociolinguistic citizenship and large-scale state education provision (Section 4.6). Finally, Section 4.7 turns reflexively to our own positioning, considering the contribution to sociolinguistic citizenship that universities can make at the present time.

4.2 The Idea of 'Linguistic Citizenship'

Stroud's notion of linguistic citizenship first emerged in a 2001 paper that compared it with 'Linguistic Human Rights' as a concept in the assessment of mother-tongue education programmes in Africa. The article focused on the success and failure of programmes that used local rather than ex-colonial metropolitan languages as media of instruction, and it argued that although it was widely invoked, the idea of Linguistic Human Rights (LHR) was inadequate as a framework for understanding and promoting mother-tongue programmes that actually worked. Stroud characterised LHR as an approach to language education that involved:

(A) the selective provision for a specific group, usually designed to overcome historic disadvantage;
(B) the identification, description and introduction of the group's distinctive language as an entitlement in institutional activity – in schools, in law courts, in aspects of state bureaucracy;
(C) an expectation that the courts and other bodies overseeing the nation-state will grant and monitor all this. (Stroud, 2001: 349)

With constitutional recognition given to 11 official languages after apartheid, the LHR perspective had been very influential in South Africa, where Stroud is based, but he pointed to a number of serious limitations of the kind articulated in the IPPR report (Stroud & Heugh, 2004):

(a) The LHR approach marginalises people who use non-standard versions of the group's language, generating new sociolinguistic inequalities.
(b) It promotes an arbitrary and essentialist view of language and ethnicity – it creates artificial boundaries between ways of speaking that are actually continuous and it overlooks mixing and hybridity.
(c) It appeals to a rather top-down and managerial politics, it presupposes membership of a single state and it neglects population mobility. It is not well adapted to the fact that 'individuals now find themselves

participating in a variety of sites in competition for resources distributed along multiple levels of scale, such as the nation, the supranation, the local and the regional' (Stroud, 2010: 200).

The advocates of Linguistic Human Rights, one could say, talked to government with a sociolinguistic map that *distorted* the ground it was supposed to represent. Instead, Stroud proposed linguistic citizenship, which differed from LHR in

(i) putting democratic participation first, emphasising cultural and political 'voice' and agency rather than just language on its own;
(ii) seeing all sorts of linguistic practices – including practices that were mixed, low status or transgressive – as potentially relevant to social and economic well-being, accepting that it is very hard to predict any of this if one is merely watching from the centre;
(iii) stressing the importance of grassroots activity on the ground, often on the margins of state control, outside formal institutions.

Going beyond the critique of LHR, Stroud also contended that an enhanced understanding of sociolinguistic processes should actually be central to emancipatory politics. LC 'aims to make visible the sociolinguistic complexity of language issues' (Stroud & Heugh, 2004: 192) and to promote 'the idea of language as a political and economic "site of struggle"', alongside 'respect for diversity and difference' and 'the deconstruction of essentialist understandings of language and identity' (Stroud, 2001: 353). This perspective should be 'inserted into political discourses and made into a legitimate form, target and instrument of political action' (Stroud, 2001: 343), and it has the potential to help marginalised people change their material and economic conditions for the better.

Stroud saw these principles at work in successful language education programmes (Stroud, 2001: 346–347) and, turning to currently dominant discourses that could increase its appeal, he also argued that the notion of LC could dovetail well with the 'new discourses of *entrepreneurialism* that are the order of the day' in South Africa (Stroud & Heugh, 2004), even though it was still difficult to promote in a wider public debate:

> In the African context, speakers move into ... and across many different associational and sociogeographical units ... exhibiting multiple and varied practices of language use, such as language crossing and mixed registers. Mozambican 'commerciantes', for example, regularly travel from the Southern Mozambican province of Gaza to South Africa, Malawi and Zimbabwe, where they conduct their purchases and sales in various forms of indigenous *African* languages, not metropolitan

languages … From an actor-oriented, or grassroots, perspective, the relevant language communities to which speakers need to refer on a daily basis may be both larger and smaller than the traditional nation-state, comprising 'communities' delimited by both transnational varieties and local ways of speaking subnational languages. As these languages generate value, they provide a basis for political action.

However, … when social and economic issues are debated in relation to language, the debate continues to deal with the rights and obligations that accrue to mastery of the ex-colonial, metropolitan and official language alone, and refer only to official and public arenas. [So …] there is a mismatch between the traditional, state-based institutions dealing with language issues, and the … sociolinguistic realities. We need some way of capitalising on the insight that local language practices are closely connected to generation of capital, and develop and promote economic models for these languages as a form of resistance to the market hegemony of ex-colonial languages. (Stroud, 2001: 350)

We will come back to the relationship between non-elite, everyday linguistic practice 'on the ground' and the ways in which state institutions conceive of language when we turn to language education in the UK. But before doing so, it is worth considering LC's links to the sociolinguistics associated with Hymes and Gumperz, founding figures in contemporary sociolinguistics, also reflecting on the ways in which this connection helps to overcome some of the criticisms levelled at the idea of linguistic citizenship.

4.3 Sociolinguistic Underpinnings in Linguistic Citizenship

According to Hymes, ethnographic sociolinguistics is a primarily analytical rather than a political or normative undertaking, focusing first on 'what is' rather than 'what should be'. But the careful comparative empirical study of communicative repertoires and practices ultimately serves the ethical objectives of achieving *Liberté, Egalité, Fraternité* because it 'prepares [sociolinguists] to speak concretely to actual inequalities' (Hymes, 1969, 1977: 204–206; Santos, 2012: 46). This interplay of the academic and the ethical/political can be seen in operation in Stroud's criticism of the way in which language and ethnicity are conceptualised in the LHR perspective.

The ideological and emotional power and persuasiveness carried by common-sense ideas about named languages and notions like 'native speaker' and 'mother tongue' is self-evident, but there is now a great deal of sociolinguistic research that challenges the idea that distinct languages exist as natural objects, and that a proper language is bounded, pure, and composed of structured sounds, grammar and vocabulary designed for referring to things (e.g. Joseph & Taylor, 1990; Makoni & Pennycook, 2007; Stroud, 1999; Woolard *et al.*, 1998). The idea of named languages – 'English', 'German', 'Bengali' – emerged with the formation of European nation-states in the 19th century (and linguistic scholarship played a very prominent part in this). But contemporary sociolinguists argue that it is far more productive *analytically* to focus on the very variable ways in which individual linguistic features with identifiable social and cultural associations get clustered together whenever people communicate (Blommaert, 2005; LePage, 1988), and that named languages are actually rather shallow and restrictive constructs when it comes to understanding how people really communicate. When people talk, they use all sorts of visual and bodily signs, and they are guided by the particularities of the genre and activity, their background knowledge, their attitudes and expectations of each other (cf. Sections 2.3 and 3.3 above). And even if we focus only on the linguistic ingredients, it soon becomes clear that the forms people use are associated with a host of different groups and situations – groups and situations that range from the very local to the transnational. Along similar lines, traditional ideas about the 'native speaker of a language' and the vital contribution that early experience in stable speech communities makes to competence in grammar and coherence in discourse have also been critiqued. These beliefs were central to a good deal of linguistic model building for much of the 20th century, but they are very difficult to reconcile with the facts of linguistic diversity and mixed language practices (Leung *et al.*, 1997). Instead, sociolinguists now generally work with the notion of linguistic repertoire, which dispenses with a priori assumptions about the links between origins, upbringing, proficiency and types of language, and refers instead to the very variable (and often rather fragmentary) grasp that individuals have of a plurality of styles, registers, genres and practices, which they have picked up and maybe then partially forgotten over the course of their lives (Arnaut *et al.*, 2015, 2017; Blommaert & Backus, 2011).

This deconstruction of essentialist ideas about language represents one way in which in sociolinguistic theory can 'prepare ... [sociolinguists] to speak concretely to actual inequalities more effectively' (Hymes, 1977: 204–206). Politically, both LHR and LC oppose the exclusion of people who do not have officially approved linguistic resources in their repertoires. But while LHR focuses on the recognition of named or nameable languages associated with specific groups judged to have been marginalised, LC works with developments in sociolinguistics that allow a more open and inclusive position, attending to the diversity of linguistic practices that people use/need to get themselves heard in arenas that affect their well-being.

But there is a question about the potential political effectiveness of the 'actor-oriented' focus on practice in LC. Petrovic and Kuntz (2013: 142) are concerned that the processes addressed by LC are rather small scale, and that LC risks relinquishing the wide-angle view and the potential to affect relatively large numbers of people identified in the debates about LHR. But in response, it is worth pointing out that in both contemporary sociolinguistic and social theory, practices are seen as the basic building blocks in the production of society, and instead it is now often said that studies of *state-level* policy run into problems if they neglect practice, because they miss all the unpredictable complexity that the formulation, implementation and enactment of policy actually entails (S.J. Ball *et al.*, 2012; Jessop, 2007): 'policy never just "is", but rather "does" ... We do not restrict our analysis to ... official policy declarations and texts ... but place these in context as part of a larger sociocultural system ... inferred from people's language practices, ideologies and beliefs' (McCarty, 2011: 2).

At the same time, however, if we are to understand how units 'both larger and smaller than the traditional nation-state' enter the account (Stroud, 2001: 350), we need to move beyond practice to the networks in which it is embedded. In fact, this is implied in the notion of voice itself.

In the first instance, we might define 'voice' as an individual's communicative power and effectiveness within the here-and-now of specific events. But beyond this, there is the crucial issue of whether and how their contribution is remembered and/or recorded and subsequently reproduced in other arenas, travelling through networks and circuits that may vary in their scale – in their spatial scope, temporal durability and social reach. This is studied in research on 'text trajectories' which focuses (a) on the here-and-now activity in which some (but not other) aspects of what is said get turned into textual 'projectiles' that can carry forward into other settings ('entextualised'), and then (b) the ways in which they are interpreted when they arrive there ('recontextualised') (Section 3.3 above). This kind of account can cover both 'top-down' and 'bottom-up' trajectories, involving a variety of people, practices, media and types of text, working in cooperative and/or conflictual relationships within and across specific events, and it can of course be turned to political processes. So, for example, we could focus on directives formulated in government offices that are turned into curriculum documents, transmitted to schools, and then interpreted by teachers interacting with children in class, or alternatively we could look at parents complaining at a school meeting, the local press reporting the matter, and local politicians then taking it up or dismissing it (see, for example, Kell, 2015; Mehan, 1996). These are obviously simplified sketches, but the essential point is that a 'trans-contextual and multi-scalar' framework of this kind allows us to investigate the resonance of particular communicative acts and practices. This then has two further implications.

First, this view of voice and text trajectories means that sociolinguists actually have to be flexible in their response to named languages and the essentialisation that they involve, accepting that there may be occasions when the discourse of LHR is strategically warranted. Certainly, when faced with data on linguistic practice situated in the here-and-now, sociolinguists first listen for the diversity of the communicative resources in play. But selection and reduction are unavoidable parts of the entextualisation process, and if someone's viewpoint is to be heard elsewhere in unfamiliar situations, it needs to be represented in a repeatable form that, regardless of its eloquence, inevitably simplifies the first-hand experience that motivated it (e.g. Haarstad & Fløysand, 2007). Named languages may form part of persuasive rhetorics that travel, and even though sociolinguists may worry about the negative (side-)effects and watch out for opportunities to reassert the ideological constructedness of named languages (Stroud & Heugh, 2004: 212), an analytic interest in the trajectory of voices has to accept the possibility that, in certain circumstances, the invocation of named languages helps to advance political causes that sociolinguists deem progressive. So although Stroud's account of LC includes mixed, low-status and transgressive language practices, we certainly should not assume that notionally purer, higher status and more standard ones are thereby necessarily excluded (Blommaert, 2004: 59–60; Stroud & Heugh, 2004: 191).

Second, it is necessary to move beyond the 'freedom to have one's voice heard' to what Hymes (1996: 64) calls the 'freedom to develop a voice worth hearing'. People in the networks through which a particular voice seeks to resonate inevitably have their own ideas of what is important, and if its message is to be taken seriously, it needs to understand and connect with these concerns. This brings education – formal and/or informal – into the reckoning. Stroud's (2001) discussion of LC centres more on the taking of control over language education programmes than on what these programmes actually teach (although see, for example, Bock & Mheta, 2014; Stroud & Heugh, 2004: 201). But if the practices that promote democratic participation and persuasive voices from the grassroots are to sustain themselves, it is vital to consider the organisation of institutionalised arenas for learning and socialisation that are at least partly sheltered from the cut and thrust of political struggle.

So the central ideas that Stroud *et al.*'s linguistic citizenship builds on – the deconstruction of named languages and the focus on linguistic repertoires and practice – finds a great deal of support in ethnographic sociolinguistics, where Hymes also outlined broadly comparable objectives at the interface of research and politics. At the same time, these links qualify some of the radicalism in Stroud's articulation of LC: if claims and voices want people elsewhere to listen to them, they have to make themselves relevant, and the entextualisation required to do so often results in messages that simplify and partly compromise the original intention. It can also take time to develop a 'voice worth listening to', and this raises the question of institutional support.

Indeed, more generally, a reflexive understanding of the interface between research and politics is also important when Stroud and colleagues argue that LC offers a 'transformative' politics, drawing on Nancy Fraser's distinction between '*affirmative* remedies for injustice aimed at correcting inequitable outcomes of social arrangements *without disturbing* the underlying framework that generates them', and '*transformative* remedies [are] aimed at correcting inequitable outcomes precisely by *restructuring* the underlying generative framework' (Fraser, 1995: 82; also Isin, 2008: 38; Stroud, 2001, 2018).[1] According to Stroud and colleagues, LHR takes the affirmative path, while LC is transformative, challenging traditional ideas about the distinctiveness and homogeneity of language groups and named languages, 'interrogat[ing] the historical, sociopolitical, and economic determinants of how languages are constructed' (Stroud, 2018: 20).

These claims about transformation are quite often greeted with scepticism, but to this there are two responses. First, the analytic difficulties involved in determining whether change is major or minor, radical or merely adaptive, certainly have been widely noted (e.g. Williams, 1977: 123),[2] and sociolinguistics also presents claims about rupture and transformation with a series of quite acute questions. Every communicative act entails a huge range of partly autonomous and partly interwoven structures (themselves 'generative frameworks'), operating at the linguistic, interactional and institutional levels.[3] Saying for any given intervention which of these generative frameworks is and is not being ruptured, for and by whom, and with what subsequent effects, is hard, and of course it is likely to become even harder with the introduction of analytic schemes from sociology, politics, economics and so forth. But while analysis has an *invaluable* part to play in *alerting* us to the intricacies of change, putting a brake on romantic over-readings in which the observer attributes radical creativity to actions that participants see as rather mundane and inconsequential (Blommaert & Rampton, 2011a: 9; Rampton, 2014), the assessment of whether an action is transformative, affirmative, reproductive or indeed repressive ultimately involves a holistic, all-round judgement that is inevitably also informed by understandings and commitments that go well beyond the scientific expertise of the observer. And this kind of shift from the technical to the ethical and subjective is wholly compatible with Hymes' view of an ethnographic sociolinguistics aligned with political values like *Liberté, Egalité, Fraternité* (e.g. Hymes, 1977: 194).

Second, it is essential to consider the locations where transformation is being discussed, and here Burawoy and von Holdt's (2012) *Conversations with Bourdieu: The Johannesburg Moment* provides important contextualisation. When it comes to claims about radical transformation, Bourdieu is the arch-sceptic, taking the view that *tout ça change, tout c'est la même chose*. But Burawoy and von Holdt are writing from South Africa, and they emphasise just how context specific Bourdieu's work is. In stable post-war bourgeois France, 'habitus' and 'bodily hexis' may fit seamlessly into social structure; however, in South Africa bodies are marked by colonial domination, racial classification generates endless physical and cultural assault, there is a habitus of *defiance*, and Bourdieu's merely *symbolic* violence looks distinctly genteel. The word transformation might sound naively optimistic in western Europe, but in South Africa it actually has a great deal of public currency.

How far, though, and in what ways can a concept developed in discussions of language policy in Southern Africa transfer elsewhere? To consider this, it is first worth asking what ideologies of language and citizenship currently dominate public discourse and debates about language education in a country like England.

4.4 Ideologies of Language and Citizenship in England

In recent years, two state-level discourses that link language to citizenship have gained currency in the UK. One of these discourses derives from the European Union, and it focuses on the development of 'plurilingual citizens', proposing that everyone should learn and use three languages. These should be: a person's mother tongue; a 'language of international communication'; and a 'Personal Adoptive Language', conceived as a language from another EU member state selected by the individual. But sociolinguists have noted at least two characteristics in this advocacy. First, 'all the linguistic practices considered worthy of mention conform to standardising ... assumptions: they are named languages with unified, codified norms of correctness embodied in literatures and grammars. No other configurations of speaking are recognized' (Gal, 2006: 167; Moore, 2011; Pujolar, 2007: 78, 90). Second, it is elite forms of multilingualism that are emphasised. So with the Personal Adoptive Language, fluency 'would go hand in hand with familiarity with the country/countries in which that language is used, along with the literature, culture, society and history linked with that language and its speakers' (Maalouf Report, 2008: 10, cited in Moore, 2011: 9). As Moore elaborates, this 'conjures up scenarios of culturally-enriching and self-actualizing travel: "mobility", yes, but of an ideally *voluntary* sort. Thus: the *Wanderjahr* or international residence of the cosmopolitan elites of traditional upper middle-class consciousness' (Moore, 2011: 9).

The second discourse about language and citizenship focuses on immigrants, and in the UK it proposes that they need to learn English for social cohesion and national security, claiming (without any evidence) that a lack of proficiency in the national language increases the threat of radicalisation and terrorism, particularly among Muslims (for a fuller account, see Section 9.4, this volume). In 2005, a *Life in the UK* test was introduced for migrants seeking British Citizenship (and for those seeking Indefinite Leave to Remain in 2007). Over time, increasingly demanding English proficiency requirements were tied into this with, for example, a language requirement being introduced for the reunification of non-EU, non-English speaking spouses in 2011 (Cooke & Peutrell, 2019). The spirit of these developments can be seen the words of Home Secretary (and then Prime Minister) Theresa May (2015):

> Government alone cannot defeat extremism so we need to do everything we can to build up the capacity of civil society to identify, confront and defeat extremism wherever we find it. We want to go further than ever before helping people from isolated communities to play a full and fruitful role in British life. We plan a step change in the way we help people learn English. There will be new incentives and penalties, a sharp reduction in translation services and a significant increase in the funding available for English. (May, 2015)

These two state discourses are not compatible with linguistic citizenship in Stroud's sense. But even though they are very influential, they are not universally accepted, and there are other accounts and aspirations for the UK that LC can align with much more easily. A different view is evident in the 2010 report from the Institute of Public Policy Research cited at the start of this chapter, and LC is also compatible with a substantial body of research showing that the UK is actually highly multilingual, and that many of its citizens have language repertoires that involve the kinds of variety and mixing that Stroud *et al.* describe (compare, for example, Anwar in Chapter 8 below with the 'commerciantes' referred to in

Section 4.2 above; also, for example, Britain, 2007; *Working Papers in Translanguaging & Translation*). Indeed, the next section describes two educational initiatives that seek to cultivate this diversity in London, and in considering the transposition of Stroud's conception to the UK, it makes sense to speak of '*sociolinguistic citizenship*', both to differentiate it from the two official discourses we have sketched above, and to flag up its pedigree in sociolinguistics.

4.5 Two Recent Projects Promoting Sociolinguistic Citizenship

Educational projects that, like LC, promote the voice of relatively marginalised people through the recognition of mixed/non-standard language practices and sociolinguistic awareness have a substantial pedigree in critical pedagogy and beyond, as in, for example, work with hip hop (e.g. Alim, 2009; Malai Madsen & Karrebæk, 2015; www.rapolitics.org). But we will discuss two projects that we have been involved in.[4]

The first represents an alternative to British government discourses on citizenship and immigration – an ESOL course entitled *Our Languages*. It took place within a small charitable organisation called English for Action (EfA; www.efalondon.org) which was set up in 2009 to support London Citizens' campaigning work. The vision that motivates EfA involves 'UK migrants hav[ing] the language, skills and networks they need to bring about an equal and fair society' (EfA, 2016: 7), and according to its 2015–16 Annual Report, EfA is

> absolutely committed to community organising; that is listening to people's concerns in our classes and communities, connecting people, training people to listen and take action, taking action to effect change and building powerful groups to be able to hold powerful people and organisations to account. Our approach is above all, to develop the capacity of our students to effect change. Campaigns, such as to secure better housing or living wages, emerge from classroom work and our community organising. (EfA, 2016: 5)

During 2015–16, 391 people accessed the 19 free-of-charge ESOL courses that EfA ran in seven London Boroughs, and 'over 100 students took action on a range of social justice issues' (EfA, 2016: 11). The courses were taught by a staff team of 10, with volunteers attending 85% of the classes, and this activity was supported with an income of £178,000, mostly raised from about a dozen charitable foundations.

Our Languages ran in 2017 as one strand in a three-year linguistic ethnography on 'Adult language socialisation in the Sri Lankan Tamil diaspora in London', funded by the Leverhulme Trust (2015–2018;

£227,500). The course was designed to explore how far the linguistic experience of the Sri Lankan Tamils studied in the ethnography resonated with other migrant groups, and it involved participatory education (aligned with Freire, critical pedagogy and democratic education; see www.ourlanguages.co.uk for the materials). This takes an overarching theme and then allows the exact shape of the course to emerge from session to session.[5] Working in two classes (36 students from 18 countries), the courses began by playing a recording of someone from Sri Lanka talking about how he had practised his English while working in an off-licence, and by the end of the eight weeks, the students had covered: non-standard language varieties; bi/multilingual language practices; language identities; intergenerational language transmission; multilingual communicative repertoires; language ideologies; language discrimination; and the social processes of learning English in the UK. In this way, the course addressed what Stroud and Heugh (2004: 209–210) see as a substantial problem for LC: the 'problem ... is that much current theorisation of language and politics is often unavailable to those communities who are theorised ... [L]inguistic knowledge needs to be built in dialogue with communities'.

In any programme of this kind, the outcomes are mixed. On occasion, students themselves expressed racist ideas. The session on intergenerational language transmission generated quite a lot of frustration and guilt when students talked about their children's lack of heritage language competence, and there was also quite strong support for an 'English only' policy in ESOL lessons, even though the students had been encouraged to draw on their multilingual repertoires. But at the end of the course, one of the groups said they wanted another eight weeks to continue the discussion, and there were gains in language learning, in pragmatic and 'multilingual narrative' competence and in vocabulary: one of the students reported 'jokingly but proudly – that her family had commented that she was coming home from class "sounding like a dictionary", [using] research related terms such as "theme", "data" and "participant"' (Cooke *et al.*, 2018: 25). In fact, one of the groups also made representations to the All Party Parliamentary Group (APPG) on Social Integration, whose chair happened to be the local MP (Chuka Umunna). The APPG was conducting an inquiry into the integration of immigrants, and its interim report was picked up by the *Daily Mail* with the headline 'ALL migrants should learn English before moving to UK: Verdict of Labour MP ... it's time to ditch failed multiculturalism' (Martin, 2017). Students objected to the negative stereotyping, to the way in which learning English was presented as an obligation rather than a right, and to the lack of any reference in either the Interim Report (APPG, 2017a) or the *Daily Mail* article to major cuts in state funding for ESOL (*c*.60% since 2007) and the long waiting lists for classes that these produced. EfA subsequently submitted written evidence to the inquiry (along with 66 other individuals and organisations) and Umunna was invited to the class. He came and admitted that the interim text should have taken more care to avoid interpretations like the *Daily Mail*'s. In fact, the APPG's final report was entitled *Integration not Demonisation*, and it warned against rhetorics that encouraged racism (APPG, 2017b: 16), discussed the adverse effects of the ESOL funding cuts at some length (APPG, 2017b: 69–70) and acknowledged EfA and 'the testimony of ... community group members' (APPG, 2017b: 83, 89).

In bringing students' multilingualism into the classroom and engaging with their experience of transnational, national and local structures and processes, both EfA and the *Our Languages* project illustrate the kind of reorientation proposed by Peutrell and Cooke when they suggest that there is

> a marked difference between, on the one hand, seeing ESOL students as non-citizen outsiders, who we assist to acquire the language and cultural norms of their adopted homeland, and on the other, as *diasporic locals*, with their own linguistic, cultural, social, affective and other resources, whose very presence reshapes the locality they live in. (Peutrell & Cooke, 2019: 229, emphasis added)

A comparable commitment to sociolinguistic understanding, to linguistic inclusivity and voice and to identities that are simultaneously diasporic and local was also central to a second project, this time targeting a younger age group. *Multilingual Creativity* (www.kcl.ac.uk/Cultural/-/Projects/Multilingual-Creativity.aspx) ran from January 2015 to November 2016, and the question guiding it was: 'How can plurilingualism among young people be harnessed for creativity?'. It recognised that there were a lot of unconnected projects in universities, schools and arts and cultural organisations that engaged with young people's hybrid multilingualism, and it set out to build links between them, seeking to develop something of a 'sector' for this kind of work.

There were three elements in the programme: research on current practice, the development of a website (www.multilingualcreativity.org.uk), and a series of events that focused on language communities, multilingual projects, performing and visual arts, print and multimedia texts and networking. These involved 52 cultural organisations (from education, museums, libraries, publishing and the arts sector), 17 artists, 12 academics and 32 members of the public. The research part surveyed existing projects and identified five pedagogic principles in something of a manifesto, illustrating them with examples of filmmaking in Arabic supplementary schools, German teaching with hand-puppets for primary children, three-day workshops in creative translation, and a national language challenge (Holmes, 2015). The five principles were: plurilingualism over monolingual usage (the use of different 'languages' within the same utterance or activity); exuberant smatterings over fluency ('bits of language' as opposed to 'fluency' as a legitimate goal in language learning); reflexive sociolinguistic exploration over linguistic 'common sense' (focusing on participants' own language practices); collaborative endeavour over individualisation (drawing on the pooling of repertoires within a group); and investment over 'immersion' (fostering a genuine desire to participate, rather than insisting on exclusive use of the 'target' language).

Multilingual Creativity raised important questions about the positioning of these pedagogic strategies within broader institutions. The 'Felix und Franzi' glove puppet activity with which Holmes illustrates the 'exuberant smatterings over fluency' principle was produced by the Goethe Institut, which receives large-scale, long-term financing from the German government to promote German language and culture at all levels worldwide, using German 'as the teaching language ... right from the start'.[6] So Felix und Franzi is, relatively speaking, just a tiny innovation in which language mixing is a tactic to take small children on their first steps into a much larger programme of monolingual *Deutsch*, perhaps ultimately leading to the kind of plurilingual citizenship advocated by the EU. As pedagogic methods can be adopted and recontextualised in different kinds of programme and organisation, this obviously does not make it irrelevant to sociolinguistic citizenship. Even so, the Goethe Institut stands in sharp contrast to virtually all of the other projects involved in *Multilingual Creativity*, which depended on relatively short-term, project-specific funding from charitable foundations and local communities and institutions (as did the *Multilingual Creativity* initiative itself – it relied on five or six grants, amounting to *c.*£67,000). This in turn depends on the initiative of a few dedicated individuals and their perseverance and success in raising income from a plurality of funding sources. The crucial issue of sustainability emerges here, both for the projects and for the linguistic repertoires and capacities that they seek to develop.

In Stroud *et al.*'s account, LC develops at the margins of state provision and control, and the two cases we have described seem to corroborate this view. But there is in fact no essential incompatibility between substantial state funding and the principles of sociolinguistic citizenship, as can be seen in a brief sketch of language education from the 1960s to the late 1980s in England.

4.6 Sociolinguistic Citizenship in English State Education from the 1960s to the Late 1980s

Language education in England in the period from the 1960s to the late 1980s was dominated by 'progressive' pedagogies, supported by major Committees of Inquiry (DES, 1967, 1975) which stated, for example, that the aim of language education 'is not to alienate the child from a form of language with which he has grown up ... It is to enlarge his repertoire so that he can use language effectively in other speech situations and use standard forms when they are needed ... No child should be expected to cast off the language and culture of the home as he crosses the school threshold' (DES, 1975: paras 10.6, 20.5, 20.17; Carter, 1988). Local authorities, teaching unions and subject associations had much more influence than central government and, in contrast to the system operating from the 1990s onwards, there was no national curriculum and regular standardised assessment testing (apart from the school-leaving exams), and 'no pressure of a stringent accountability framework that would make ... teachers ... or their senior managers in school ... risk averse' (Gibbons, 2017: 40). There were certainly different lines of thinking within broadly progressive language education (Cox, 1990: 21; Hewitt, 1989: 127–133; Stubbs, 1986: 78), and not all would fit the model of sociolinguistic citizenship outlined by Stroud. But there was a great deal of emphasis on voice. Together with the idea that English teaching should seek to broaden the child's *repertoire* rather than impose Standard English on its own (DES, 1975, 1981), this itself created openings for mixed and non-standard language (the leading language educationalists also knew about Hymes and were sensitive to contemporaneous developments in ethnographic sociolinguistics; Burgess, 2002; Rosen & Burgess, 1980: 140). Work of this kind was supported by several very large-scale curriculum development initiatives, and the last of these, the 1989–1992 Language in the National Curriculum Project, argued, for example, that:

- 'some aspects of language resist systematisation' and 'language and its conventions of use are permanently and unavoidably unstable and in flux' (Carter, 1990: 17);
- '[b]eing more explicitly informed about the sources of attitudes to language, about its uses and misuses, about how language is used to manipulate and incapacitate, can *empower* pupils to see through language to the ways in which messages are mediated and ideologies encoded' (Carter, 1990: 4, emphasis in original);
- teachers in multilingual classrooms can 'create the conditions which enable children to gain access to the whole curriculum by encouraging

> them to use, as appropriate, their strongest or preferring language', accepting that 'many bilingual children operate naturally ... switching between languages in speech or writing in response to context and audience' (Savva, 1990: 260, 263).

This was supported with £21 million from central government (£165 million at 2018 values), and it involved 25 coordinators and more than 10,000 teachers in over 400 training courses (Carter, 1990: 16), generating professional development materials for teachers that involved 12 units supported by BBC TV and radio, each designed to take up 1–1.5 days of course time (Carter, 1990: 2).

In the end, the Conservative government refused to allow publication of these training materials, objecting, among other things, to a chapter on multilingualism (Abrams, 1991) and asking, in the words of the Minister of State: 'Why ... so much prominence [is] given to exceptions rather than the norm – to dialects rather than standard English, for example ... Of course, language is a living force, but our central concern must be the business of teaching children how to use their language correctly' (Eggar, 1991). Indeed, this ushered in a period of top-down curriculum reform that has left 'English teachers with the underlying sense that the critical decisions about what to teach and how to teach are no longer theirs to make. So hegemonic seems the discourse around standards, accountability, performance and attainment that it can appear that this is just the way things are' (Gibbons, 2017: 3). Nevertheless, this retrospective glimpse of language education from the 1960s to 1980s suggests that the promotion of sociolinguistic citizenship – with its commitments to democratic participation, to voice, to the heterogeneity of the linguistic resources that these entail, and to the political value of sociolinguistic understanding – is not inevitably confined to relatively short-term projects, and that it may be possible to work on a scale that reaches far beyond local initiatives involving critical pedagogy or creative production that symbolically challenges the linguistic status quo (see Rampton *et al.*, 2018a: §7 for fuller discussion).

But what of the situation today? In the UK at present, there is little hope of persuading central government to provide financial resources to support the kind of sociolinguistic citizenship conceived by Stroud and his associates. But regional bodies may well be more receptive, and in the final section of this chapter it is worth turning reflexively to our own positioning and the practical contribution that universities can make to sustaining initiatives that promote LC.

4.7 Universities as a Durable Resource for Sociolinguistic Citizenship

According to an OECD-based study of higher education (HE) in 12 countries with advanced economies, universities are expected to play a larger role in their local areas as economies become more regional (Goddard & Pukka, 2008: 19). Shifts in HE pedagogy are implicated in this: 'learning and teaching activities ... are becoming more interactive and experiential, drawing upon, for example, project work and work-based learning, much of which is locationally specific ... [T]he most effective technology and knowledge transfer mechanism between higher education institutions and the external environment is through ... staff and students via the teaching curriculum, placements, teaching company schemes, secondments, etc.' (Chatterton & Goddard, 2000: 480, 488). This reaches right across the disciplinary spectrum, 'from science and technology and medical faculties to the arts, humanities and social sciences' (Goddard & Pukka, 2008: 14), and similar shifts can be seen in the UK. The actual and/or potential 'non-academic impact' of research is now evaluated both in individual project proposals and in the large-scale national assessments of research conducted every five or six years and, as elsewhere, there is increasing pressure for teaching to cultivate employability and social responsibility among students.

In ethnographic sociolinguistics, there is a very well established tradition of action research and outreach, with university staff and students working with local groups to promote the kind of LC we have been discussing (see, for example, Gumperz *et al.*, 1979; Heath, 1983; Hymes, 1980a; Van de Aa & Blommaert, 2011). Perhaps 'unexpectedly', 'growing [neoliberal] emphasis on the economisation of research, commodification of teaching, and a need to demonstrate a "return on investment to clients and sponsors" creates favourable conditions' for strengthening this sociolinguistic tradition (Matras & Robertson, 2017: 5). Both of the projects described in Section 4.5 draw on these developments, and if opportunities for placements and practical work outside the academy are to become an established feature of the university curriculum, then individual modules could be built around efforts to promote sociolinguistic citizenship, providing them with greater institutional durability, introducing undergraduates or Masters students to the underlying ideas on an annual basis, involving them in placements where they have the chance to explore these ideas in action.

Exactly what this kind of module covered would depend on the requirements and support provided in the particular institution where it was taught, on the sorts of non-academic organisation that it was linked to, and staff experience, expertise and interests (at least to begin with).[7] Embedded like this in the teaching module, one of the core structures of the university, the promotion of sociolinguistic citizenship could spread in other ways, and Manchester University's *Multilingual Manchester*[8] is a spectacular example of this (Matras & Robertson, 2017). It began in 2009 with 'a new second year undergraduate module on Societal Multilingualism' and 'benefit[ed] from the new opportunities for digital learning and the emerging Social Responsibility agenda' (Matras & Robertson, 2017: 8). Since then it has grown very substantially: by 2017, it was supported by three fixed-term project managers (Matras & Robertson, 2017: 10); it had been adopted as one of Manchester University's flagship regional engagement programmes; and it 'bring[s] together university students, experienced researchers of international repute, community representatives, and members of local services', inviting 'contacts, offer[s] for collaboration, and requests for information, from school, local authorities and local services, businesses, media, related research projects, and students wishing to carry out research on one of Manchester's many community languages, or on language policy and community multilingualism' (MLM website as at 1 July 2015). Admittedly, continuity and stability are major challenges for a programme of this size, because without 'a long term commitment to providing core resources', it is caught up in the university's 'volatile processes of prioritisation and internal competition for resources' (Matras & Robertson, 2017: 11, 10). But working on a smaller scale, within the boundaries of the individual module, acute issues of sustainability like these are less likely to arise.[9]

Even in the highly developed programme developed at Manchester University, this is all still a long way off the £165 million central government grant for sociolinguistic work in schools seen in the late 1980s, and at the time of writing in the UK at least (January 2020), national government itself stands out as a major obstacle to sociolinguistic citizenship, slashing the budgets of local government[10] while promoting a far-reaching 'hostile environment for migrants' policy, explicitly designed to spread fear and suspicion in everyday multi-ethnic urban life, turning teachers, academics, health workers, landlords and employers into border guards (Yuval-Davis *et al.*, 2019: 17–18; Part 3, this volume). But many argue that universities should be a significant source of opposition to developments like these, and the heritage of Hymes and Gumperz provides a strong rationale as well as plenty of rigorous content for courses that can also align with the values articulated in Stroud's LC – the commitment to democratic participation, to voice, to the heterogeneity of linguistic resources and to the political value of sociolinguistic understanding. From a course of this kind, 20–30 people (or more) can emerge every year, equipped with an understanding of how language diversity privileges some and disadvantages others, and an at least incipient sense of what might be done to change these relationships. In their interaction with university students, third sector organisations like those mentioned in Section 4.5 can get tasks done that they would not otherwise have the resources to complete, potentially engaging with frameworks for understanding their activity that are different and maybe more elaborate than those they are used to. In settings like this, students and organisations can now get to know each other, and opportunities emerge to develop their relationship in all sorts of unanticipated ways.

The idea of sociolinguistic citizenship is not itself discussed in any further detail in what follows, although in Part 3 we return to some of the conceptions of language and citizenship that are diametrically opposed to it. But before that, the account moves to a much fuller portrayal of the linguascapes where the relevance of sociolinguistic citizenship stands out, and the speech practices of adolescents and adults who also qualify as diasporic locals move into focus.

Notes

(1) Fraser and Stroud illustrate this in different political responses to discrimination against gay people. Affirmative action in the 1970s and 1980s gave legitimacy to claims for equal treatment by giving positive recognition to gay identity, while transformative politics would follow queer theory and question 'the very basis of the distinction between heterosexual and homosexual, acknowledging instead the variable and amorphous sexuality of each individual, ... destabilising sexual identities in the process' (Fraser, 1995: 85; Stroud, 2001: 344).

(2) 'new meanings and values, new practices and relationships and kinds of relationship are continually being created ... but it is exceptionally difficult to distinguish between those which are really elements of some new phase of the dominant culture ... and those which are substantially alternative or oppositional to it' (Williams, 1977: 123).

(3) Pronunciation, grammar, lexis, proposition, text organisation, etc. ⇔ turn sequence and construction, participation and production format ⇔ media, genre, role, etc.

(4) Our account sidesteps the question of transformation, accepting that 'all classrooms must be approached as complex interactive settings where, rather than simply accepting what is offered, pupils always negotiate what is put on the table (curricula, teaching styles, teachers) and develop different strategies depending on their short- and long-term ambitions, the classroom climate, and local socio-economic conditions' (Charalambous *et al.*, 2016; Jaspers, 2017: 11). So our description takes a relatively cautious line, linking these two projects to LC because of the political *intentions* driving them (democratic participation, voice, linguistic inclusivity, sociolinguistic understanding), focusing more on questions of scale and sustainability than transformative impact.

(5) Sub-themes are drawn out and elaborated on through the use of a range of tools, activities and texts – see the accounts of two previous short courses in *Whose Integration?* (Bryers *et al.*, 2013) and *The Power of Discussion* (Bryers *et al.*, 2014; Cooke *et al.*, 2014).
(6) See https://www.goethe.de/en/spr/kup/kon.html (accessed 22 December 2017).
(7) Our own effort to set up a module of this kind covers most of the sociolinguistic concepts outlined in this paper (language & superdiversity; 'named languages' and language mixing; repertoires, practices, voice and trajectories of text), as well as citizenship and insecuritisation. The module gives students the option of placements in adult ESOL organisations (including EfA), and it promotes an ethnographic stance and a readiness to push sociolinguistic theories into open-ended dialogue with the rationales and practices 'on the ground' in organisations where students are interning, thinking hard about the ways in which concepts are variously complicated and simplified as they travel in and out of the academy and other contexts. Our work has also been very actively supported by the Linguistics Department at the University of the Western Cape and the Educational Linguistics Division in the Graduate School of Education at the University of Pennsylvania.
(8) See http://mlm.humanities.manchester.ac.uk/.
(9) See Rampton and Cooke (2021) for a much fuller discussion of the organisational practicalities of collaboration between universities and non-academic organisations.
(10) See, for example, https://www.ifs.org.uk/publications/14134.

Part 2

Ethnicity, Race and Class in Micro-practices of Differentiation and Alignment

5 Ethnicities without Guarantees[1]

(co-authored with Roxy Harris)

5.1 Introduction

What can the close study of the everyday interactional life in a multi-ethnic urban setting reveal to us about contemporary ethnicity?

Both in public debate and in social science research over the last 50 years or so in the UK, the discussion of race and ethnicity has centred on conflict, discrimination, racism/anti-racism, equal opportunities policies and so on, placing in the foreground the ongoing struggle between clearly demarcated dominant and subordinated racial and ethnic groups. In the process, overwhelming attention has been given to explicit (and often sincere) propositions and statements, whether these are the utterances or labels produced by social actors in the public arena, the views expressed by research subjects in qualitative interviews, or the conclusions drawn by quantitative survey research about race/ethnicity and differential outcomes in, for example, educational achievement.

There have been very good reasons for the dominance of this idiom, and this chapter in no way seeks to underplay the continuing prevalence and pernicious effects of racism (see Part 3). But the dominant perspective rarely looks beyond explicit statements to *non-propositional* expression and the many ways in which race and ethnicity are *indirectly* evoked, performed or noted in the ordinary interactions of everyday life. This chapter starts to repair this neglect. Focusing on the spontaneous activity of a group of 14-year-old girls at a multi-ethnic, multilingual London comprehensive school in 2005–2006, it uses linguistic ethnography to go beyond the surface meaning of words to dimensions of race and ethnic relations that are often overlooked.

The chapter begins by outlining the forces that have shaped the dominant race/ethnicity idiom in Britain (Section 5.2), and then moves to the reconceptualisations of ethnicity provided by Hall and Gilroy (Section 5.3). There are grounds, though, for questioning the success of empirical social science in coming to terms with Hall and Gilroy's 'new' and 'convivial' ethnicities. So, in the rest of the chapter, Section 5.4 provides a glimpse into the kinds of everyday interaction in which such ethnicities emerge, Section 5.5 takes a closer look, drawing on the resources of linguistic ethnography, and Section 5.6 concludes by pointing (a) to the kinds of account that linguistic ethnography helps us *circumvent* and (b) to reasons for preferring it to research based primarily on interviews (or questionnaires).

5.2 Talking about Race/Ethnicity: The Dominant Idiom

What we are calling the dominant idiom on race/ethnicity has been influential throughout the period from 1945 to the present day, but with a little arbitrary licence, it can be divided into phases.

The period 1945–1975 began with the dominance of social, economic and political systems that were explicitly committed to racial hierarchy, sustained by direct colonial rule in the European Empires (British, French, Dutch, Belgian, Portuguese, etc.), by segregation (USA) and by apartheid (South Africa). The challenge to these systems increased throughout the period, and culminated in their overthrow or serious weakening. There was an important catalyst to this process of change in the rhetorical claim that the allies were fighting World War II to preserve freedom and democracy – in 1941, Churchill and Roosevelt had initiated the Atlantic Charter, a ringing declaration that democracy and human rights for all were essential international requirements. In London in 1944, black and brown colonial subjects responded with a Charter for Coloured Peoples which they circulated worldwide, demanding that the British state make good its Atlantic Charter commitments (Ramdin, 1987). The following year, the historic Fifth Pan-African Congress was held in Manchester to articulate a demand for colonial freedom (Adi & Sherwood, 1995), and after World War II, challenges to explicit systems of racism took a variety of forms. There were: (i) *independence struggles*, movements for independence from colonial rule taking the form of mainly mass movements of civil protest (e.g. the Caribbean, West Africa, India); (ii) *liberation movements*, armed struggles for independence from colonial rule (e.g. Kenya, Malaya, Mozambique, Angola, Guinea Bissau); and (iii) *civil rights movements*, particularly in the US (e.g. Martin Luther King, the Black Power Movement [Black Panthers and Malcolm X]).

Changing gear away from attempts to suppress these challenges, a settlement emerged in the US and UK in the 1970s, acknowledging that racial discrimination existed, was wrong and should be countered (as a minimum) by state interventions in support of (nominal) racial equality and against discriminatory practices (cf. the UK Race Relations Acts, 1965, 1968, and the comprehensive 1976 Race Relations Act). The definition of *institutional racism* provided by Stokely Carmichael and Charles V. Hamilton in the US played a key part in precipitating this change:

> Racism is both overt and covert. It takes two, closely related forms ... The first consist of overt acts by individuals, which cause death, injury or the violent destruction of property. This type can be recorded by television cameras; it can frequently be observed in the process of commission. The second type is less overt, far more subtle, less identifiable in terms of *specific* individuals committing the acts. But it is no less destructive of human life. The second type originates in the operation of established and respected forces in the society, and thus receives far less public condemnation than the first type. (Carmichael & Hamilton, 1967: 20, emphasis in original)

This stimulated the idea that state institutions could counter racism with systems of ethnic monitoring for all official bodies. Monitoring would provide a ready and practical way of disclosing racially inspired discrimination and disadvantage, leading in turn to remedial action, at least by implication. These schemes typically involved special funding allocations, building on the racial/ethnic classifications and labels through which the obligatory ethnic monitoring procedures were conducted. At the turn of the century, for example, the 'New Labour' Government consolidated legally backed actions against institutional racism in a relatively comprehensive Race Relations Amendment Act (2000). This was supported by moves to strengthen the visibility of black and brown people in Parliament and at the highest levels of the governmental apparatus and, more generally, their appearance in wider spheres of public life has become more normal.

Critics would argue that state interventions of this kind were only ever symbolic, tokenistic and deliberately designed to leave racially constructed power structures and relations intact, and certainly, following 9/11 and the 'war on terror', race and ethnic relations in Britain have been very adversely affected by British government policies, both in the UK and abroad (see Section 9.4). But throughout the post-war period, group classifications have been highly problematic. The British Empire was deft in its use of both *racial* and *ethnic* categories: on the one hand, notions of race reinforced a common sense in which 'white European' was superior, 'black' was inferior and 'brown' was in between (as in the North American rhyme, 'if you're white you're all right; if you're brown stick aroun'; if you're black get back'), while on the other, ethnicity was deployed as a subtle tool to divide and rule subordinate colonised populations (e.g.

within Africa, Asia or the Caribbean). With ethnic monitoring from the mid-1970s onwards, 'ethnicity' started to displace race as the pre-eminent discursive construct, but there was still a tension between a residual concentration on relations of dominance (race) and the emerging focus on relations of difference (ethnicity). Monitoring itself tended towards a tripartite conceptualisation of '*white*' (the majority of the British population), '*black*' (people of Caribbean and/or African descent) and '*Asian*' (Indian, Pakistani, Bangladeshi), and there was often a confusion of *colour* (with implied notions of biological race – 'White', 'Black'), *nationality* ('Pakistani', 'Bangladeshi'), and *ethnicity* ('Asian'). Even policymakers acknowledged the practical problems involved in ethnic monitoring, with 'other' and 'unclassified' becoming an increasingly significant category in survey returns (for example, more than one-third in the monitoring of schools; DfE, 1995; Harris, 1997: 16–18).

More fundamentally and whatever the labelling used, there was an essentialist tenor to all of these discourses, and for different reasons this was widely accepted by both the dominant majority and subordinate minorities (cf., for example, Bauman, 1996). The crucial *break* with these modes of thought and action came with Stuart Hall's (1988) seminal formulation of a 'new ethnicities' perspective and with Paul Gilroy's (1987) critique of ethnic absolutism, extended more recently in his conceptualisation of urban 'conviviality'.

5.3 Hall and Gilroy's Alternatives

Insisting that race and ethnicity have 'no guarantees in Nature', Hall challenged the dominant idioms of classification and saw the search for 'goodies' and 'baddies' as limiting. He argued for

> the 'end of innocence', or the end of the innocent notion of the essential black subject. ... What is at issue here is the recognition of the extraordinary diversity of subjective positions, social experiences, and cultural identities which compose the category 'black'; that is, the recognition that 'black' is essentially a politically and culturally *constructed* category, which cannot be grounded in a set of fixed transcultural or transcendental racial categories and which therefore has no guarantees in Nature. What this brings into play is the recognition of the immense diversity and differentiation of the historical and cultural experiences of black subjects ...
>
> Once you enter the politics of the end of the essential black subject you are plunged headlong into the maelstrom of a continuously contingent, unguaranteed, political argument and debate: a critical politics, a politics of criticism. You can no longer conduct black politics through the strategy of a simple set of reversals, putting in the place of the bad old essential

> white subject the new essentially good black subject .... (Hall, 1988: 254–255)

In the perspective that Hall develops, discourse plays a crucial role (Hall, 1988: 253–254), and picking up this view of ethnicity as discursively constituted and situationally contingent, Gilroy considers the implications for everyday life in British cities:

> Largely undetected by either government or media, Britain's immigrants and their descendants have generated more positive possibilities. Other varieties of interaction have developed alongside the usual tales of crime and racial conflict. These patterns emerge, not from a mosaic pluralism along US lines, in which each self-sustaining and carefully segregated element is located so as to enhance a larger picture, but with an unruly, convivial mode of interaction in which differences have to be negotiated in real time.
>
> Britain's civic life has been endowed with a multi-culture that we do not always value or use wisely. In many instances, *convivial* social forms have sprouted spontaneously and unappreciated from the detritus of Roy Jenkins' failed mid-1960s experiments with integration. Conviviality is a social pattern in which different metropolitan groups dwell in close proximity but where their racial, linguistic and religious particularities do not – as the logic of ethnic absolutism suggests they must – add up to discontinuities of experience or insuperable problems of communication. In these conditions, a degree of differentiation can be combined with a large measure of overlapping ...
>
> There are institutional, demographic, generational, educational, legal and political commonalities as well as elective variations that inter-cut the dimensions of difference and complicate the desire to possess or manage the cultural habits of others as a function of one's own relationship with identity. Conviviality acknowledges this complexity and, though it cannot banish conflict, can be shown to have equipped people with means of managing it in their own interests and in the interests of others with whom they can be induced to heteropathically identify.
>
> Recognising conviviality should not signify the absence of racism. Instead, it can convey the idea that alongside its institutional and interpersonal dynamics, the means of racism's overcoming have also evolved ... In this convivial culture, racial and ethnic differences have been rendered unremarkable, ... they have been able to become 'ordinary'. Instead of adding to the premium of race as political ontology and economic fate, people discover that the things which really divide them are much more profound: taste, life-style, leisure preferences. (Gilroy, 2006: 39–40)

At the same time, it is difficult for most social scientists to describe in any detail how convivial culture actually works (Gilroy, 2006: 28), and indeed

Hall (2006) also admitted 'that "new ethnicities" (like almost everything I have ever written) was not very empirically based'.

This is where sociolinguistics can make a contribution, and in what follows later, the linguistic ethnographic analysis of ordinary interaction is presented as a productive way of describing the kinds of ethnicity identified by Gilroy and Hall. But first, here are some data.

5.4 An Interaction Involving Text Messages, Mobile Phones and Racialising Statements

The data in this section come from the project 'Urban Classroom Culture and Interaction' (2005–2008). This followed nine adolescents (5F, 4M) over two years in a London secondary school, and data collection involved participant-observation, interviews, radio-microphone recording (180 hours) and playback interviews focusing on the radio-mic data. To set the scene for the interactional episode that follows, two points are in order.

First, the episode is not particularly unusual in the attention that the girls give to popular and new media culture (PNMC) in general, and to text messages in particular. In an observational survey of kids' involvement with PNMC at school, we listened to 80 hours of radio-mic recordings of five pupils over two years (3F, 2M), identifying over 530 episodes in which they audibly used, referred to or performed: music, TV, mobiles, mp3s, PSPs, PCs, internet, electronic games, magazines, newspaper, fashion, body-care, 'recreational food' and sport (cf. Dover, 2007; Rampton, 2006: Ch. 3). There was considerable variation between individuals – 237 episodes with one girl, 24 with another – and there were also striking differences in how (and with what degrees of success) young people drew PNMC into the negotiation of their school and peer group relationships. Even so, these five youngsters' involvement with non-curricular, popular and digital culture at school averaged out at about seven episodes an hour, and for Habibah, one of the main protagonists in the transcript below, there were 122 episodes in 16 hours of radio-mic recording.

Second, although we were on the alert for any evidence corroborating the dominant idiom on race and ethnicity (and had four minority ethnic researchers in our team of six), we found very little in our 100+ days of observation and radio-mic recording to justify an emphasis on racial/ethnic trouble. Adolescents certainly recognised ethnic differences – in Nadia's friendship group, for example, whiteness had lesser value in popular culture contexts, and in looks, mixed race and light brown rated highest. But this was not a crisis. References and allusions to ethnic difference featured as subsidiary issues in conversations addressed to far more insistent concerns – friendship responsibilities, male-female relations, popular media culture, etc. – and indeed there is evidence of this in the episode that follows.

In this interaction, some 14-year-old girls of South Asian and Anglo descent are talking about boys, text messages and phoning, and in the course of their conversation, one of them says:

> `I don't mix with` [kaɭeː] `((=` *`'black boys' in Punjabi)`*`)` `I don't like` [kaɭeː], `cos they... cos you know what they're like... that's why I don't like them` (Lines 92–95 below)

What significance can we attach to this? Within the dominant discourse, the temptation would be to jump in and accuse the girls of making a racist statement, but the ethnographic discourse analysis we are proposing cautions against taking words too literally, insisting instead on paying serious attention to the discursive and social contingencies involved. To start building an understanding of these contingencies, here is quite an extensive transcript of the episode in which this statement was made.

An episode in which ethnicity becomes salient

Participants (all pseudonyms): Habibah (Indian descent); Lily (White British); Masouda (Pakistani descent); (and Mena, who makes a brief appearance around line 97).

Background: Wednesday 18 May 2005 – Habibah is wearing a lapel radio-microphone. A drama lesson, in which as a 'treat', the class is watching a video because quite a lot of pupils are absent at a residential week. But Habibah and Lily aren't interested, and have instead been chatting near the door, singing duets for the last 10 minutes or so. At the start of the episode, they are joined by Masouda, who has left the video viewing, motivated, it seems, by a text message she's just received on her mobile from a boy. So far this morning, Habibah and Lily's relations with Masouda have been strained, following a falling out over recent weeks, and later on, Habibah and Lily say it's been about a week or two since they've spoken with her.

Transcription conventions:

`[text` `[text`	overlapping turns
`text=`	two utterances closely connected without a noticeable overlap, or different parts of a single speaker's

=text	turn
( )	speech that can't be deciphered
(text)	analyst's guess at speech that's hard to decipher
((*italics*))	stage directions
(2)	approximate length of a pause in seconds
te::xt	the colons indicate that the word is stretched out
>text<	words spoken more rapidly
TEXT	capitals indicate words spoken more loudly
[kaɭeː]	phonetic transcription of Punjabi
text	text message read out loud
text	singing
text	speech in an Indian English accent

```
1   Habibah:  ((referring to trainers which they've found in a boy's bag by the
2             door:)) he's got some big feet boy (.)
3             ((Masouda comes up with her mobile))
4   Habibah:  [fuck you scared me
5   Masouda:  [(      ) pick it up and say "Um she left my phone with you"
6             I was so fuckin scar[ed
7   Habibah:                      [>woa::h< ((sounds excited))
8             who is it (.) who is it
9   Masouda:  I just got this text (.)
10  Habibah:  sha' I answer it (.)
11            ((proposing a response:))
12            "well can you fuckin fuckin stop callin' my fuckin phone
13            what the fuck is your problem bitch="
14  Lily:     = >no no< I'll do it I'll do it
15  Masouda:  I'm gonna missed call the person
16            I don' wanna look
17            I'm so scared now (.)
18  Habibah:  ((reading the text message slowly and in monotone: ))
19            "do you (want) me
20            I  [want you
21  Masouda:     [I don't like this black boy
22  Habibah:  "(it's) me ((Lily joins in the reading:)) (the black boy)
23            [come to (my house)                my name is
24  Masouda:  [I don't know who the FUCK he is he knows who I am
25  Habibah:  "ANDREW"
26  Lily:     ["black boy come to
27  Habibah:  ["call me [or
28  Lily:               ["see me I
29  Habibah:  "me and you can do something today
30            so call me
31            you've seen me
32            and I want you to be [(          )"
33  Masouda:                       [give me it
34  Habibah:  what
35            I know what number it is
36  Lily:     missed call him then init=
37  Masouda:  =yeah
38  Lily:     and then if he-
39            when he ring[s I'll answer
40  Masouda:              [Lily I want you to do it
```

```
41             I'm so scared
42             I ain't jokin I'm so scared
43  Lily:      I'll do it
44             I'm a gangster
45             I'll do it
46             (.) [gangsta
47  Habibah:       [what shall I say
48             can I do it
49             [I know I know
50  Masouda:   [any of you two
51             as long as one of you two do it
52  Lily:      [let me do it let me do it
53  Habibah:   [yeh go on
54             what you gonna say
55  Lily:      I'm gonna say (    )-=
56  Habibah:   =shall I fuck him off
57             (.)
58             boy him off
59  Lily:      no I'll [(fucking                          )
60  Habibah:           [((rehearsing reply:)) "cn can you stop fucking fucking
61             calling my phone yeh
62             [don't fucking call my phone"                   01.08
63             [((some conversation in the background too))
64  Masouda:   I missed called him ([and it's gonna               )
65  Lily:                           [when it ring yeah
66             I'll go like this yeah
67             I'll go "hello (West      ) yeah
68             Masouda left her phone"
69             can [I-
70  Masouda:       [NO no
71             he doesn't know my name
72  Lily:      [alright
73  Masouda:   [my name   he thinks my name is Aisha
74             yeh
75  Lily:      alright=
76  Masouda:   =Aisha
77             Alright I'll say 'hi' >yeah yeah yeah<
78  Habibah:   ((directing her attention to Masouda in particular:))
79             see! [kal̪e:] (('kale:' = 'black boys'))
80             [that's it    you're gone
81  Lily:      [why d-you why d-you keep ringin' me
82  Masouda:   ((responding to Habibah:))
83             NO I didn't
84             no::
85             I I know one of his friends
86             that's why
87             (.)
88  Lily:      that's a [lie
89  Masouda:            [I know one of his friends
90             I don't-  I d-
91             Ha- Ha- Habibah
92             I don't mix with [kal̪e:]
93             I don't like [kal̪e:]
94             cos they're   cos you know what they're like
95             that's why [I don't like them
96                        [((A banging of the door opening and closing))
97  Lily:      ((addressing Mena, the girl causing the banging?:))
98             stop stop stop
99             (Miss ) gonna come (.)
100            I'll say why-
101 Masouda:   >Mena stop it<
102 Habibah:   Mena stop
```

103 Masouda: [cos they're tryin to-
104 Lily: [( )plea:se
105 (.)
106 Masouda: I've got credit *((for the phone))*
107 Habibah: *((singing to herself:))* "*when you're not here*
108 *I sleep in your T-shirt"*
109 Masouda: don't understand [why]
110 Habibah: (eh) eh speak speak *((is Habibah referring to the radio-mic?))*
111 Lily: "ello Moto"
112 Habibah: Masouda say something (.) *((into the radiomicrophone))*
113 Masouda: oh
114 Lily: "ello Mo[to"
115 Habibah: [*((laughs))*
116 >no no don't take it off< *(('it' = the radio-mic?))*
117 (.)
118 *((sings:))* "*when you're not here*
119 *I sleep in your T-shirt"*
120 (.)
121 Masouda: [that's why I don't like [kɑɭe] man
122 Habibah: [*wish you were here* [*to sleep in your T-shirt"*
123 Masouda: [oh [
124 Lily: [there's some buff black boys man
125 seriously
126 Habibah: half-caste (I go)
127 Masouda: [>half-caste<
128 Lily: [na na
129 Masouda: [yeah but this guy is blick
130 this er- bu- [not
131 Lily: [na blood
132 I'm not fucking about (.)
133 [(d-you know that) buff man that boy
134 Masouda: [he's burnt toast
135 Lily: that tall black boy is
136 (.)
137 buff
138 don't fuck about
139 Masouda: *((with a hint of laughter in her voice))* he's bu::rnt toast man
140 *((in a constricted voice:))* he's burnt toast
141 Lily: *((exhaling:))* na::
142 Habibah: fucking why's it not ringing
143 Lily: *((quieter, with the argument dying down:))* he's bu:::ff
144 *((very quietly:))* (buff)
145 (.)
146 Habibah: how the fuck did he get your number
147 Masouda: I don't know
148 (.)
149 cos I don't- [
150 Habibah: [*((singing:))* "*I wish you were here*
151 *to sleep in your T Shirt*
152 (.)
153 *then we make lo::ve*
154 (.)
155 *I sleep in your T-shirt"*
156 Masouda: (he picked up *(('he' = Andrew, returning the missed-call))*
157 *((half-laughing:))* (jus as you were singing)
158 Lily?: did he pick it up
159 Masouda: yeh he picked it up (.)
160 just (killed it)
161 (4.0) *((teacher talking in the background))*
162 Lily: mad cow
163 Habibah: does he go to this school

164 Masouda: no
165 (2.0)
166 somewhere in (Shepherd's Bush)
167 (5.0)
168 ?Masouda: is it ringing
169 Habibah: how the fuck do you get
170 yeh- pass-
171 (.)
172 Masouda: yeah (just) flash *(('flash' = let the phone ring once and hang up))*
173 [(cz my minutes)
174 Lily: [(that's what I thought)
175 and then I go
176 "eh eh (.) (ex-blood)"
177 (.)
178 Habibah: Say ((*in Indian English*)) "***hell:o who this calling me***
179 ***don't call me next time***"
180 Lily: I'll go like this
181 *((carrying on in Indian English))* "***eh hello please***
182 ***who you ringing***
183 ***this my phone (not)***
184 ***gil[this ol lady***"
185 Masouda: [and (wants) to
186 come to ((St Mary's)) on Friday
187 Habibah: ((*laughs*))
188 Lily: ((*continuing in IE*)) "***this is ol' lady***"
189 Habibah: ((*deeper voice, with an Elvis impersonation?*)) 'hello hello'
190 Lily: I'll be like [hello
191 Habibah: shall I do that
192 do you dare me to
193 ((*deeper voice, Elvis impersonation?*))'hello'
194 Lily: [( )
195 Masouda: [([ )
196 Habibah: [((*continuing the rehearsal in IE:*)) "***this is her dad***
197 ***leave her alone***"
198 Girls: [((*loud laughs*))
199 Habibah: [*((not in IE:))* "I'm gonna kill [you"
200 Lily: [let do
201 do you dare me to do that-
202 do you dare me to do that
203 Habibah: yeh go on
204 if you can but don't laugh
205 Lily: *((more rehearsing Indian English for the phone-call:))* "***hello hello***
206 ***this her dad***
207 ***how can I help you***
208 Girls: ((*laughter*))
209 Lily: ***okay bye bye***"
210 Girls: ((*laughs & giggles*))
211 Habibah: no let's talk normal
212 Lily: yeh >I'll be like<
213 hi (.)
214 yeah (.) yeah I-
215 Habibah: >>oh he's (ringing)<<
216 Masouda: pick it up
217 Lily: (J) (it's flashed) again
218 Masouda: oh you fucking shit
219 is that the number though that he (gave) me?
220 ?: (I bet-)
221 Masouda: Yeah this is what Asif sent to me (.)
222 *((discussion turns to the text-message sent by another boy))*

Presented in a fuller context like this, it is not so straightforward reading racism into Masouda's original statement about not liking 'kale'. But are the prospective gains made in moving past a simplistic interpretation immediately cancelled out by the rather daunting task of trying to get to grips with everything else that seems to be going on in this episode? This is where linguistic ethnography and interactional sociolinguistics can help, providing relatively systematic frameworks and procedures for working one's way through the complicated organisation of an episode like this *without* losing sight of all the situated and emergent particularities which, if we follow Hall and Gilroy, are actually crucial to the meanings of ethnicity.

5.5 Linguistic Ethnography and an Initial Analysis of the Girls' Interaction

Contemporary linguistic and interactional ethnography generally takes a 'practice' view of identity, concentrating on how identities affect and get configured in people's social activity together (Chapters 2 and 3, this volume). In studying the embedding of ethnicities in everyday life, the aim is to understand their significance without either exaggerating this or ignoring the flexible agency with which people process ethnicities in everyday encounters. Analysis starts with careful description of real-time interactional discourse, but from there it looks to the relationship between communicative practices, social actors and the institutional processes in which they are participating. In this way, race and ethnicity can be conceptualised and empirically explored in three closely interlocking 'sites'. So for example:

- if the analyst's main interest is in *social actors*, then ethnicity is construed as those aspects of a person's (semiotically manifest) resources, knowledge, capacities, dispositions and embodiment that have been shaped over time in networks regarded as distinctively different from others in the locality;
- when *institutional processes* are the central concern, race and ethnicity are treated as elements in well-established ideologies which frame the situations in which social actors find themselves, inclining them to particular kinds of action and interpretation before, during and/or after an encounter;
- where the interest is in *communication* itself, race and ethnicity are located in the semiotic activity – in the signs, actions and practices that reflect, invoke or produce the resources, capacities and ideologies associated with actors, networks and institutions.

At the same time, however, even in highly racialised and ethnically marked situations, racial and ethnic identifications exist alongside a myriad of other role and category enactments, and it is in their dynamic interaction with these other identity articulations that much of the meaning of ethnicity and race takes shape. Zimmerman (1998) usefully suggests at least three kinds of identity at play in any social encounter:

- *discourse (or interactional) identities*, such as 'story teller', 'story recipient', 'questioner', 'answerer', 'inviter', 'invitee', etc., which people are continuously taking on and leaving as talk progresses;
- *situated (or institutional) identities*, such as 'teacher', 'student', 'doctor', 'patient', which come into play in particular kinds of institutional situation;
- *'transportable' identities* which are latent, travel with individuals across situations and are potentially relevant at any time (e.g. 'middle-aged white man', 'working-class woman', 'adolescent black boy', etc.).

These identities can either be 'oriented to', actively influencing the way in which people try to shape both their own actions and the subsequent actions of others, or they may be merely 'apprehended' – tacitly noticed but not treated as immediately relevant to the interaction on hand. And the interactional and institutional identities that a person projects at any moment may be ratified, reformulated or resisted in the immediately following the actions of their interlocutors.

To see how different kinds of identity get activated, displayed and processed in situated interaction, the analysis of interactional discourse focuses on the ways in which participants handle a wide range of linguistic/semiotic materials in their exchanges together – pronunciations, accents, words, utterances, gestures, postures, ways of speaking, modes of address, texts, genres and so on. But – and here we return again to the contingency emphasised by Hall and Gilroy – the meaning and interpretation of a linguistic or semiotic form is always influenced by the way in which people read its very particular *context*, with context minimally understood as:

(i) the *institutional and social network relations* among the participants and their *histories of interaction* both together and apart (here institutional and 'transportable' are most immediately relevant);
(ii) the *type of activity* in which participants are currently engaged, the stage they have reached in the activity and their different interactional roles and positionings within it (cf. institutional and interactional identities);

(iii) their position and manoeuvring in and around institutional *discourses* and circumambient *ideologies* (institutional and transportable identities);
(iv) what has just been said and done, and the options for doing something right now *(the moment-by-moment unfolding of activity)* (interactional identities).

Of course it is often hard to know exactly *which* aspect of context is relevant to an utterance (and how), and it only takes a small shift in how you conceive of the context to change your understanding of what an utterance means (see Section 2.3 on contextualisation and Section 3.3 on context-as-process). But this is an issue that participants themselves have to address throughout their interaction together, and so, to prevent the analysis becoming an interpretive free-for-all, researchers can try to track the way in which participants develop, monitor and repair an intersubjective understanding together from one moment to the next.

Putting all of this together, we can see that in the interactional negotiation of meaning, things move very fast, and people are extraordinarily adept at using very small pieces of linguistic/semiotic form to guide or challenge the understandings of the world emerging in the talk – the choice of one word rather than another can introduce a different issue, a particular pronunciation can reframe the significance of what is going on, a shift in facial expression can convey a specific stance or attitude (to give just a fraction of the possibilities). And so as well as looking closely at semiotic forms and slowing things down to capture the processes of adaptive improvisation from one moment to the next, analysts also need a lot of background knowledge of the local contexts if they are to have any chance of picking up and understanding what it is that these crucial nuances and intimations are pointing to. People generally do manage to communicate fairly well together, but they do not just go around expressing themselves in explicit, well-formed and readily quoted sentences.

This perspective is consonant with Gilroy's (2006) interest in 'mode[s] of interaction in which differences have to be negotiated in real-time', 'largely undetected by government and media' (see above), and our contention is that for a fuller – or indeed maybe for even only an *adequate* – understanding of what people mean when they speak, the combination of linguistics, interaction analysis and ethnography provides valuable support. To illustrate this, it is worth now returning to the episode in Section 5.4 above.

Analysts interested in race and ethnicity could, of course, draw attention to a number of different aspects of this episode, and there are many ways in which the girls are living the historical and institutional effects of large-scale racial/ethnic processes well beyond what they are either consciously aware of or actually discuss. Nevertheless, to illustrate our larger point about the importance of meanings that are not explicitly stated, it is worth focusing on two fairly conspicuous sequences in the interaction when the girls themselves orient actively to race/ethnicity:

- *Focal sequence 1*: Lines 78–95 and 121–140, from Habibah's 'see! *kale*' to Masouda's 'he's burnt toast';
- *Focal sequence 2*: Lines 178–211, when the girls switch into Indian accented English ('IE') in their rehearsals of speaking to Andrew over the phone.

Following Hall and Gilroy's injunctions, as well as the methodological tenets of linguistic ethnography, these moments of racialisation/ethnification need to be situated in their contexts, taking context as:

(i) the institutional and social network relations among the girls, and their (recent) histories of interaction together;
(ii) the types of activity they are involved in;
(iii) the broader discourses, ideologies and moralities they live amidst; and
(iv) the acts and utterances immediately leading up to and following racialising/ethnifying utterances.

The tables below take the first three of these as the point of entry into analysis of '*kale*', the Indian English voicing and of the episode as a whole. They explicate in a little more detail both how and where these contexts are relevant to the interaction, and try to show how one might start to navigate the structuring of this episode while also beginning to reckon with some of its vital particularities.

Table 5.1 Institutional and social network relations, histories of interaction, etc.

Institutional identities	Schoolgirls in Year 9 (aged 13–14)
Family networks	Family links with different countries: Habibah (India); Masouda (Pakistan); Lily (white, England
Peer relations and recent interactional history	Habibah and Lily are good friends, and they spend a lot of time together talking about boys. Masouda has recently fallen out with them, but is keen to re-establish friendship (later during break, she gets a friend to tell Habibah that she wants to say sorry for anything she's done, but Habibah tells the friend not to interfere and to get lost).

Table 5.2 Types of activity

The main activity in this sequence	
RESPONDING TOGETHER TO A TEXT MESSAGE FROM A MEMBER OF THE OPPOSITE SEX – Masouda, Habibah and Lily. The girls are active in protecting this from potential interruption/disruption by the teacher or others.	Lines 5–219
Subsidiary activities (These are either abbreviated or ignored as the girls' attention shifts back to texting/phoning, the main activity)	
AVOIDING INTERRUPTION FROM THE TEACHER	96–102
RESUMING A DISPUTE (Habibah and Masouda) Prompted by the discovery that Masouda has actually played an active part in soliciting the text message (telling the boy she was called Aisha), Habibah puts an accusation to Masouda ('See! [*kale*] That's it, you're gone') which Masouda denies. (See Table 5.3 below for further discussion.)	78–95, 109, 121–140, 146–149, 169
SOLO-HUMMING AND SINGING – Habibah Habibah sings snatches of a song by Destiny's Child to herself ('T shirt')	107–108, 118–119, 122, 150–155
BEING RESEARCHED –Habibah, Lily, Masouda	110–116

Table 5.3 Ideologies and institutional and moral codes variously in play in this episode

	Lines
THE PROPRIETIES AND POSSIBILITIES OF CONDUCT AND CONVERSATION DURING LESSONS These are largely **suspended** (although there is a risk of their being reasserted at any time)	
THE CONVENTIONS AND EXPECTATIONS OF FRIENDSHIP: For the most part, these are **enacted** – they are implied, negotiated or indeed questioned in the way these girls initiate, reciprocate or refuse actions and activity together. But drawing on our ethnographic knowledge of Habibah's friendship with Masouda, as well as on what she says later, there is a good case for saying that issues of friendship and loyalty are central to Habibah's 'See! [*kale*] That's it, you're gone' in Lines 78–80. Later in the recording (not in this extract), Habibah says: 'that was funny, boy … see, see, how the fuck did she get in contact with those boys, and then she calling me a whore'. So it looks as though her 'See! – *kale*' alludes to the defamatory claims that Habibah thinks Masouda has made about Habibah's contact with black boys in particular. 'See!', in other words, seem to be implying that Masouda is a hypocrite. In the event, of course, Masouda's response in Lines 82–95 fails to address these rather inexplicit accusations of defamation and hypocrisy, and instead she responds by denying an interest in black boys. But Habibah never explicitly accepts this, and she never lets her off with e.g. an 'okay'. Instead she carries on with questions about the contact ('how the fuck did he get your number'; Lines 146, 169), and then she blanks Masouda's answer in Lines 147–149 by singing to herself (Lines 150–155).	5–222

Table 5.3 *(Continued)*

THE PROPRIETIES AND POSSIBILITIES OF CONTACT BETWEEN GIRLS AND BOYS/WOMEN AND MEN These are **explicitly debated in talk, written in text messages and sung** – they constitute topics that all the girls are interested in, and that serve as a source of laughter, excitement, stories, and argument (both more and less light-hearted), etc. Within this broad field of interest, ethnically marked moral codes also become salient ...	
PUNJABI PROHIBITIONS ON GIRLS ASSOCIATING WITH (BLACK) BOYS are **evoked** by the introduction of elements from the Punjabi language (vocabulary and pronunciation).	
But the girls shift their stance on the (relatively stable) view that Asian girls shouldn't associate with black boys. In the 'kale' sequence, Masouda appears to accept the prohibition, and denies that she has transgressed, but in the phone voicings, the prohibition is subject to comic impersonation and implicit ridicule. These shifts are an effect and articulation of fluctuations in the spirit of Habibah's relationship with Masouda.	
Focal sequence 1: Habibah: 'See! *kale*' ((*'kale' = 'black boys' in Punjabi*)) • Habibah's switch to Punjabi introduces a co-ethnic angle on her 'See! That's it – you're gone'. This seems to be forceful. Rather than responding to Habibah's 'See!' with 'So what?', or to 'you're gone' with 'why?' or 'how', Masouda dwells on the issue of black boys in her rebuttal, first appealing to a shared ethnic understanding ('I don't like '*kale*' cos you know what they're like') and then claiming that Andrew is 'burnt toast' (Lines 134, 139, 140). • But there is a strong case for saying that Habibah is more concerned with Masouda's hypocrisy about Masouda's own contacts with black boys and with her gossiping, than she is with the notion of contact with boys of the wrong race and colour *per se* (see above). Indeed, in a subsequent playback interview, Habibah made it clear that she likes black boys ('I think they're buff, innit'), Masouda confirmed this, and talking to the researcher (who was a black woman), both of them were embarrassed about using the word '*kale*'.	78ff
Focal sequence 2: Rehearsing for the phone conversation with Andrew with Indian English accents – Habibah and Lily • Indian English is widely used as a stereotypic voice, even by Lily who is white British – as Masouda comments in a playback interview, 'Lily uses it A LOT. I've got this video clip in my phone – oh my gosh – she done this Indian accent, it was so funny'. • More than that, Habibah had previously been seen being severely reprimanded by her father for being alone with some boys from school, and his reproachful injunction 'don't look at 'em' has temporarily become a jocular Indian English catch-phrase directed at Habibah by her peers. • So Habibah's dad doesn't like her hanging around with boys – indeed, he doesn't allow her a mobile and he has cut back on her MSN contact list. *But* he doesn't actually speak English with an Indian accent – 'my dad don't speak like that, my dad speaks proper English' (playback interview). In addition, Habibah also says subsequently that she partly understands his views – 'it looked wrong [being alone with the boys], but still... I wasn't doing anything wrong'. Overall, she considers her parents 'not strict, they have- we have limits like', and her mum 'understands everything... she knows I won't do anything wrong'.	178ff

This description is very preliminary and says hardly anything about the turn-by-turn sequencing in the interaction ('context [iv]' above). But it already opens several potentially productive lines into the investigation of contemporary ethnicities, and we might dwell, for example, on the resonance of African American popular culture (Habibah's humming and singing), processes of ethnic boundary crossing (the acceptability of Lily's Indian English impersonations), or new technologies and the renegotiation of sexuality, gender and generational relations. But rather than elaborating on these here (cf. Georgakopoulou, 2008; Harris, 2006), the argument in this chapter dictates that we turn instead to the types of interpretation *eliminated* by data and analyses like ours.

5.6 Understanding Better

If we allowed our interest in ethnicity and race to take us straight to '*kale*' and the Indian English voicing, hurrying past the contexts of activity, interactional history, network relations and circumambient discourse sketched out in Tables 5.1–5.3, we might find it hard to resist several stock interpretations from a rather well rehearsed repertoire of racial/ethnic analyses:

- in Lines 78–80, Habibah's '`See` *`kale!`* `That's it, you're gone`' might be treated as the expression of ethno-moral purism, upholding traditional values in the face of Masouda's alleged deviation. Linguistic ethnographic description, though, makes it clear that instead of reflecting the irrepressible dictates of a compelling ethno-moral conscience, '*kale*' points to the fragility of the girls' on-and-off friendship, and constitutes a moment of retaliation to the moral character assassination that Habibah thinks Masouda has been engaged in.
- In Lines 92 and 93, Masouda's '`I don't mix with "`*`kale`*`", I don't like "`*`kale`*`"`' might be read as straight racial hostility. But even a cursory reading of the transcript shows that this is a defensive protestation, and our wider ethnographic knowledge repositions this in the very active interest in black boys that Masouda, Habibah and Lily all share.
- The shift in tone between our focal sequences – the switch between the rather serious argument about '*kale*' and the very light-hearted Indian English voicings – might be viewed as a contradiction or confusion in the girls' ethnic ideologies and perspectives on Punjabi/South Asian sexual codes, tempting us into a 'caught-between-cultures' formulation. But if we reckon with the interactional purposes driving these

invocations of ethno-morality at the particular moments when they are produced, then the girls' utterances seem perfectly coherent, very effective (in terms of their impact on the recipients) and actually rather assured. If there is trouble and contradiction, it has far less to do with East versus West than with (a) Habibah and Masouda's friendship and (b) the general business of male-female relations among adolescents.

In saying all this, we are certainly not denying that the episode reveals ethnically linked differences in sexual morality, as well as ethnically inflected conflict between the peer group and home-based proprieties. If it were not for these tensions, then, as rhetorical actions, the switches into Punjabi and Indian English would have been entirely inert. *However*, it cannot be claimed that conflict around race and ethnicity was the girls' principal preoccupation in this episode, or that it somehow incapacitated them. Instead, they were obviously much more concerned with the tensions and excitement of prospective boy-girl relations and the vicissitudes of adolescent female friendship, and rather than being disempowering, ethno-moral conflict featured as a resource that the girls exploited quite skilfully in pursuit of their really pressing interests.

In fact, even though there were lots of allusions and evocations of the kind shown here, it was very rare in our dataset of 180 hours of radio-microphone recordings to see race or ethnicity pushed into the foreground as the central issue in an interaction. Contrary to the claims of what we have characterised as the dominant idiom, race and ethnicity featured for the most part as subsidiary and incidental issues, very much in the 'unruly convivial mode of interaction' identified by Gilroy and illustrated in Section 5.3. And indeed all this points to one of the most general ways in which our data and analysis can contribute to wider discussions of ethnicity and race. Holding closely to the contexts of everyday life, linguistic ethnography helps get ethnicity and race *into perspective*, as significant but by no means all-encompassing processes, intricate but much more ordinary and liveable than anything one might infer from the high-octane, headline representations of the political and media arena.

As the work of Hall and Gilroy amply demonstrates, linguistic ethnographies of routine practice are certainly not the only path to this kind of perspective – participant observation in non-linguistic ethnography is another route, as is first-hand experience of everyday urban life. But our account does raise quite serious questions about the adequacy of the standard social science interview as a means of assessing the significance of race and ethnicity amidst all the other social relations that people live (see also Savage, 2007: 893–894). In the transcript we have presented,

(i) the talk is jostling, allusive, multi-voiced, partisan and interwoven with physical movement and action;
(ii) racial/ethnic issues are introduced amid a range of other concerns, contested and collaboratively reformulated over time (and across settings); and
(iii) it is obvious that you need a lot of contextual knowledge to understand what is going on.

In contrast, research interviews

(a) typically privilege orderly progression, explicitness, relatively detached (and detachable) commentary, illustrative narrative, and speech separated from movement and action;
(b) seldom serve as sites for the contestation of identity claims against a background of shared knowledge; and
(c) researchers often lack the local understanding to pick up on allusions, looking for quotably literal encapsulations instead (see also Georgakopoulou, 2008).[2]

All of this favours the dominant idiom in the representation of ethnicity and race. If researchers do not grasp (i), (ii) and (iii) – if they lack access to local activities and to the ongoing co-construction/renegotiation of racial or ethnic meanings among everyday associates amid a host of other concerns – then the accounts of context produced in interview research are not only likely to be limited. There is also a risk that in trying to identify a context for what interview informants say, researchers draw on (and position their informants 'intertextually' within) only the most obvious discourses at large. Unfortunately, these tend to be essentialist and crisis-oriented, and if these are used as the main framing for the utterances of interviewees, then research cedes the terms of engagement to dominant formulations, making it much harder to pick up on the articulation of alternative/different agendas, more likely to find itself confined to 'the strategy of a simple set of reversals' (Hall, 1988, cited above).

When we presented our perspective at a seminar on ethnicity organised by the ESRC's Identities Programme, Hall agreed that it represented an empirical advance.[3] But he also wondered 'how you ever get back to the larger field' from all the contingent detail. As both of us are committed to using fine-grained data to address much bigger questions (about, for example, ethnicity, race, class, education and contemporary culture), we see this as a vital question, and elsewhere we have made extended attempts to address it (Harris, 2006; Harris & Rampton, 2003; Rampton, 1995/2018, 2006). Nor, as we said at the start, do we want to underplay the significance of contemporary racism, and we know that in order to address it, sometimes it certainly is necessary to go straight to the big concepts, in acts of strategic essentialism. So we are not advocating a retreat from larger generalisations about ethnicity and race in contemporary society, either in analysis or politics. We do hold, though, that in the process of abstracting and simplifying, it is vital to refer back continuously to the everyday, and that ultimately both academic and political generalisations must be made accountable to the kinds of activity represented in the transcript in Section 5.4.

Without that anchoring – without a sense of how, in one way or another, most people *do* manage in the generally rather low-key practices of the day-to-day – it is impossible to identify changes in the terms of everyday ethnic/racial encounters, and discussion is left vulnerable to the dramatisations of the dominant idiom, panicked and unable to imagine how anyone copes. And we are also not convinced that, on its own, talk of 'multiple, fluid, intersecting and ambiguous identities' provides recovery from this, assuming as it often does (a) that the identities we mention all count, and (b) that it is really hard working out how they link together. In our view, it is essential to look hard at how, in their everyday practices, people do make sense of things, work them through, and bring quite a high degree of intelligible order to their circumstances. This sometimes reveals that people are not as preoccupied, fractured or troubled by particular identifications as we initially supposed, and that they are actually rather adept at negotiating 'ethnicities without guarantees', inflecting them in ways that are extremely hard to anticipate in the absence of close empirical observation. And then this in turn prompts some crucial critical reflection on the relationship between political, academic and everyday constructs and practices. Of course there are no pure truths or easy readings in/of the everyday – no 'guarantees' – and its empirical study and representation require a host of historically located interpretive frameworks and procedures, as we have tried to illustrate. Still, we see ordinary activity as a vital resource and reference point for discussion about identities in general, quite often cutting the ground from dominant accounts, pointing in new or different directions.

The next chapter takes a closer look at two linguistic practices used by young people to bring intelligible order to their circumstances, and instead of dwelling on the contrast with established ideological discourses, it develops a comparative account that highlights the ground-level creativity with which the practices of language crossing and stylisation can collectively express rather specific ideological perspectives and positionings, here focused on migration and on class.

Notes

(1) The ethnographic fieldwork and data collection for the chapter was carried out by Lauren Small, and as well as drawing on Lauren's work, we are highly indebted to other members and associates of the Urban Classroom Culture and Interaction project team – Alexandra Georgakopoulou, Constant Leung, Caroline Dover and Adam Lefstein.

(2) We recognise, of course, that interviews take many shapes, are often embedded in ethnography, and can themselves be productively analysed as culturally situated interactional events. Indeed, when we interviewed senior teachers in this school and conducted focus groups with others, ethnicity did not emerge as more of a pressing issue than in our recordings of youngsters' spontaneous interaction, and in this regard, the interview and radio-mic data are complementary. Still, although our characterisation may be a little too stark, we do not think it completely misses the mark, and it actually also extends to survey questionnaires.

(3) '[W]hat I have heard is a very substantial deepening of the [new ethnicities] paradigm … I think the move to ethnography, the move to discursive analysis, discourse analysis of interviews, is a way of methodologically exemplifying the conceptual complexity that the paradigm talked about …. I hope you learn very much more exactly what it means to say the end of the essential social subject – how to look at this question when we don't have fixed, essentialised subjects who are the endless bearers of these positionalities whether they are race identity, ethnic identity, etc. What that actually means methodologically and conceptually – very important work' (Hall, 2006).

6 Style Contrasts, Migration and Social Class

6.1 Introduction

Since the 1990s, in the study of multilingualism and language style more generally, there has been a major shift, away from the traditional emphasis on the conditioning of social structure towards an interest in the agency of speakers and recipients, so much so, that the linguistic anthropologist Jane Hill was

> struck by the attention ... give[n] to what has come to be called 'agency': The capacity, even among young people who are members of disadvantaged racialised populations, to recruit what might be thought of as unpromising semiotic materials for the construction of vivid and dynamic identities. However, in a sort of contradictory reaction, the papers made me think about agency's opposite, 'structure' ... Into what kind of ... system do these speakers fit? (Hill, 2004: 193)

In a similar vein, in a discussion of multilingualism Monica Heller accepts that 'we can no longer see the [constraints on multilingualism] as fixed, natural, essentialised or objective'. But like Hill, she is reluctant to 'give up entirely any notion of system and boundary, any notion of constraint', arguing instead that we need to 'understand [system, boundary and constraint] as ongoing processes of social construction occurring under specific ... conditions' (Heller, 2007a: 341).

A good deal of my own research has contributed to this emphasis on agency, focusing on stylisation and crossing, two pointedly non-habitual speech practices that break with ordinary modes of action and interpretation and invite attention to creative agency in language use (Rampton, 1999: 422–423). *Stylisation* involves reflexive communicative action in which speakers produce specially marked and often exaggerated representations of languages, dialects and styles that lie outside their own habitual repertoire (at least as this is perceived within the situation at hand). *Crossing* is closely related, but involves a stronger sense of social or ethnic boundary transgression. The variants being used are more likely to be seen as anomalously 'other' for the speaker, and questions of legitimacy and entitlement can arise (Auer, 2006; Quist & Jørgensen, 2007; Rampton, 1995/2018: Ch. 11.1–2, 2009b: 151–153). How, though, is the analysis of relatively agentive practices like these to address Hill and Heller's challenge? Exactly what kinds of structure and system were there in the crossing and stylisation I have studied, and how far, for example, can these systems be seen as 'ongoing processes of social construction'?

There are of course many systems that ethnographic research can attend to, operating in many different macro/meso/micro linguistic, cultural and social processes, and there is also always a risk of over-schematisation, building elegant analytic models for processes that are actually more indeterminate. Nevertheless, this chapter examines the agency of British teenagers within two types of system: semiotic and socioeconomic.

The *semiotic* systems it attends to are binary style contrasts of the kind described by Ferguson (1959), Irvine (2001) and many others. In the fieldsites that the chapter describes, there were a large number of languages, dialects and speech styles, but from within this sociolinguistic diversity, particular varieties were highlighted and placed together in contrastive pairs, and these oppositional pairings were reproduced in public discourse, in the media, in education and in everyday practice. In the two settings to be discussed, posh and Cockney formed one contrastive pair, and Creole and Asian English formed another.

The *socioeconomic* system is Britain in the late 20th century, a stratified class society in which wealth and opportunity are unequally distributed and where, among other things, post-war employers have relied on a continuing flow of immigrant labour to do low-paid work.[1] This socio-economic system is obviously far more complex than just a style contrast, involving all sorts of political, economic and institutional processes that I am hardly qualified to discuss. But plainly, semiotic representations play a central part in the ongoing construction and reproduction of this large-scale social system (e.g. Bourdieu, 1991: 234 *et passim*; Williams, 1977) and, according to Parkin (1977), contrasts in style can themselves play a rather significant role (see also Irvine, 2001: 22, 24). Studying urban multilingualism in newly independent Kenya, Parkin described how the values and connotations associated with different local, national and international languages converged in a complex system of symbolic oppositions. This system of contrasting varieties provided

> a framework for [the] expression of [both emergent and established] ideological differences, ... [It was] a kind of template along the lines of which social groups [might] later become distinguished ... [Indeed more generally w]ithin ... polyethnic communities, diversity of speech ... provides ... the most readily available 'raw' classificatory data for the differentiation of new social groups and the redefinition of old ones. (Parkin, 1977: 205, 187, 208)

But if Parkin points to at least one potential connection between the two kinds of system, one semiotic and the other social/political, where does agency feature? For sign-users situated in the lower levels of a stratified society, the scope for agentively reshaping the social system as a whole is obviously limited. But that does not mean that they have no scope at all for agentive engagement with the conditions shaping their lives. As Hill notes, speech stylisation and language crossing are practices where agency is particularly pronounced, and according to Parkin, style contrasts act as rather clearly coded orientation points for the navigation of social space and social relations. And that at least is the focus of this chapter – adolescents positioning themselves in a multi-ethnic class society through their active involvement with two binary style contrasts, posh and Cockney, Creole and Asian English.

The chapter draws on two datasets, the first focusing on kids doing exaggerated posh and Cockney in a multi-ethnic secondary school in the 1990s, and the second involving stylised Creole and Indian English in multilingual friendship groups in the 1980s. Drawing on these data, I shall argue that:

- the posh/Cockney binary was intimately tied to social class, and it permeated the ordinary urban English habitually spoken by my British-born informants. But when, agentively, they put on stylised posh and Cockney voices, adolescents *accentuated* and *denaturalised* class stratification;
- the Creole/Asian English binary was related to ethnicity and migration, and in their agentive stylisations of Creole and Asian English, youngsters actively *reworked* the ethnolinguistic imagery circulating in the dominant ideology, *adapting* it in ways that made much better sense of their multi-ethnic lives together;
- these reworkings of the Creole/Asian English binary were actually grounded in a broadly shared working-class position, and the Creole/Asian English binary was also influenced by the high/low dualism central both to posh and Cockney and to social class. So although migration and ethnicity certainly mattered a great deal, the structuring processes associated with class seemed to be more fundamental;

- within globalisation, nation-states are giving more recognition to minority bilingualism, but they base this on a model of monolingual standard languages. As standard language multilingualism becomes the new cosmopolitan posh, polylingual hybridity emerges as a core marker of multi-ethnic urban working-class identity.

In developing a relatively panoramic account like this, there are times when this chapter is unavoidably synoptic, thin on interactional evidence, cursory in the discussion of the examples it does give, and dependent on summary interpretations based on a very large number of cases it leaves out. In an effort to compensate, I shall quite often refer back to the two monographs where these datasets are treated in much more detail (Rampton, 1995/2018, 2006). This still leaves a lot of data, analysis and interpretation 'black-boxed', but this is necessary in order to reach the vantage point emerging at the conjunction of these two datasets, working from there to a response to the questions that Hill and Heller pose, bringing out the ideological distinctiveness of the collective ground-level responses to particular social conditions that crossing and stylisation can articulate.

We can start with the style contrast tuned to traditional British social class stratification.

6.2 The Posh/Cockney Style Binary at Central High

In the 1990s, I studied 'Central High', a state-funded inner London secondary school for 11–16 year-olds (with a sixth form for 16–18 year-olds as well).[2] About one-third of its students came from refugee and asylum families; a substantial proportion moved away from the school (and sometimes back) before they completed their compulsory education; almost one-third were registered as having special educational needs and over half of the school's pupils received free school meals; and in the national 16+ school-leaving exams, the school performed substantially worse than the local borough average (see Rampton, 2006: Ch. 2.1, for more detail). Judged by the metrics of educational policy research, this was very far from being an affluent middle-class school in a settled suburban community (cf. Gillborn & Gipps, 1996).

Among other things, I analysed the ways in which adolescents spontaneously stylised posh and Cockney accents. They did this on average about once every 45 minutes and, in doing so, they drew on a high/low, mind/body, reason-and-emotion dualism that is deeply embedded both in British class culture and in the schooling process (e.g. Cohen, 1987; also

Bourdieu, 1991: 93). So, for example, in Extract 1 below involving two girls at the end of a tutor group lesson, Joanne's performance articulates quite a sharp contrast between the stances associated with standard and vernacular speech. Standard language gets linked to sceptical reasoning while Cockney is tied to passionate indignation.

Extract 1: Posh, then Cockney

During the tutor period while Mr Alcott is talking to the class, Joanne (wearing the radio-mic) has been telling Ninnette a bit about her parents and grandparents, and has just talking about her mum's difficult pregnancy (for a much fuller discussion, see Rampton, 2006: 338–341).

Key: STANDARD/POSH, **London vernacular**

```
1   Joanne:  (.)
2            ((quietly: )) she could have lost me ((light laugh))
3            (3)
4            ((with a hint of tearfulness in her voice: ))
             n you'd all be sitting here today without me ((laughs))
                               [sɪtʔɪn    hɪə ]
5   Tannoy:  ((eleven pips, followed by the din of chairs moving))
6   Jo:      ((louder, and in literate speech: ))
             but   you  ˈWOULDN'T  ˈCARE
             [bt   jə   wʊdʰntʰ    kɛə ]
7            cos   you  ˈWOULDN'T ˋknow ((laughs))
             [kəz  jə   wʊdʰntᵘ    næ̃u ]
8   ?N:      (                           )
9   Jo:      nothing I'm just jok-              )
10           I'm being st-
11           ((high-pitched)) ^oooh::
                                      [u::]
12           ((moving into broader Cockney:)) ^Ninne::tte
13           you've got eˌnough with you to\day
             [ju     gɒt   enʌf   wɪᶿ   juː   tədẽĩ]
14           and ˌthen you ˌgo and \ chee::k \me::
             [æn    en    jə  gəʊ  n     tʃiːk      miˡ]
15           ˌyou    \little::   ˌbuggˌ ayeˌ  aye  ˌayeˌ  aye
             [ju     lɪtʔʊ::ʔ    bʌg    ãĩ    jãĩ   jãĩ   jãĩ ]
16           (15) ((the teacher is giving clearing up instructions))
17           ((Joanne leaves the classroom and then hums quietly to
             herself))
```

When Joanne shifts to careful 'literate' speech in Lines 6 and 7 (Mugglestone, 1995: 208), she uses logic to *undermine* sentiment, whereas in contrast, when she pretends to *intensify* the emotion in her speech in Lines 12–15 – when she abandons her apology, and issues an indignant reprimand – her speech becomes markedly Cockney. Setting this episode next to many others where kids used exaggerated posh and Cockney in greetings, taunts, commands, rebukes, summonses, etc., or referred to physical prowess, social misdemeanours, sexuality and so forth, there was rather a consistent pattern (Rampton, 2006: Ch. 9). In one way or another Cockney evoked solidarity, vigour, passion and bodily laxity, while posh conjured social distance, superiority, constraint, physical weakness and sexual inhibition. And youngsters also positioned themselves around this ideological structure in a range of different ways – on some occasions they put ironic distance between themselves and the image of, for example, an over-sexed lowlife or a patronising snob, but on other occasions they seemed to identify with the indexical possibilities, using Cockney to soften the boundary between sociability and work, or adding piquancy to sexual interest by introducing posh.

From the description so far, posh/Cockney stylisation certainly did seem to fit Hill's characterisation of agency as a 'capacity ... to recruit [even] ... unpromising semiotic materials for the construction of vivid and dynamic identities'. But the account becomes more complicated when it is remembered that this high/low contrast stretches back several centuries, and that there is a strong case, for example, for seeing the binary materialised in the institution of schooling itself. As Packer and Goicoechea (2000: 236) note, '[t]he costs of membership of and participation in the classroom community of practice are paid in the form of binary divisions that become lived: dualisms of mind and body, reason and emotion, and thought and action' (also see, for example, Foucault, 1977; Varenne & McDermott, 1998: Ch. 2). 'Mind over body' can be seen in the tight constraints on physical activity in classrooms. The curriculum prioritises the production of lexico-grammatical propositions in thematically connected strings instead of humming, singing and the modalities of popular culture – a case, one might say, of reason over emotion; and of course high-low ranking is central to the whole organisation of education. And when we recognise the high/low binary's extensive institutionalisation in schooling like this, the purchase offered, for example, by an 'acts of identity' idiom decreases (Auer, 2007b; LePage & Tabouret-Keller, 1985). Instead of simply suggesting that these youngsters were 'projecting' a particular ideological imagery (as in 'acts of identity' theory), it becomes more accurate to describe their stylisation as 'spotlighting' or 'illuminating' elements of a structure that they already inhabited. And this certainly fits much better with the fact that it was often at particular institutional and interactional junctures that kids stylised posh and Cockney – they shifted into stylised posh and Cockney in moments when they felt humiliated or offended by a teacher, when faced with separation from their pals, and at sharply felt states and changes in the structured flow of social relations. So here, for example, is Hanif's response to some patronising over-explanation from Mr A:

Extract 2

A Humanities class, working on how lawyers in an upcoming role-play will introduce their cases (see Rampton, 2006: 284–312, for more detailed discussion and other examples).

Key: STANDARD/POSH

```
1   Mr A:   how can y- (.) how can you introduce your speech
2           like writing an essay
3           you have t-
4   Rafiq:  I would like to bring up
5   Mr A:   I would like to::
6   Hanif:  bring forward
7   Masud:  bring forw[ard
8   Anon:             [(ex      )
9   Mr A:   or even (.) I ˌin\te::nd ˏto
10  Anon:   pro[secute)
11  Hanif   [((loudly, in a posh accent, stretched, with an exaggerated
            rise-fall: )) ^O:::H
                           [əɪʊ]
```

But even this is not enough. Beyond the specific occasions in which youngsters put on exaggerated posh and Cockney voices, they continuously adjusted themselves to the high-low binary in their tacit speech practices. In a small quantitative Labovian study of style-shifting among the four core informants, I compared their use of standard and vernacular speech variants in 'formal' and 'informal' settings (reading aloud, speaking in front of the class, etc., as opposed to arguing with friends or telling them a story; see Rampton, 2006: Ch. 7.3). Table 6.1 presents the results for these students, and Extract 3 shows Ninnette, a black girl of mixed Caribbean/African descent, recoding her self-presentation in increasingly standard grammatical and phonological forms in an attempt to catch the teacher's attention:

Extract 3[3]

A drama class where, working in pairs, everyone has been told to prepare and rehearse a short role-play discussion involving one character who is going to have a baby. They will then be expected to perform in front of the rest of the group, but Ninnette and Joanne are fairly emphatic about not wanting to, and they have used their time joking around putting pillows up their jumpers. In the end, they successfully manage to avoid having to perform, but during the final moments allocated to preparation and rehearsal, just prior to their coming together to watch individual performances, Ninnette is recorded as follows (see Rampton, 2006: 258–261):

Key: STANDARD, **London vernacular**

1 Ninnette: ((*calling out to the teacher, loudly:*))
2 MISS
3 (.)
4 MISS
5 WE ˈ**AIN'T** ˈ**EVEN** ˈ**DONE** ˋ**NU' IN**
[nʌʔĩᵑ]
6 (.)
7 ((*even louder:*)) MISS WE ˈ**AIN'T** ˈ**DONE** ˋ**NOTHING**
[nʌfiŋ]
8 (2)
9 ((*not so loud, as if Miss is in closer range:*))
10 miss we ˈaven't ˈdone ^ANYTHING
[enɪθɪŋ]
11 (2)

These data show that my informants had absorbed the high/low posh and Cockney dichotomy into their ordinary, *non*-stylised speech (cf. Bourdieu, 1991: Part I; Rampton, 2006: 253, 258; Stroud, 2004: 198–199). Indeed, to push the 'spotlighting' metaphor one step further, here one might say that these youngsters had been *irradiated* by the high/low posh/Cockney

Table 6.1 Percentage (and proportions) of STANDARD variants in four informants' production of six variables in formal and informal contexts

	Simon (White Anglo descent)		**Hanif (Bangladeshi descent)**		**Ninnette (African Caribbean)**		**Joanne (White Anglo)**	
	Formal	**Informal**	**Formal**	**Informal**	**Formal**	**Informal**	**Formal**	**Informal**
1. Word-medial voiced TH (o*th*er)	(9/9)	(3/4)	(6/6)	(1/1)	(4/10)	–	(2/5)	(3/7)
2. Word initial voiced TH (*th*e)	**96%** (27/28)	**100%** (35/35)	**97%** (32/33)	**70%** (35/50)	**82%** (40/49)	**79%** (34/43)	**100%** (37/37)	**94%** (16/17)
3. Word-initial H (not proforms)	**88%** (23/26)	**86%** (13/15)	**100%** (16/16)	**86%** (12/14)	**100%** (14/14)	**79%** (15/19)	**86%** (12/14)	**44%** (4/9)
4. Pre-consonantal, post-vocalic L (o*l*d)	**89%** (16/19)	**50%** (6/12)	**66%** (6/9)	**64%** (9/14)	**42%** (11/26)	**23%** (5/21)	**47%** (18/38)	**66%** (8/12)
5. Word-medial intervocalic T (bu*tt*er)	**87%** (7/8)	**0%** (0/4)	**66%** (2/3)	**20%** (3/13)	**70%** (7/10)	**0%** (0/5)	**14%** (2/14)	**0%** (0/11)
6. -ING in participial suffixes (runn*ing*)	**86%** (12/14)	**40%** (4/10)	**100%** (17/17)	**33%** (2/6)	**66%** (6/9)	**0%** (0/6)	**61%** (8/13)	**22%** (2/9)
Overall scores	**90%** 94/104	**76%** 61/80	**94%** (79/84)	**63%** (62/98)	**69%** (82/118)	**57%** (54/94)	**65%** 79/121	**51%** 33/65

binary – it was a fundamental structuring principle in their routine, everyday English speech.

To return to Hill and Heller, yes we *can* see agency in posh and Cockney stylisation (evidenced, for example, in the (more and less) artful stylisations in Extracts 1 and 2). But agentive stylisation fits into a much more widespread, multi-layered and enduring system of sociocultural stratification, and in their routine Labovian style-shifting, these kids tacitly ratified and reproduced the semiotically marked distinctions and hierarchies that configure British social class. So amid class structuring that was both institutionally entrenched and individually internalised like this, it makes most sense to see agentive posh and Cockney stylisation as practices of *denaturalisation*, throwing an ideological system into high relief that was otherwise hegemonic, omni-pervasive and taken-for-granted.[4]

Denaturalisation like this certainly is not the only way in which stylisation operates as an agentive response to systemic conditions, and in the next section I shall describe a rather different dynamic. But by way of introduction, there is one more point to make about posh, Cockney and social class at Central High. Even though they stylised posh and Cockney more than any other variety, and even though they displayed traditional British patterns of sociolinguistic stratification in their Labovian style-shifting, this was very much a multilingual, multi-ethnic school with a very high migrant and refugee population, and this makes it hard to explain the reproduction of classed speech simply in terms of intergenerational transmission within the family (cf. Hill, 1999: 542). Of the four focal informants cited in Table 6.1, for example, Ninnette's mother came from the French-speaking Caribbean and Hanif spoke to his mum in Sylheti (and neither lived with their fathers). So instead of seeking an explanation in cultural inheritance and family reproduction, it is necessary to locate the development of a class sensibility in ongoing activity, in peer-group processes, in popular culture and in school experience. Indeed, it looks as though there could be a rather complicated relationship between class, migration and ethnicity, and this provides the cue for an overview of my second dataset, involving crossing and stylisation in Creole and Asian English in the 1980s.

6.3 The Creole/Asian English Style Contrast in Ashmead

In the 1980s, I researched multi-ethnic adolescent peer groups in 'Ashmead', a working-class neighbourhood in the town of 'Stoneford' in the south Midlands of England.[5] Stoneford had a population of about 100,000 and a substantial post-WWII history of labour migration, with people coming to work in local heavy industry, first from Poland, the Baltic states, Croatia and the Ukraine, then from Italy, then from 1958 onwards from the West Indies and Indian subcontinent, and finally, after 1972, from Bangladesh and East Africa. Ashmead was the most ethnically mixed area of migrant settlement in Stoneford, and in the local middle school the pupils were 9% African-Caribbean, 20% Anglo, 12% Bangladeshi, 28% Indian, 28% Pakistani and 0.7% Italian. Three-quarters of the houses in Ashmead were constructed between 1875 and 1914; in 1976 it accounted for one-third of all Stoneford's 'high stress' housing, and the inhabitants generally recognised that, elsewhere in the town, the discourses about their neighbourhood were predominantly negative.

My research investigated several speech varieties, and revealed rather a sharp symbolic opposition between Creole and Asian English. There is a glimpse of this in Extract 4, which comes from a playback interview:

Extract 4: Asian English, then Creole

Participants: Asif (15 years old, male, Pakistani descent), Kazim (15, male, Pakistani descent), Alan (15, male, Anglo descent), Ben (the researcher/author, 30+ , male, Anglo descent).

Setting: An interview, in which Ben is struggling to elicit some retrospective participant commentary on extracts of recorded data, and is on the point of giving up (see Harris & Rampton, 2002: 39–44; Rampton, 1995/2018: 123–124, for much fuller analysis).

Key: Creole accent ***Punjabi accent***

```
1  Ben:    right shall I- shall we shall we stop there
2  Kazim:  no
3  Alan:   no come [ on carry on
4  Asif:           [ do another extract
5  Ben:    le- lets have (.) [ then you have to give me more =
6  Alan:                     [ carry on
7  Ben:    = attention gents
8  Asif    ((quieter)): yeh [ alright
9  Alan    ((quieter)):     [ alright
10 Asif    ((quieter)):     [ yeh
11 Ben:    I need more attention
12 Kazim   ((in Asian English)): I AM VERY SORRY BEN JAAD
                                 [aɪ æm veri sɑri ben dʒɑːd]
13 Asif    ((in Asian English)): ATTENTION BENJAMIN
                                 [əthenʃɑːn bendʒəmɪn]
14 :       [ ((laughter))
15 Ben:    [ right well you can- we cn-
16 Alan:   [ BENJAADEMIN
```

```
17 Ben:    we can continue but we er must concentrate a bit
18         [ more
19 Asif:   [ yeh
20 Alan:   alright                    [ (go on) then
21 Asif    ((in Asian English)):  [ concentrating very  hard
                                  [ kɑnsəstɾetɪɳ   veɾi  ɑɾ]
22 Ben:    okay right
23 :       ((giggles dying down))
24 Kazim   ((in Asian English)): what a stupid (     )
                                 [vʌd  ə  stupɪd ]
25 Ben     ((returning the microphone to what he considers to be a
               better position to catch all the speakers)):
               concentrate a little bit-
26 Alan:   alright then
27 Kazim   ((in Creole)): stop movin dat  ting  aroun
                                     [dæt tɪŋ  əɹɑʊn]
28 Ben:    WELL YOU stop moving it around and then I'll won't need to
29         (.)           r[ight
30 Kazim   ((in Creole)): [stop moving dat  ting  aroun
                                       [dæʔ tɪŋ  əɹɑʊn]
31 Ben:    right okay [
32 Kazim:             [ BEN JAAD
33 Alan:   ((laughs))
34 Ben:    what are you doing
35 Alan:   ben jaa[ad
36 Ben:           [ well leave ( ) alone
37 Kazim:  IT'S HIM that ben jaad over there
38 Ben:    right
((Ben continues his efforts to reinstitute the listening activity))
```

Things are not going quite as I had planned, and at the point where I threaten to stop the interview, Asif and Kazim switch into exaggerated Indian English in a sequence of mock apologies. Then a moment later in Line 27, just as I seem to be signalling 'back-to-business' by repositioning the microphone, the boot moves onto the other foot; Kazim switches into Creole and directs a 'prime' at me, this time constructing *my* activity as an impropriety. This difference in the way Asian English and Creole are used fitted with a very general pattern in my data. When adolescents used Asian English, there was nearly always a wide gap between self and voice, evident here in Asif and Kazim's feigned deference. In contrast, switches into Creole tended to lend emphasis to evaluations that synchronised with the identities that speakers maintained in their ordinary speech, and in line with this, Creole was often hard to distinguish from young people's ordinary vernacular English (cf. Rampton, 1995/2018: 215–219).

Away from stylised practices like this, Ashmead youngsters encountered many different uses of Asian and Creole English, and inside minority ethnic networks, the forms, functions and associations of Creole and Asian English were obviously much more complex and extensive than I recorded in the interethnic settings where my fieldwork was located (see Sharma, 2011: 482, on non-distanced/ing uses of Asian English by young people at home). But in spite of this, the images evoked in stylisation were quite specific, and across a wide range of instances, there was a sharp polarisation. Creole indexed an excess of demeanour over deference, displaying qualities like assertiveness, verbal resourcefulness and opposition to authority, whereas Asian English stood for a surfeit of deference and dysfluency, typified in polite and uncomprehending phrases like 'jolly good', 'excuse me please', 'I no understanding English' (cf. Goffman, 1967b).

This contrast certainly was not just autonomously generated within Ashmead. Undoubtedly, there were a lot of local influences, experiences and histories that, in one way or another, could give this contrast a strong and complex emotional resonance, but it also tuned to a much more widely circulating imagery which polarised black and Asian people in threat/clown, 'problem/victim couplet[s]' (Dummett, 1973: 212; Gilroy, 1987; Hebdige, 1979: 2, 88; Walvin, 1987), echoing 'a common-sense racism that stereotypes African Caribbean youth as violent criminals and all Asian people as the personification of victimage' (Gilroy & Lawrence, 1988: 143). In the UK at the time, Asians were often stereotyped as compliant newcomers, ineptly oriented to bourgeois success, while African Caribbeans were portrayed as troublemakers, ensconced in the working class and adept only in sports and entertainment (Hewitt, 1986: 216; Jones, 1988: 217–218). And within the education system itself, there was also some powerful contrastive stereotyping in institutional responses to the ethnolinguistic difference of Caribbean and Asian migrants (cf. Rampton, 1983, 1988).

In Ashmead, awareness of racist imaging like this meant that in the wrong mouth at the wrong moment, stylised Creole or Asian English could certainly get very negatively sanctioned (Rampton, 1995/2018: Ch. 2), and in the cross-ethnic production and reception of these expressive practices, local youngsters generally developed quite a reliable sense of what they could and couldn't do, where and with whom (Rampton, 1995/2018: Ch. 12.4 *et passim*). Even so, the public imagery was appropriated, reworked and recirculated at a local level, so that crossing and stylisation became significant local currency.[6]

Creole was clearly much more attractive to youngsters of all ethnic backgrounds, and it was often reported as part of the general local linguistic inheritance, particularly among Asian informants, who described it as something 'we been doing ... for a long time' (Rampton, 1995/2018: Ch. 2.2). In the interpretation in my 1995/2018 book, I situated this socio-symbolic polarisation in the larger context of migration (Rampton,

1995/2018: 217). On the one hand, I suggested, *Creole* indexed an excitement and an excellence in youth culture that many adolescents aspired to, and it was even described as 'future language'. On the other hand, *Asian English* represented distance from the main currents of adolescent life, and it stood for a stage of historical transition that many youngsters felt they were leaving behind. In fact, though, this symbolisation of a large-scale historical trajectory, this 'weight[ing mediated] by the speaker[s'] social position and interest' (Irvine, 2001: 24), went deeper. There was also a class dimension to the path indexed in the binary opposition of Creole and Asian English, and this showed up in at least four ways.

First, crossing and stylisation themselves figured as something of a local emblem of the neighbourhood's positioning within the town's socio-economic stratification, signifying the difference between Ashmead's mixed adolescent community and the wider Stoneford population. When my informants described the kinds of people who *wouldn't* do crossing and stylisation, they referred to groups who were vertically placed at either end of a bipolar hierarchy of wealth and status, a hierarchy that matched the economic and demographic facts quite closely (Rampton, 1995/2018: Chs 1.7 and 2). Up above, there were the 'posh wimpies' living in wealthier districts outside Ashmead, and down below, there were Bangladeshis living in the very poorest parts of town. So this, for example, is how Peter referred to youngsters from outside the neighbourhood:

> 'gorra' – 'white man' ((*in Panjabi*))… always call the people who didn't go to [our school] gorras, yet I'm white myself… cos we reckon they're a bit you know upper class (most of them)… the gorra gang. (Peter, cited in Rampton, 1995/2018: 62)

A second reason for linking the Creole/Asian English contrast to social class lies in a significant overlap in the evaluation of Creole and local non-standard English. When Asian and Anglo kids described the efforts of their mums and dads to get them to speak properly, in styles associated with the more educated classes, it was often the intrusion of swear-words, question tags and verb tense forms in *Creole* that were targeted (Rampton, 1995/2018: Ch. 5.6), and here is Ian (white), explaining how his American cousins were disappointed by his English:

> they think we speak really upper class English in England… they they see on the… they say that Englishmen has got such beautiful voices, and they express themselves so well… ((*shifting into an approximation to Creole:*)) **'eh what you talkin' abaat, wha' you chattin' about, you raas klaat'**, and they don't like it! They thought I was going to be posher.

Indeed, beyond the confines of my own research, this broad functional equivalence of Creole and traditional non-standard British speech was widely celebrated (and extensively noted) during the 1980s in a code-switching record called 'Cockney Translation' by the black British MC Smiley Culture (see Gilroy, 1987: 194–197; Hebdige, 1987: 149–152; Jones, 1988: 54–56).

Third, the Creole/Asian English contrast can itself be mapped into the high/low, mind/body, reason-and-emotion oppositions outlined in Section 6.2. As Cohen explains, this dualistic high/low idiom was generated 'from within certain strategic discourses in British class society' from the 17th century onwards, and 'from the very outset [it was] applied across a range of sites of domination, both to the indigenous lower orders and ethnic minority settlers as well as to colonial populations overseas' (Cohen, 1987: 63). In the light of the overlapping evaluation of Creole and non-posh English identified immediately above, it is not difficult to see Creole linked to the low side of the traditional British class semiotic. But just as important, the high side of the class binary was linked to Asian English. English is a prestige variety in the Indian sub-continent, and when my informants compared themselves with relatives there, they saw their own varieties as inferior:

> in India right, the people that I've seen that talk English... talk strict English, you know. Here, this is more of a slangish way... the English that people talk round here you know, they're not really talkin' proper English... if you go India right... they say it clear, in the proper words.

> my cousin come ((*over from India*))... he's got a degree and everything, he speaks good English, but he didn't used to speak in English with us though, cos they sort of speak perfect English, innit. We sort of speak a bit slang, sort of innit - like we would say 'innit' and all that. He was scared we might laugh at this perfect sort of English... the good solid English that they teach 'em'.

At the same time, there was very little evidence in these kids' stylised Asian English that this status carried over into Ashmead. Transposed to the UK and re-entextualised in stylisation, Ashmead kids depicted an Indian English orientation to the high, proper and polite as comical, its aspirations hopelessly marred by foreignness.

Lastly, there was little indication of a commitment to education in ethnolinguistic crossing and stylisation in Ashmead.[7] Of course, schools were a vital meeting point for kids from different ethnic backgrounds, and the general pastoral and extra-curricular ethos played a very significant part in promoting good interethnic relations. But Creole, which many admired, hardly featured at all on the curriculum, and rather than being tolerant of learners of English as a second language, or respecting them for their progress (as the teaching staff might hope), adolescents generally stigmatised pupils who had not yet been fully socialised into the vernacular ways of ordinary youth. Instead of curriculum learning, the activities and codes of conduct characteristic of playground and after-school recreation tended to be central to the cross-ethnic spread of minority languages and, if anything, this was facilitated when a style got used in opposition to school authority.[8] Certainly, there were complex bodies of knowledge, skill and experience associated with different types of ethnically marked music and performance art, and there were, for example, white girls who were very interested in finding out more about reggae or bhangra. But a lot of this interest was embedded in heterosexual relations, and learning was much more a matter of legitimate peripheral participation in recreational 'communities of practice' than classroom study (cf. Lave & Wenger, 1991; Rampton, 1995/2018: Part III).

Putting all this together, there is a case for saying that the Creole/Asian English contrast oriented Ashmead adolescents to *two* major social processes. Not only did crossing and stylisation situate them at an end-point in the migrant transition from outside into Britain, but then also, once inside, the binary lined them up with cultural values much more associated with lower than higher classes. Yes, iconically, Creole was first and foremost associated with Caribbeans, Asian English with Asians, and local cross-ethnic respect for these ownership rights was evidenced in the way that, in some contexts, 'non-owners' either often avoided the use of these varieties and/or only invoked them in specially licensed interactional moments. But in the problems, pleasures and expectations of non-posh adolescent life together, these kids experienced enough common ground to open up ethnolinguistic speech styles, realigning them with the high/low valuations hegemonic in British society, respecifying their significance in crossing and stylisation practices that recognised and cultivated the shared social space that labour migration had now created.

It is worth now trying to pull the threads of this description together, first by discussing similarities, differences and the relationship between posh/Cockney, Creole and Asian English in England, and then by commenting on late modern multilingualism, ethnicity and social class more generally.

6.4 Comparing and Connecting Posh/Cockney and Creole/Asian English

High/low, mind/body and reason/emotion polarisation are central to English schooling and, at Central High, adolescents broadly ratified the institutional embodiment of this binary in their routine style-shifting. But posh and Cockney *stylisation* interrupted the routine patterning of everyday talk, exaggerating and elaborating evaluative differentiations that were otherwise normally treated as non-problematic in their practical activity. Stylisation made the sociocultural structuring of everyday life more conspicuous, and denaturalised a pervasive cultural hierarchy, disrupting its authority as an interpretive frame that might have otherwise been 'accepted undiscussed, unnamed, admitted without scrutiny' (Bourdieu, 1977: 169–170).

In Ashmead, crossing and stylisation registered ethnicities in the first instance, recognising differences but integrating them in a repertoire of ethnically marked styles that adolescents could now more or less share (in speech reception, if not always in production). Partially reproducing but also appropriating and recasting racist imagery circulating more widely in public culture, peer-group crossing and stylisation figured Asian English as an emblem of ethnic difference rooted outside Britain and/or in older generations, and treated Creole as a powerful model of youth ethnicity grounded now in the UK. In addition, crossing and stylisation were reported as signs of mixed multi-ethnic community, and against a background of local agreement on ethnic groups getting along together, adolescents learnt – and got told – how and when to follow the lead of the owners of an ethnic speech variety in their crossing and stylisation, avoiding derogatory Creole, for example, and confining Asian English to particular interactional sites (Rampton, 1995/2018: Ch. 7.9). In short, Ashmead's active and explicit ideological commitment to multiculturalism produced significant levels of *normative conventionalisation* in local practices of crossing and stylisation (cf. Agha, 2007; Johnstone & Danielson, 2006), attested in rules of cross-ethnic avoidance and licence of the kind documented in detail not only in Rampton (1995/2018) but also in Hewitt (1986).

There was nothing comparable to this in the stylisation of posh/Cockney at Central High. Of course, there were plenty of representations of posh twats and vernacular slobs circulating in British public culture generally, but with nothing like anti-racism to challenge them, they were not particularly controversial. Kids did have a class-related sense of futures being potentially better and worse for them as individuals; they could be quite articulate in their images of lives to either aim for or avoid; there was a lot of very animated political debate focused on sexuality, race and ethnicity. But there was little evidence of any explicit, collectively mobilising, specifically *class* consciousness among the youngsters at Central High (Rampton, 2006: Ch. 7.2), and nothing to compare with the normative conventionalisation of Creole/Asian English stylisation in Ashmead. In Ashmead, you risked offending the putative owners if/when you did exaggerated Creole or Asian English or were seen to endorse racist representations. But at Central High, you could stylise posh and Cockney with much more freedom, relatively unconcerned about transgressing core codes of collective solidarity and, consistent with this, the patterns of alignment between self and voice in acts of stylisation were also much more varied (Rampton, 2006: 366–367).

So overall, the social problematics that were thematised in these two sets of contrastive crossing and stylisation practices were very different and, in summarising this, we can return to the relationship between stylisation, structure and agency:

- at Central High, posh and Cockney stylisation seemed geared to the *deconstruction of a system of sociocultural differentiation* that was very well established and that adolescents *already inhabited*. This multi-scalar system was geared to the reproduction of class hierarchy and it governed the vertical trajectory of individuals, elevating some and degrading others. In school contexts, stylised posh and Cockney generally *denaturalised* this.

In rather stark opposition to this,

- in Ashmead, crossing and stylisation in Creole and Asian English oriented to the *collective construction of a shared habitation from group differences* which had only been encountered relatively recently and was represented in problematic ways in public culture generally. Crossing and stylisation 'domesticated' these differences – *made them orderly, familiar and acceptable* – by, among other things, articulating a contrast which depicted ethnic styles as different moments in group trajectories with a common destination in British class culture.

Viewed as simple but powerful semiotic systems like this, style polarities like posh/Cockney and Creole/Asian English allow people to plot positions and paths in the territory between, just as Parkin proposed, and in their exploitation of these contrasts, adolescents actively oriented themselves to two absolutely central axes in the organisation of British society – on a 'horizontal', ethnic axis, the movement from outside Britain in, and then once inside, on a 'vertical' class axis – up/down, high/low. So evidently, when seen as the agentive practice of historical actors engaging with the conditions where they find themselves, stylisation can support different ideological projects, and in Creole/Asian English stylisation, adolescents articulated collective commitments that were quite distinct from the kind of micro-political positionings entailed in stylised posh and Cockney. Whereas one, one might say, reinterpreted the dominant version of ethnicity and replaced it with the kinds of 'new ethnicity' described by Stuart Hall (1988) in the unruly convivial modes of interaction referred to by Gilroy (2006; Section 5.3 above), the other intimated the kind of 'partial penetration' of social class, the only partly articulated consciousness of class hegemony, described by Paul Willis (1977; Rampton, 2006: Ch. 9.6).

At the same time, these data also suggest that underpinning all this, sociocultural class stratification was the most powerful systemic process, configuring the ground from which adolescents spoke. In *both* of the datasets that have been discussed, it seemed to be interethnically shared alignments with values and activities marked as non-elite in English class culture that gave crossing and stylisation so much of their shape, intelligibility, currency and resonance. Admittedly, my account has nothing to say about the dynamics within homes and intra-ethnic community settings. But in the account so far at least, it is hard to see posh and Cockney stylisation being directly shaped by ethnicity and migration, whereas in contrast, there was substantial evidence that the style polarisation of Creole and Asian English reflected class sensibilities in England. Of the two binaries that stylisation played on, the high/low contrast was omni-pervasive, whereas the sense of collective trajectory from past to future was much more specific to the projection and recognition of ethnic and migrant identities.

With this view of class sensibilities influencing the stylisation of Creole and Asian English in Ashmead, as well as the stylisation of posh and Cockney at Central High, it is worth concluding with some general observations about developments in the political and institutional recognition of multilingualism.

6.5 Globalisation and Social Class: Standard Multilingualism and Vernacular Heteroglossia

As a number of commentators have noted, in recent years many nation-states have become significantly more proactive at promoting multilingualism, especially with indigenous minorities:

> [p]olitical economic conditions are changing; the new economy places much greater emphasis on communicative skills in general, and multilingualism in particular, than did the old ...; nation-states try to reposition themselves advantageously on the dynamic and increasingly globalised market. (Heller, 2007b: 15)

Influenced also by supra-national bodies and NGOs, '[m]inority language education is now becoming the standard policy in the territories inhabited by linguistic groups other than that of the nation-state' (Pujolar, 2007: 77). At the same time, however, the promotion of minority language bilingualism is often based on traditional monolingual models of literacy, schooling and language codification:

> the kind of public typically imagined within minority language revitalisation and/or ethnic nationalism movements ... are typically bourgeois and universalistic in nature: the nation or linguistic community is imagined in the singular and envisioned primarily as a reading and writing public .... [L]anguage politics tend to be oriented towards normalisation, expanding literacy, and gaining legitimacy within the terms of state hegemonic language hierarchies. (Urla, 1995)

Jaffe spells out the significance of this:

> [M]inority language movements like the Corsican one have often made monolingual minority language competence the centrepiece of their discourses about language and identity ... *[This] makes the mixed cultural and linguistic practices and identities that are found in societies that have undergone language contact and shift 'matter out of place'*. (Jaffe, 2007: 53, 60, emphasis added)

Influenced by a number of processes associated with globalisation, standard language multilingualism is more widely seen as desirable, positioning an expanded range of bilingual repertoires as (cosmopolitan) posh. But this accords little value to the kinds of mixed cultural and linguistic practices described in Ashmead and at Central High. Indeed, there is a good case for seeing this type of heteroglossic hybridity as a lower-class counterpart to the respectability of the more recently encouraged bilingualisms.

This claim certainly fits with my reanalysis of the data from Ashmead, and there is broad support for it in a growing body of research which describes the hybrid language practices of young people in multi-ethnic working-class locations in European cities (e.g. Auer & Dirim, 2003; Jaspers, 2005; Jørgensen, 2008b; Keim, 2007; Lytra, 2007; Quist & Jørgensen, 2007). At the same time, if this claim is to be sustained, it needs to be nuanced, because heteroglossic multi-ethnic practices can also circulate beyond their territories of origin. Translinguistic switching, mixing, crossing and stylisation may well thrive in demographic sites where there are migrant and minority populations in poorer housing and underfunded schools, but some of these practices get taken up by the popular media, relayed much more widely and subsequently reproduced by people in very different socio-economic locations. Androutsopoulos (2001) documents the process very clearly (cf. also Stroud, 2004), and there is a vivid description in Cutler's account of how African American Vernacular English gets adopted by 'Mike', a very wealthy young white New Yorker (1999; also Bucholtz, 1999b; Depperman, 2007). This kind of appropriation muddies our view of the class distribution of this ethnically marked mixed speech, and with youngsters like Mike using it, maybe we should say that the associations of ethnically marked mixed speech are really just 'non-work' rather than 'working-class'. Indeed, if, instead of economic subordination, it is actually more a matter of simply 'letting your hair down', recreation, informality or 'fun', then perhaps we ought to use a class-neutral label like 'youth language' to characterise speech practices like these.

But it is important not to overlook the subjective dynamics of social class. Sherry Ortner describes how class binaries become internalised psychologically, how class opposites affect individuals as an emotionally charged imagery of alternative possibilities and how all of us live with 'fears, anxieties' and an insistent sense that people in higher and lower class positions mirror our 'pasts and possible futures' (Ortner, 1991: 177):

> we normally think of class relations as taking place *between* classes, [but] in fact each class contains the other(s) within itself, though in distorted and ambivalent forms ... [E]ach class views the others not only ... as antagonistic groups but as images of their hopes and fears for their own lives and futures ... [M]uch of working class culture can be understood as a set of discourses and practices embodying the ambivalence of upward mobility, [and] much of middle-class culture can be seen as a set of discourses and practices embodying the terror of downward mobility. (Ortner, 1991: 172, 175, 176)

Stallybrass and White (1996: 194) provide further elaboration: this class-based self-other relationship is actually rather unstable and, mixed in with the bourgeois disgust and fear of the lower orders, there is also fascination and desire. So when middle-class majority kids use speech forms historically associated with the urban ethnic lower classes, this does not mean that class no longer matters. There is a long tradition of relatively well-to-do young people temporarily 'slumming it', taking time off from the journey to higher-class futures, and with Ortner, Stallybrass and White, there is a stronger case for seeing the ethnolinguistic crossing and stylisation of affluent teenagers as exactly the kind of exception that proves the rule, the rule being that this kind of ethnically marked mixed speech emerges among people positioned in the lower realms of class structure, developing there its strong vernacular connotations.

Notes

(1) Discussing empirical traditions and methods in the massive literature on 'class', Bradley usefully distinguishes between 'those who study class structure and patterns of social mobility using highly sophisticated statistical techniques, and those who focus on class formation and consciousness employing historical or ethnographic approaches' (Bradley, 1996: 45; see also Ortner, 1991: 168–169 on research in the US). Although there is some cursory, loosely statistical contextualisation, the analysis in what follows aligns with the second approach, centring on class formation and consciousness (see Rampton, 2006: Ch. 6, for a fuller discussion).

(2) This was part of a 28-month ESRC-funded project, 'Multilingualism and Heteroglossia In and Out of School' (1997–1999), and data collection involved interviews, participant observation, radio-microphone recordings of everyday interaction, and participant retrospection on extracts from the audio-recordings. Analysis focused on four youngsters (2M, 2F) in a tutor group of about 30 14-year-olds, and the account of posh and Cockney stylisation centred on *c*.65 episodes identified in 37 hours of radio-mic audio-data.

(3) The linguistic changes produced over turns in this sequence can be charted as follows:

Non-standard ←===========================→ *Standard*

Line 5	Line 7	Line 10
ain't	ain't	=> aven't
n't (= not) + nothing	n't + nothing	=> n't + anything
nasalised -ING [ĩɳ]	=> velarised -ING [ŋ]	velarised -ING
glottal TH [ʔ]	labio-dental TH [f]	=> dental TH [θ]

(=> indicates the point where the variable becomes (more) standard.)

(4) It is worth adding here that although the adolescents I studied talked a lot about ethnicity, gender and sexuality, they did not have a great deal to say about social class as an explicit topic (cf. Rampton, 2006: 7.2 and below).

(5) This was an ESRC-funded project entitled 'Language Use in the Multiracial Adolescent Peer Group', and it involved two years of fieldwork with 23 11–13 year-olds of Indian, Pakistani, African Caribbean and Anglo descent in 1984, and approximately 64 14–16 year-olds in 1987. Data collection focused mainly on a youth club and on lunch and break time recreation at school, and included radio-microphone recording (approximately 145 hours), participant observation, interviewing, and retrospective participant commentary on extracts of recorded interaction (see Rampton, 1995/2018, for further details).

(6) Overall in my corpus of field observations, interviews and more than 100 hours of radio-mic recordings, I identified more than 250 episodes where there was a clear Creole influence in the speech of whites and Asians and about 120 exchanges involving stylised Asian English (as well as 68 episodes with black and white uses of Punjabi).

(7) At the same time, it is important to emphasise that for the most part, my research in Ashmead focused on a rather particular set of collective perceptions and conventional practices, and it would be a mistake to extrapolate from these to the more general attitudes, aspirations and trajectories of individuals. As a group, my informants' crossing and stylisation were embedded in practices and pastimes that were popular rather than elite, and looked towards (lower) class solidarity. But these kids also engaged in lots of other types of practice which I have not considered, and in fact in my data collection there was an explicit bias towards recreational sites. So it is very possible – in fact highly likely – that when, say, they settled down to work in lessons, a lot of kids could put aside the stances and alignments displayed in crossing – the attraction to Creole's street credibility, the pleasures of Punjabi abuse, the mockery of Asian English deference. All of that might well be sectioned off quite easily as just having a laugh, messing around with friends.

(8) As well as Creole and Asian English, Punjabi had a very significant place in the local interethnic repertoire, and it was also beginning to be taught as a subject at school. But nobody white or black attended these classes, and hardly any of my informants said they would be interested, even in principle. Instead of being book-learned, the lexicon of cross-ethnic peer group Punjabi consisted of nouns referring to parts of the body, bodily functions, animals, ethnic groups and kin, as well as verbs to do with sex, violence and ingestion. And in the two situations where most crossers got interested in Punjabi, the ethos was broadly anti-establishment. First, Punjabi was quite useful as a language for excluding teachers and other white adults and, second, it had entered the kind of traditional playground language and lore of school-kids described by the Opies, figuring in incrimination traps, jocular abuse and chasing games.

7 From 'Youth Language' to Contemporary Urban Vernaculars[1]

7.1 Introduction

In the late 1990s, the heteroglossic practices of young people with migrant backgrounds became a major focus for sociolinguistic research, and there has also been a great deal of interest in the spread of such practices among both other-ethnic and non-migrant peers (Chapter 6, this volume; Alim *et al.*, 2009; Androutsopoulos & Georgakopoulou, 2003; Auer, 2007b; Harris, 2006; Hewitt, 1986; Jaspers, 2005; Jørgensen, 2008b; Malai Madsen, 2015; Rampton, 1995, 1999; Rampton & Charalambous, 2012; Reyes & Lo, 2009). Young people certainly have not been the only focus,[2] but practices of stylisation and crossing have been much more extensively researched among young people than anyone else, and youth is often taken as central to their social distribution, to the extent that these ways of speaking are regularly described as 'youth language'.

But what happens to these practices as young people grow older? Here the research literature has far less to say, and a somewhat mixed picture emerges from the few studies that exist, some suggesting that these ways of speaking decline, others that they continue (Cutler, 1999: 430; Hewitt, 1986: 193). So there is a substantial lacuna in our knowledge about the durability of these practices, and this has major consequences for any more general interpretation: are these heteroglossic practices just an 'adolescent phase', a 'stylistic flirtation', or do they instead point to the emergence of cultural formations that are actually enduring? Indeed, if these ways of speaking are dropped in early adulthood, then the claim in Chapter 6 that heteroglossic mixed speech marks the development of new urban working-class sensibilities looks rather overblown.

To investigate these issues, there are at least four questions that we should ask:

(a) Is this kind of heteroglossia simply an evanescent phenomenon within the particular environments where it has been studied? Is it simply a brief stage in, for example, a longer process of language shift – a transitional moment as new populations shift from dominance in the migrant language to dominance in the language of the 'host' society?
(b) If it is not simply an ephemeral phase that new populations pass through in the process of assimilation to majority norms, is it just an age-graded phenomenon, something that successive generations of young people with (and without) migrant roots pick up for a while, but then abandon as they get older?
(c) If it is not just age-graded, if it does actually last into adulthood, then just how significant is it? Exactly what place does it hold in the speech repertoire of individuals and social groups?
(d) If it is actually significant, then how should we conceptualise it, and what should it be called? Clearly, neither 'youth language' nor something like 'multi-ethnic adolescent heteroglossia' will be enough.

Before starting on this sequence of questions, my account begins with a résumé of some of the earliest findings, drawing on my own research on multi-ethnic adolescent peer groups in the 1980s, cross-referring to Hewitt (1986) as well (Section 7.2). With the baseline for historical comparison laid out, Sections 7.3 and 7.4 address Questions (a) and (b), mainly drawing on interview data from a study in 2008–2009 focusing on people of South Asian descent in west London, also alluding to Harris's analysis of adolescents from the same area in the mid-1990s. These data show that the patterns and practices identified in the 1980s *have* persisted, and there are also indications that they are not necessarily abandoned as adolescents move into adulthood. Section 7.5 confirms this with extracts of telephone interaction involving a man in his 40s, and the discussion then turns to Question (c) – if the practices of youth persist, what kind of place do they hold in an adult speech repertoire? Section 7.6 explores this, first by comparing the man's most heteroglot speech with the way he talks to a lawyer, and then by reporting his own retrospective account of talk and friendships formed at school. With both the historical and biographical durability of this way of speaking now established, the chapter turns to Question (d). After characterising the speech in focus as a hybrid style that has emerged at the intersection of migration and class, that is strongly linked to youth in its indexical associations but not in its social distribution, and that is closely related but still distinct from other languages in the vicinity,

Section 7.7 proposes 'contemporary urban vernacular' as a solution to the terminological uncertainty and dispute that characterises recent work in this field, drawing on Agha (2004, 2007).

We should begin with the research from the 1980s, summarising key points from Section 6.3 and adding a few extra findings relevant to the overall argument.

7.2 Crossing and Stylisation in the South Midlands in the 1980s

As indicated in the previous chapter, the research published in Rampton (1995/2018) focused on crossing and stylisation in a multi-ethnic working-class neighbourhood in 1984 and 1987 and it showed that:

- Creole was the most attractive to youngsters of all ethnic backgrounds. It was associated with qualities like assertiveness, verbal resourcefulness and opposition to authority, and was often reported as part of the general local linguistic inheritance (Rampton, 1995/2018: Ch. 2.2).
- In sharp contrast, Asian English stood for a surfeit of deference and dysfluency, typified in polite and uncomprehending phrases like 'jolly good', 'excuse me please', 'I no understanding English'.
- Beyond the peer group, there was a great deal of public discourse that polarised black and Asian people in threat/clown, problem/victim binaries (Gilroy, 1987; Rampton, 1995/2018), and awareness of racist imaging like this meant that, with crossing and stylisation, local youngsters generally developed quite a reliable sense of what they could and could not do, where and with whom (Rampton, 1995/2018: 301–303 *et passim*). Even so, within these constraints, both varieties could figure in joking cross-ethnic interaction between friends, they could be used competitively and they could be used against teachers and authority.
- These patterns invited three broader lines of interpretation. First, even though it did not stand for a seamless racial harmony, as a general practice language crossing carried solidary interethnic meanings. Second, the socio-symbolic polarisation of Creole and Asian English seemed to locate youngsters in a larger context of migration. On the one hand, Creole indexed an excitement and an excellence in youth culture that many aspired to, while on the other, *Asian* English represented distance from the main currents of adolescent life. But then once inside – third – ethnolinguistic crossing and stylisation expressed largely working-class alignments, and there was very little indication of any commitment to education in these practices.

So, overall, it looked as though in these heteroglossic practices, youngsters had developed a set of conventionalised interactional procedures that reconciled and reworked their ethnic differences within broadly shared experience of a working-class positioning in British society. Race and ethnicity were very big and controversial issues in the media, education and public discourse generally, but in language crossing and stylisation, kids had found and affirmed enough common ground in the problems, pleasures and expectations of local adolescent life to navigate or renegotiate the significance, risks and opportunities of ethnic otherness.

For what follows, two additional findings from this research are significant, the first relating to Punjabi and the second to these adolescents' non-stylised, more routine speech.

- With both Asian English and Creole, crossing by people *without* family connections to these two varieties was generally more inhibited in the presence of people who *did* have inherited ties to them, but with Punjabi crossing, the participation of Indian and Pakistani peer 'inheritors' was central. Asked to compare it with Creole, informants agreed that while the latter was tough and cool, Punjabi was ordinary, funny or just like English, and bilinguals were generally enthusiastic about Punjabi crossing, explicitly denying that it was disrespectful: 'if they're our friends, we teach them it', 'most of them ... who hang around with us lot, you see, they all know one word, I bet you' (Rampton, 1995/2018: 58; see Chapter 6, this volume, note 8).
- Looking beyond crossing and stylisation, I also carried out a small-scale quantitative study of my informants' more ordinary talk, focusing on the pronunciation of post-vocalic, prepausal or preconsonantal L and word-initial voiced TH in the speech of three Caribbean, three Anglo, one mixed Anglo/Caribbean, four Indian and seven Pakistani boys in informal interviews in 1984 (Rampton, 1987). All of the informants made some use of the standard English variants (even though 'dark' L does not typically occur in Punjabi or Creole and fricative TH is generally absent from Punjabi and rare in English in India; Wells, 1982: 629). But non-standard variants were much more common. Everyone used traditional non-standard Anglo variants – vocalic L was used by adolescents of Indian, Pakistani and Caribbean descent as well as whites (Wells, 1982: 258), and all the informants used zero TH (coalescences and other sandhi forms in post-consonantal environments; Wells, 1982: 329). In addition, variants with a notionally minority language provenance had spread into the speech of Anglos – everyone used stopped TH, and traditionally Creole and Punjabi clear

L was also used post-vocalically by the three white informants, one of whom also used retroflex L, a variant typically associated with Punjabi and Indian English (Shackle, 1972: 11; Wells, 1982: 5, 70). So even though subtle ethnolinguistic differences had not been eliminated from these youngsters' routine speech and you could still generally tell someone's ethnic background from their pronunciation, there were also clear signs of non-standard accent convergence in their ordinary English, and this was broadly consistent with the overarching interpretation of crossing and stylisation as expressions of multi-ethnic youth community.

In fact even in the 1980s, it was clear that Ashmead was not unique as a site for ethnolinguistic crossing and the spread of migrant speech forms into the everyday English of white youth. Hewitt's pioneering research in broadly working-class areas in South London in the early 1980s did not include people of South Asian descent, but his account revealed crossing and stylisation practices among youth with Caribbean and Anglo backgrounds that bore a good deal of similarity to the ones that I subsequently identified (see also Back, 1996; see Jones, 1988: 146–150, on Birmingham). In addition, Hewitt discussed more routine, non-stylised ways of speaking of the kind noted immediately above, and he called these 'local multi-ethnic vernaculars':

> There has developed in many inner city areas a form of 'community English' or multiracial vernacular which, while containing Creole forms and idioms, is not regarded as charged with any symbolic meanings related to race and ethnicity, and is in no way related to boundary maintaining practices. Rather, it is, if anything, a site within which ethnicity is deconstructed, dismantled and reassembled into a new, ethnically mixed, community English. The degree of Creole influence on the specific local vernacular is often higher in the case of young black speakers, but the situation is highly fluid and open to much variation. [This] de-ethnicised, racially mixed local language [operates as] ... a constraining, taken-for-granted medium subsisting through all interactions. (Hewitt, 1986, 1989: 139, 1992/2003: 192–193)

So clearly, during the early and mid-1980s, broadly comparable practices were becoming widespread at the intersections of language, migration, ethnicity and class. But how long did they last?

The durability of the patterns identified in Ashmead and elsewhere is in fact well-attested in public culture, and representations include: the (originally Birmingham-based) rap musician Apache Indian from 1990 onwards (described in Back, 1995/2003); the comic TV character Ali G of the 'West Staines Massiv' (1998–2006; see, for example, Sebba, 2007); the teenage Bhangra Muffins ('kiss my *chuddies,* man') in the radio and TV show, *Goodness Gracious Me* (1996–2001); and Gautam Malkani's 2006 *Londonstani*, a novel about a white boy growing up in west London. But to supplement this with ground-level data, it is worth turning to the project in west London in 2008–2009, supplementing this with cross-reference to Harris's findings from roughly the same area in 1996–1997 (Harris, 2006).

7.3 Was this Evanescent? Southall 25 Years on

Since the 1950s, west London has been a major area of settlement for people with links to South Asia in general and the Punjab in particular. According to the 2001 Census,[3] the *c.*89,000 population in Ealing Southall was 47.8% Asian (23.2% Sikh, 12.4% Hindu, 13.3% Muslim), 37.6% white and 8.9% black, 43% being born outside Britain. Southall is a great deal larger than Ashmead, a suburb in a metropolis rather than just a neighbourhood in a provincial town, but in spite of these size differences, there are broad similarities in patterns of migrant settlement. Neither are affluent areas and, according to Ealing Council, 'areas within Southall appear within the top 5% most deprived in the country in terms of income deprivation, crime and barriers to housing and services'.[4] Both have strong histories of voting Labour in elections, and in both places the Punjabi cultural presence has been very strong, with Southall often referred to as 'little India' and 'little Punjab' (Gillespie, 1995: 35). So the demography provides some initial warrant for their comparison.

In the fieldwork we conducted in 2008–2009, there were >70 informants with mainly Punjabi ethnic backgrounds, aged between 14 and 65, born both in the UK and abroad (in India, Pakistan, East African, Malaysia and Hong Kong). Data collection was carried out by Devyani Sharma (Principal Investigator) and Lavanya Sankaran (Research Officer), and it involved participant observation, interviews (including the elicitation of social network data) and self-recordings conducted by a smallish subset of the informants. This generated a dataset that differed from the Ashmead corpus in two obvious ways. First, with only eight informants who were under 20 years old (and only two under-16s), the 2008–2009 informants were generally a lot older than my 1980s Ashmead informants and, second, most of them were now engaged in occupations that could be categorised as either middle class or lower middle class.

In spite of these differences, there was good evidence that some of the main patterns and practices identified in the 1980s continued into the noughties, and the following account draws on content analysis of eight interviews (with four males and two females under 30, and two men in their 40s) as well as some interactional sociolinguistic micro-analysis of self-recordings by one of the 40-year-olds.[5]

Just as Harris (2006: 128–129) had found in the mid-1990s, there were reports of the continuing influence of Caribbean speech features:

Extract 1

Jeet (M, 14, born in London, Punjabi background) and friend (M, 14, Asian) in interview with DS (F, 30+, Indian background) (simplified transcript 1651ff.; 32.17ff.)

```
1  DS:    do some (.) is there like a black style of speaking, an Asian style of
                                                                       speaking
2  Jeet:  yea::h it's like (.) 'wha's gaaing, blood', that's black
       ((a little later:))
13 DS:    and Indian?
14 Jeet:  (.) ehm
15 Nav:   they speak exactly the same as black people
       ((a little later:))
26 DS:    but Indian kids like like Punjabi like Asian British kids,
27        so your kind of [kids
28 Jeet:                  [they mainly talk the black style
29 DS:    really
30 Jeet:  ye::ah
```

In Harris's 1996–1997 sample of 17 female and 13 male adolescents with predominantly Asian backgrounds, '[o]n the whole the ... boys were more likely than the girls to claim a greater usage of Jamaican influenced speech beyond the expression of individual words, and a greater affiliation to them' (2006: 131), and this was also reported in 2007–2008:

Extract 2

Sameer (student, M, 23, born in London, Punjabi background) and friend in interview with DS (simplified transcript 1367; 56.52)

```
1  DS:  what's the slang that you think is quite local here that you guys use?
2       can you think of examples of slang or words (.)
3  Sam: 'innit' (.) that's one there they all use 'innit'(.)
4  DS:  yeh
5  Sam: um:: (.) 'why not man'(.) they always say 'man' at the end.
6  DS:  yea
7  Sam: yea like a- like a kala ((black)) word.
8       er they will always say 'yea man' or whatever
9  DS:  yeh
10 Sam: they always use 'man' at the end for some reason
     ((a little later:))
21 DS:  do you think girls- do boys do it more:-
22      girls and boys here? (.) speak the same-
```

```
23 Sam:  do you know what
24       girls actually are a bit- (.) different actually
25       girls don't (.) er yea girls: (.) ain't really (.) got like a Southall
                                                                      lingo-
26       some girls have (.) but not most of them
27       they still sound fluent English like
28       they still like sound posh or something.
```

But it did not look as though females categorically dissociated themselves from non-posh slang:

Extract 3

Rita (student, F, 19, born in London, Punjabi background) in interview with LS (F, 25+, Singapore background) (simplified transcript 1798; 90.30)

```
1  Rita:  in terms of generation
2         English is different.
3         um we have uh:: very- we use slang (.)
4         a lot of slang as in (.)
5         a lot a lot of slang
6         slang which I'm not even aware of sometimes (.)
7         um whereas er:: other people:: use (.) f- (.) proper version of English
8         like the full English
9         as in we say 'innit' (.)
10        they say 'isn't it'
```

Indian English was also widely noted, just as it had been in Ashmead in the 1980s. Jeet interrupted his account in Extract 1 with: 'the Indians (.) they (just) speak it like (.) *((shifting into a mock Indian accent:))* "what is going on" hhahaha'. This was now supplemented with the term 'freshie' (from 'fresh off the boat'), a word that had not featured either in my dataset from the 1980s or Harris's from the mid-1990s, and that was said to be a relatively recent innovation: 'I think we made that up innit (.) I think seriously I think that we did make that up in school innit', 'that started in our era', 'that happened yea:: that was when our age started all that off' (Sameer, London-born student, M, 23, Punjabi background and friend). Invoked, invested and contested from a range of different positions, 'freshie' is too complex a term for adequate discussion here,[6] but there is an account of its joking use in Extract 4:

Extract 4

Anand (student, M, 23, born in London, Punjabi background) in interview with DS (simplified transcription 1200; 51.10)

```
5  Anand: I get called a freshie myself
6  LS:    you!
7  Anand: yea I get called it because I'm so: (.)
8         cos when I speak with my friends in sort of really (.)
```

```
9          um you know er Punjabi accent or whatever (.)
10         I speak Punjabi really well,
11         they just (.) think I'm a complete freshie (.)
12         well (.) some of my mate- cos they don't understand it to that extent
13 LS:     but you can speak Punjabi but they can speak-
14 Anand:  they can speak Punjabi too but they're probably not as fluent or as-
15 LS:     so it's sort of like an affectionate thing? like '[ah you freshie( )'
16 Anand:                                                  [ yea..you freshie yea
17         it's not an offensive thing
```

Lastly, as in Ashmead, there were reports of other-ethnic crossing with Punjabi:

Extract 5

Rita (student, F, 19, Punjabi background) in interview with LS (simplified transcript 1665; 83.46)

```
1  Rita:  yea oh my god another thing (.)
2         a white person
3         if you were to go right 'you gora'  ((Punjabi = 'white person'))
4         (he) would understand that now (.)
5         he would understand it (.)
6         and if I er swear at him in Punjabi he would understand it for some
                                                                   reason (.)
7         it's like 'damn! ((snaps fingers)) they've taken over' heh
8  LS:    so is it in Southall that they can understand?
9  Rita:  anywhere now
10        even in Ha:yes, in Southa::ll. and old Southall
       ((a little later [1898 94.41:))
41        I talk to my white friends like this (.)
42        and I will say 'hunna' and they'll be like 'yea' (.)
43        cos they- they've once or twi- they've-
44        at the beginning they'll be like 'what does hunna mean'
45        I'll be like 'do you agree with it' (.)
46        and then they get used to it and now she uses that word
47        she says 'hunna' (.) so:
```

So the comparison of datasets about a quarter of a century apart points to significant continuities – the continuing pre-eminence of Creole/Jamaican in accounts of non-standard speech, Asian English as a point of derogatory or comic reference, non-Asian uses of Punjabi, and the association of all this with slang, non-proper speech and emblematic 'innit' (Extracts 2, 3; Harris, 2006: 99; Hewitt, 1986; Rampton, 1995/2018: Chs 5.5 and 5.6). Given public representations like those cited at the end of the previous section, this evidence of durability is not really news, but even so, it confirms the answer to our first question – Has multi-ethnic heteroglossia of the kind described in Ashmead proved historically ephemeral? No. It also sets the stage for the second question: Is it all just an adolescent phase?

7.4 Adolescents Only?

In my research in the 1980s, the identity of mixed multi-ethnic English as a *youth* style was suggested, among other things, in teenagers' tales of 'innits' and bits of Creole getting corrected by adults (Rampton, 1995/2018: Ch. 5.6), and in its more recent public media depictions, this kind of heteroglossic speech has been associated with youth rather emphatically. In our fieldwork in 2008–2009, most of the informants were post-adolescent, and so this offered an additional perspective.

Namrita, a professional in her late 20s, discussed young people's language with a degree of critical detachment:

Extract 6

Namrita (freelance broadcaster, F, 28, born in the UK, Punjabi background) in interview with LS (simplified transcript 51.16)

```
1     the younger people speak (.)
2     the English they speak (.) is very (.) umm (.) colloq- colloquial (.)
3     umm lots of slang (.).
4     umm they don't speak the best English (.)
5     purely because their parents don't speak the best English (.)
6     umm (.) I'm not sure that the role models they're looking at (.)
7     sometimes that the artists they're looking up to speak (.) the best
```

Naseem – a successful businessman in his late 40s – provided a parental perspective:

Extract 7

Naseem (businessman, M, 48, Punjabi background, came to the UK aged three) in interview with DS (simplified transcript 1693; 15.15)

```
1  DS:   do you think that young (.) kids in Southall are speaking English
                                                                 differently
2        [like their own
3  Nas:  [too fast (.)
4        they they have their own lingo their own dialect
5  DS:   what's it li I mean do you
6  Nas:  it's very- I can't (.) I don't understand
7  DS:   do your kids speak (.) a bit like
8  Nas:  when they're speaking with me
9        I I I always emphasize the fact that you must speak properly (.) you know
10       and when they're with their friends (.)
11       yeah 'how you doing man'
12       you know that sort of thing
13       but it's very difficult to pick up you know
14       like sometimes I'm (.) trying pick up but they try
15       but it's so difficult you know
16 DS:   so with their friends they speak very differently
17 Nas:  it's a different language they speak (.)
18       the dialect the tone the eh eh eh the syllables
```

And Ravinder gave a personal account of shifting away from a style thought 'black':

Extract 8

Ravinder (student, M, 19, born in London, Punjabi background) in interview with DS (simplified transcript 542; 21.38)

```
15 Rav:  two years ago I:: I used to- I used to think I-I'm I'm acting too
                                                                  black (.)
16       it's getting a bit er- it's getting old now
17       everyone will make fun of me cos I'm- not-
18       not make fun of me but everyone's saying
19       'oh you why you Asian boys acting all black' (.)
20       so I started acting like bit more (.) a bit more Asian like (.)
21 DS:   now?
22 Rav:  yea (.) yea (.) changed my earrings and um:: (.)
23       I don't know (.) basically acting more Asian.
```

Twenty-three year-old Sameer also referred to younger kids doing styles that were judged too 'black':

Extract 9

Sameer (student, M, 23, Punjabi background) and friend in interview with DS (simplified and abbreviated transcript 60.02)

```
1  Sam:  some youngsters I've seen on the road (.) when they see each other (.)
2        all they talk about i- (.) like (.) 'BLOOD' (.)
3  DS:   heh heh you don't do that
4  Sam:  nah we're too old for that kinda stuff
5  Sam:  some of them think they're proper kale
                                   ((Punjabi for 'black people'))
6        'what's going on 'pant dig gaya''
                   ((= 'your pants fallen down?' in Punjabi))
7        once this guy was walking past and my friend said
8        he said 'hey bro your pants falling down man what's wrong with
                                                            you' heh heh
9  DS:   heh heh heh so you're not like-
10 Sam:  nah not now. not anymore. not anymore. not anymore ( )
11       used to (.) that's when I was really young though
```

But Sameer's reflections on stylistic development also looked ahead as well as backwards, and in an account of growing into more mature and peaceable forms of masculine sociability, his description of going to a pub outside the locality included cross-ethnic heteroglossia:

Extract 10

Sameer again, as before (1120; 46.48)

```
1  Sam:  if you go to the one ((the pub)) in your own area (.)
2        you know you're gonna (.)
3        it's jus (.) you're gonna to see the same face:s (.)
4        and sometimes fights start off:
5        cos there are so many Indian people in one area (.)
6  Sam:  so we got out of the area and we go to ((name of pub))
7        where there's bunde ((= 'men' in Punjabi))
```

```
8          like proper gentlemen that go there
9          like men go there (.) and we go there (.)
10         the first time they saw us they were like [ yea ]
       ((a few moments later:))
21         you get gore ((= 'white people' in Punjabi)) there as well
22         you get white people there:: (.)
23         you get Jamaican people there (.)
24         and everyone's alright
25         and it's like you even see black people they try talk Punjabi-
26 DS:     really?
27 Sam:    kiddan:: kiddan tiikiya yea
           ((= 'what's up? what's up? you okay?' - greeting in Punjabi))
       ((a little later:))
38         probably everyone has problems
39         but like they- they ((= older pub-goers))
40         probably grown out of all their little fighting or whatever
41         whereas we might see someone-
42         cos we're only twenty-three twenty-four::
43         maybe when we're like twenty-six twenty-seven
44         everything would have died out
```

Most of the other extracts run with the association of heteroglot speech with adolescence, variously characterising it as inferior (Extract 6), hard to comprehend (Extract 7) or comical (Extract 9, Lines 6–9). But in this one, it is linked with 'proper gentlemen' who've grown out of their problems, who understand the ways of Sameer and his friends, and whose multi-ethnic conviviality provides them with a bit of fresh air. This complicates the picture of adolescents-only age-grading sketched out in the earlier data, and there is a further challenge to this if we now turn to some evidence from interaction.

7.5 Middle-aged Complications

Here is a successful 40-year-old businessman on the telephone:

Extract 11

Anwar (businessman, M, early 40s, born in London, Punjabi background) phoning Ronni (M, early 40s, Punjabi background) on his mobile

Key: Creole; **London vernacular;** ***Punjabi***

```
5            ((ringing tone))
6   R:       ((inaudible))
7   Anw:     ((in Jamaican accent:)) WA:APN  RA:NNI
                                     [wɑːm]  [ɑː]
8            ((in a more London accent:)) ow's 'ings man
                                          [øʌuz ɪŋz]
9   R:       ((inaudible))
10  Anw:     nice one man
11           ((in Punjabi:)) kiddaan
             ((Translation: 'what's up'))
```

12 everything alright?
13 R: *((speaks for 2.0 - inaudible))*
14 Anw: wha's happening
15 R: *((speaks for 3.5 - inaudible))*
16 Anw: yeh man yeh yeh (.)
17 hows every**f**ing
everyf**f**ing cool
18 R: ((speaks for 2.5 - inaudible))
19 Anw: ((with sigh?:)) yes bru**v** yeh yeh yeh yeh (.)
((the conversation is interrupted by an incoming call. When the incoming call is completed, Anwar rings Ronni back and they discuss a business arrangement. Then in Line 73, Anwar shifts the topic:
72 R: *((speaks for 1.4 - inaudible))*
73 Anw: ***aor kiddan*** - wha's **goin** **down** man every**f**ing cool
((trans: 'what else is up?')) [æʊ]
74 R: *((speaks for 2.3 - inaudible))*
75 Anw: how's 'ings a' e yard
[haʊ s ɪŋz æ ə jʌɖh]

There are a number of linguistic features in Anwar's talk that align it with the interview descriptions of an English style infused with Creole and Punjabi, and we can also see a contribution from traditional London vernacular forms (Table 7.1).

There are also other features that mark this as colloquial speech, several reproducing other characteristics identified in the interview extracts: vernacular vocatives – 'bruv' (Line 19) and 'man' (Lines 8, 10, 16, 73) (classed as black in Extract 2, Line 5); phonetic elisions associated with rapid speech, 'aa s ings' (Line 8) and 'a e yard' (Line 75) (see Naseem's complaint in Extract 7, Line 3); and words like 'cool' (Lines 17 and 73) and 'nice one' (Line 10).

However, the complication is that in spite of bearing all these hallmarks of the transgressive, working-class adolescent style discussed in Sections 7.1 and 7.2, the speech in Extract 11 is produced by a successful

Table 7.1 Some of the linguistic resources in play in Extract 11

Creole features	Punjabi	Traditional London vernacular
• Line 7: 'waapn' used as a greeting (Hewitt, 1986: 130); • Line 7: fronting of [ɒ] to [a] in the friend's name (Sebba, 1993; Wells, 1982: Ch. 7); • Line 75: 'yard' used for 'home'.	• Lines 11 and 73: 'kiddaan' (a phrase that is also used by black and white people); • Line 75: Jamaican 'yard' pronounced with short central vowel [ʌ] and a retroflex D.	• Lines 8 and 75: zero-TH in 'aa's [ø]ings' (Wells, 1982: 329); • Line 8: H-dropping in 'ow's' • Lines 17, 19, 73: TH-fronting in 'bruv' and 'everyfing'; • Line 73: alveolar -ING in 'goin'; • Line 73: centring diphthong in 'down' – [dæʊn] (Wells, 1982: 305).

middle-aged businessman. More than that, it is a style that he incorporates into the transactions of his trade, as illustrated in Extract 12:

Extract 12

Anwar being phoned on his mobile by a business associate (M, 30+, Punjabi background) on his mobile

Key: Creole; **London vernacular;** ***Punjabi***

1	Anw:	*((ring tone))* (1)	01.00
2		hallo (.)	
3	Man:	hallo	
4	Anw:	***o kiddaan vei*** (.)	
		((= 'what's up bro' in Punjabi))	
5	Man:	**a'righ'**	
6	Anw:	Anwar here	
7		(.)	
8	Man:	how you **doin' a'righ'**	
9	Anw:	yeh man I'm fine thanks	
10		whas happen**in** wi' yiu	
		[wɒs hæpnɪn wɪ jʏ]	
11		(.)	
12	Man:	er **nu'in** man	
		[nʌʔɪn]	
13		(.)	
14	Anw:	yeh every**f**ing good	
15		(.)	
16	Anw:	[ah	
17	Man:	[nah business is slow	
18	Anw:	(.) yeh well why is it slow man?	

There is no Creole pronunciation in this episode, but there are similar greetings and vocatives – 'o kiddaan vei' (Line 4), 'wha' happenin' wi' yiu' (Line 10), 'everyfing good' (Line 14), 'man' (Lines 9 and 18) – and some comparable accent features – alveolar -ING (Line 10) and TH-fronting (Line 14).[7]

So if we put these two extracts together with the glimpse that Sameer provided of a style enduring into maturity, it looks as though this *is not* just an adolescents-only age-graded way of talking. So what is going on? Just how significant is this style, and how do we reconcile its middle-aged currency with what everybody else has said?

7.6 How Significant is this Style? Placing it in the Repertoire

It is important to set the style that Anwar used with Ronni and the trading associate in a broader view of his speech repertoire, and so here he is on the phone to a barrister about a matter of business:

Extract 13

Anwar (businessman, M, early 40s, Punjabi background) phoning Bilal (lawyer, M, late 20s/early 30s, Punjabi background) on his mobile

Key: Creole; **London vernacular**; ***Punjabi***; STANDARD ENGLISH PRONUNCIATION/RP

```
1  Anw:    ((phone rings))
2  Lwyer:  hello
3  Anw:    hi Bilal HOW you doING
4  Lwyr:   yeah alhamdulillah not too bad
5          how you doing
6  Anw:    yeah I'm I'm I'm fiNe THank you veRy much..
7          I THough['  -
                   [ʔ]
8  Lwyr:           [you've caught me at a good moment
9          cause I just finished courts
10         s[o just going back to chambers
11 Anw:     [o-
12         oh oh OKAY yeah
13         'a's great
           [øæs]
14         .hh e:::hm BILal
15         THE REASON why I called you is e::h
16         I jus' WANTED TO LET you KNOW THat Xxxxxxxxx((a name pronounced in
                                                                 Punjabi))
17         He came.. ande::h we DECIDED not tu pursue His case
```

Although Bilal now lives in another part of London, he grew up in Southall, and Anwar has known him since he was a boy (and he comments elsewhere on how hard it was for Bilal to become a barrister). So the style here is not highly impersonal or formal.[8] Even so, the differences from the opening of his conversation with Ronni are very striking (Table 7.2).

The contrast is even sharper when we compare the way in which Anwar shifts the topic from business to ask about the family. With the lawyer, he does this as follows:

Extract 14

Anwar on the phone with Bilal the lawyer (1.17)

```
53 Anw:   ((finishing the business topic:))
          bu'  I I I'LL keep you iNformed iN whaT's HappeNING
          [bʌʔ ɑː ɑː ɑːɫ]        [n]      [n]  [t]   [hæpnɪŋ]

54        HOW's everyTHING ELSE
                    [θɪŋ  eɫs]

55        How's the famili:
```

Table 7.2 Stylistic differences between Extracts 11 and 13

Conversation with lawyer Lines 3–13 (Extract 13)	Conversation with Ronni Lines 7–18 (Extract 11)	Comment
Line 3: 'hi B*ɭɭ*al HOW you doING'	Lines 7 and 8: 'wa:apn ranni **ow's 'ings** man'	(a) Greetings in informal Anglo with the lawyer versus Creole with Ronni; (b) lawyer's name pronounced with Punjabi retroflexion versus Jamaicanisation of Ronni's name.
Line 13: ''a's great' Line 6: 'I'm fine'	Line 10: 'nice one' Line 17: 'everyfing cool'	(c) Talking to Ronni, A's lexis is more idiomatic ('nice one') and colloquial ('cool' versus 'fine').
Line 6: 'THank you' Line 7: 'THough''	Lines 17, 19: 'every**f**ing', 'bru**v**'	(d) Standard pronunciation of TH with the lawyer versus vernacular London with Ronni.
Lines 3–13: no vocatives other than the lawyer's name	Lines 8, 10, 16: 'man' Line 19: 'bruv'	

With Ronni, it was:

Extract 15: (taken from Extract 11)

```
73    Anw:    (kor kiddan - wha's goin  down man everyfing cool
                            [wɒs  gəʊɪn  dæʊn]

74    R:      ((speaks for 2.3 - inaudible))

75    Anw:    how's 'ings a' e yard
              [haʊ s  ɪŋz   æ  ə jʌɖh]
```

So it is clear that Anwar is not mono-stylistic, and elsewhere in our recordings of him talking on the phone, his English becomes more Cockney (his own term), while in another with a woman from Sri Lanka who does not speak much English, it is more 'bud bud', a description that he says his daughter gives to the 'broken English' foreigner talk he uses with non-Hindi/non-Punjabi speaking South Asians whose English is limited (see Rampton, 2015a for further discussion).

But exactly how is this particular way of speaking best characterised? In fact, just before he talks to Ronni on the phone, Anwar provides his own gloss: 'Ronni's a schoolfriend of mine and we speak our- (.) different type of dialect which is a- a typical Southallian language'. He elaborates on this in an interview:

Extract 16

Anwar in interview with DS (Simplified and abbreviated transcription. 1174 66.46)

```
1   Anw:   when we were at school (.)
2          w- the way we were speaking (.)
3          Southall had its own language (.)
4   DS:    its own English.
5   Anw:   its own- its own English-
6          you know like you saying um: (.)
           ((in a more Caribbean accent in Lines 7 & 8:))
7          'w' ya gaing man, w' y' aaff to' you know
8          'w' y' aaff to' you know and er::
           ((with glottal T in 'laters':))
9          'I see you la'ers' 'la'ers' 'I see you la'ers' you know.
10         this type of language,
           ((a little later: ))
23         when I see my friends right
24         I (.) er::m
25         like he would say to me 'w' ya goin' (Anwar)'
26         er er I mean this is-
27         I'm talking about friends
28         who've got er:: you know who are [forty-
29         forty- forty year old people
30         from school yea from from from from school
```

His experience of schooling seems to have been important: 'you see I had a- a lovely childhood (.) ok (.) I loved my school days (.) every part of my school days'. He started out in a mainly white middle-class school where 'we were like p- the poor kids because all of us Asians were- (.) living in this part of Southall' but 'we mixed so well (.) that I don't remember any racist type of er- er:: (.) act or even by the teachers'. Then he went to the local state secondary school and 'again (.) we had brilliant times'. At this school, 'we didn't have many whites left at that time (.) we had Afro-Caribbean and Indian and Pakistani', but religious differences were 'on the back burner' – 'we were like living in each other's pocket... I acted like a Hindu (.) I acted like a Sikh, acted like a Muslim'. These ties, he says, have been lasting – 'my best friends are from my high school and my junior school (.) I still meet with the guy who is my friend, er who is in er my junior school (.) and er::m er (.) they're in very good positions in the civil service and and one is working for the Times and you know', 'our high school was not like friendship, we had a bond like brothers bond you know I mean'.

Anwar's contextualisation of the mixed speech that he uses with Ronni is consistent with the other accounts in so far as he describes a style forged in youth. But 25 years later, it looks as though this style still has affectively powerful connotations of peer-group familiarity, very much rooted in personal experience in a particular milieu. This is not a way of speaking used with just any co-ethnic of roughly equivalent age – in another phone conversation, Anwar sticks much more closely to straight Cockney when talking to a Pakistani mechanic brought up in the East End, while conversely, just after the business conversation in Extract 12, he describes his interlocutor as a friend. Nor is this some kind of Peter Pan refusal to grow up – like Anwar himself, a number of his school friends now have responsible jobs, and it is clear from his comments on texting that he's not uncritical of the verbal styles of youth today:

```
you know what annoys me in texting and emailing is you know when the
children and when people u::m when I get a text with abbreviated text
(.) slang text I don't like it (.) and when I do text I never abbreviate,
I write the who::le thing (.)
```

Instead, there are signs of the mixed style being adjusted to the concerns and constraints of adulthood. Even among the teenagers that I studied in the 1980s, there were signs of mellowing as youngsters moved from primary to secondary school (Rampton, 1995/2018: Ch. 7.6), and in place of the humorous, transgressive or ludic practices described in so much of the literature on adolescent heteroglossia, Anwar uses this mixed style in an effort to counsel Ronni on serious difficulties in his personal life:

Extract 17

Anwar talking to Ronni on his mobile (02.58)

Key: Creole; **London vernacular;** ***Punjabi***; STANDARD ENGLISH PRONUNCIATION/RP

122 Anw: both of you come home man
123 ***edda yaar*** *((= 'here man' in Punjabi))*
124 THA**a's i'** man
[ðæøs ɪʔ mæn]

125 *((tuts))* **yer my bruv** man **wha's 'e ma'er wid yiu**
[jə mʌ bɹʌv mæn wɒs ə mæʔə wɪd jʏʊ]
((a little later:))
145 R: *((inaudible, but speaking for 1.1 seconds))*
146 Anw: **na na na** you can't do TH**a'** man
[nʌ nʌ nʌ] [ðæʔ]
147 you can't do TH**a'**
[ðæʔ]
148 R: *((inaudible, but speaking for 1.2 seconds))*

```
149  Anw:  yeah lets lef i' man
                  [les  lef ɪʔ]

150        jus' LEAV-  le- jus' lef  i'
                [liːv   le   dʒəs lef ɪʔ]

151        if she seiys righ'    (.)              3.48
                  [seɪz  raɪʔ]
152        abou' dis
           [əbɑː  dɪs]

153        jus give her wha' Her dues are (.)
                   [hɜː  wɒʔ hɜː  ɖjuz ɑː]
```

In accounts of adolescent heteroglossia, a great deal of the movement between different ethnolinguistic forms looks ambivalently 'double-voiced', as if 'a variety of alien voices [are] enter[ing] into the struggle for influence within an individual's consciousness' (Bakhtin, 1981: 348; Jaspers, 2005; Rampton, 1995/2018: Ch. 8.5). But given both the account of its origins and the context in which it is used here – serious advice to a close friend in trouble – it would be hard to argue that in Extract 17, Creole, Punjabi and traditional London vernacular features come together in anything other than straight, serious talk – in Bakhtin's (1984: 199) terms, 'direct unmediated discourse'.

So in addition to being active in urban locations in Britain for at least 25–30 years, it looks as though this style of speaking can endure across the lifespan.[9] The acts and activities in which it is articulated may change as people get older, but crossing is not incompatible with the process of maturation (Extract 10), and a dense vernacular mix of Creole, Cockney and Punjabi forms can still be a valued and quite flexible resource in the repertoire of successful middle-aged professionals (Extracts 11, 12, 17). Plainly, phrases like 'youth language' or 'multi-ethnic adolescent heteroglossia' are no longer adequate as a description of this. But what should we call it instead?

7.7 Contemporary Urban Vernaculars

To address this terminological question, it is first worth summarising the key characteristics of the way of speaking that we have been addressing.

The style in focus has emerged in a sociohistorical context of migration from the Indian subcontinent, closely linked to enduring socioeconomic stratification in the UK. This has created a sociolinguistic space where a number of languages and named varieties of English circulate: 'standard

English', 'proper' or 'posh'; 'bud bud' or 'freshie'; 'black', 'kala' or 'Jamaican'; and 'Cockney' as a traditional local vernacular distinct from Geordie, Brummie, etc. The style outlined in the previous sections is related to these, but it is still felt to be distinctive:

Key characteristics of the style described in this chapter:

(a) it draws on black speech (Extracts 1, 2, 8, 9; Section 7.2) but people who go too far and 'think they're black' are seen as rather comical (Extracts 8 and 9; also Rampton, 1995/2018: 53–54);
(b) it features a significant number of traditional local – here London – vernacular features (Table 7.1; Section 7.2)[10] and is judged non-posh, not the 'proper version of English' (Extracts 2 and 3), even though, of course, the presence of (a) above and (c) and (d) below prevent it from being heard as historically monolingual white[11];
(c) it features some Punjabi in ritualised utterances (e.g. greeting, swearing, etc.), but it does not require high levels of proficiency in the language,[12] and white and black people use Punjabi words (Extracts 5, 10; Section 7.2);
(d) Punjabi phonological features like retroflexion carry into the local English, both in casual and in more formal speech (e.g. Extract 11, Line 75; Section 7.2).

But in spite of its widely sensed distinctiveness, there is not a commonly agreed term for this way of speaking – a situation that seems to be quite widely replicated in Europe (e.g. Bijvoet & Fraurud, 2010: 182).

As a way of talking which *recognises* many of the other varieties circulating in the intersection of migration, ethnicity and class stratification but *reproduces* none, this style has a hybridity that may itself complicate the business of labelling:

Extract 18

Ravinder (student, M, 19, born in London, Punjabi background) in interview with DS (simplified transcript 858ff.; see Extract 8 above)

```
DS:        Is there a particular way of speaking English in west
           London among Punjabis who've grown up here?
Ravinder:  yea there is (.) there is, like it's different to (.)
           it's different to like how other people
           like- say the white peoples speak and er::
           yea it's different (.) the accent- the accent is different (.)
           ((referring to Punjabis who have grown up in West London:)) they
           don't have like a British accent (.)
           they don't have like um the- or or an Indian accent (.)
```

```
          it's in between somewhere- it's not in between but (.)
          it's just not- it's not like an English accent (.)
          I don't know I don't know how to describe it
          it's like (.) I just can't describe it
DS:       do you think you speak it?
Ravinder: yea I think I speak it (.)
          cos when I w- when I went to America (.)
          my cousins there said 'aw you have a British accent'
          and over here when I compare myself to other British people, the
          white people, I- I don't think I have (.)
          a British accent.
```

Indeed, when informants were more definite, their labelling sometimes seemed to reflect aspects of their own social positioning (Agha, 2004: 29; LePage & Tabouret-Keller, 1985: 180–186). So, spending a lot of time cooped up in school, a 14-year-old like Jeet might well be inclined to link this style to transgressive acts like 'swearing' and 'slang' (see also Extracts 3, 6; Harris, 2006: 99 *et passim*), but for a 40-year-old with an active role in local politics, it was more readily identified as an emblem of community (Anwar on 'Southallian'; also Sameer in Extract 2, Line 25).

Most commonly, of course, the style *was* associated with school-aged youth (Section 7.3), and this could well derive from the contexts of its emergence within the lifespan of the individual. It is easy to imagine the style developing new vitality in successive generations of school kids as they venture into the field of sociolinguistic possibilities formed at the juncture of ethnic plurality and the stratifying regimes of schooling, and this could be the age when the style is practised most intensively (on adolescence as a period of increasing vernacular usage generally, see Androutsopoulos & Georgakopoulou, 2003: 4; Chambers, 1995; Romaine, 1984; van Hofwegen & Wolfram, 2010). Indeed, its recurrent association with 'youth' might also reflect its conspicuously relational identity, connected to all points of the sociolinguistic compass but identical to none. Typically, 'youth' designates an intermediate, transitional social positioning, increasingly attracted to a range of pleasures and possibilities beyond the horizons of childhood, sensitive but not necessarily submissive to governing norms and authorities, and it has a strong positivity of its own, linked to intense forms of sociability either in spite of or because of its non-canonical positioning. On these grounds, it is quite easy to see how, at least indexically, 'youth' might be a powerful association for this way of speaking (Agha, 2007: 22). Even so, terms like 'youth style' fail to capture the contemporary facts of its users' age profile, its durability or its embedding in an area with a 50-year history of immigration, and at least for the purposes of analytical discussion, it is necessary to look for alternatives.

In recent years, particularly in Europe, a number of cover terms have been proposed for urban language practices like the ones described in this chapter: not only 'youth language' and 'youth talk' but also, for example, 'ethnolect', 'multi-ethnolect' (Quist, 2008), 'polylingual languaging' (Jørgensen, Møller), 'late modern urban youth style' (Jørgensen, Malai Madsen) and 'Multicultural (London) English' (Cheshire *et al.*, 2008: 1).[13] In the UK, Hewitt's conception of 'local multi-racial vernaculars' has been influential (Harris, 2006; Hewitt, 1986, 1989: 139, 1992/2003: 192–193, above; Rampton, 1995; Sebba, 1993: 59–60), and in my own argument in favour of the label 'contemporary urban vernacular', I would like to start with this (accepting, of course, that as in any naming, the terms chosen are heavily influenced by the context and concerns of the namer, not just the properties of the referent).

As used in the British research, 'local multi-racial vernaculars' are viewed as follows:

The characteristics of 'local multiracial vernaculars' described in Britain:

(i) a hybrid combination of linguistic forms (cf. 'multi-racial'/'multi-ethnic'): 'a bedrock of traditional working class ... English (straightforwardly identifiable lexically, phonologically and grammatically/syntactically), elements of language from parental/grandparental "homelands", elements of Jamaican Creole speech ... and elements of Standard English' (Harris, 2008: 14; also Hewitt, 1992/2003: 192–193);
(ii) variation from locality to locality (cf. 'local'), responsive to differences both in the 'bedrock' of traditional working-class English – Cockney, Brummie, Geordie, Glaswegian, etc. – and in the local migrant diaspora/heritage languages (Punjabi, Bengali, Turkish, Polish, etc.);
(iii) social and individual variation involving both 'broad' and 'light' uses and users, as situations and biographical trajectories draw people towards other styles in the polycentric environment to different degrees, shaping their pathways in line with, inter alia, lifespan, work and gendered interests and demands (see Sharma, 2011; Sharma & Sankaran, 2011).

This is consistent with most of the preceding account,[14] and comparing it with other terms that have been proposed, 'vernacular' is preferable to 'lect' or just 'English' because it gives fuller recognition to the non-standardness and non-posh/popular connotations of this mixed speech. 'Vernacular' also recognises the collective durability of this way of speaking better than 'style'. Indeed, there are also good reasons for replacing Hewitt's 'local multi-racial/multi-ethnic' with just 'contemporary urban'. 'Local' risks excluding important elements of diasporic and global popular culture that circulate in the urban linguascape, and although it might be worth sometimes preserving in other places, in the UK 'multi-ethnic' is maybe now already implied by 'urban'. 'Contemporary' invites a historical perspective and pushes for consideration of exactly how far these styles are similar to or different from the non-standard styles that pre-dated migration, a line of enquiry which is also likely to show that amid all the forms identified as relatively new, there is also often an abundance of quite traditional non-standard speech in multi-ethnic networks. Finally, the phrase 'contemporary urban vernacular' has the advantage of terminological simplicity over more complicated formulations like 'multi-ethnic urban heteroglossia' or 'late modern youth style', and as such it suggests that very widespread styles like these should be moved out from the 'marked' margins of study and debate and instead recognised as an established part of the mainstream, not only in sociolinguistics but maybe also in public discourse more generally.

There is, though, one major disciplinary obstacle to using the phrase 'contemporary urban vernacular' to describe the full range of sociolinguistic practices addressed in this chapter.

Sociolinguistics has traditionally worked with a rather sharp dividing line between stylised and routine uses of language and, as Svendsen and Quist note, a good deal of the work on multi-ethnic urban speech prioritises one or the other of two general perspectives:

> the *variety* approach in general examines the linguistic traits in relation to a standard language and the broader (national) speech community, [while] the *practice* approach analyzes the ways speakers create and negotiate meaning in interaction. (Svendsen & Quist, 2010: xvii, emphasis added)[15]

This distinction has been heavily influenced by the pioneering work of William Labov, who laid a great deal of emphasis on the degree of self-consciousness in speech, and argued that the term 'vernacular' should be reserved for routine, unself-conscious speech, prioritising this as the best data for systematic description of linguistic regularities.[16] As a result, relatively conscious, reflexive practices like crossing and stylisation have been allocated to pragmatics and interactional sociolinguistics rather than to dialectology and variationism (the variety approach), and indeed, discussions of the 'local multiracial vernacular' have tended to assume that this is something distinct from practices like code-switching, crossing and stylisation (see e.g. Eckert, 2012; Hewitt, 1986; Rampton, 1995/2018: Ch. 5.5; Svendsen & Quist, 2010). So by this logic, many of the practices described here and in Chapter 6 would be disqualified from categorisation as 'Ashmeadian vernacular', while the range of practices eligible for classification as the Southallian vernacular would also be greatly reduced. We can rehabilitate them, however, if we turn to Agha's discussions of 'register' (see also Section 3.3 above).

Agha insists that reflexive metapragmatic/metalinguistic practices play a vital role in the life of a register or style. Through processes of 'enregisterment', particular sets of linguistic (and other semiotic) forms are linked to particular social typifications (types of people, groups, situations, etc.; Agha, 2005: 46, 2007: 81), and this can be seen in a very wide variety of reflexive practices operating in combination, ranging from small-scale metapragmatic actions – the use of register/style names, stylisations, accounts of usage, next turn responses – to institutional fields and discourses like lexicography, schooling and literary representation (Agha, 2004: 27, 2007: 151–152).[17] Agha (2004: 27) argues that 'overt (publicly perceivable) evaluative behaviour … is a necessary condition on the social existence of registers', and this insistence that metapragmatics and language ideology play a central, active role in the existence of registers distinguishes Agha's account from more objectivist definitions of 'variety' in sociolinguistics, which simply describe a variety as 'a set of linguistic items with a similar social distribution' (Holmes, 2001: 6; Hudson, 1996: 22). If we accept this – that reflexivity is built into the very definition of a register/style/variety – we can circumvent the Labovian separation of routine unself-conscious uses of a particular vernacular from expressive practices like stylisation and crossing. By Agha's logic, vernaculars simply would not be identifiable as such if it were not for stylisation, crossing and a range of other relatively conscious metapragmatic activities (Agha, 2004: 30–32). Following this through, we can now suggest that in places like Ashmead and Southall, local discourses about language, crossing, stylisation and unself-conscious phonological convergence are all integral facets of the same sociolinguistic process – different sides of the same coin.

If we pursue this, points (i), (ii) and (iii) listed above under 'local multiracial vernaculars' now need to be supplemented so that the characterisation includes

(iv) stylisation, crossing and a wide range of other metapragmatic practices alongside routine speech.

This in turn leads us to formulate *contemporary urban vernaculars* as

- *sets of linguistic forms and enregistered and enregistering practices (including commentary, crossing and stylisation)*
- *that have emerged, are sustained and are felt to be distinctive in ethnically mixed urban neighbourhoods shaped by immigration and class inequalities*
- *that are seen as connected-but-distinct from the locality's migrant languages, its traditional non-standard dialect, its national standard and its adult second language speaker styles, as well as from the prestigious counter-standard styles circulating in (sometimes global) popular culture, and*
- *that are often widely noted and enregistered beyond their localities of origin, represented in media and popular culture as well as in the informal speech of people outside.*

This definition recognises the significance of crossing and stylisation as practices that explore the linguistic affordances of the multi-ethnic spaces in which contemporary urban vernaculars develop. And in doing so, it does more than simply suggest that urban vernaculars occupy a sociolinguistic space adjacent to purer versions of Punjabi, Jamaican, and standard, Indian and traditional vernacular Englishes, or that they draw on linguistic forms that can be traced back to varieties like these. Instead, it proposes that the distinctiveness of this vernacular is continuously marked out by reflexive practices in which other styles are invoked and variously valorised and counter-valorised. Distantiation and the cognisance of stylistic options *not taken* can count as much as the alignments indexed in any utterance, and the suggestion is that with varying levels of awareness, vernacular speakers are continuously affiliating or dissociating themselves from a range of circumambient images of language and speech, some of them echoing back from media representations of the kind mentioned at the end of Section 7.2. Encompassing both tacit *and* spectacular appropriations of purer styles nearby, this definition also allows for the fact that, empirically, it is sometimes very difficult to differentiate stylised from ordinary speech, and this uncertainty can actually be very important on the ground, where, for example, Hewitt found that if 'a white youngster wishes to use a certain [Creole] word ..., he or she may have to make it appear "natural" to their speech if they are to avoid the possibility of being challenged' (1986: 151; Rampton, 1995/2018: 130–132).[18]

But is this definition of contemporary urban vernaculars impracticably overcomplicated? It certainly sets a more challenging agenda for research than the structuralist sociolinguistic notion of a 'variety', simply conceptualised as a distinctive set of phonological, lexical and grammatical features and systems. But like Agha's notion of register, this essentially dynamic definition is consistent with Silverstein's observation that 'the datum for a science of language is irreducibly *dialectic* in nature[,] an *unstable mutual interaction* of meaningful sign forms, contextualised to situations of interested human use and mediated by the fact of cultural ideology' (Silverstein, 1985: 220, emphasis added). Indeed, it fits with the sociolinguistics of Hymes and Gumperz. Rejecting the equation of linguistic competence with internalised grammar, Hymes' early attempt to integrate psychological processing, linguistic structure, social action and cultural patterning in the notion of 'communicative competence' (Hymes, 1972a: 280) is one example of the kind of framework needed to conceptualise the capacities underpinning this definition of urban vernacular speech. Bourdieu's practice theory offers another possibility, allowing us to think of a person's facility with the urban vernacular as the habitus (or disposition) developed in a particular kind of social field (Bourdieu, 1991; Coupland, 2007b: 222; Hanks, 2005).[19] And drawing on Raymond Williams, a third option would be to conceive of urban vernaculars as the expression of situated 'structures of feeling' (Williams, 1977; Harris, 2006: 77–78; Rampton, 2006: 344–345).[20]

Since the purpose here is simply to point to a post-structuralist pedigree for my definition of contemporary urban vernaculars, there is actually no need to deliberate on the choice between (more encompassing) lingua-cultural theories like these. Indeed, in the next chapter, I shall also use the term 'sensibility' as an approximation for the kind of capacity and understanding underpinning particular ways of speaking. All these theories of course also carry the implication that urban vernaculars are not the only registers produced in the dynamic interplay of linguistic structure, interactional practice and cultural ideology – a comparable approach can be taken to, for example, any standard language, asking what constellation of styles operate as the most significant 'others', appropriated in what way (Agha, 2004: 36).[21] Indeed, the same perspective can be applied to another very important element in the urban linguascape, the new language acquired by adult migrants, as I shall show in the next chapter.

Notes

(1) In different ways – fieldwork, analysis, interpretation – this chapter owes a very great deal to my colleagues on the project 'Dialect Development & Style in a Diaspora Community' – Devyani Sharma, Lavanya Sankaran, Pam Knight and Roxy Harris (2008–2009). The project was funded by the UK Economic & Social Research

Council (RES-062-23-0604), as was the one described in Section 7.2 (00 23 2390; 1985–1988).

(2) Unrelated to youth, there is also important work on stylised performance in, for example, public and media discourse (e.g. Androutsopoulos, 2007; Bell, 1999; Coupland, 2001, 2007a; Hill, 2008; also e.g. De Fina, 2007 and Kotthoff, 2007).

(3) See http://ukpollingreport.co.uk/guide/seat-profiles/ealingsouthall (accessed 12 June 2010).

(4) See http://www.visitsouthall.co.uk/Local_Info/southall_middlesex.php (accessed 12 June 2010).

(5) We made much more comprehensive use of the dataset in the pursuit of other questions about local varieties of English.

(6) See, however, for example: Shankar (2008) on 'FOB' in a south Indian community in California; Talmy (2009) on FOB in a Hawai'ian high school; Sarroub (2005) on 'boater' among Yemenis on the US east coast; and Pyke and Trang (2003).

(7) There is also fronting of the GOOSE vowel in 'you' in Line 10, noted as a feature of multicultural London English by Cheshire *et al.* (n.d.: § 3).

(8) See, for example: the shift from 'hello' to 'hi' across Lines 2 and 3; Anwar's selection of 'how you doing' rather than 'how are you' in Line 3; Bilal's 'yeah' rather than 'yes' in Line 4 (as well as the word-final glottal-T in Line 7 – 'though?' – and the word-initial zero TH in Line 13).

(9) This finding complements Møller's in a longitudinal study of bilinguals over a period of 17 years in Copenhagen (2009). Møller finds that 'polylingual languaging' continues among young men in their mid-20s, and that 'the linguistic features ascribed to Turkish and Danish get more and more integrated over the years, [with] "mixing" becom[ing] their "natural" way of speaking' (Møller, 2009: 188).

(10) It is in the nature of traditional British sociolinguistic variability in Britain, of course, that standard and local non-standard speech forms alternate in even rather vernacular styles (Rampton, 2006: 360). So as well as the traditional London vernacular features identified in Table 7.1, even in Anwar's greeting to Ronni in Extract 13, one of his *everything*s has an RP alveolar TH (Line 12), and in 'happening' in Line 14, neither the H is dropped nor the –ING is fronted.

(11) According to Ravinder again (213/8.27; 230/9.02): 'if you're too like um er if you're too British, then people make fun of you ( ) (.) saying "aww you- you you became white" or something like that (.) so you have to be- you have to be in- inbetween (.)', 'if you were very white behaving the- then they call you a coconut'.

(12) Namrita (freelance broadcaster, F, 28, British-born, Punjabi background) gives a good view of its availability to (middle-aged) Punjabis whose command of the language is otherwise limited:

Extract 19

```
2  I was driving a couple of artists just up to Birmingham
3  and and (.) we were listening to some songs (.)
4  and he kept saying to me 'so what does this mean?'
5  I was thinking,
6  'you're nearly forty, why don't you understand what this means' (.)
7  umm I still class him as young though he's nearly forty but (.) umm (.)
8  you know I was like 'why don't you- (.)
9  you should understand what this means
10 I shouldn't have to explain it to you, but it's beautiful' (.)
11 so (.) i- it's sad
12 so they- while they're very happy to know
```

```
13 and they know that it's a good sound
14 and know something good's being said
15 they're not quite sure what's being said (.)
16 you know
17 but they always- they're always using the love- lovely Punjabi swear words
18 Punjabi slang and your 'kiddaan'
19 and you know 'chakka de futte' and your 'bulle'
```

(simplified transcript 950; 49.26)

(13) See Jaspers (2008) for critical discussion.

(14) Vis-à-vis individual variation ([iii]), it was clear in the Southall data that even siblings differed considerably in their alignments with Punjabi or standard English (Rampton, 2015a: 150–151).

(15) Admittedly, this division is not absolute (and indeed there is a case for saying that instead of simply being contemporaneous alternatives, the practice perspective is now superseding the variety approach). So both in variationist and in speech evaluation research, for example, there are now important variety-focused studies which have drawn practice theories about the social world's interactional construction into their interpretation of quantitative patterns in the demographic distribution of linguistic forms (Aarsæther, 2010; Bijvoet & Fraurud, 2010; Eckert, 2000; Maegard, 2010; Quist, 2008).

(16) 'Not every (speech) style ... is of equal interest to linguists. Some styles show irregular phonological and grammatical patterns, with a great deal of "hypercorrection". In other styles, we find more systematic speech, where the fundamental relations which determine the course of linguistic evolution can be seen most clearly. This is the "vernacular" – the style in which minimum attention is paid to the monitoring of speech' (Labov, 1972: 208).

(17) To identify the register/style sketched in (a)–(d) above, I have drawn on accounts of usage and register names elicited in interviews, and I have referred to literary and media representations, as well of course as works of linguistic scholarship (Harris, 2006; Rampton, 1995/2018). In addition, Agha proposes that 'the utterance or use of a register's forms formulates a sketch of the social occasion, indexing contextual features such as interlocutor's roles, relationships, and the type of social practice they're involved in' (Agha, 2004: 25), and we have seen Creole-influenced 'Southallian' used both in a shift of topic (and footing – Extract 15), and in Goffmanian interpersonal rituals (Goffman, 1981: 20–21) – in the opening of phone conversations, establishing a particular kind of social relationship for the talk coming up (Extracts 11, 12 and 10, Lines 25 and 27; Rampton, 1995/2018: 90–92), in expressions of disapproval (Extract 17), and elsewhere in closings, providing reassurance of continuing affiliation in the period of separation coming up.

(18) The 'naturalness' of this use could be justified either by claiming family ties to the ethnic group with which the forms are associated (1986: 165, 195) or, much less dramatically, by delivering the word in such a way that it seems like a routine element in the local multi-ethnic vernacular.

(19) 'From a language perspective, habitus corresponds to the social formation of speakers, including the disposition to use language in certain ways, to evaluate it according to socially instilled values, to embody expression in gesture, posture, and speech production ... [Habitus] was developed to explain reproduction without rules. It follows that in a practice approach to language, regularities of "usage" are ... explained ... by embodied dispositions and schemas, which are ... actualized in speech' in specific fields, fields being 'form[s] of social organisation [characterised by] (a) [particular]

configuration[s] of social roles, agent positions, and the structures they fit into and (b) the historical process in which those positions are actually taken up, occupied by actors (individual or collective)' (Hanks, 2005: 72).

(20) In Williams' account, 'structures of feeling' are socially and historically shaped, and they draw on experiences prior to the communicative present, to the extent that one can speak of the structures of feeling characteristic of a person, a set of people, a collection of texts, a set of situations or indeed a period. The 'structure' part of 'structures of feeling' involves 'a set [of affective elements of consciousness and relationships] with specific internal relations, at once interlocking and in tension' (Williams, 1977: 132), and in their relationship with interaction, structures of feeling 'exert pressures and set effective limits on experience and action' (Williams, 1977: 132). But they 'cannot without loss be reduced to belief-systems, institutions, or explicit general relationships' (Williams, 1977: 133). Instead, structures of feeling are 'practical consciousness of a present kind, in a living and interrelating continuity', and 'can be defined as social experience *in solution*, as distinct from other social semantic formations which have been *precipitated* and are more evidently and more immediately available' (Williams, 1977: 133). Williams' 'structures of feeling' offers an account of more stable dimensions of subjectivity, related to particular aspects of sociohistorical experience, but this is nevertheless incessantly recoloured and slowly reshaped amid the pressures and contingencies of everyday practice.

(21) Local non-standard vernaculars may be vital, indeed constitutive, points of contrastive reference for a register like standard English, but what about migrant, minority and modern foreign languages (French, German) or indeed a school language like Latin? How far and in what ways are processes of standard and vernacular reproduction similar or different in the manner and extent to which circumambient styles get acknowledged, ignored or derogated, and how similar or different are the practices that give standards their hegemony and vernaculars their vitality? What kinds of relationship between self and voice get projected in the stylisation of standard codes – are these stereotyped or flexible, affiliative or mocking – and how does this differ for people in different social positions (Bucholtz, 1999; Rampton, 2006: Part III)? What differences in 'ideological becoming' are involved in the practices of troping and reflexive enregisterment that emerge when different groups and individuals orient to particular standards (cf. Bakhtin, 1981: 348)? And finally, of course, if we follow the momentum of contemporary urban vernaculars, these questions have to be properly located in conditions of globalisation, going beyond the confines of the nation-state to investigate the sociolinguistic sensibilities associated with 'elite cosmopolitanism' (Hannerz, 1990).

8 Styling in a Language Learnt Later in Life[1]

8.1 Introduction

The three preceding chapters have together provided sociolinguistic elaboration of Gilroy's observation that in spite of widespread racism, civic life in Britain has seen the emergence of an 'unruly, convivial mode of interaction in which differences have to be negotiated in real-time' (Gilroy, 2006: 39; Section 5.3 above). From the evidence assembled, this looks broadly compatible with the sensibility associated with what I have called contemporary urban vernaculars, and these have been a feature of the British urban linguascape for decades, sometimes lasting as a stable element in the speech repertoire of individuals beyond youth into adulthood and middle age. Within the sociolinguistic terrain where these vernaculars have developed, migration has been a central formative influence, but despite this, speakers of English as a second, third, or n^{th} language have in fact appeared only indirectly in each of the chapters, mainly as figures performed in stylisation and crossing – Lily's impersonation of an angry father on the phone (Section 5.4), Ashmead's Stylised Asian English (Section 6.3), the 'freshies' reported in Southall (Section 7.3). It has been people born and brought up in the UK who have been in the foreground of my analyses so far, despite the fact that, for example, in the area inhabited by Anwar and others in Chapter 7, more than 40% of the residents were born *outside* Britain.

The present chapter seeks to correct this omission, shifting the focus away from contemporary urban vernaculars to the English spoken by a middle-class man with a professional background (Mandeep), who says that he really only started to speak the language when he migrated from India to London in his late 20s. In doing so, it makes several moves that are somewhat non-canonical within mainstream research on the acquisition, development and use of a second language (henceforth 'SLA' and 'L2 research'), at least until relatively recently (Bremer *et al.*, 1996: 1; Douglas Fir Group, 2016; Ortega, 2019).

First, rather than placing second language speakers and the unpredictabilities of L2 speech a priori in a separate analytical category, the analysis places migrant learners of English in their local speech economies, reckoning with the fact, among other things, that long-standing transnational links can blur the boundaries between 'host' and 'migrant', so that what sounded 'foreign' 30 years ago may no longer do so today. As Blommaert, Collins and Slembrouck (2005: 201) note, '[p]rocesses such as diaspora ... develop over long spans of time ... and result in *lasting* ... social, ... sociolinguistic and discursive reconfigurations which have effects across a wide range of situations'.

Second, it brings the same analytical focus to bear on L2 speech that was applied to the urban vernacular, examining Mandeep's stylistic performance and the ideological categories, social scenes and stances that he evokes through the non-referential, socially indexical possibilities of English. In L2 research, there is theoretical recognition that 'imagined identities, projected selves, idealisations or stereotypes of the other ... seem to be central to the language-learning experience', but 'they are difficult to grasp within the current paradigms of SLA research' (Kramsch, 2009: 5).

Third, it analyses Mandeep's speech within the same overarching framework as before, investigating the dynamic three-way interaction of linguistic form, situated discourse and ideology associated with Gumperz's pursuit of a 'closer understanding of how linguistic signs interact with social knowledge in discourse' (Gumperz, 1982: 29), and with Silverstein's 'Total Linguistic Fact (TLF), the [irreducibly dialectic] datum for a science of language' (Silverstein, 1985: 220). For L2 research, this dialectic has not been a foundational priority and, indeed, like a number of other (substantial and productive) traditions in linguistics, it has generally tended to focus on only two dimensions of the TLF at a time.[2] So, for example, SLA's 'input and interaction' paradigm has addressed linguistic structure and interaction but overlooked ideology, while in the critical tradition, the focus has been on interaction and ideology without much sustained attention to linguistic form.[3] Certainly, L2 research has sometimes drawn quite heavily on sociolinguistics, but it has often been influenced by the quantitative variationist approach, which has itself been relatively slow to address the TLF and is typically much stronger on the interface between linguistic form and ideology (attitudes and evaluations) than situated interaction (see Section 8.3 below).[4]

For research on L2 speech, the potential significance of studying the interplay of formal structure, situated activity and cultural ideology lies in at least two directions, the first affecting the analysis of data and the second affecting the interpretation of findings.

First, as Hanks says of analysis,

> [i]t is tempting, depending upon one's own commitments, to try to treat activities as if they were formal systems, or language structure as if it were no more than the temporary product of activity, or ideology as merely the projection of verbal categories or the misconstrual of action. But all such attempts distort their object by denying its basic distinctiveness. The challenge … is not reduction of this to a by-product of that but integration of distinct phenomena into a more holistic framework. (Hanks, 1996: 231–232)

If we take this seriously in our approach to L2 speech, we need to address the possibility that in an L2, the formal, interactional and ideological dimensions of sociolinguistic sensibility develop at different rates, and be ready to spot this kind of asynchronous development in, for example, an L2 speaker's ability (i) to distinguish different social types, (ii) to recognise the ways of speaking associated with them, and then (iii) to reproduce them with the right linguistic forms (Preston, 1989: 254; Sharma, 2005: 215; van Lier, 2000: 248).

Second, a *failure* to study form, discourse and ideology together can have restrictive effects on how linguists imagine the people that they research, particularly if these are L2 users. If analysts do not look empirically at the missing third element – whichever it happens to be – then they tend to fill the gap with the default assumptions characteristic of their subdisciplines. Potentially crucial aspects of their informants' social, political, rhetorical or linguistic positioning are obscured, and this allows in the romantic celebration of difference and creative agency that has been so common in sociolinguistics, or the presumption of deficit and remedial need endemic to a great deal of L2 research. With a neglect of proficiency with linguistic form, it is all too easy for specific instances of rhetorical success to tempt the sociolinguist to forget the longer term constraints that individuals face, while in SLA, informants are intuitively framed as 'learners' if there is no engagement with ideology. So the challenge is to chart a line between the Scylla of SLA exceptionalism and the Charybdis of sociolinguistic romanticisation. Analysing L2 immigrants alongside L1 locals is one step towards de-exceptionalising them. At the same time, it is important to stay alert to issues of proficiency in accounts of style – plainly, migration is often associated with an unequal distribution of material, cultural and linguistic resources, and this should not be erased either.

In sum, this chapter brings L2 speakers much more fully into Part 2's account of contemporary urban linguascapes than the previous chapters, and it seeks to develop an account that acknowledges the changing particularities of the localities they inhabit, that attends to their ideological self-positioning in sociolinguistic space, that reckons with the unevenness with which individual sociolinguistic sensibilities develop and that reflects their ordinariness.

To pursue this, I shall analyse data from Southall in southwest London, the area that was the primary focus in Chapter 7 (Section 7.3) and that also served as one of the fieldsites in Gumperz and Roberts' ground-breaking research on intercultural communication from the 1970s to the 1990s (Bremer *et al.*, 1996; Gumperz, 1982; Gumperz *et al.*, 1979; Roberts *et al.*, 1992). This has had a very substantial South Asian population for over 50 years and, as already noted, according to the 2001 national census, 43% of its 89,000 inhabitants were born outside the UK. In our study, conducted in 2008–2009, there were approximately 75 mostly adult and mainly ethnic Punjabi informants, born both in Britain and abroad, and the focal informant here, Mandeep, came to London in 2001 aged 28. With Mandeep, our data collection involved approximately 5½ hours of audio-recordings – two interviews with Lavanya Sankaran, and four self-recordings (with a group of colleagues at work [one Anglo and several people born in India], with an Indian-born friend, with a newly arrived relative and on his own in the car).

My attempt to build an understanding of Mandeep's social and ideological positioning starts with what he told us about his experience of coming to the UK and learning and using English (Section 8.2). It then reports a quantitative variationist analysis of his style-shifting, comparing the patterns of linguistic variability in Mandeep's speech with British-born Anwar's (Section 8.3). After that, it turns to his stylised performance of different voices in narrative discourse (Sections 8.4 and 8.5), before summarising the analysis and its broader implications for our understanding of urban linguascapes (Section 8.6).

8.2 What Mandeep Told us in Interview

In interview, Mandeep told us that he had been a teacher in the Punjab, and that he had left India to find a better life. Soon after arriving, he had found work as a newsreader and editor at a local Southall Punjabi-language radio station, but now he was working there only part-time because he wanted to do postgraduate teacher training and first he had to do a year's maths enhancement course. He had not had any family in London when he had arrived, but he had known three or four people from home, and now he had married a healthcare professional from India. His taste in music and media had not changed, he said, but 'it's developed ...

opened up new branches', and although he did not get any spare time to watch the game, he said he would support England in cricket against India – after all, there were now two Punjabis in each team (in 2008–2009, Harbhajan & Yuvraj versus Panesar & Bopara).

Mandeep said that he 'wasn't speaking English at all' until he came to England aged 28, but actually, he had had a lot of exposure to the language through study, and among other things, most of his MA in economics had been in English. Since arriving in the UK, he had done a year's GCSE in English, and he regarded soaps-with-teletext on British TV as a great resource for language learning. With the British-born English speakers on his maths course, he said 'it's fine, you always mingle with them, talk with them, joke with them – obviously you don't know every single joke', but that was no reason for feeling 'you are ... being excluded'. He did not like it when people with Punjabi backgrounds born in Britain called him a 'freshie', but he was convinced that 'if you are calibre enough, no one can stop you', and his stock reply was that at least he was not 'worn out' and stale like them. With the Anglos in his Maths classes, he said he avoided the Punjabi pronunciation of his name, while with people who were weak in English but could not speak Punjabi, he would *de*-anglicise his pronunciation of English. Lastly, he was conscious of social stratification in English speech:

> accent is to do with… watching telly, talking to the other people… Sometimes, say in English, you're swearing a lot, and 'yo mate yo mate' or something you're doing, and then- you're glorifying yourself, some other people are glorifying you, then you develop that accent for the whole of your life. Then your family says, 'no, that's not the way how you speak'.

And dispositions like these were not just restricted to Anglos:

> the children of Indian sub-continent, [the] third generation… know other things as well - pub culture, these sorts of things - [and] now they are as bad as white partners and as good as white partners - they are now normals… of this country.

So to sum up before moving into an investigation of how Mandeep actually used English himself, there are at least three points to take from his interview commentary:

(a) second language learning is not just our own external analytic attribution: learning to speak English as an additional language had been a significant issue for Mandeep in London, even though English had also been important in his education in India;
(b) it is worth looking at at least *two* major axes of local sociolinguistic differentiation: not just Indian versus Anglo, or newcomer versus local, but also high versus low, posh versus vulgar (see Chapters 6 and 7);

(c) at the same time, it looks as though the stereotypic links between language, ethnicity and class have all been scrambled up, and we could go seriously wrong if we just accepted the traditional image of a minority ethnic L2 speaker migrating into a host society dominated by an L1 ethnic majority.

In fact, we will see the significance of Mandeep's residence among born-and-bred Londoners with family links to the Indian subcontinent if we now turn to a quantitative analysis of stylistic variation.

8.3 Quantitative Analysis of Style-shifting across Contexts

The quantitative analysis of style-shifting is a central element in variationist sociolinguistics, and it correlates patterns of phonological variation with, inter alia, different situations (Labov, 1972). As noted above, this approach generally overlooks the rhetorical significance and interactional effects of alterations in speech style (although see Coupland, 2007a: 41–42, 2007b: 219; Schilling–Estes, 1998: 55; Sharma & Rampton, 2015), but it can reveal relatively tacit changes in orientation as speakers shift settings, and this quantitative patterning has in fact played a significant part in Bourdieu's theorisation of 'habitus', taking 'habitus' as the preconscious disposition to hear and speak in specific ways inculcated into the individual through long-term experience of the purchase that their language resources provide in different kinds of setting (Bourdieu, 1991: Part 1). In addition, variationist research usually involves quite extensive surveys of different kinds of speaker, and this allows the style-shifting of any given individual to be placed in a wider empirical view of speech in the area where he or she resides.

For the analysis of Mandeep's style-shifting, Devyani Sharma and Lavanya Sankaran focused on the four linguistic variables indicated in Table 8.1, each involving variants linked to Punjabi or British English in the research literature, and one also involving a vernacular form: T, L, 'e' as in 'FACE' and 'o' as in 'GOAT' (see also Sharma, 2011: particularly 469–471).

Using auditory analysis, they then assessed the percentages of Punjabi versus British variants in Mandeep's speech in three settings: in self-recorded interaction with an Indian friend who was himself a fluent speaker of standard Indian English; in one of the interviews with Sankaran (brought up in southern India and Singapore, and a non-speaker of Punjabi); and at work, conversing together with an Anglo L1 English speaking man and several Indian L2 English speaking women. This revealed style-shifting very clearly.

Table 8.1 Linguistic variables used in the analysis of Mandeep's situational style-shifting

Linguistic variable	Punjabi variant	Standard British English variant	Vernacular British English variant
(t) in the environments vt#, #tv and vtv (as in 'eight', 'time', 'thirty')	Retroflex [ʈ]	Alveolar [t]	Glottal [ʔ]
Post-vocalic (l) as in 'will' or 'deal'	Light [l]	Dark [ɫ]	
(e) – 'FACE' (e) as in 'say' and 'game'	Monophthong [e]	Diphthong [eɪ]	
(o) – 'GOAT' as in 'don't' and 'road'	Monophthong [o]	Diphthong [əʊ]	

Mandeep used most Punjabi variants with his Punjabi friend at home, and fewest at work (in the presence of an Anglo colleague; see Tables 8.2–8.4), and this pattern is broadly in line with the findings of other studies of L2 speech (e.g. Beebe, 1977; Beebe & Zuengler, 1983; Dickerson, 1975; Ellis, 1994: Ch. 4; Rehner *et al*., 2003; Tarone, 1983).

In addition, Sharma and Sankaran conducted quantitative style-shifting analyses with eight other local informants who produced self-recorded as well interview data (Sharma & Sankaran, 2011), and among these, there were three adult males who had been speaking English since early childhood whose style-shifting was broadly similar to Mandeep's: when talking to people who had marked non-British accents linked to the Indian subcontinent, there was greater use of Punjabi variants, whereas in

Table 8.2 Mandeep's English with an Indian friend

	Retro-flex [ʈ]	Mono-phthong [e]	Mono-phthong [o]	Light [l]	Glottal [ʔ]	[t]	Dipht-hong [e]	Dipht-hong [o]	Dark [ɫ]
%	57.5	69.2	86.7	61.5	0	30	30.8	13.3	38.5
Tokens	23	9	13	8	0	12	4	2	5
Total *n*	40	13	15	13	28	40	13	15	13

Table 8.3 Mandeep's English in interview

	Retro-flex [ʈ]	Mono-phthong [e]	Mono-phthong [o]	Light [l]	Glottal [ʔ]	[t]	Dipht-hong [e]	Dipht-hong [o]	Dark [ɫ]
%	0	50	76.9	40	3.3	97.8	50	23.1	60
Tokens	0	7	10	6	1	44	7	3	9
Total *n*	45	14	13	15	30	45	14	13	15

Table 8.4 Mandeep's English in mixed white and Indian company at work

	Retro-flex [ʈ]	Mono-phthong [e]	Mono-phthong [o]	Light [l]	Glottal [ʔ]	[t]	Dipht-hong [e]	Dipht-hong [o]	Dark [ɫ]
%	4.4	0	13.3	0	6.7	82.2	100	86.7	100
Tokens	2	0	2	0	2	37	15	13	15
Total *n*	45	15	15	15	30	45	15	15	15

the company of people brought up in the UK, the use of British variants increased. Figure 8.1 shows Mandeep's style-shifting and Figure 8.2 shows Anwar's, the successful 40 year-old British-born businessman who travelled a lot between London and Pakistan (see Chapter 7).

Mandeep is obviously different from Anwar in his non-use of glottal T, and I will return to this below. But before that, the comparison suggests that:

(a) nowadays, retroflexion, postvocalic clear Ls and monophthonged 'FACE' and 'GOAT' vowels are no longer foreign in British-born London speech, and Mandeep would not have to completely erase them in order to sound local;
(b) the directionality of Mandeep's stylistic adjustment with these four variants was broadly in line with the directions of shift produced by people who have been speaking English all their lives, so on the Anglo versus Indian axis of social differentiation, Mandeep's socio-stylistic sensibility seemed to be roughly in tune with that of natal residents.

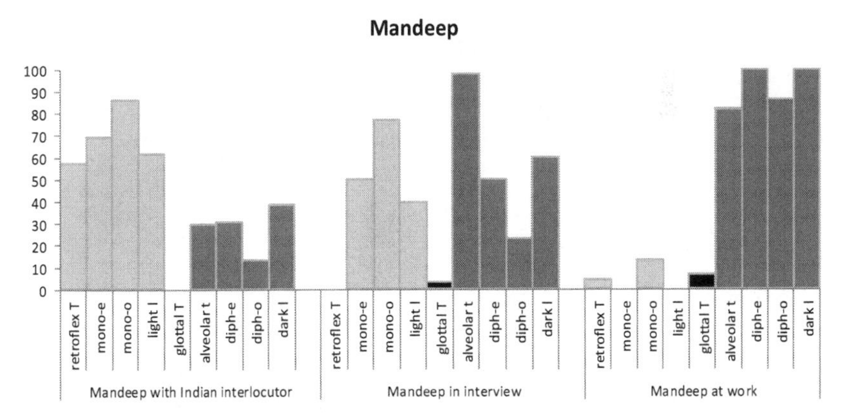

Figure 8.1 Mandeep: distribution of Punjabi and Anglo variants across three settings

Notes: light grey = Punjabi origin; dark grey = Anglo origin; black = vernacular London.

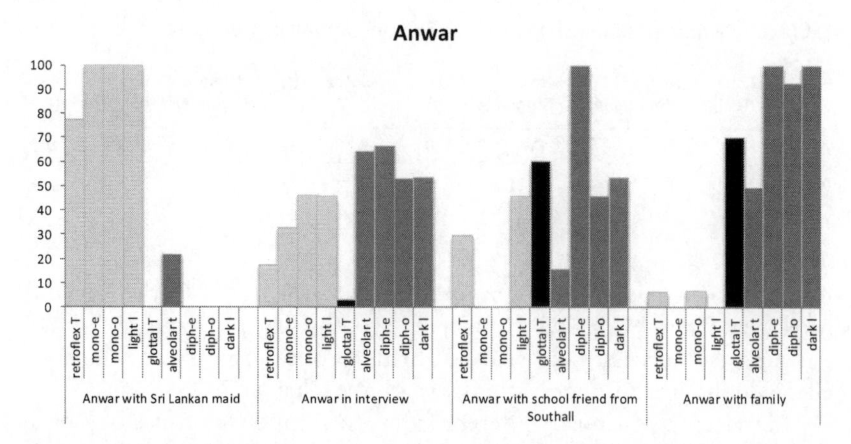

Figure 8.2 British-born Anwar: distribution of Punjabi and Anglo variants across four settings

Notes*:* light grey = Punjabi origin; dark grey = Anglo origin; black = vernacular London. 'Family' here refers to his UK-born children.

In interview, Mandeep said that if you come from Punjab to Southall, 'you won't feel like you are living abroad', and there is support for this in these quantitative analyses of style. In addition to the fact that the Punjabi language itself has a lot of local currency in Southall, the Britain-India link is inscribed in the patternings of *local* Southall English.

Admittedly, there is no control for the talk's discursive development in quantitative measures like these – for changes of footing, topic, genre, etc. – and if one looks at only four out of potentially umpteen linguistic variables, it is impossible to tell whether, overall, Mandeep's speech sounded more Anglo or more Indian at different times with different people. So at this point, it is worth now turning to some discourse.

8.4 Styling in Narrative Discourse

Mandeep told a lot of stories in his interviews with Lavanya Sankaran, and it was in the performance of character speech in narrative that his accent became most Anglo. Here is an example from an account of the difficulties he had in finding a job when he first arrived in England, where he found that all the employers were asking for experience, even for basic jobs:

Extract 1: 'okay wait wait'
Mandeep in interview with Lavanya Sankaran (female; aged 25–30)

Key: ANGLO VARIANTS; ***Punjabi variants***

1 ˍTHEN I was SAying
[ðen ɑ wz seɪɪŋ]

2 "↑\no: I d**o**n have any- **th**aT sorT of ex|p**e**rience"
[nəʊ aɪ dɔ̃ hʌv ənɪ d̪æt sɔt ɒv əkspiːɹɪəns]

3 ↑s**o** .hhh
[sɒ]

4 |**th**ey **w**ere giving me "O:\KAY:
[d̪ᵉ vʌ gɪvɪŋ mɪ əʊkʰeɪ]

5 (0.3) |WAIT |WAIT'
weɪtʰ weɪtʰ]

6 and **th**en ˉafter- (0.5) \TWO- (0.3)\TWO months
[ən d̪ən ɑft'ə tʃʰu tʰu mʌns]

In Line 5, Mandeep marks the difference between the narrating and the reported speech with shifts in tempo, becoming much slower in reported speech, and he renders the voice of the employers in exclusively British variants.

So Mandeep could do some pure Anglo, and indeed, the fact that he mixed Anglo and Punjabi features elsewhere in the story – for example, in Line 2's '↑\no: I d**o**n have any- **th**aT sorT of ex|p**e**rience' – does not itself necessarily mark Mandeep as an L2 speaker. Mixing occurred even in the relatively formal English of Punjabis born and raised in the UK, and we could see this, for example, in Anwar's business talk with an RP-speaking barrister (Chapter 7, Extract 13):

THE REASON why I ca***lled*** you is e::h I jus WANTED TO LET you KNOW THA***t Xxxxxxx*** *((name))* He came.. and e::h we DECIDED ***not tu*** pursue His case

Even so, when we looked across our dataset more generally, there were very clear differences in the length of the utterances in which Mandeep and Anwar maintained exclusively Anglo-accented character speech: whereas Anwar produced one stretch of almost completely Anglo-sounding multi-clause direct speech that lasted 29 syllables, Mandeep's exclusively Anglo-accented voicing never exceeded 12, and as we shall see, it was actually rather rare to find a consistent separation of Anglo and Punjabi forms in the speech of the figures in his narratives.

Of course that in itself raises a question: if Mandeep's 'O:\KAY: (0.3) |WAIT |WAIT' was actually rather rare in the consistency of its phonological anglicisation, how did he actually manage to style narrative character speech as distinctly Anglo? If his mobilisations of linguistic code resources were somewhat unpredictable, how did he achieve stylistic effects?

To address this, we should now turn to his stylisation of the local Anglo-English vernacular, moving from an Anglo-Indian axis of differentiation to socially stratified class styles. As we do so, we will begin to see how important it is to address linguistic forms, discourse and ideology each in their own right.

8.5 Styling the Traditional London Vernacular

In the interviews, there were signs of Mandeep's class consciousness when he talked about 'pub culture' and linked accent to watching telly, swearing and behaving in ways that got you into trouble with your family. How far did this translate into his own dramatised speech performances, and with what kinds of rhetorical success?

The excerpt below forms part of an argument that people make too much of a fuss about racism, and that you should not overgeneralise about racism on the basis of single incidents. In it, Mandeep is presenting the hypothetical scenario of a white man shouting racist abuse:

Extract 2: Sun reader (MI. 50.01, 0.59.9)
Mandeep in interview with Lavanya Sankaran

Key: ANGLO VARIANTS; ***Punjabi variants***

```
1  Mandeep:   if |someone jusT misbe\haves wiTH you
2             .hh ↑\someone |drunk |whiTe |Person and uh (.)
3             .hhhh you are just |passing by or |somethhing,
4             he |saw you
5             ((pitch step-up and shift to non-modal phonation:))
              ↑"you \bloody 'ASians 'why you 'come to 'my 'counTry"
6             or somethhing
7             ((high pitched:)) ↑↑thats not \RAcism-
8             -that's- he::- .hh mAY be 'reading 'Sun \only (0.5)
9             'SO: m- m- he may be just \listeni:ng a|bOU:T s-som-|so:me like
10            ((shift in voice quality similar to Line 5:))
11            ((non-modal phonation on first three words:))
              " \why 'they 'Came to our 'country"
12            e- 'he 'may 'noT \know (.)
13            ((faster:)) what the e'conomy is
14            what the contribution of .hhh
15 LS:        [as-
```

```
15 Mandeep:   [\migranT ˈPeoPle to ˈBridish eˈconomy is-
16            so ˊhe don know ↑↑any↓\thing
17            ˈh:e jus ↑ˈshouTing a \/you and then /\swearing ˎeven
```

Mandeep describes the character as ignorant, drunk, uncouth, informed only by the (very lowbrow) popular press – in effect, as a stereotypical lower-class white racist – and there are two things worth noting.

First, Mandeep locates the white British lower class in a global economy, and he portrays this group as the ignorant victim of restricted mobility and very limiting national horizons (Lines 12–16). Second, the segmental phonology used to enact the man's speech in Line 5 sounds more Anglo than Indian – ↑"you \bloody ˈAsians ˈwhy you ˈcome to ˈmy ˈcounTry" But does it sound more *vernacular*? Here it is again in a more detailed transcript:

Extract 3

```
((pitch step-up with shift to tense muscular phonation)):
"↑you \bloody  ˈAsians  ˈwhy  youˈ  come  to  ˈmy  ˈcounTry"
 [jʊ   bᵘɫʌdi:   eɪʃn̩z    waɪ   jʊ   kʰʌm   tʊ   mɑɪ  k'ʌntɹi:]
```

Segmentally, the onsets of the diphthongs in '<u>A</u>sian' and 'wh<u>y</u>' sounded RP, as they lacked the backed vowel quality of traditional working-class London,[5] and in fact there was also a detectably Punjabi influence in *<u>c</u>ountry*'s unaspirated word-initial consonant. Even so, there are a number of other semiotic cues showing that Mandeep was aiming for more than just ordinary British:

- segmentally, the onset of the diphthong in 'm<u>y</u>' was relatively backed, as in traditional vernacular London speech[6];
- 'you bloody Asians' is also very marked supra-segmentally with abruptly raised pitch and tenser muscular non-modal phonation. This gives the impression of shouting without actually doing so, and when this is linked to swearing, it is often typed as vulgar;
- in addition, of course, Mandeep used an explicit metalanguage of social types to characterise the speech/speaker both before and after ('drunk', 'white', 'reading *Sun*').

So even though the segmental phonetics were not especially vernacular, this was not rhetorically incapacitating. If one *extracted* this impersonation of a 'white London lout' from its narrative context, it probably would not carry very far, and the groups and networks where it would be rated or even recognised for what is intended might be limited. But within the specific narrative world and narrating event in which it was produced, the social typification worked reasonably well, and the voice can be heard as traditional Anglo vernacular English.[7]

So even though Mandeep was not very good at doing traditional London vernacular vowels and consonants, he knew that they sounded different and he did not mind trying to impersonate it. In fact, there is other evidence that he was aware of vernacular London features without accurately reproducing them, and here we can also see that his apprehension of the vernacular's indexical potential extended beyond social group stereotypes to typifications of stance.

In his interview comments on accent, Mandeep linked 'swearing a lot' to saying 'yo mate yo mate', and in fact he pronounced 'mate' as 'yo [meɪ] yo [meɪ]'. In contemporary vernacular London, the post-vocalic T in 'mate' is a glottal, not an alveolar stop, and it looks as though Mandeep went half-way – he removed the alveolar, but did not replace it with the glottal, doing a zero realisation instead. In fact, the analysis of quantitative style-shifting showed that he hardly ever produced glottal Ts – three out of 88 possible realisations (Tables 8.2–8.4), and Sharma and Sankaran's survey showed that he was very similar in this to a great many other informants born in India.[8] But this did not stop Mandeep using zero T strategically in constructed dialogue.

In the excerpt below, Mandeep is continuing the argument that accusations of racism are often exaggerated. He has just been talking about the notorious Shilpa Shetty episode in *Celebrity Big Brother*, and he has taken the line that when the other contestants criticised Shilpa for touching some food, they were not being racist – the complaint was 'just normal talk'. He now follows this up with a story about being ticked off by his mother when he was small, the overall point being that there is very little to distinguish these two episodes:

Extract 4: Spoiled carrots

Mandeep in interview with Lavanya Sankaran (cf. Extract 5; MI 50.01, 0.59.9)

Key: ANGLO VARIANTS; ***Punjabi variants***

```
33      one \DAY (.)
        .hh I was 'very \liTTLE (.)
            [ɑ]    [w]      [t]
```

34 and er my mum ˌboughT some \caRROTS (.)
[t] [t]

35 an I puT ˈaLL the \carriTS in::- (.)
[aɪ] [t] [ɔɫ d̪ə] [ɾ] [t]

36 er- as ˈouTside in- on the \sand
[t]

37 so I ˈspoiled \everything
[d] [t̪ʰ]

38 so ˈshe ˈsla:pped \me (.)

39 L: *((very quiet laugh:))* hehe

40 M: *((half-laughing in 'bought' and 'that':))*

➔ 41 thaT "ˈI ˈbough ˈtha fo ˈus 1.04
[d̪ ætʰ aɪ bᵊhɔːø d̪æø ɸɔːʷ ʌs]

42 (0.2)

➔ 43 a:nd ˈyou pu the \everything aˌWAY" (.)
[ænd jɪu pʊø ‿d̪ ə? evɹɪ t̪ʰɪŋ ʔəweɪ]

44 hh ˉso
[əʊ]

45 th- th- th- ↑tha s not \RAcism (.)
[d̪æø] [ø]

46 ˉtha s \simple ˈTalk as ˈwell
[ø]

47 ˉand that was the- (0.2)

48 and \other thing is
((Mandeep continues about another aspect))

The distribution of alveolar and zero Ts is shown in Table 8.5.

In the part leading up to the reprimand, there are seven potentially variable T sounds, and all of them are alveolar.[9] But in the direct reported reprimand in Lines 41–43, all three Ts are zero realisations ('bough[ø]', 'tha[ø]', 'pu[ø]'), and after that, the zero realisations are carried into the evaluation in Lines 45–46 ('tha[ø]', 'no[ø]', 'tha[ø]').

In the quoted utterance in Lines 41 and 43, Mandeep's approximations of vernacular London contribute to a character portrait that is very different from the white working-class figure in the *Sun* reader episode. Here, the speaker is Mandeep's mum; she is saying the kind of thing that Mandeep approves of ('simple talk' that only the misguided would read

Table 8.5 Realisation of the post-vocalic Ts in Mandeep's 'spoiled carrots' story

Environments	The setting, events and actions leading up to the reprimand (Lines 33–38)			The reprimand in direct reported speech (Lines 41–43)			The evaluation (Lines 44–46)		
	[t]	[ʔ]	[ø]	[t]	[ʔ]	[ø]	[t]	[ʔ]	[ø]
V_#C, V_#V, V_C	7/7	0	0	0	0	3/3	0	0	3/3

as racism); and indeed in its incorporation of zero Ts in the evaluation, there is a 'fusion' of the narrating and the quoted voices (Bakhtin, 1984: 199). So if it is not just unruly working-class types that Mandeep is trying to index with the concentration of zero-Ts in Lines 41–43, what is it? If we turn back to *Anwar* and look at the quantitative data on Anwar's style-shifting, T-glottaling increased with family and friends (Figure 8.2), and of course this pattern is repeated not just with other locally born individuals in our survey, but in British society much more generally. Vernacular forms often index not only types of person but also types of stance and relationship, and in the quoted speech in the carrots story, the glottal-T approximations seem designed to evoke the intimacy or informality of a mother-son relationship,[10, 11] a relationship that Mandeep seemed quite happy to inhabit. So yes, Mandeep's reproduction of the linguistic specifics of emblematic vernacular English forms is only partial, *but* his grasp of the social meaning *is not* restricted to the stereotypes of people and groups that one might expect with speech styles seen from afar.

This is not to say, however, that the partiality of this approximation was itself cost-free, or that the impersonation was as effective as it had been with the white lout in the earlier extract. Compared with the extract earlier, there is very little supplementary characterisation of Mandeep's mother in the tale of spoiled carrots, and the sociolinguistic iconography associated with 'mums' is generally much more indeterminate. Admittedly, our larger sociolinguistic survey indicated that low levels of T-glottaling were common in the English of Southall residents born in India, so local people born in India might well constitute a social network where the social indexicality of the zero-Ts in the 'carrots' narrative could be easily appreciated.[12] But beyond those networks – and maybe even within them – Mandeep's stylised performance of his mum sounds odd rather than indexically resonant, and it certainly took our research team quite a lot of time and analysis to generate a plausible interpretation of the social typification being attempted.

At this point, we can move to a more general discussion, placing the account alongside the findings from previous chapters, as well as other earlier and contemporaneous studies of Southall. I will focus first on London as a sociolinguistic space; second, on Mandeep's position there as an L2 speaker; third, on the key methodological moves underpinning the analysis, and their implications for different schools and traditions within linguistics; glancing finally at the wider relevance of this kind of analysis.

8.6 The Sociolinguistic Development of a Diasporic Local Sensibility

At the start of this chapter, I quoted Blommaert, Collins and Slembrouck on the lasting reconfigurations produced by the development of diaspora over long periods of time, and we can glimpse sociolinguistic aspects of this in research on Southall over the last half-century. So in accounts from the 1970s, 1980s and 1990s produced by Gumperz, Roberts and others (e.g. Bremer *et al.*, 1996; Gumperz, 1982a, 1982b; Gumperz *et al.*, 1979; Roberts *et al.*, 1992), we are shown the discrimination and intercultural misunderstanding experienced by adult newcomers to the UK in their interaction with mainstream British institutions. But at the same time, their children were growing up in the more convivial multi-ethnic environments described by, for example, Anwar in Section 7.6 and by the research on crossing and stylisation in Ashmead (Sections 6.3 and 7.2). More recently, Sharma and Sankaran's research shows the emergence, by 2008–2009, of local adult styles of English which combine Punjabi, standard and vernacular English features in ways that are influenced not only by the immediate situation but also by social network differences, by the local dynamics of gender, and by degrees of exposure to racist hostility in British society, itself experienced more intensely growing up in the 1970s and 1980s than the 1990s and early 2000s (Sharma, 2011; Sharma & Sankaran, 2011).

The upshot of all this was that, for a newcomer like Mandeep, it did not feel like you were living abroad if you came to London from the Punjab. You could find work capitalising on your abilities in Punjabi, you found that children of the Indian subcontinent were fully incorporated into London pub culture and you saw Punjabis playing cricket for England. Mandeep had settled in a space formed at the historical intersection of socio-economic stratification within the UK on the one hand, and migration and movement between Britain and the Indian subcontinent on the other. Here, class, ethnic and racialisation processes have drawn different sets of linguistic forms, practices and evaluations into the environment and, over time, a number of these forms and practices have been configured in a series of conventionalised sociolinguistic contrasts – in Southall and Ashmead, Punjabi versus English, vernacular/low versus standard English/high, Creole versus Asian English. In earlier chapters, we have seen these style contrasts operating among very competent speakers of English, both adult and adolescent. How can we best characterise the participation of someone like Mandeep, who classified himself as coming to speak English later in life?

When compared with people who had grown up in the neighbourhood such as Anwar, Mandeep's English appeared more limited in a number of ways: in the range of English phonological variants that he commanded; in the number of identifiably distinct English styles that he performed (Anwar's English style repertoire was much more extensive, and included Cockney, standard Indian English, Indian English foreigner talk and the London urban vernacular (which itself included elements of Jamaican)); in the duration of the speech in which Mandeep sustained artful stylisations; and in the discursive actions achieved with switches of style (Anwar's shifts of style occurred with a far wider range of footing changes, and contributed to the management of non-stylised, non-artful, routine interaction as this moved between business and personal matters, between greeting and reason-for-call in telephone conversations and so forth; see Sharma & Rampton, 2015).

Nevertheless, in spite of these comparative limitations, it would be wrong to locate Mandeep as an L2 speaker outside the London sociolinguistic economy, aspirationally looking in. Familiarity with being on the receiving end of the locally circulating 'freshie' stereotype had led to the formulation of his standard response ('you're stale'), and instead of starting to develop the sensibility associated with contemporary urban vernaculars, he was continuing the professional teaching career path he had started in India. He insisted that in his maths class, 'I am perfectly fine', and in the interview stories, he presented himself as a now-established citizen of multi-ethnic London – among other things, siding with the Anglos criticising Shilpa Shetty and dismissing white racism as just parochial lower-class ignorance.

Beyond this explicit self-placement, there were a number of similarities between Mandeep's stylistic practices and Anwar's that invited us to treat both of them together as active participants in broadly the same sociolinguistic space. Anwar was more fully engaged with the stylistically differentiated positions in the local sociolinguistic economy, but Mandeep also actively oriented to these schemata. In the quantitative analysis, several of the context-sensitive variables in Mandeep's speech were similar to other people's, and the directionalities of shift were also broadly similar (more Punjabi variants with speakers of English brought up in South Asia, and more Anglo ones with people brought up in England). He referred to high/low and Anglo/Indian contrasts explicitly, and he performed them in narrative stylisations. The Southall urban vernacular might not have featured in Mandeep's repertoire, but his stylised performances involved comparable processes of reflexive self-positioning, affiliating and dissociating himself from circumambient images of language and speech, contrastively displaying, for example, his middle-class self-identification through his impersonations of traditional Anglo vernacular.[13] His reproduction of the high–low, standard–vernacular binary traditional in Anglo English had its limitations, but he could exploit the contrast between Punjabi- and Anglo-accented English,[14] and far from being simply confined to people born abroad, this Punjabi–Anglo contrast was itself widespread and well-established as a local practice. Indeed, Sharma and Sankaran (2011) have shown that over time, the presence of people like Mandeep, born and brought up in Punjabi in India and Pakistan, have made a major contribution to the development of local Southall English.

What about the methodological aspects of this account, and its broader implications for sub-fields of linguistics?

First and most obviously, we avoided the a priori separation of L1 and L2 English speakers in our analyses, and discovered that the differences between newcomers and people speaking English from childhood were not as sharp as one might initially assume (see also Aarsæther, 2010, on Oslo; Fraurud & Boyd, 2006, on Stockholm). Even though Mandeep had only started to speak the language as an adult, he displayed a practical sensitivity to key dimensions of local English sociolinguistic structure, and a label like 'immigrant learner of English' does not do justice to his position in the local London speech economy. So in the context of second language learning research, it is important not to take the 'target language' for granted, and to be empirically circumspect both in a specification of forms that compose it, and in an assessment of the linguistic distance that newcomers need to travel to reach it. Instead of classifying Mandeep as an L2 learner, he could be more aptly categorised, alongside Anwar and others, as a 'diasporic local' (Section 4.5), like them embedded in the neighbourhood while simultaneously linked to the Indian subcontinent. Certainly, he was more challenged than them by the intricacies of spoken English, but even so, there were substantial overlaps in communicative repertoire (itself always differentiated by experience and aspiration, biography and networks; Blommaert & Backus, 2011; Section 7.7 above).

This conclusion emerged in part from our use of the quantitative methods developed by Labov, which themselves have a long history of use with L2 speakers, on occasion leading to similar findings about the plurality of potential targets (Beebe, 1985). Turning to the qualitative account of Mandeep's styling, my analysis oriented to the 'total linguistic fact' and it slowed right down: it looked at stylistic moves individually; it broke them down into the linguistic forms, the discursive acts and the socio-ideological typifications that composed them, considering each of these in turn; and then it looked at the effects of their combination. This produced a rather nuanced picture of Mandeep's L2 English, showing how it formed part of larger sociolinguistic structures and processes, *without* (I hope) either romanticising or remedialising Mandeep by erasing or exaggerating the differences and limitations. So with Extract 4, we saw that a grasp of the indexical relationship between stance and vernacular style need not be matched by accurate reproduction of the canonical structural forms, and this could make the interpretation quite tricky. At the same time, Extract 2 showed that an imperfect grasp of vernacular Anglo forms *was not* automatically an expressive handicap in the impersonation of a lower-class white man.[15]

Stepping back for a broader overview, taking in the other chapters in Part 2 as well, my analyses have gone beyond the traditional focus of interactional sociolinguistics on work and bureaucratic encounters. But they still follow Gumperz in seeking a 'dynamic view of social environments' – in this case, urban England – 'where history, economic forces and interactive processes ... combine to create or to eliminate social distinctions' (Gumperz, 1982: 29).

Styles of English shaped in the interplay of Punjabi, Creole and standard and vernacular British Englishes have provided the point of entry into this investigation, and they have illuminated processes of stratification and differentiation among adolescents and adults, born locally and abroad, in a range of relationships (friendship, business, school, research interviews). The account certainly draws on the quantitative variationist methods that have been most prominent in descriptions of regional speech (Sections 6.2 and 8.3 above), and it shares with variationist sociolinguistics an interest in the language used in particular geo-historical locations. But rather than taking variation and change in linguistic structure as the main topic, the analyses have centred on the ways in which these linguistic resources are used in practices of social alignment and distancing, orienting at particular interactional junctures, in specific rhetorical moves, to ideological models of the social world shaped within migration, diaspora and social class over half a century.

The 2010 IPPR Report cited in Chapter 4, *You Can't Put Me in a Box* (Section 4.1) highlighted social identity's dynamic complexity, but Gumperz pioneered ways of charting the details of this. He recognised much earlier that 'the relationship of ... social factors to speech form is quite different from what the sociologist means by correlation among variables' (Gumperz & Hernández-Chavez, 1972: 98), and he argued instead that 'culture is essentially a communicative phenomenon, constituted through talk' (Gumperz & Cook-Gumperz, 2008: 536). Major commentators like Hall and Gilroy have certainly also addressed identity dynamics of the kind I have described, and they have provided an important warrant for my own analyses with their much more broadly based accounts of the cultural politics of class, race and ethnicity (Sections 5.2 and 5.3). But interactional sociolinguistics takes us close into the negotiations and struggles over social categorisation that unfold in everyday practice, and it delivers at least two key messages for social science more generally. First and most obviously, it confirms in vivid empirical detail that the identities that people align with cannot be predicted a priori from a distance – there are, in Hall's phrase, 'no guarantees' (Chapter 5). But second, just as important and maybe more distinctively, this absence of guarantees does *not* justify the claim that these identity processes are 'fluid'. On the contrary, there is structuring 'all the way down', and a complex and unending interplay of expectation and (agentive or accidental) deviation can be found at every level of social interaction (Blommaert, 2018a), right down into the details of pronunciation.

* * *

In this part of the book, my argument is that the sociolinguistic sensibilities evidenced in the practices I have described amount to what Gilroy calls a 'convivial multiculture', a multiculture which, he suggests, is capable of inspiring 'us to demand a more mature polity that, even if not entirely free of racism, might be better equipped to deal with racial inequality and cultural plurality as matters of politics' (Gilroy, 2006: 40). But the title of the article carrying Gilroy's characterisation is 'Multiculture in times of war', and he counterposes convivial multiculture to a very different discourse that builds on 'the tendentious political and theoretical assumption that solidarity and diversity cannot co-exist', arguing that if 'Brits are to be united and robust in the face of terror, Islam, unwanted immigration and European meddling, we must now become fundamentally and decisively the same' (Gilroy, 2006: 30). The 'proponents [of this discourse] turn wilfully ... away from the exhilarating cultural interaction common in cities', and their case is articulated alongside the 'militarization of everyday life and the elevation of security over the other functions of government' (Gilroy, 2006: 29, 30, 31).

Relevant though it might be, I am unable to provide any detailed account of how everyday communicative practices in England are affected by the ongoing tension and conflict between these perspectives. But the first chapter of Part 3 includes Kamran Khan's account of how the 'elevation of security' has affected UK policies on citizenship and language, in a broader discussion of what the 'militarisation of everyday life' means for sociolinguistics (Chapter 9). This is followed by an account of how one of the central concepts in Part 2, language crossing, can take a very different form when transposed to a context that has been heavily affected by violent conflict (Cyprus; Chapter 10). And then in the last chapter, Chapter 11, the distinctive contribution that socioculturally situated micro-analysis can make to our understanding of social process is asserted once again, this time turning to Goffman and the description of non-verbal conduct under surveillance.

Notes

(1) Much fuller and more fully referenced treatments of this dataset can be found in Rampton (2011b, 2013).
(2) Historically at least, Conversation Analysis has focused on interaction, cared about linguistic form but neglected ideology (see Section 2.4), whereas Critical Discourse Analysis has tended to emphasise form and ideology with not enough situated interactional processing (Blommaert & Bulcaen, 2000).
(3) This situation seems to be changing (Douglas Fir Group, 2016; Duff, 2012), and Young (2009: 1), for example, brings to L2 research an interest in practice as 'the construction and reflection of social realities through actions that invoke identity, ideology, belief and power'. But he also suggests that 'in studies [of L2 discursive practice], rich descriptions of context are illustrated with superficial analyses of language, whereas in other studies, a close analysis of a newcomer's developing utilization of verbal, non-verbal, and interactional skills is explained by a rather thin description of context' (Young, 2009: 230).
(4) Even in Eckert's ground-breaking work, the analysis of practice stops short of the micro-analysis of talk, dwelling instead on cultural styles, tastes and activities captured through ethnographic observation (Eckert, 2000; cf. Coupland, 2007a: 51; for exceptions see, for example, Kiesling, 2004, 2005; Schilling-Estes, 1998: 55; Sharma & Rampton, 2015; Snell, 2010).
(5) [eɪ], not [ʌɪ], and [aɪ], not [ɒɪ]
(6) [ɑɪ], not [aɪ]
(7) Admittedly, immediate audience response would be the best indication of the success of Mandeep's performances. Audible laughter followed Mandeep's quoted speech performances elsewhere, and there were other signs of the story recipient's involvement: laughter elsewhere, and supportive intervention at moment of disfluency. So

overall, it sounded as though the interview was enjoyable for both participants, but in the absence of a video-record, it is impossible to track the impact of all Mandeep's narrative performances in any detail, and we have to rely on the more distantiated analytic assessment offered above.

(8) Across the wider population we sampled, glottal Ts were very rare among people born in India, more common among Punjabi-descended people born in the UK in the 1960s and very often used by those UK-born in the 1980s (Sharma & Sankaran, 2011). The analysis of glottal-T involved 18 informants born in India (9F, 9M), 10 born in the UK in the 1960s (6F, 4M), and 14 born in the UK in the 1980s (6F, 8M). The results are shown in Figure 8.3:

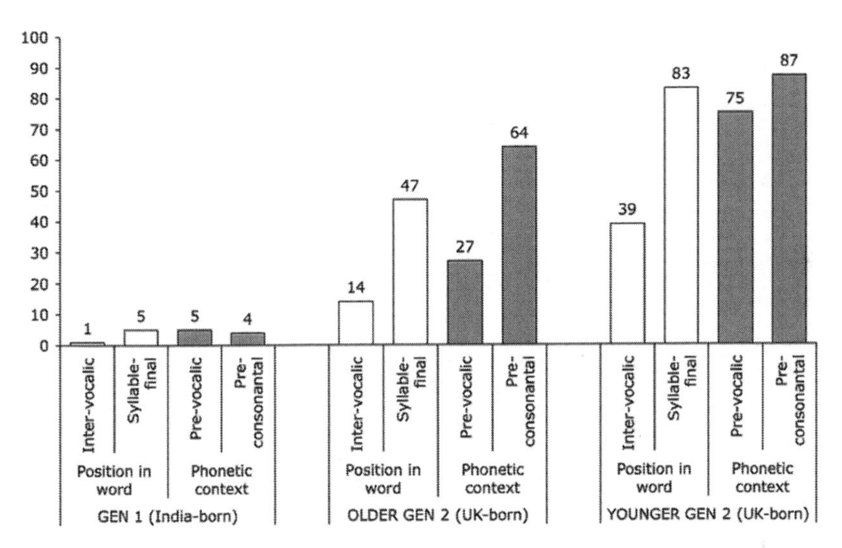

Figure 8.3 T-glottaling by generation

(9) Lines 33–38: 'li[t]le', 'bough[t]', 'carro[t]s', 'pu[t]', 'carro[t]s', 'ou[t]side' 'tha[t]'.

(10) As Mandeep told us elsewhere that his mum had always lived in India and only talks to him in Punjabi, we can be confident that it is not an accurate copy of her speech.

(11) In another rendering of a scolding from his mum later in the interview, Mandeep brought off a glottal T: "If I have to shou[t] at my wife so I will be getting a shou[t] from my mum 'how dare you to say tha[ʔ]' yea so it is always good" *((laughter from interviewer))* (MI 627; 39.58).

(12) Elicitations tests could be developed to investigate this (cf. Gumperz, 1982: 31).

(13) Within what Bakhtin calls processes of 'ideological becoming', the impersonation of traditional Anglo vernacular in Extract 2 constituted the kind of 'experimental' practice performed by 'someone ... striving to liberate himself from the influence of ... an image and its discourse by means of objectification, ... striving to expose the limitations of both image and discourse' (Bakhtin, 1981: 348).

(14) Rampton (2013: 369–371) gives a fuller account of this, showing how in his narrative character speech, Mandeep shifted between Punjabi and Anglo pronunciations of 'okay', evoking the ethnicity of the figure he was portraying.

(15) The dynamic relationship between form, activity and ideology is a staple concern in linguistic anthropology, and its role in linguistic development is also studied in research on adult/L2 as well as child/L1 language socialisation (Bremer *et al.*, 1996; Duff, 2012; Duranti *et al.*, 2012). But the stylisation practices of people speaking an L2 have not been extensively examined, despite prima facie relevance to second language learning in the very definition of stylisation as communicative action in which speakers produce representations of languages, dialects and styles that lie *outside* their own habitual repertoire. Of course, without sustained longitudinal data analysis, there is no scope for examining whether there was any relationship between stylisation and longer term linguistic change in Mandeep's speech (although see Turner, 2017), but there is theoretical plausibility in the idea that in certain types of stylisation, we may be able to detect new ways of speaking first taking hold in the L2 speech of individuals (Eckert, 2000: Ch. 1; Tarone, 2000; Woolard, 2008). The element of heightened metalinguistic reflexivity in stylisation practices makes them relevant to L2 researchers' longstanding interest in the relationship between linguistic development and language awareness (cf. 'focus on form', Doughty & Williams, 1998; 'noticing', Schmidt, 1990), and this interest could be enriched by the detailed accounts of interaction and ideology customary in studies of stylisation.

Part 3

Everyday (In)securitisation

9 Sociolinguistics and Everyday (In)securitisation

(co-authored with Constadina Charalambous, Panayiota Charalambous and Kamran Khan)

9.1 Introduction

Fears and experiences of large-scale, institutionally authorised violence certainly are not new for linguistics. The very term 'applied linguistics' sprang from the marriage of Bloomfield's structuralism with language training in the American army in the 1940s (Howatt, 1984: 265–269), and 'there is a long history of linguists cooperating with intelligence services in areas like language teaching and cryptology' (Jones, 2020b; Scollon & Scollon, 2007), raising a host of important moral and political issues, both for individuals and for the discipline (Heller & McElhinny, 2017; Price, 2004). As well as being a shaping influence, processes associated with security have also been the focus of analysis, and there are now substantial sociolinguistic studies covering, for example: intelligence gathering, translation/interpreting, language instruction and personnel coordination in ongoing military conflict, sometimes close to the battlefield (see Foottit & Kelly's [2012] *Palgrave Studies in Languages at War*); language policy during and after conflict (Liddicoat, 2008); narrations of militarised violence in reconciliation commissions (e.g. Verdoolaege, 2015); and language in applications for asylum (e.g. Maryns, 2006) (P. Charalambous, 2017, provides a bibliography). There is a good deal of critical discourse research showing how, in recent years, policy and media texts portray particular groups as threats to the state (e.g. Hodges, 2011, 2013; Macdonald & Hunter, 2013), and some sociolinguistic studies have developed very general theoretical frameworks, reaching far beyond the specialised sites of acute insecurity that they serve as their empirical starting point (cf. Blommaert, 2005, 2010a; Busch, 2016a, 2016b; Jacquemet, 2011).

Since 9/11, however, suspicion and the fear of existential threats have become much more widespread in everyday life in liberal democracies in Europe, North America and elsewhere. In the UK, for example, racism is often treated as less significant than the threat of Islamist terrorism, and schools, nurseries, hospitals and community centres are becoming sites of security surveillance, with ordinary people (medical and education staff, landlords, employers and so forth) pressured to check the residence rights of their patients/students/ tenants, etc. Even within university workplaces, central government's *Prevent* strategy enjoins academics to watch their own students for signs of radicalisation and terrorist leanings (Section 9.4, below); university security surveils students and staff with CCTV footage and access gate information; faculty are instructed to be more rigorous in checking international students' attendance to ensure that they are bona fide; and scholars from Africa and the Middle East are routinely denied visitor visas to participate in UK conferences (APPG, 2019). Much of this is underpinned by the British government's coordinated, cross-ministry strategy promoting a 'hostile environment for migrants' (Liberty, 2018), in which new forms of racism become official policy, to be enacted both by the state and by the organisations, businesses and NGOs contracted or compelled to carry it out (Yuval-Davis *et al.*, 2019).

So it is more difficult now for sociolinguists in Western democracies to think that fear and suspicion only operate as political principles somewhere else, at some other time, and there are at least two reasons why these developments call for sociolinguistic analysis. First, in the tradition associated with Gumperz and Hymes, sociolinguistics involves the study of everyday communicative practice in changing social conditions, and it follows from this that if fear and suspicion are growing more widespread and intense in everyday experience, the need to address them as mainstream sociolinguistic concerns is also increasing. Second, this tradition has never been politically indifferent. Sociolinguistics may be a primarily analytical rather than normative undertaking, focusing first on 'what is' rather than 'what should be', but in the formulation from Hymes (1977) cited in Section 4.3 above, the careful comparative empirical study of communicative repertoires and practices ultimately serves the ethical objectives of *Liberté, Egalité, Fraternité* because it 'prepares [linguists] to speak concretely to actual inequalities' (Hymes, 1977: 204–206).

The processes associated with growing insecurity deserve careful consideration. But can sociolinguistics provide some distinctive illumination of these shifts? Are there implications for its theories, frameworks and procedures? What kinds of interdisciplinary collaboration are needed to understand them better? What are the consequences for sociolinguists' moral or political positioning and their professional roles and identities?

In a programmatic rather than detailed empirical discussion, the following chapter begins with the relevance of recent work in a critical strand of International Relations research (IR, also covering Security Studies and Peace & Conflict Studies). This points to how everyday life is increasingly influenced by processes that were formerly only conceptualised in the realm of international geopolitics (Section 9.2). Following on from this, it briefly identifies a range of topics meriting closer sociolinguistic consideration ('enemy' as a social identity; 'bordering' and surveillance; Section 9.3), and it then outlines the ways in which security policies in the UK have been licensing and normalising new forms of racism, redefining the responsibilities of professionals, respecifying the goals for language education (Section 9.4). After that, it turns to Cyprus, where it sketches some of the challenges to mainstream theories of language education that emerge in a cultural climate shaped within a legacy of large-scale conflict (Section 9.5) and then, finally, it reflects on implications for the positioning of sociolinguistic research and researchers.

9.2 Critical IR as a Resource for Sociolinguistics[1]

Traditionally in the study of politics and IR, as well as in a good deal of common-sense, the state has been seen as a sovereign entity that governs and protects a specified population within a given territory, and it exists alongside others in an international order made of similar sovereign states. But Foucault's account of the state has become increasingly influential in recent years (e.g. Huysmans, 2006), and instead of seeing it as a monolithic power, this approach sees the state as a plethora of different people, processes, types of knowledge, technologies, actions, arguments, etc.:

> [t]he study of power should begin from below, in the heterogeneous and dispersed micro-physics of power[; it should] explore specific forms of [the exercise of power] in different institutional sites, and consider how, if at all, these were linked to produce broader and more persistent societal configurations. One should study power where it is exercised over individuals rather than legitimated at the centre; explore the actual practices of subjugation rather than the intentions that guide attempts at domination; and recognize that power circulates through networks. (Jessop, 2007: 36)

For Foucault, the state is a 'polymorphous crystallisation' of these ground-level practices, one of the 'broader and more persistent societal configurations' that emerge when these practices are coordinated, through mechanisms and organisations like policy, diplomacy and the military (Jessop, 2007: 36–37). But the whole assemblage is still rather precarious, and this bottom-up, practice-centred approach to the state feeds internal critique within IR research, stepping away from IR's traditional idealisation of the nation-state, its dislike of 'details, local events, or precise and complex life stories' and its tendency to limit 'the thickness of history and anthropology … to a varnish' (Bigo, 2014: 190–191). Instead, this critical work looks at how everyday life in Europe and elsewhere is increasingly permeated by micro-practices of securitisation.

Within this approach, security is no longer seen as the condition of being safe from external threat, but is instead regarded as

> a practice of making 'enemy' and 'fear' the integrative, energetic principle of politics displacing the democratic principles of freedom and justice …. [S]ecurity can thus be understood as a political force. It is not simply a policy responding to threats and dangers. Neither is it a public good or value. It is a practice with a political content. It enacts our world as if it is a dangerous world, a world saturated by insecurities. It invests fear and enmity in relations between humans and polities rather than simply defending or protecting political units and people from enemies and fear. (Huysmans, 2014: 3)

The conceptualisation of borders also shifts away from the common-sense view of them as relatively static geographical facts – lines around the perimeter of the territory governed by a particular state. Globalisation makes this definition increasingly difficult to operate, and the distinction between inside and outside loses a great deal of its fixity in the activities of the agencies set up to manage state borders. The division between police holding the monopoly on legitimate violence within the nation-state and military operating in a more anarchic international order no longer obtains (Bigo, 2008: 14) and, instead, there is a growing body of 'security professionals' engaged in 'border work' – police with military status, border guards, customs agents, immigration officers, intelligence officers, private security companies, specialist lawyers, academics and others. Their interests and specialisms form a complicated, interconnected but also relatively disorganised transnational field which often operates outside the auspices of the nation-state, but which nevertheless converges 'towards the same figure of risk and unease management, the immigrant' (Bigo, 2002: 77).

In monitoring who belongs where, who is entitled to stay or visit, who presents what kinds of need, benefit or threat, border work extends well beyond the moment when a person crosses from the territory of one state into another. Security professionals also make increasing use of digital technologies, building risk profiles of individuals and groups with computational algorithms that work on datasets assembled from the information traces left behind whenever people encounter bureaucracy or themselves use digital technologies (Bauman *et al.*, 2014; Bigo, 2008; Huysmans, 2014). And of course it is not only migrants who are affected by this surveillance. As a matter of routine, most people in the West go online, visit websites, use a swipe cards, carry cell-phones, etc. For much of the time, the data generated by these swift, convenient and pervasive technologies are used commercially, as a resource for targeted marketing, promoting and monitoring consumption (Bauman & Lyon, 2013; Haggerty & Ericson, 2000; van Dijck, 2013a). But these data can also be used to generate a risk profile for someone who wants health cover, insurance or a mortgage, and there is only a thin line between commercial and security surveillance (see also Staples, 2014). Admittedly, there is no overall coordination between all the private, state and transnational organisations involved in this surveillance and there is also a good deal of political argument over privacy rights, so that in the view of scholars of security in the West, this does not all amount to *1984*'s Big Brother totalitarianism (Bauman *et al.*, 2014; Bigo, 2008: 11). But as Edward Snowden's revelations show, the US National Security Agency and the UK's GCHQ collect phone calls, emails, text messages, Skype communications and other data on a massive scale without public consent. Digital intelligence work starts with a particular suspect and then extends to friends of friends of friends. So 'for a suspected person with 100 friends at the first hop, the person in charge of surveillance at the NSA or one of its private subcontractors can, without warrant, put under surveillance all 2,669,556 potential connections at the third hop' (Bauman *et al.*, 2014: 123–124).

The processes covered in this critical IR agenda are often referred to as '*(in)securitisation*'. The '-isation' suffix reflects the attention to practices, and the parenthetic prefix '(in)-' captures the fact that the effects of these practices are both unstable and relational: 'depending on power relations, the[se] measures and routinised practices will be called either violence [and] insecurity or security and safety' (Bigo & McCluskey, 2018: 126) – security to one person is insecurity to another, and this may change with the situation, sometimes quite quickly.

For sociolinguists struggling with the growing significance that 'terrorist' and 'security' have as officially generated terms in the cultural and discursive climate where they try to describe everyday communication, this critical IR literature can be very informative, illuminating the interaction of state, supra-state and private organisations in the security field, the development and management of counter-terrorism programmes, the mechanisms of surveillance, the security dimensions in humanitarian support, the intersection between security, peace and neoliberalism and so forth. Indeed, critical IR scholars are themselves very receptive to cross-disciplinary dialogue, and they have started looking to ethnography, going beyond the empirical study of security professionals and political elites to the experiences of people who are insecuritised by these developments, also connecting with an emerging anthropology of security (Goldstein, 2010; Maguire *et al.*, 2014; Mc Cluskey, 2017, 2019). Critical IR refers quite extensively to the same major social theorists that sociolinguists and linguistic anthropologists often invoke (for example, Bourdieu as well as Foucault), and indeed key figures in sociolinguistics are themselves also sometimes cited.[2] Admittedly, for the most part, these cross-references are pointers to possibilities for the future, as yet unsupported by a substantial body of sociolinguistic research analysing the practices that 'enact our world as if it is a dangerous world, a world saturated by insecurities' (Huysmans, 2014: 3). But critical IR is likely to be receptive if sociolinguistics is successful in providing thick descriptions of (in)securitisation, detailing the lived experience of (in)securitisation as an intensifying apprehension of institutionally authorised vulnerability and existential threat, produced and received in communicative practice in a range of social settings. Where, though, should these descriptions begin?

9.3 Aspects of (In)securitisation Calling for Sociolinguistic Analysis

Since it is increasingly pervasive, it is difficult to delimit the scope and foci for sociolinguistic analyses of (in)securitisation. But it is worth noting right at the start that as a category active in everyday life, 'enemy' is not well-established as a staple term in mainstream sociolinguistics. Certainly, there is a great deal of sociolinguistic work where conflict and struggle feature very prominently, but for the most part this is seen to occur inside nation-states, and it is more about domination and subordination, competition, rivalry or politics than actual war with violence, casualties and fatalities. Likewise, 'the Other' – 'Other-with-a-capital-O' – is a very significant figure in sociolinguistic analysis, but on the whole this stops a long way short of 'enemy'. 'Identity' has been a central sociolinguistic theme for over four decades, and the contrasting Other is crucial to identity definition. There is a plurality of Others around us – others identified in terms of taste, style, wealth, age, expertise, gender, area of residence, etc. – and it is the salience and significance of particular Others that provides people with their identities as individuals and as members of particular social groups. Even so, the figure of enemy differs from the usual types of Other analysed in sociolinguistics. In liberal democracies, there is cooperation between 'Others' – there is cooperation between people occupying different, even opposite, categories – and some of the cooperation is intimate and long term. Certainly, some of these Others may be very low-prestige and unpopular, but it is their integration into society that is at issue. With *enemies* it is different: actual or potential enemies should be kept out, defeated or destroyed. Enemies are usually embedded in substantial social systems of their own, and if they are an imminent threat, then in the societies they are threatening, people are supposed to sink their differences in the interests of united self-defence. Typically, interaction with an enemy is either forbidden or it is associated with well-organised violence, and the moral and legal codes governing interaction between fellow-citizens do not apply. In addition, of course, 'enemy' links into a range of other institutional categories and processes: types of person like soldier, casualty, veteran, hero, prisoner, spy, terrorist, traitor, refugee, etc.; types of action – bombing, killing, wounding, torturing; types of mobility – invasion, occupation, escape; and types of collective change – victory, defeat, reconciliation. The ramifications of this for policy and practice in language education are discussed in more detail in Sections 9.4 and 9.5 and Chapter 10 below, but before addressing these, it is worth mentioning several other issues calling for investigation within and beyond interactional sociolinguistics.

The relationship between 'gatekeeping' and inequality has been a foundational IS research topic (cf. Erickson & Shultz, 1982; Gumperz, 1982), and scholars like Blommaert (2009b), Maryns (2006) and Jacquemet (2011) have extended these analyses to asylum application procedures, where the stakes are raised from wealth and status stratification to territorial exclusion (see also Erickson, 2004: Ch. 4 *et passim* on military conscription) (Section 2.6). But the notion of 'everyday bordering' takes this further, operating well beyond a direct concern with territorial border control. This entails a set of discourses and practices that determine who is and who is not protected by rights policies and legislation 'on the basis of the citizenship and immigration status as they intersect with[, for example,] racialised and gendered identities' (Yuval-Davis *et al.*, 2019: 98):

> [e]veryday bordering has become a major governance technology, controlling diversity and constructing hierarchies of exclusion and exploitation. As such, it affects not only migrants and racialised minorities; and it affects other people not only when they actually cross a border or are in employment in a border zone. Bordering has become a new citizenship duty and major influence on social and communal solidarities ... [I]n different and new contexts, citizens are required to become untrained

> and unpaid border guards, and more of us are falling under suspicion as illegitimate border crossers. (Yuval-Davis *et al.*, 2019: 162, 17; also Section 9.4)

Related to this, surveillance itself is another central process in (in)securitisation that deserves much closer attention. Working in surveillance studies, Ball (2009: 640) notes that 'the experience of surveillance has not yet been addressed in any detail', and somewhat remarkably in view of the fact that surveillance involves relations of communication, there has been hardly any research on this in sociolinguistics. Interactional sociolinguistics has now started to address this gap (see Jones, 2015, 2017, 2020a; Rampton, 2016, 2017: 11–12; Chapter 11, this volume), but the challenge is actually much broader. So, for example, analyses of multilingual signage in linguistic landscape studies risk a reductive account of the communicative dynamics of space, ethnicity and migration if they neglect the placement, use and effects of CCTV (see Eley, 2018; Jones, 2017; Kitis & Milani, 2015; Stroud & Jegels, 2014). Equally, in foregrounding the ways in which globalised mobility undermines established bureaucratic and academic systems of demographic classification, research on language and superdiversity now needs to engage with the flexibility of digital surveillance (Arnaut, 2012; Rampton *et al.*, 2015b: 8–10), because in online digital surveillance,

> a category like gender is not determined by one's genitalia or even physical appearance. Nor is it entirely self-selected. Rather, categories of identity are being inferred upon individuals based on their web use. Code and algorithm are the engines behind such inference[, constructing] identity and category online. (Cheney-Lippold, 2011: 165)

As 'a mode of governing that seeks to quickly adapt delivery of services, control and coercion to changing behaviours deriving and processing information directly from the everyday "doings" of people' (Huysmans, 2014: 166–167), the technologies of contemporary surveillance build on the assumption that identities are dynamic and (re)shaped in (online) interactional practice. Certainly, these technologies are insensitive to the subtleties, and their interpretations of online activity are heavily skewed by the preoccupations of their designers and users. But even so, they play a very significant part in institutional categorisation processes, and if sociolinguistics is to continue to speak to contemporary identity construction, it now needs to engage with the challenging complexities of the surveillant digital (Rampton, 2016).

Much of this empirical agenda lies beyond the scope of this book, but in the next section we sketch the ways in which concepts like 'enemy' have become an active principle in UK policy (see also Khan, 2017), directly impacting on the multi-ethnic terrain described in Part 2 of this book.

9.4 The (In)securitisation of Citizenship and Language Policy in the UK

As we have already noted, the work of security professionals tends to converge on 'the same figure of risk and unease management, the immigrant' (Bigo, 2002: 77), and the negative portrayal of Muslims is long-standing in Britain. But over the last 20 years, securitising discourses that construct British Muslims as a 'suspect community' have intensified, 'singl[ing them] out for state attention as being "problematic" in terms of policing, [targeting] individuals ... not necessarily as a result of suspected wrong doing, but simply because of their presumed membership to that sub-group' (Pantazis & Pemberton, 2009: 649). Since 2000, a number of events, both in the UK and internationally, have resulted in Muslims becoming primary targets of suspicion. In the summer of 2001, there were riots in three northern English cities involving (mainly Muslim) British Asians, far-right extremists and the police, and these led to calls for more emphasis on citizenship as a way of fusing together 'parallel communities' (Cantle Commission, 2002). The 9/11 bombings occurred a few weeks later, and in 2005, the view of Islamic communities as poorly integrated and a security risk became entrenched with the 7/7 London bombings, where three of the four bombers were born in the UK (Fortier, 2008). In 2007, Glasgow Airport was attacked by two Muslims driving a Jeep packed with petrol canisters into a terminal; in 2013, Fusilier Lee Rigby was murdered in Greenwich by Islamic militants. The Charlie Hebdo murders in Paris in 2015 once again focused attention on an Islamic 'enemy within' and, more recently, the scale of ISIS's recruitment of young Muslims willing to leave a comfortable existence in the UK has intensified the portrayal of British-born Muslims as weakly integrated, potentially dangerous, with questionable loyalty.

Over this period, the expression of hostility in public discourse has become much more explicit (see also Cooke & Simpson, 2012: 124–125), and this can be seen in, for example, Prime Minister Cameron's claim that too many Muslims 'quietly condone' violent extremism (*Daily Mail*, 18 June 2015), as well as in the rise to prominence and acceptability of anti-immigration parties such as UKIP (the United Kingdom Independence Party). The public is now told that it is constantly under threat, and the 2015 guidelines in the British Government's *Prevent* policy stated three objectives: 'Respond to the ideological challenge of terrorism and the threat we face from those who promote it; prevent people from being drawn into terrorism and ensure that they are given appropriate advice and support; work with sectors and institutions where there are risks of radicalisation that we need to address' (HM Government, 2015: 5). The institutions identified 'for partnership with *Prevent*' include local authorities, education (from early childcare to universities and colleges), health services, the prison service and the police (HM Government, 2015), and the signs of this effort to alert the public to the threat of terrorism are now unavoidable in everyday life, whether these take the form of classroom surveillance, new measures in airports or public signage about how to report suspicion (see 'everyday bordering' above). These developments are widely contested, and to cite just one example, the trades union for Further Education and Higher Education stated: 'the *Prevent* agenda will force our members to spy on learners, is discriminatory towards Muslims, and legitimises Islamophobia and xenophobia, encouraging racist views to be publicised and normalised in society' (UCU, 2015: 4). But they have also affected language policy, repositioning languages within policies on citizenship, anti-radicalisation and recruitment for the military and intelligence services.

In the English education system, after extensive multicultural interest in the 1970s and 1980s, support for the multilingualism of minority ethnic students declined sharply in the 1990s, making way for a much more exclusive commitment to Standard English (Section 4.6; Rampton *et al.*, 2001).[3] But the events and discourses sketched above have led beyond this to an intensified emphasis on the need for adult migrants to learn English, and ESOL teaching (teaching English for speakers of other languages) has been advocated as an essential ingredient in citizenship, an antidote to the ills of segregated communities and a vital instrument of 'social cohesion'. The 2001 riots were followed by a series of political speeches and policy documents calling for more attention to British citizenship, arguing that to be a citizen is to be a speaker of English (Blackledge, 2005; Cooke & Simpson, 2012: 125). In 2005, the *Life in the UK* test was introduced for migrants seeking British Citizenship and, over time, increasingly demanding English proficiency requirements were tied into this, with, for example, a language requirement being introduced for the reunification of non-EU, non-English speaking spouses in 2011. The spirit of these developments can be seen the words of the Home Secretary (and later Prime Minister), Theresa May, proposing a spurious correlation between extremism and proficiency in English:

> Government alone cannot defeat extremism so we need to do everything we can to build up the capacity of civil society to identify, confront and defeat extremism wherever we find it. We want to go further than ever before helping people from isolated communities to play a full and fruitful role in British life. We plan a step change in the way we help people learn English. There will be new incentives and penalties, a sharp reduction in translation services and a significant increase in the funding available for English. (May, 2015)

Alongside the reduction in translation and interpreting services promised here, Prime Minister Cameron targeted other multilingual spaces, proposing that 'as we develop our Counter-Extremism Strategy ... we will also bring forward further measures to guard against the radicalisation of children in some so-called supplementary schools or tuition centres' (Cameron, 2015). Consistent with this, funding for a number of modern and heritage language courses declined (Steer, 2014).

Of course, policy initiatives of this kind require the involvement of professionals from a range of sectors – immigration, education, city councils, etc. – and the complexity of the coordination of the ensemble of people, practices, knowledges and mechanisms that constitute the state is captured in Khan and Blackledge's (2015) detailed description of a citizenship ceremony. On the one hand, officials watch the mouths of participants to ensure that they utter the affirmation/oath to become British. At the same time, this gravity can be softened by the conduct of the officers in charge, as noted in Khan's fieldnote:

> All the citizens are standing together; they then make the pledge. As they go through the pledge, some are proud and speak clearly and loudly. Some people are a little more reserved and some look plain shy and embarrassed. B [the officiating dignitary] makes a joke: 'we can't speak your language, so we need you to say it in English. Even if understanding English is difficult – do your best.' He then makes the citizens aware that another hurdle remains. He even says: 'I know you have jumped through a lot of hoops, but there is still a hurdle to go.' He then says: 'we'll be watching. Do your best. Try and do your best.' (Khan & Blackledge, 2015: 399)

The precarities of implementation emerged on a much larger scale when in 2014 Home Secretary May suspended the English language tests for immigration run by the Educational Testing Service (ETS), following allegations of widespread abuse ('fake sitters', and passes guaranteed for £500; *Times Higher Education*, 10 February 2014; *Daily Mail*, 10 February 2014). And when political calls for English language proficiency as a prerequisite for citizenship coincided with extensive cuts to ESOL and adult education budgets (*Times Education Supplement*, 20 July 2015), the counter-extremist emphasis on English for citizenship looked incoherent to the point of self-defeating.

In fact, for the British intelligence and security services, a dramatic fall in the number of students graduating with foreign language (FL) degrees gave the multilingualism of the UK's ethnic minority population considerable strategic significance. So in a 2013 response to potential cuts in heritage language qualifications, GCHQ (Government Communications Headquarters) stated that it was 'concerned that there may be a move away from offering qualifications spoken by [minority ethnic] native speakers ... We would ... support any initiative to increase the number of languages qualifications which cover native speaker or heritage languages' (British Academy, 2013: 30). In its recruitment efforts, GCHQ undertook outreach work in schools and, in a similar vein, the British Army made a concerted effort to recruit more Muslims, not just because of its diversity targets but also for their linguistic skills (British Academy, 2013; Carter, 2015). The difficulty was, of course, that just at the time when intelligence and the military wanted their linguistic abilities more than ever, Muslims were being portrayed as a 'suspect community', subjected to high levels of surveillance, scrutiny and distrust (Khan, 2015).

So language policy has been no more unified than other aspects of this securitisation process. Even so, security concerns have become far more prominent in the discourses around domestic language policy, and they generate a model of citizenship and language education that is very different from, for example, the *Our Languages* project described in Section 4.5. Their overarching message is that cultural and linguistic difference is a security risk, and regardless of whether or not these policies have been coherent or efficiently implemented, their effect is to insecuritise the everyday lives of many people with Muslim, migrant, diasporic and/or multilingual backgrounds, making them increasingly vulnerable to 'exceptional measures', watched by a growing number of people pushed into the role of 'security professional' (Bigo, 2014: 198–202, 2008).

These ongoing processes are certainly not restricted to the UK,[4] and in the UK the arguments that have fed into Brexit are far from concluded (Dorling & Tomlinson, 2019). But rather than dwelling on these political developments, our second sketch points to the challenges to mainstream theories of language education emerging in environments where security has been a very longstanding concern.[5]

9.5 Challenges to Foreign Language Education Theory from a Legacy of Conflict

In the Council of Europe's *Common European Framework of Reference for Languages*, FL education is generally assumed to contribute to peaceful coexistence. But what happens to dominant assumptions in a well-established field like this when teaching takes place in a conflict-ridden or post-conflict setting where the language taught is associated with people who have been portrayed for many years as a threatening enemy?

Cyprus has a long history of interethnic conflict between the Greek-Cypriot and Turkish-Cypriot communities, going back to the beginning of the 20th century. In an era of intense nation-building in both Greece and Turkey, the island's two main religious communities, Christians and Muslims, came to imagine themselves as incompatible 'Greeks' and 'Turks' under the influence of antagonistic nationalist discourses (Bryant, 2004). A bi-communal Republic of Cyprus was established in 1960 but in spite of this, interethnic violence broke out between 1963 and 1967, and in 1974 the political turmoil culminated in a military intervention by Turkey that left the island de facto divided into a (Turkish speaking) north and a (Greek speaking) south. Since then, a buffer zone patrolled by military personnel and UN peacekeeping forces has served as a physical border that separates the two communities and substantially inhibits communication between them.

Language played a crucial role in the historical development of these ethnic identities in Cyprus. It served as a tangible way of differentiating the population into two communities and was perceived as a precondition for their survival (Karoulla-Vrikki, 2004; Kizilyurek & Gautier-Kizilyurek, 2004). At earlier points in history, Turkish-Cypriots (the minority) used both Turkish and the local Cypriot variety of Greek, but during the conflict, nationalist discourses on both sides not only discouraged but also penalised bilingualism (C. Charalambous, 2012; Ozerk, 2001). Speaking the language of the national 'archenemy' (Papadakis, 2008) became undesirable and a sign of betrayal. So in the southern part of the island, the focus of our research, Turkish never featured in official Greek-Cypriot educational curricula, and learning the language was largely restricted to Greek-Cypriot police and intelligence services (Papadakis, 2005).

In 2003, however, after 29 years of total isolation and 'ethnic estrangement' (Bryant, 2004), in the midst of negotiations for Cyprus' entry to the EU and the search for a political settlement of the Cyprus Conflict, the Turkish-Cypriot authorities announced the partial lifting of the restrictions of movement across the buffer zone and, for the first time, people were allowed to cross the dividing line. Language was also drawn into a central role in this period of rapid political developments: just a week after the opening of the buffer-zone checkpoints, the (Greek-)Cypriot government announced the establishment of language classes for Greek-Cypriots wishing to learn Turkish as a foreign language, in both secondary schools and adult institutes, as well as classes for Turkish speaking adults who wanted to learn Greek.[6] In educational documents, in interviews with senior ministry officials and among many people who decided to attend the classes, these initiatives fitted into a rhetoric of reconciliation and were seen as an emblematic gesture of government goodwill (see C. Charalambous, 2012, 2013, 2014).

On the ground, though, things were more difficult, as the setting up of Turkish classes was not accompanied by an immediate change in educational and public discourse, which continued to construct Turks as the enemy posing an imminent threat to the Greek-Cypriot community (see Adamides, 2014). As a result, teaching and learning Turkish was often seen as threatening Greek-Cypriot education's Greek-centred – 'Hellenocentric' – orientation. For Turkish FL teachers and learners, this generated a series of practical complications. In our 2006 study (see C. Charalambous, 2012), almost all interviewees reported being called a 'traitor', a 'Turk' or 'Turkophile' by peers, friends and occasionally by family members and other teachers, and as a result they often hid their Turkish books, avoided mentioning the classes they taught or attended and/or developed careful justifications in defence.

Formulated in terms from security studies, the lifting of border restrictions and the introduction of Turkish classes can be seen as *de*-securitising moves. Rather than seeking to shift a group from the sphere of ordinary politics into a zone of exceptional measures (securitisation), de-securitisation pushes in the opposite direction and seeks to normalise relations with what has hitherto been seen as an existential threat (cf. Aradau, 2004; P. Charalambous *et al.*, 2015). But this involves discursive struggle and resistance, and analysis of the enactment of Turkish FL policy in Cyprus points to practices and stances that challenge mainstream applied linguistic accounts of FL education, thereby relativising them, while also suggesting unanticipated ways in which language education can contribute to processes of reconciliation.

In a great deal of the theory underpinning FL education policy, lessons are seen as occasions for practising communication, with a view to engaging with speakers of the FL outside class. Role-plays and materials with a degree of resemblance to the everyday world inhabited by the FL speakers are often recommended ('authenticity'), and in recent years there has been increased emphasis on students developing intercultural competence, the capacity to understand and manage cultural differences (Byram *et al.*, 2001; Council of Europe, 2001). But in the de-securitisation process in Cyprus, Greek-Cypriot society was itself engaged in a still highly contested process of negotiating whether and how to move Turkish issues *into* the realm of ordinary civic life, *out of* the exceptional measures required for an existential threat. So for many Turkish language students, imagining oneself in the world of the target language was far from straightforward. A number of secondary school students told us that they had no intention of ever talking to a Turkish speaker, and as one teacher complained, 'how am I going to practice dialogues in the classroom between sales-men and buyers, when students are not supposed to cross to the other side and buy things from the occupied territories' (Fieldnotes, 2006). Indeed, if a teacher made a positive comment about Turkish speaking people even in passing in the classroom, this could spark intense reactions and at least momentarily jeopardise their authority, as C. Charalambous (2013) documents in detail.

So how did teachers cope? They developed several strategies, but the most common was to treat Turkish as just a lexico-grammatical code (see Section 10.8). Some scholars may suggest that in contexts of violent conflict, language educators should make 'culture ... the starting point of every individual class session' (Allen, 2004: 287), but instead of emphasising the communicative and cultural aspects of the language, encouraging learners to 'cope with the affective as well as cognitive demands of engagement with otherness' (Byram, 1995: 25), a lot of teachers tried to suppress the socio-indexical/socio-symbolic side of Turkish, and instead they presented it in class as a neutral set of lexical items and syntactic structures. Of course there is a strong philological tradition that supports pedagogy like this, but these teachers were quite explicit about the risks of attempting a communicative or intercultural approach (P. Charalambous *et al.*, 2017). Their 'de-culturalisation' of Turkish, in other words, was driven by acute cultural sensitivity.

And what of the young people? Why did they choose Turkish in the first place? 'Because it's easy and gets you good marks' was one of the most common answers provided in interview, and liking a particular teacher also played a part (Section 10.6). But this oversimplifies the experience of learning the language of an enemy, and for a fuller understanding it is important to look beyond the usual unit of analysis in the study of FL learning motivation – the individual – and to situate learners in their families and family histories. In violent conflicts of the kind experienced in

Cyprus, collective life is profoundly disrupted, with widespread loss of life and a great deal of forced relocation (Greek-Cypriot refugees moved south, and Turkish Cypriots fled north). After the cessation of hostilities, the language of the enemy – in this case, Turkish – is likely to be bound up with lived, learned and taught histories that are vividly remembered, indexing a set of experiences and relationships that families still have very deep feelings about. So to grasp how adolescents positioned themselves as learners of Turkish, we had to understand their intergenerational family relationships, and it was clear in interview that family discussions could either constrain or enhance their scope for studying the language. Family losses, anger and pain produced visible reservations among some learners, who worried about venturing too far with things Turkish, while for others, more positive family experiences in the pre-1974 period before the war – stories of friendship, collaboration and exchange with Turkish-Cypriots – contributed to greater engagement, gradually reworking the negative associations of Turkish, often in continuing dialogue with older family members. In sum, secondary school students participated in these classes as the younger members of multigenerational families, balancing loyalty and responsibility to their kin with an awareness of geopolitical processes increasing the possibility of reconciliation. So here and more generally in post-conflict situations, an analysis that follows the usual route of focusing only on the motivation, aspirations and choices of individuals is likely to be insufficient.

In the mainstream paradigm, FL teachers prepare their students for visits abroad to the country where the language is widely spoken, but the situation was much more complex in Cyprus. While the political situation remained officially unsettled on the island, crossing to the other side was often treated as morally unacceptable. For some, the act of passing through a checkpoint gave recognition to an imposed dividing line which they regarded as illegitimate, bringing accusations of betrayal; some crossed occasionally but avoided economic transactions as a matter of principle, and others crossed more frequently and had ongoing relationships with people in the north. These differences were experienced among both adults and adolescents, and in the adult classes they were quite often acknowledged and discussed. When adults and adolescents did cross to the north, their perspective was also radically different from the 'touristic' gaze most commonly assumed in FL education (e.g. Sercu, 2005). Instead, especially among adolescents, accounts of visits to the Turkish speaking north often carried the aura of *pilgrimage*, and they were formulated as 'narratives of return', either to their parents' former home in the case of students from refugee families, or to places emblematic of Greek Orthodox identity.

Indeed, even when talking about Istanbul in class, teachers tended to highlight its Greek roots, history and character. In sum, locating the 'target language' in time and space always bore the stamp of a troubled past, and it was far more difficult in these Turkish classes than is usually assumed in discussions of FL education (C. Charalambous, 2013).

Admittedly, in defence of orthodox FL education theory, one might argue that, given the long history of Turkish in Cyprus, it is a mistake to call it a 'foreign' language. But this was the categorisation used by the Greek-Cypriot education authorities, who placed it alongside Italian, French, Russian and other languages in the secondary curriculum. Moreover, there is a case for saying that its very position as an everyday curriculum subject, as just one among a number of FLs, made a significant contribution to the reconciliation process (see Section 10.7). As we have said, it was very hard to normalise relations between Greek- and Turkish-Cypriots because it ran counter to the historic securitisation of Turks and Turkish-Cypriots. But for this, the very 'ordinariness' of the FL class was itself a resource. Curricular FL learning is an unspectacular but long-term, widely established, institutionally organised activity that demands a significant investment of time and effort, and these Turkish language classes meant that Greek-Cypriots regularly shared a space where things and practices linked with Turkish had a low-key presence close at hand, travelling back and forth between school and home in homework bags, accessible for closer association if students wanted and were able. According to Aradau, effective de-securitisation in a liberal democracy needs to restore the 'possibility of scrutiny as well as the expression of voice', practices that securitisation suppresses. To achieve this, de-securitisation requires a '*slowness* in procedures that ensures the possibility of contestation' (Aradau, 2004: 393, emphasis added), and 'a different relation from the one of enmity ... has to be *inscribed institutionally*' (Aradau, 2004: 400, emphasis added). Slowness and institutionalisation were intrinsic to these Turkish classes. They brought people into the vicinity of otherness as a matter of routine (a teaching period twice a week for one or two years in the secondary curriculum), and they occupied their attention over periods of time that were long enough to host small and gradual shifts in outlook. Such shifts were, of course, far from guaranteed, but there was some evidence that Turkish lessons helped a number of students orient more constructively towards a peaceful future (Charalambous *et al.*, 2021).

These processes are described in more detail in the next chapter, and at this point it is sufficient to say that the case illustrated here certainly is not the only situation in which young people learn a language that is closely associated with violent conflict. There are other examples in Uhlmann's research on Jewish secondary school students learning Arabic in Israel (e.g. Uhlmann, 2011) and Karrebaek and Ghanchi's (2015) study of children and adolescents of Iranian descent learning Farsi in the divided Iranian refugee community in Copenhagen.[7] Certainly, there are important differences between these environments, but here too circumambient discourses of security, and/or serious conflict in the background, lead to the exclusion of the 'target' culture in culturally responsive language classrooms, along with anticipations of casual contact and tourist travel. So Cyprus is not alone in challenging the orthodoxies of FL education theory.

With these two sketches in place, one narrating the securitisation of language policy in Britain and the other pointing to challenges to orthodox language education theory in Cyprus, it is worth turning to consider the stance that sociolinguists should take when turning to the potentially intense, dangerous and highly consequential situations that (in)securitisation often involves. Are sociolinguists moving out of their depth in doing so, putting themselves and others at risk?

9.6 The Positioning of Sociolinguists

Interaction with people from disciplines with more experience in areas of acute insecurity is often helpful, as we have found in our ongoing dialogue with critical IR scholars (see www.kcl.ac.uk/liep). It is also possible for sociolinguists to contribute 'from the sidelines', providing sociolinguistic training to researchers (from different disciplines) who are themselves working in conflict-affected fieldsites. So, for example, in an eight-hour/four-session doctoral training short course on 'Security, Ethnography & Discourse' at King's, we teach the rudiments of multi-layered linguistic ethnography, Goffman and situated discourse analysis to students in fields like IR, area studies, international development and healthcare, making space for their own projects and focusing heavily on data relevant to themes like 'the institutional enactment of security policy', 'everyday surveillance' and 'interviewing geopolitical elites'. At the same time, however, in IR as elsewhere, there is also substantial concern that work in troubled sites is often carried out by researchers who 'parachute' in with little local understanding (Mac Ginty & Richmond, 2013), and here sociolinguistics may have its advantages. It is hard to imagine starting a linguistic ethnography without quite a high level of communicative competence in a local language, and in our own work, long-term ongoing involvement in the fieldsite has been crucial, identifying the research questions, negotiating fieldsite access, appreciating discursive tropes, nuances and silences, and formulating academic accounts alert to continuing tensions.

Within the process of knowledge production, researchers rooted like this in the settings being investigated have to grapple with personal questions of positionality more intensely than those living far away, and especially if they come from minoritised 'suspect communities', they themselves may risk being (in)securitised (Khan, 2017, 2020; Mangual Figueroa, 2020). Researchers in conflict-affected settings who deviate from heavily securitised discourses may be perceived as traitors posing a threat; ethnographic data collection may be treated with suspicion and distrust among highly surveilled groups, to the point of being unworkable; and research with groups and institutions in conflict can present serious dilemmas about how to represent different voices and perspectives and what to disclose or conceal. So, for example, as Mangual Figueroa (2020: 97) notes, sociolinguists need to think carefully about celebrating the resistance of their informants, since 'documenting ... grassroots efforts to resist surveillance ... can in fact increase police gaze'.

At the same time, despite the challenges, locally based researchers are well placed to put their work to practical use, in university teaching, youth workshops, policy committees and so forth.[8] But to do so, they may have to give up the attempt to remain 'neutral' (treating equally the different voices encountered in research), instead taking a stance that is normative as well as active. Alternatively, they may need to strategically mitigate some of their own views to reach a wider audience. So, for example, C. Charalambous *et al.* (2013) describe how in peace education teaching workshops, they used a familiar and well-accepted 'humanist discourse', appealing to the participants' sense of the shared humanity of traditional enemies, as a basis for introducing otherwise controversial peace education ideas to teachers, even though they had critiqued this discourse in their academic work. These ethical issues are not new, but they become more intense in situations of acute insecurity when lives and livelihoods are threatened, requiring researchers to think about ethics, politics, relationships and roles with potentially different lenses.

Finally, if sociolinguistics engages more fully with everyday (in)securitisation, what should this field of enquiry be called? It would be a mistake to call it the 'sociolinguistics *of* (in)security' for at least three reasons. First, this could separate (in)security-focused sociolinguistics from ordinary sociolinguistics, when in fact the tense and unpredictable relationship between the ordinary and the exceptionalised can be a key issue. Overwhelming sociolinguistic emphasis on exceptionality could miss the way in which many people do still produce liveable lives in very difficult conditions (Papadopoulos & Tsianos, 2013), and if analysts thematise fear and suspicion in their description of sociolinguistic actors as a matter of routine, they could end up supporting rather than interrogating the (in)securitising discourses that call for special measures for particular groups. Second, by imaging a viewing lens (sociolinguistics) apart from and above its object of inspection ((in)security), the phrase 'sociolinguistics of (in)security' suggests a transcendent vantage point separate from (in)securitisation processes. This would risk obscuring the close relationship between power and disciplinary knowledge, and the fact that linguistics is often a significant part of the security apparatus. In contrast, 'sociolinguistics *and* (in)security' allows more room for reflexivity about this relationship, a reflexivity that is of cardinal significance for future work. Third, the 'sociolinguistics *of* (in)security' suggests a well-defined field, with its own canonical readings and empirical reference points. But this would risk underestimating (in)securitisation's pervasiveness, its protean character and significance across a plurality of sites and processes. Sociolinguistics *and* (in)securitisation provides for much wider ranging analysis and debate.

The next chapter discusses the Cyprus case study in more detail, exploring the implications of the legacy of conflict for the sociolinguistic concept of language crossing.

Notes

(1) In most of what follows, we only distinguish between IR and 'critical IR', but the field is much more differentiated than this, and within critical IR, International Political Sociology is our main reference point (see Basaran *et al.*, 2017).

(2) In Balzacq's edited volume on the discursive processes involved in declaring a particular group or phenomenon to be an existential threat and persuading people that special measures are now warranted, Sapir, Goffman, Schegloff, Fairclough, Kress, Wetherell, Duranti and Goodwin (as well as Austin and Searle), are all indexed. According to Bigo (2017: 31), 'the vision [of] sociolinguists when they analyse everyday interactions' can capture the complex workings and effects of (in)securitisation.

(3) For a critical overview of 50 years of language education policy in England, see Rampton *et al.* (2020).

(4) In the study of a town in Pennsylvania with a large community with links to Mexico, Gallo describes the enactment of 'Secure Communities' from 2011 onwards: '"Secure Communities" is a data sharing program in which local police officers submit a person's information to Immigration and Customs Enforcement (ICE) when a person is stopped for any infraction, ranging from an arrest for an aggravated felony to a minor infraction such as a speeding ticket ... If this person does not have documentation for U.S. residency, he or she can be apprehended by ICE and undergo the deportation process' (Gallo, 2014: 477). Ninety per cent of those deported are not released from detention prior to deportation, often not having the chance to say goodbye to their

families (Gallo, 2014: 490), and Gallo describes in detail the traumatic effects on children and community (as well as the difficulties that schools hamstrung by test-oriented curricula have in engaging with this) (de Genova, 2002; Gallo & Link, 2015).

(5) The discussion draws on findings from two periods of linguistic ethnographic research focused on Turkish language classes organised in Greek-Cypriot schools and adult institutes (2006–2009; 2012–2015). For a succinct overview, see Section 10.2.

(6) For Turkish-Cypriots coming into the south, the language classes were only offered in afternoon governmental institutions, as schooling in both communities has been historically separate.

(7) See P. Charalambous *et al.* (2017: §1) on differences between them, as well as C. Charalambous and Rampton (2012: 203) for other cases. Also Zakharia (2020) on very different pedagogies.

(8) For example, Constadina Charalambous regularly runs teacher training workshops in Cyprus, and serves as a member of the Bi-communal Technical Committee on Education which makes education policy recommendations to the Government of Cyprus, and also organises ongoing bi-communal training for children across the buffer zone.

10 Crossing of a Different Kind[1]

(co-authored with Constadina Charalambous and Panayiota Charalambous)

10.1 Introduction

In order to elaborate on the claim that established sociolinguistic concepts need to be reconsidered in situations where there is a strong orientation to security and large-scale conflict, this chapter returns to the Greek-Cypriot setting introduced in Section 9.5, and it focuses on the notion of language crossing. The practices that were first called 'crossing' occurred in principally recreational interaction among adolescents in multi-ethnic neighbourhoods affected by several decades of migration into the UK, and they were often linked to popular cultural media (cf. Sections 6.3 and 7.2). But this chapter moves away from these vernacular sites to explore the relevance of crossing to learning and teaching another language at school, focusing on young people in the Greek-Cypriot education system learning Turkish, the language of the (former) enemy. This is a situation where the legacy of war makes ongoing interethnic hostility much more intense than in the UK sites that I originally studied in the 1980s. But we will argue that participation in these language classes also constitutes crossing, and that our case study can enrich the conceptualisation of crossing practices, contribute to the understanding of language education and add to our knowledge of how language features in changing intergroup relations.

We begin with theory and methodology, defining crossing and stylisation, explaining why our account attends more to ideology and institutional processes than to the micro-details of interaction, also outlining our fieldwork and dataset (Section 10.2). After that, we briefly recap on the history of conflict in Cyprus and the roles that state and supra-state actors played in the introduction of Turkish as a curriculum subject in 2003 (Section 10.3). We then turn to the ideological controversy around Turkish, attending first to students' perceptions and the influence of family history, and then to obstacles to Turkish language provision encountered at different institutional levels (Sections 10.4 and 10.5). We then turn to processes and practices that supported crossing into Turkish: the justifications that students offered (Section 10.6); the institutional affordances and normalising routines of foreign language learning at secondary school (Section 10.7); and the ways in which learning Turkish was interactionally framed in class (Section 10.8). After that, we compare this case study with other accounts of crossing, bringing out its distinctiveness (Section 10.9), and in the concluding section (Section 10.10) we draw out the broader implications, reaffirming the specificity of crossing as a practice, arguing for the contribution that analyses of crossing can make to our understanding of language education in conflict-riven settings in particular, and peacebuilding more generally.

10.2 Theory and Methodology

In our definition of it, crossing involves reflexive communicative action in which a person performs specially marked speech in a language, dialect or style that can be heard as anomalously 'other', raising questions of legitimacy and entitlement for the participants (Rampton, 1995/2018: Ch. 11.1–2, 2009b: 151–153). Crossing is closely related to stylisation and, as clearly non-habitual speech practices, they both break with ordinary modes of action and interpretation. But crossing entails a stronger sense of social or ethnic boundary transgression. When hearers encounter the transgressive disjuncture between a speaker's voice and background that crossing involves, the questions with which they make sense of it go beyond 'why that now?' to 'by what right?' or 'with what licence?' (Auer, 2006; Quist & Jørgensen, 2007; Rampton, 2009b: 151–153).

From the outset, the concept of crossing has been aligned with interactional sociolinguistics, following Gumperz in the search for a 'closer understanding of how linguistic signs interact with social knowledge in discourse' (Gumperz, 1982: 29; Rampton, 1995/2018: App. I). Consistent with this (and with Silverstein's 'total linguistic fact' (cf. Chapter 8)), I originally focused on strips of interaction in which there was a conspicuous disjuncture between social identity and linguistic code selection, and I analysed the discursive strategies that led to the acceptance or rejection of this, also drawing on ethnographic and historical data to identify the ideological and institutional processes that threw the legitimacy of these linguistic switches into question. The present study also orients to the 'total linguistic fact', but the historical, institutional and ideological dimensions of language crossing feature more prominently than transcripts of interaction. In my earlier research, the linguistic switches that constituted crossing were generally both conspicuous and relatively brief and, as in many other studies, this meant that crossing could be illustrated with relatively short episodes analysed in a good deal of micro-interactional detail. Here, however, Greek-Cypriots' involvement and exposure to Turkish occurred almost continuously throughout the twice-weekly 'foreign language' lessons that they attended, and even when students were not producing it themselves, the controversial other-language was there in front of them, in their exercise and textbooks, on the whiteboard, in their teacher's speech. So in the first instance, the scale of this activity substantially reduces the capacity of short but closely analysed transcripts of audio-data to capture these students' experiences of crossing during these lessons. Instead, ethnographic description of the institutional setting necessarily plays a larger role. Second, the performance of these lessons was actually rather similar to many of the classes described in the literature on foreign language learning, and transcripts of typical episodes of Greek-Cypriots producing Turkish in class could leave the reader wondering whether and how these lessons were any different. So rather than, as previously, seeking to evidence crossing in the micro-interactional analysis of specific shifts into the other language, our categorisation of participation in these classes as language crossing relies on an understanding of the ideological and institutional background, combined with interactional *theory* and more broadly drawn empirical description.

Most of the data that inform this understanding come from fieldwork in Turkish language classes in Greek-Cypriot secondary schools and adult institutes conducted in 2012–2013,[2] building on an earlier ethnography of such classes by Constadina Charalambous (2009, 2012, 2013). The secondary students were 16–17 years old, and the adult learners were aged between 25 and 70. The project combined analysis of interviews and classroom discourse with consideration of historical, sociopolitical and institutional processes, and initial data analysis involved 18 months of data processing and produced 20 thematic reports.[3] In addition, the account draws more indirectly on broader knowledge of Greek-Cypriot schools shaped in, for example, Panayiota Charalambous's doctoral project (P. Charalambous, 2010) and in the study of a peace education initiative in 2012–2014 (cf. Zembylas *et al.*, 2016).

In view of this chapter's central aim – to explore whether and how Greek-Cypriots learning the language of the traditional enemy represents a significant expansion to existing accounts of language crossing – our account of crossing in Cyprus is theoretically pointed, not comprehensive. As my earlier work on crossing focused on youth (as have many studies), we will also concentrate on the adolescent data, summarised in Table 10.1, to sharpen the comparison. But at least two simplifications in the portrait

Table 10.1 Overview of the dataset

Secondary schools	
Classes observed and no. of participants	2 teachers (Savvas, Stella), 6 classes, 101 students
Classroom recordings	51 hours
Classroom observations	78 hours
Interviews	62 students in 21 interviews, 2 teachers
Other	93 questionnaires
Adult institutions	
Classes observed and no. of participants	2 teachers, 2 classes, 25 students
Classroom recordings	34 hours
Classroom observations	68 hours
Interviews	15 students, 3 teachers
Other	22 questionnaires

need to be recognised: (i) there were actually many more sites in Cyprus where both adolescent and adult Greek-Cypriots could learn Turkish than those we describe, displaying potentially very different dynamics. These included a Turkish Studies programme at the University of Cyprus, private tuition, and inter-communal centres committed to reconciliation. (ii) Cyprus is itself now actually very multi-ethnic and multilingual, even though the historic antagonism between Greek- and Turkish-Cypriots can easily suppress recognition of this diversity (Zembylas *et al.*, 2016).

With this account of the focal concept and of our approach, our fieldwork, our dataset and key caveats in place, we can start with a preliminary sketch of the historical and political background.

10.3 Reconciliatory Policy Initiatives against a Background of Division

In Cyprus, interethnic conflict between the Greek-Cypriot and Turkish-Cypriot communities began in the early 20th century, when the island's two main religious groups were transformed into ethno-national groups – 'Greeks' and 'Turks'. In 1960, a bi-communal Republic of Cyprus was established, but there was interethnic violence between 1963 and 1967, and approximately 20,000 Turkish-Cypriots moved into ethnically pure enclaves. In 1974, after a *coup d'état* backed by Greece, the Turkish army intervened, occupying the northern third of the island.[4] The war had devastating consequences and involved the violent relocation of around 196,000 Greek-Cypriots and 34,000 Turkish-Cypriots into, respectively, ethnically homogenised sectors in the south and north of the island

(Canefe, 2002), which are still separated by a UN buffer zone. Since then, there has been little violence, but in the government-controlled (southern) areas where our research has been based, hostile images of Turks and Turkish-Cypriots have been perpetuated in the media (Adamides, 2014), in public debate and mainstream education (Christou, 2007; Papadakis, 2005).

Turkish has been spoken in Cyprus for about four centuries and when Cyprus gained independence from British Administration in 1960, both languages were recognised as official languages in the constitution. Indeed, Turkish is still considered to be the second official language of the (Greek-Cypriot) Republic of Cyprus, and it is used alongside Greek on stamps and bank notes and in official documents (Karyolemou, 2003).[5] But rising nationalism and growing hostility between the two communities in the latter part of the 20th century had a negative impact on Greek-Turkish/Turkish-Greek bilingualism on the island. Language was seen as essential to being 'Greek' or 'Turkish' and to each community's survival (Karoulla-Vrikki, 2004). Speaking the language of the other community became not just undesirable but a sign of 'betrayal' (Ozerk, 2001), and Greek-Cypriot education was monolingual, Turkish never being taught in the school curriculum before 2003.

In 2003, however, this situation was somewhat disrupted. With the EU Accession Treaty in focus and negotiations for a political settlement of the Cyprus Conflict ongoing, the Turkish-Cypriot authorities lifted some of the restrictions of movement across the buffer zone in Nicosia, so that people could cross the dividing line for the first time in nearly 30 years. Very soon afterwards, the (Greek-)Cypriot government announced that among other things (including access to healthcare), it would set up voluntary language classes for Greek-Cypriots who wanted to learn Turkish, in both secondary schools and adult institutes, as well as classes for Turkish speaking adults who wanted to learn Greek. In educational documents and in interviews with senior ministry officials, all of this fitted into a rhetoric of reconciliation, and the new classes were presented as an emblem of government goodwill (C. Charalambous, 2012). These political intentions were not, however, reflected in any straightforward way either among the young people who took up the opportunity to study Turkish, or in the schools that provided it.

10.4 Students' Mixed Perceptions of Turkish

The adolescents studying Turkish had very mixed political views, and these were linked to their perceptions of Turkish and its speakers.

When we asked them whether they spoke Turkish outside class, only 16 of the 62 students that we interviewed in 2012–2013 claimed to know Turkish-Cypriots personally.[6] We asked everyone whether they would like to meet a Turkish speaker, or to know one in order to be able to practise their Turkish with them. Thirteen students (in 10 out of 21 interviews) said they did not 'want any relations with them', occasionally elaborating with expressions of dislike or hatred ('I don't like them'; 'I don't want them'; 'I wish they were effaced'). They said they did not like seeing Turks or Turkish-Cypriots in the streets, did not want to visit Turkey, and preferred to stay 'friends and apart', 'the further the better'. Such views were regularly linked back to the 1974 war and the suffering of Greek-Cypriots (15 interviews), which was described as hugely traumatic. For these students, the Turks were violators who committed great and disproportionate injustice: they felt 'bitterness' and 'hostility', because the Turks 'inflicted evil over here' – 'they are the enemy that uprooted my family'.

Other students, however, spoke of Turkish as being useful if ever there was a solution to the Cyprus problem (nine interviews out of 21): 'it's not a bad thing to learn a language that lives in Cyprus'; 'in the future we may need them, to talk wi::th-' 'Turkish girls ((*laughs*))' (Marinos & Michalis). But more positive views tended to be articulated in relatively general terms, in expressions of inter-communal goodwill or in criticisms of their own community, rather than emerging from close personal alignment with other-ethnic individuals.[7] Some drew on the distinction between 'Turks' and 'Turkish-Cypriots', shifting the blame to 'Turks': Turkish-Cypriots were 'more towards our side', 'more friendly towards us'. For others (in 12 interviews), the distinction between Turks and Turkish-Cypriots was dissolved in a regard for their common humanity and instead, the 'big actors' that take political decisions and affect the course of history – the 'state', 'people higher up', 'big interests' – were distinguished from 'simple people', including women and children, who were innocent victims. Indeed, in 12 of the interviews, adolescents voiced criticisms of their own community: 'we also did a lot, it's not only them', 'we gave them [Turkish-Cypriots] a hard time'. Those expressing views like these described themselves as 'more open-minded', 'searching things more', and they were also critical of one-sided nationalism with which they were 'brainwashed' in their families, their communities and their schools: 'there is fanaticism on both sides'.

Turning to the non-school experiences that informed these young people's perceptions of Turkish, it was clear that intergenerational relationships were very significant (cf. Section 9.5). All but seven of the 62 adolescent interviewees had crossed the border on visits to the Turkish speaking part of the island, usually only once or just a few times, and most of them made these trips with their families. They described day excursions, going around 'out of curiosity' to 'see the place' and 'see how it is', visiting major cities, religious monuments and archaeological and historical sites – visiting places that 'we had been hearing about since we were babies'. Impressed by the natural beauty but struck by what they saw as a general state of dilapidation, these visits had much more the character of pilgrimage than tourist recreation, and in 17 interviews, informants from refugee families said they visited family homes and occupied villages and towns where their parents or grandparents had lived before 1974, with very mixed reactions:

Extract 1

Interview with Panayiota. Here and in all the other extracts in this chapter, the speech is translated from Greek.

Charis:	eh whenever we go there, those who live there now are really really nice, they preserve the house very much, eh whenever we go let's say they welcome us there and they have food and invite us to go and sit, or before we leave they give us fresh vegetables they produce themselves
Yiota:	yes yes
Charis:	it depends on the character of each person, and of course how you behave to them too

Extract 2:

Interview with Panayiota.

Christi:	eh over there in the occupied areas they have brought many people from Turkey, and they are not Turkish-Cypriots, they are <u>Turks</u>, they are the bad Turks let's say, it's unacceptable for my father to go to his house and not to let him in his house, his parents' house, just to enter, not in order to take something, just to see it, to see where he used to sleep and to leave, nothing, he wouldn't bother them, this thing is absurd, to take our property like that [...] a::nd my father doesn't want to go again since then, he says this can't be, it's unacceptable

Extract 3

Interview with Panayiota.

Nikos:	becau::se they [*parents*] give you this impression before you go, tha::t it was wonderful, it was a house in the mountains, we had our chicken there, and then you see a ramshackle there, wha::t- it ruins your psychology, you change a lot, you change a lot, you go through a shock

Filippos: or when you go like with your grandmother, my mother and my grandmother and all
Nikos: yes and they cry let's say

So attitudes to Turkish and its speakers were strongly affected by the history of violent interethnic conflict, and although the language had first been introduced to Greek-Cypriot secondary education within a rhetoric of reconciliation, this was far from universally reflected among the adolescents who chose to study it. The implementation of this policy initiative also encountered a range of obstacles in schools.

10.5 Reactions and Impediments at School

Both teachers and students reported a lot of adverse reactions to their involvement with Turkish. Admittedly, the teachers told us (in 2012) that hostility to Turkey and Turkish-Cypriots had 'simmered down' since the first years when Turkish was introduced. Then, there had been damage to classrooms, anti-Turkish slogans and swear words were written on the boards in class, and there were requests in lessons for the translation into Turkish of nationalist slogans like 'a good Turk is a dead Turk'. Indeed, over the course of seven months' fieldwork in 2012, we ourselves witnessed only a few incidents of hostility from other students. But learning Turkish was not something students could pursue discreetly unnoticed – the people who had chosen Turkish were conspicuous to everyone when they all went off to different language classes twice a week – and both in informal interaction and in interviews, adolescents studying the language complained about being called 'traitors' by their peers, and about negative reactions from other teachers (see Extract 6).

The structural organisation of the language curriculum also made the provision of Turkish somewhat precarious. In 2012, there were 873 students learning Turkish in 61 classes in the Greek-Cypriot secondary system, but these were taught by just eight teachers, all Greek-Cypriot, and they worked peripatetically. Learning Turkish was not compulsory, so teachers had to recruit final and next-to-final year students in sufficient numbers to justify running these classes. Although they certainly encountered some help and encouragement from other colleagues, they often faced substantial challenges and 'institutional sabotage'. At crucial points in the options selection process, there had been lapses in government support. Although classes were approved in 2003, Turkish was omitted from the 2004 and 2006 editions of the Ministry booklet advising secondary students on their option choices; in 2007, it was only publicised in an addendum circulated belatedly to schools, and in 2010, even though it was taught as part of the foreign language curriculum, it was left out of the section on 'Foreign Languages' and presented separately. School management could also create obstacles:

Extract 4

Savvas in interview with Panayiota.

Yiota:	em:::, to what could we attribute the fact that in some schools we have 4 classes of Turkish and in others one or none?
Savvas:	there are many reasons, first it has to do with the way in which they [students] get informed by the career advisors, second, the way the school timetable organiser allows things to happen, the collaboration between the career advisor and the timetable organiser, our guidelines from the school management

And other staff could be difficult, as one of the teachers made clear in her account of 'European Languages Day', an important marketing event:

Extract 5

Stella (Turkish language teacher) in interview with Panayiota.

Yiota:	on the Day of Languages do you do anything with Turkish?
Stella:	no, and [Savvas] made a big issue of the fact that many schools say-, in their own way they tell us not to do [things][...] there was an incident this year in one Lyceum in Paphos where the teacher [of Turkish] wanted to take part as a European language and the English teachers reacted, and the philologists, "but it does not belong to the European Union", but we said "it's languages day" and so on, and they made a big issue out of it, and then the inspector called and also made an issue of why they did this to the Turkish-language teacher

So, plainly, there was rather more involved in studying Turkish than one normally associates with 'learning a foreign language at school', and issues of legitimacy – crucial to the definition of crossing – loomed very large. All this adds salience to the questions as to why students should actually choose Turkish in the first place, how they would subsequently justify their choice, and how teachers could deal with this controversy – issues to which we now turn.

10.6 Justifying the Learning of Turkish

In our interviews, the decision to study Turkish was relatively easy to explain for students who expressed goodwill towards Turkish speakers and were well-disposed to the possibility of reunification. For others (in more than half of the interviews), there seemed to be good *security* reasons for 'knowing the language of the enemy'. Some referred to war in the future, while others said that they would be able to detect if they were being insulted in the street and swear back. Indeed, even those who were quite interested in reconciliation said that this security rationale was a very good way of warding off their critics:

Extract 6

Maria (F, 17), Kostis (M, 17), Chrysanthi (F, 17) and Sokratis (M, 17) in interview with Panayiota.

Maria:	or one day [...] Mrs G. came, a historian ((*laughs*)) her nation is high up there let's say, ((*laughs*)) and she tells me "why did you choose Turkish?" and she is also my teacher, I was scared, I me::an
Kostis:	((*laughs*))
Maria:	eh I tell her "Miss, whether we like it or not Turkish-Cypriots are there, we have to learn too th-, and I have an uncle who is in the- a military officer and he tells me, 'eh to combat the enemy you have [to know his culture too, everything, you have to know everything'".
Sokratis:	you have to learn his language
Chrysanthi:	hey what mark did she give you?
Maria:	eighteen [out of 20]
Chrysanthi:	eh that's ok ((*laughs*))
Kostis:	((*laughs*))

But most often, students invoked a local language ideology that was closely connected to the exigencies of upper secondary schooling and centred on similarities between the Cypriot dialects of Turkish and Greek (cf. Hadjipieris & Kabatas, 2015). When describing the learning of Turkish, students frequently referred to shared lexis, saying that Turkish was 'very close to the Cypriot dialect that we use', we 'speak it without realizing it', 'it's familiar, it's not the first time we hear it'. This, it was said, made learning Turkish easy, along with familiar pronunciation and the readability resulting from the correspondence between grapheme and phoneme (nine interviews). Although it was very much contrary to our own and other Greek-Cypriot adults' perceptions of how hard it is to learn Turkish, the discourse of 'easiness' provided a justification that sidestepped ideological controversy, and in fact it was also actively propounded in workshops and guidelines for teachers. According to the advisory teacher for Turkish, 'the guidelines we give to the teachers during our seminars ... are "prove to them how easy Turkish is, in order for them to love the subject"'. Other teachers picked this up: 'if they have the impression that it's easy they will try and they like it ... I mean I know which bits of Turkish are difficult, eh, in those parts I will cover them painlessly let's say, so that they don't get scared' (Stella). The word was not in any of the interview questions we planned in advance, but the idea that it was 'easy' ('*efkola*') was actually by far the most commonly given reason for learning Turkish (20 interviews): 'from all languages I believe it's the easiest' (Despina); 'it's more for the marks and for the fact that it's an easy language' (Christina).

Especially in the last two years of secondary school, students were under a lot of exam pressure if they wanted to get a place at a Greek or Greek-Cypriot university. They had to study foreign languages, and choosing a language option that was easy to study could both increase their overall GPA and 'reduce workload' pressure, allowing them 'to have a lighter schedule'. There was a strong consensus that it was a good way 'to get an A' or '20', 'to have a sure mark' and, for very weak students, even 'to pass the class'. More than that, its easiness as a school subject provided students who were anti-Turkish with a good reason for studying the language:

Extract 7: Interview

Minas:	am I going to learn [the language] of our conqueror, the one let's say who is above me? I don't like this thing
Yiota:	what do you mean?
Minas:	I'm I going to sit and learn the language of the one who conquered me and has me underneath [his power] for so long let's say?
Yiota:	but you chose it [yourself]
Minas:	eh?
Yiota:	you chose it yourself
Manos:	he took it as a course
Minas:	myself, I took it as a course, for the marks let's say, a foreign language and all "all right fuck it, let's take it" but apparently I didn't take it so that I learn to speak with one or the other
Manos:	but we said that [already], it's a language, we took it in order to pass [the class], at least to learn 2-3 words to speak

So far, our account has centred on the ideological contestation associated with Greek-Cypriots learning Turkish at secondary school: strong and divided political views on interethnic relations, shaped in family history; resistance and equivocation over policy implementation in different parts of the schooling system; long-term language contact in Cyprus strategically constructed as a resource facilitating the learning of Turkish. Clearly, teaching and learning Turkish was caught in powerful ideological cross-currents and, from our description so far, its precariousness stands out more than its sustainability. Nevertheless, these classes had managed to keep running since 2003, and to get a better sense of how this was achieved it is worth turning more fully to the institutional structures and practices in which the learning and teaching of Turkish were enacted.

10.7 The Ordinariness of School Foreign Language Learning

Although the place of Turkish in the curriculum was certainly controversial and sometimes faced substantial hurdles at particular points in the academic cycle (options recruitment), there is a good case for saying that the humdrum institutional ordinariness of foreign language learning was itself significant in the promotion and sustainability of Turkish at secondary school. Curricular foreign language learning is an unspectacular but long-term and widely established activity. There is widespread international agreement that learning a foreign language is worthwhile, it is supported by professionals with subject specific expertise (language teachers), and there are well-developed grading schemes for measuring progress. With all the administrative and delivery structures already in place, the government could slot Turkish into the system by adding it as just another language to the list of Foreign Languages options (with 'foreign' also muting its identity as an official national language).

Once Turkish had appeared among the modern language options, this could then be a first cue for students to talk to their parents about whether or not Turkish could play a part in their future, even if this reached only as far as end-of-year exams and, as we have already seen, pressures from the rest of the curriculum provided a reason for selecting Turkish as the reputedly easy language option. Once they had chosen it, then twice a week, students would find themselves participating in a space where objects and practices linked with Turkish had a routine presence close at hand, and they would also need to work out how to justify their choice to others. More than that, small linguistic tokens of Turkishness would begin to circulate through the low-key everyday activities of secondary study, travelling back and forth between school and home in homework bags, figuring in anecdotes of classroom experience, getting mentioned in chat about tests and exams. According to several students, speaking in school-learned Turkish to parents who did not know the language was the only time they used it outside class, either 'for fun' or to 'teach' them a few things like '"good morning" "how are you" "what's your name"' (Areti). Indeed, there were reports of kids inspiring their parents to start learning Turkish. Katerina, for example, told us that her parents began a year after she chose Turkish at school ('they were listening to me studying a bit and they wanted to know'), and now she uses it to teach her mum: 'I was telling her some words so that she understands them, because she is English and she doesn't get it that easily so I had to explain things to her again while she was studying'. And 19 students said that they had been encouraged to take Turkish by siblings and cousins who were learning or had learnt it themselves, most often as options at school:

Extract 8: Interview

```
Yiota:     erm, do you use it anywhere?
Mariza:    yes, all the time!
Yiota:     really? where?
Mariza:    with my siblings, my cousins, we are learning foreign languages
           and we are exchanging
Despo:     me with my brother, because he used to know it, sometimes he sits
           and we spend time together talking and learning it
Yiota:     ah really?
Despo:     yes, also new words and things like that
```

Bringing Turkish home from school certainly was not always welcomed:

> we read it ((*laughs*)) I go and read my dialogues at home and she listens to me, like I read to my mum, but to my brother no, I can't [...] he doesn't want to [...] he won't let me. (Marina)

> my mum simply doesn't like it and she told me not to speak it at home but she is ok with me learning it. (Corina)

> erm ok also because they lived through the war and they had a hard time, there's no chance that they'll want to hear the Turkish language in the home, but ok. (Froso)

Even so, despite taking limited and fragmentary forms, studying Turkish at school increased the language's currency at home, embedding it in a set of home-school relationships in which parents are conventionally expected to talk to children about their subject choices, and children are supposed to engage in school tasks with the knowledge and approval of their parents. This seemed to happen in families with very different attitudes to the Cyprus problem, and *within* families it also brought out differences in perspective and/or life experience between parents and children and sisters and brothers.

But of course, all this presupposes that lessons themselves passed off without undue commotion, so at this point we should turn to the lessons themselves, bringing in Goffman's 'keying' to elaborate on our reasons for applying the notion of crossing to the students' participation in class.

10.8 Crossing in Another Key: Learning Turkish as 'Technical Redoing'

The Turkish lessons were filled with students who held very different political views, as we have seen. So how did Turkish language teachers cope? What did they do to avoid a classroom experience that was not traumatically riven by conflict?

As detailed in P. Charalambous *et al.* (2017), we identified three pedagogic strategies. In adult classes, teachers did occasionally introduce role-plays of scenes of everyday Cypriot activity with Turkish speakers, but this never happened in the secondary classes – as one teacher complained in 2006, 'how am I going to practice dialogues in the classroom between salesmen and buyers, when students are not supposed to cross to the other side and buy things from the occupied territories?' (Fieldnotes). There was also one very gifted secondary teacher who managed to 'cosmopolitanise' Turkish, repositioning it in a globalised Europe above and beyond the Cyprus problem. The most common pedagogic strategy, however, was to de-politicise the learning of Turkish by decontextualising the language, disconnecting it from Turkish people, from Turkish culture and all its political and emotional associations (see also C. Charalambous, 2013). Instead, teachers presented the language as a neutral lexico-grammatical code, and they avoided any talk about the Turks or Cypriot politics in the classroom. In fact, there is a long line of teaching that treats language as a formal code, but these teachers were aware that they were presenting a very narrow view of Turkish, explaining that they were doing this deliberately to avoid the ideological controversy around the language: 'we have to be very careful about what we say so that students don't go out and say that we are doing propaganda in favour of Turkey ... we have to be very careful and stay in matters of language' (Stella; Charalambous *et al.*, 2017: § 4.2). As a result, for the students, participation in the Turkish lessons centred on grammar and vocabulary, not culture or politics.

There were some students who participated in bi-communal networks outside school and/or had contact with Turkish-Cypriots through their families, but for the most part they kept quiet about this in their Turkish classes (see Charalambous *et al.*, 2017: § 4.3, on the exceptions). Instead, learning Turkish involved a great deal of formal grammar: verbs were conjugated; terms like 'verb', 'suffix', 'possessive', 'pronoun', 'vowel harmony' and 'hard vowels' featured in explanations; grammatical rules were dictated or written on the whiteboard; and to understand and apply the rules they were being taught, students did lots of exercises with isolated and de-contextualised sentences. Just as in any classroom, levels of interest and engagement varied from pupil to pupil and class to class, and the analysis of classroom audio-recordings points to very different styles of participation – enthusiastic, reluctant, playful, ironic, with the mainline of instructional discourse embellished or resisted with all kinds of side-talk (C. Charalambous, 2009, 2012). This mode of analysis could certainly be very productively extended in, for example, case studies of how individuals with different stances on the Cyprus issue managed their participation, or explorations of the impact of different kinds of pedagogic activity (C. Charalambous, 2013). But our argument here is that these lessons were themselves an institutional space in which crossing was the *central* activity, and that this involved everyone who signed up to the class and continued until the end of the year.

We started to make this case in our account of the ideological controversy and acute questions of legitimacy that surrounded these classes, but at this point we need to turn to the interactional characterisation of crossing provided in earlier research on adolescents in a multi-ethnic neighbourhood in the UK.

First, previous work has shown that crossing can vary a great deal in the interactional and ideological stances that it articulates, expressing respect or disdain, approval or mockery, aspiration and revulsion (Rampton, 1995/2018: Ch. 12). So this accommodates the diversity of attitudes revealed among the students here. Second, the moments and activities that sustain crossing vary a great deal in their scale and duration, from micro-activities like greetings and self-talk to larger activities like games, jocular abuse and musical performance (Rampton, 2001b: 49). So the duration of language lessons does not disqualify them as sites for crossing. Third and most crucially, earlier work has shown that crossing occurs in moments and events where the routine flow of everyday social order is loosened and normal social relations cannot be taken for granted. Crossing's occurrence in interactional spaces marked as non-routine carries the implication that the crossers are not really claiming unqualified access to the identity associated with the language they are switching into (cf., for example, Rampton, 1995/2018: Ch. 7.9, Ch. 12.4 *et passim* on 'liminality'). To explain how this partial suspension of the ordinary world is linked to the Turkish lessons, we need to turn to Goffman's notion of keying, extending the way in which it has been used in previous theorisations of crossing (cf. Rampton, 1995/2018, 2009b).

Rampton (1995/2018) identified three recurring frames for crossing in which routine assumptions about the world are temporarily problematised and partially suspended: artful performance, games and interaction rituals. But these do not fit the Turkish lessons, which were dominated by explanations, discussions and exercises focused on Turkish grammar and vocabulary (articulated for the most part in Greek). To explain how this specifically instructional encounter with (fragments of) Turkish qualifies as crossing, and to bring out the connection with earlier work, the notion of keying requires elaboration.

When acts are 'keyed', they are framed as special, non-ordinary and not to be treated naively or taken 'straight', and Goffman (1974: Ch. 3) outlines several very basic types of keying (even though they are certainly not mutually exclusive – Goffman, 1974: 79–80; Rampton, 2009b: 151). 'Make believe' is one type of keying, and this can be aligned with artful performance: it includes playful mimicry, dramatic scriptings and activity performed to entertain and engross the participants, 'done with the knowledge that nothing practical will come of the doing' (Goffman, 1974: 48–56). Games are covered by the 'contests' key – transformations of fighting in which the 'the rules ... supply restrictions of degree and mode of aggression' and, as in drama, there are 'engrossing materials which observers can get carried away with, materials which generate a realm of being' (Goffman, 1974: 56–57). The interaction rituals that support crossing can be seen as small forms of 'ceremonial' keying. Acts and events keyed as ceremonial have 'a consequence that scripted dramas and even contests do not', and rather than pretending to be someone else (as in make believe), 'the performer takes on the task of representing and epitomising himself [sic] in some one of his central social roles – parent, spouse, national and so forth' (Goffman, 1974: 58; see Rampton, 2009b, for full discussion). Crucially, Goffman also identifies a *fourth* type of keying – what he calls 'technical redoings' – and this fits the Turkish classes rather closely.

Technical redoings include activities like rehearsals, pedagogic demonstrations and 'practicings' in which

> instructor and student ... focus conscious attention on an aspect of the practiced task with which competent performers no longer concern themselves. Thus, when children are being taught to read aloud, word pronunciation can become something that is continuously oriented to, as if the meaning of the words were temporarily of little account. Indeed, the same text can be used as a source of quite different abstractable issues: in the above case, spelling, phrasing, and so forth. Similarly during stage rehearsals, proficiency with lines may come first, movement and timing later. In all of this one sees again that a strip of activity is merely a starting point; all sorts of perspectives and uses can be brought to it, all sorts of motivational relevances. (Goffman, 1974: 64)

Practising gives 'the neophyte experience in performing under conditions in which (it is felt) no actual engagement with the world is allowed, events having been "decoupled" from their usual embedment in consequentiality' (Goffman, 1974: 59). In short, technical redoings are activities which are [i] 'performed out of their usual context, [ii] for utilitarian purposes openly different from those of the original performance, [iii] the understanding being that the original outcome of the activity will not occur' (Goffman, 1974: 59, numerals added). This matches the Turkish lessons, in which the language was extracted from its sociocultural context ([i] above) and turned into something you needed in order to pass exams rather than communicate with ([ii]), thereby accommodating students who never wanted to talk to a Turkish speaker ([iii]). And just as technical redoing also allows 'all sorts of perspectives and ... motivational relevances', these culturally sterilised lessons could accommodate students who saw Turkish as a potential weapon alongside those who hoped for better interethnic relations in the future. Of course, as Goffman makes clear, technical redoings occur in many language classrooms, and this itself added to the routine institutionality that contributed to normalising the learning of Turkish. But whereas culture usually features as an important element in foreign language education (and efforts are made to provide students with authentic representations and/or experiences of everyday life in the place where the foreign language is spoken), this was deliberately avoided in the Turkish lessons (see above, as well as C. Charalambous, 2013; Rampton & Charalambous, 2016, for detailed descriptions of the adverse interactional effects produced by references to culture). In short, the inauthenticity associated with technical redoing was crucial to the viability of secondary school Turkish language teaching.

Stepping back, we can generate a broader characterisation of what was happening in these lessons if we compare them with the adult classes that we studied. In the adult classes, a substantial proportion of students said that Turkish classes provided linguistic and cultural resources that could bring them closer to Turkish-Cypriots in a journey that some of them had been travelling for a number of years. Not every adult had a strong personal investment in this, but even if they were learning for work purposes, they anticipated encountering people who spoke Turkish. Likewise, not everyone in the adult classes visited the north, and when they did, some experienced trepidation or disappointment. But adult students linked the Turkish language to Turkish speakers, and saw learning Turkish as a way of strengthening connections severed by conflict in the past. In contrast, for adolescents at secondary school, the *lessons seemed more like a tentative and precarious prelude* to the kind of commitment that Turkish involved for adults. Rather than venturing over the threshold, they were, one might say, assembling on the porch, prevaricating in the ante-chamber. Turkish was there on the table, but they had not necessarily signed up to go any further. Students who hated the idea of contact with a Turkish speaker said that they were only doing it because they had been told that Turkish was an easy subject: for students like this, even a shift from hostility to tolerance could be a step forward. And even with students who were quite positive about the language in interview, the idea of getting closer to Turkish speakers was regularly hedged with phrases like 'so far but no further', only 'up to there', 'up to that point', 'but that's about it', implying 'that's all', 'don't think there is much more than that':

Extract 9: Interview

Yiota:	((*to Phaedra*))e::rm with your Turkish-Cypriot friends do you meet on this side only o:::r
Phaedra:	yes, I don't want to go over there, I told them, I don't care, if they want to come let them come, if they don't - "stay over there, I'll never see you again" but I'm not going over there
Yorgos:	((*laughs*))
Phaedra:	((*laughs*))I don't care
Eleonora:	what a friendship man!
Phaedra:	eh that's enough, let's not overdo it

10.9 Comparison with Other Studies of Crossing

Earlier on (Section 10.2), we defined language crossing as reflexive communicative action in which a person performs specially marked speech in a language, dialect or style that can be heard as anomalously 'other', raising questions of legitimacy and entitlement. To explain why we consider Greek-Cypriot secondary students learning Turkish to be a case of crossing, we have described the background of violent conflict in Cyprus and the introduction of Turkish lessons as a reconciliatory policy initiative, its uneven reception in secondary schools, the mixed attitudes of the young people studying it, the institutional processes that at least partially normalised it, and the keyed interactional practices in class that allowed these adolescents to cross into Turkish without over-committing to improved interethnic relations. In the preceding section, we compared these Turkish language classes with the practices analysed in earlier investigations of crossing, showing how Goffman's keying applies to both. It is now worth extending this comparative discussion, showing the ways in which the crossing described here is similar to other studies in the literature in some respects, but very different in others.

Many studies have described crossing as a local practice embedded within widespread ideological contestation about changing ethnic boundaries. In Europe, for example, a substantial number of studies have focused on crossing among youth in multi-ethnic urban working-class locales where there are substantial post-war histories of labour immigration from abroad (e.g. Auer & Dirim, 2003; Doran, 2004; Hewitt, 1986; Jaspers, 2005; Lytra, 2007; Malai Madsen, 2015; Nortier & Svendsen, 2015; Quist & Jørgensen, 2009; Rampton, 1995/2018). Widespread and intense public debate about integration, racism and anti-racism form the backdrop, but the impetus for affiliative (rather than pejorative) language crossing often develops 'bottom-up' from the experience of people with different ethnic backgrounds living together in the same spaces as friends, neighbours or workmates, attending the same schools or places of work (thereby giving the lie to the racist discourses that seek to divide them). Indeed, the ethnic outgroup affiliation is sometimes so strong that there is talk of 'wannabees' and '(white) people who think they're black' (e.g. Cutler, 1999; Hewitt, 1986; Rampton, 1995/2018; Sweetland, 2002).

Compared with accounts of crossing elsewhere in Europe, the legacy of hostile division in Cyprus was much more intense and institutionalised, with roots in armed violence and Turks routinely portrayed as the traditional enemy in other parts of the curriculum (Zembylas *et al.*, 2016). Only a minority of adolescent students of Turkish had ever met a Turkish speaker, and there was no evidence of very intense cross-ethnic identification – even the most well-disposed students wanted to go 'only so far but no further'. Rather than being a bottom-up process, opportunities to learn the language were directly derived from a government policy initiative emerging in negotiations between the Greek- and Turkish-Cypriot authorities, influenced by the EU.

Studies of crossing often attend to the interplay between institutional platforms and local practices, and popular culture and the mass and social media are highly influential, promoting the kind of heterodox language mixing that features in everyday recreation on the ground (Auer, 2003: 85–90; Rampton, 1995/2018: Pt. IV). On the one hand, there are reductive stereotypes of migrant neighbourhoods and ethnic populations in circulation that can feed mockery (Androutsopoulos, 2001, 2007; Chun, 2009; Hill, 2008; Jaspers, 2005; Lippi-Green, 1997; Quist & Jørgensen, 2009: 376–377; Rampton, 1995/2018: Ch. 3; Reyes & Lo, 2009), while on the other, mediated musical cultures influence affiliative crossing and stylisation on a huge scale. African-American Vernacular English, for example, has gained global currency through hip hop (e.g. in Brazil, Greece, Germany, Tanzania, Nigeria, Hong Kong, Japan; Alim *et al.*, 2009), and as well as displaying alignment with a larger transnational community, these appropriations are also sometimes redirected towards local political struggles (Roth-Gordon, 2009; Sarkar, 2009: 153). In places like London, Hamburg and Copenhagen, crossing is also typically associated with youth and 'youth language' (e.g. Nortier & Svendsen, 2015), and it sometimes functions as a source of discomfiture to parents (Rampton, 1995/2018: Ch. 5.6). In addition, educational institutions are generally seen to pursue purist standard language policies, and this positions crossing as a 'low', 'slang', vernacular style that departs from the forms and decorums of educated language, whether this is mono- or multilingual (see Section 6.3 above).

For young Greek-Cypriots, institutional platforms were also very significant, but in sharp contrast, it was schools and teachers sponsored by the state who were crucial to their sustained encounter with Turkish, supported by specifically educational incentives and the familiar routines of secondary school study. In addition, rather than being an expression of youth culture, crossing into Turkish was embedded in a great deal of sensitive concern for the perceptions and experience of parents and older family members who had experienced the war.

Crossing and stylisation are also often closely associated with substantial changes to the traditional local vernaculars in the areas where they have been studied (see Sections 7.2 and 7.7 above). Urban vernaculars influenced by Turkish and other minority languages have been described in Germany, Denmark and Sweden (Auer & Dirim, 2003; Kotsinas, 1988; Nortier & Svendsen, 2015; Quist, 2008), while in the UK, Jamaican Creole often plays a leading role in reinvigorating non-standard English (Harris, 2006; Hewitt, 1986; Rampton, 1995/2018). For the Greek-Cypriot adolescents we studied, there was also a close link between Turkish and their local vernacular speech. But rather than being conceived as a relatively recent phenomenon associated with youth, the mixing of Greek and Turkish features in habitual speech was deeply rooted in pre-war history, and rather than indexing a resurgent multi-ethnic (or pan-Cypriot) identity, students valued this linguistic proximity within the educational logic of studying a reputedly easy language that would get them better marks.

Overall, our study addresses a number of processes covered elsewhere in the literature on crossing: interactional keying; ideological contestation over changing social boundaries; an interplay between institutional platforms and activity on the ground; indexes of intergroup contact in habitual vernacular speech. Even so, a rather different portrait of crossing emerges from our study, showing that:

- crossing can occur in situations severely affected by violent conflict as well as in multi-ethnic cities shaped by immigration;
- it can be formally promoted in education systems, not just in popular culture and informal interaction;
- it may be keyed as a 'technical redoing' rather than as 'make believe', 'contest' or 'ceremonial';
- it can be influenced as much – or more – by intergenerational as by peer group relations; and

- the interethnically significant linguistic contact attested in habitual vernacular speech may lie in the past as much as in the present and future.

Of course, in formulating this comparison, it is important to re-emphasise that ours is not a *comprehensive* study of Greek-Cypriots crossing into Turkish in Cyprus – the analysis of adult learners would produce a different and (in some ways more familiar) picture. Instead, we have deliberately chosen to report on our encounter with specific but still very substantial empirical processes that take our understanding of the interplay of linguistic form, situated interaction and ideology involved in crossing in a new direction. But what implications flow from this account of a different kind of crossing?

10.10 Post-conflict Crossing in Education and Peacebuilding

First, our case study serves to reaffirm the specificity of language crossing. Crossing is quite often associated with what Pennycook (2016) calls the 'trans-super-poly-metro movement' in studies of urban language mixing, and in this context there may be grounds for wondering whether crossing is still relevant, asking whether the potentially tense interethnic dynamics that were said to give crossing its vitality and edge have now dissolved in the convivialities of urban superdiversity. It so happens that the first detailed studies of crossing appeared at a time of growing optimism about interethnic relations in Britain, when 'new ethnicities' more at ease with difference were gaining recognition (Gilroy, 1987; Hall, 1988; Hewitt, 1986; Rampton, 1995/2018). In addition, circumstances can actually lead to the blurring and weakening of interethnic boundaries, and this can mean that crossing becomes stylisation, which can in turn become (habitual) style (Bakhtin, 1984: 199; Rampton, 1995/2018: Chs 5 & 8.5, 2015b; Chapter 7, this volume). If these two points are put together, they facilitate the inference: changing conditions have led to the disappearance of crossing, submerging it in stylisation and style. But the case of Greek-Cypriots learning Turkish shows how important it is not to confound the broader cultural ambience in one particular sociohistorical locale with the specificity of crossing itself as a discursive practice. In parts of cities in the UK, ethnicity may well be just one identity among others in interpersonal friendships, very much secondary to 'taste, life-style, leisure preferences' (Gilroy, 2006: 40, cited in Section 5.3), and in contexts of this kind, the use of someone else's ethnic language may cease to be potentially transgressive. But in Greek-Cypriot secondary schools, Turks were the traditional enemy. Ethnic difference loomed very large in the learning and use of Turkish, and far from just slipping into their ordinary speech as an index of solidary conviviality, Turkish was marked off from routine vernacular activity by all the paraphernalia of formal language learning. So, clearly, 'crossing' is not just another word for trans-/super-/poly-/metro-lingualism.

Second, the concept of crossing sensitises us to sociolinguistic dynamics that it would be easy to miss in language learning situations affected by violent conflict (e.g. Malcolm, 2009; O'Reilly, 1996; Uhlmann, 2011). If we think of these classrooms as sites of crossing rather than ordinary language learning, we are less likely to criticise the teachers for failing to meet the expectations of dominant theories like communicative language teaching. Rather than seeing these teachers as narrowly old-fashioned in their focus on the lexico-grammatical code and in their failure to introduce authentic everyday material from the real world of the target language, we can appreciate their teaching as a keyed framing, a technical redoing, that is sensitively adapted to a setting shaped within living memory by major upheaval and war, where even the idea of talking to a real speaker of the target language can be challenging. We may also wonder whether the conventional metrics of success in a foreign language can grasp the tentative and precarious exposure to the other language that such classes involve. Foreign language assessment generally only starts to notice and measure progress when someone begins to speak the language a little, or takes an interest in the culture. Measured in this way, these secondary Turkish lessons might look like a failure, since metaphorically at least we could characterise them more as 'throat-clearing' than talk itself, more like a long, deep in-breath than an actual speaking turn. The notion of crossing, however, emphasises both the significance *and* the multivalent fragility of the part that language can play in the renegotiation of group boundaries, and its framing within interactional sociolinguistics and linguistic ethnography allows us to analyse all this empirically, demonstrating the substantiality of an intersection of linguistic, interactional and ideological processes that might otherwise remain invisible.

Third, we can also look beyond education to Peace & Conflict Studies, a field of research and intervention that is centrally concerned with rebuilding relationships after large-scale conflict. Here as elsewhere in IR (Section 9.2), there is a burgeoning interest in widening the angle of vision beyond 'elite politics and highly institutionalized security practices, towards sites of routine, individual identity and especially interaction in proximity' (Huysmans, 2009: 197). There is also increasing emphasis on 'the engagement of policymakers, peacebuilders, NGOs and donors with local civil society's potential to initiate and sustain a peaceful polity in a range of different but overlapping contextual frames' (Richmond & Tellidis, 2012: 137; Charalambous *et al.*, 2021; Gready & Robins, 2014; Leonardsson & Rudd, 2015; Mac Ginty & Richmond, 2013). Ethnographic sociolinguistics can make a substantial contribution to this, with crossing playing a significant part. There is, for example, a good deal of sociolinguistic resonance in Roger Mac Ginty's (2014: 549) notion of 'everyday peace', conceived as a set of 'routinized practices used by individuals and collectives as they navigate their way through life in a deeply divided society'. These practices are 'coping mechanisms such as the avoidance of contentious subjects ... or a constructive ambiguity' (Mac Ginty, 2014: 549), they 'allow a façade of normality to prevail', they involve 'innovation, creativity and improvisation' (Mac Ginty, 2014: 555), and they are produced within an alert sensitivity to the possibility of rapid conflict escalation (Mac Ginty, 2014: 549). This is consistent with, for example, our analysis of grammar-focused Turkish language teaching and learning as 'technical redoing' – as a practice that was carefully tuned to the risk of controversy.

At the same time, however, Mac Ginty draws a sharp line between 'bottom up and local agency' and 'top-down actors, formal institutions and conflict resolutions "professionals"' (Mac Ginty, 2014: 548), suggesting that 'everyday peace' practices are the exclusive preserve of non-elite people interacting in non-formal environments. From the vantage point of our analysis of crossing in Cyprus, this division looks questionable. The avoidance and keying practices that we identified cannot be exclusively equated with informal domains: the settings we largely focused on were official ones sponsored by the state (schools and classrooms), and the dichotomisation of formal and informal itself looks fragile when there is light-hearted talk at home in Turkish imported from the classroom (or adolescents can be seen joking with friends in lessons). More generally, when Mac Ginty distinguishes between 'everyday civilities produced by local people directly affected by conflict on the one hand, and the "expert" peacebuilding discourse of expatriates, a discourse that's standardised and professionalised though "best practice" and "lessons learned"' (Mac Ginty, 2014: 551), we can agree that locals and expatriates are likely to differ in the linguistic resources they can draw on – the genres, the languages, the styles and so forth. It is also very possible that these differences themselves get politicised, and that local communicative practices are ignored or dismissed. But as Goffman's *oeuvre* makes clear, virtually everyone produces 'everyday civilities' (ritualised politeness, blame deferral, etc.), and even though peacebuilding professionals may be pressured by their overseers to adhere to scripts and rulebooks, the subtleties of communicative interaction always exceed institutional prescriptions, and there is still room for them to produce coping practices creatively adjusted to the communicative exigencies on hand, crossing included – even though, of course, their success can never be guaranteed.

In fact, in the final chapter, Goffman moves centre stage in a multimodal situated analysis of the experience of being surveilled, a process neglected both in sociolinguistics and Surveillance Studies.

Notes

(1) Although the shortcomings are our own, we are very grateful for some very helpful feedback on this paper from Alexandra Georgakopoulou, from Jenny Cheshire and Judith Irvine and from two anonymous reviewers. We also very indebted indeed to the teachers and students with whom we conducted the fieldwork. An earlier and much longer draft of the paper was posted in *Working Papers in Urban Language & Literacies* No. 240 (at academia.edu).

(2) Entitled *Crossing Language & Borders: Intercultural Language Education in a Conflict-troubled Context*, this was funded for three years by the Leverhulme Trust and it was designed as a continuation of Constadina Charalambous' doctoral project on Turkish language classes, mirroring it methodologically (see Rampton *et al.*, 2015a). Fieldwork was conducted between September 2012 and May 2013, in (a) three Lyceums (secondary schools) in different districts in Nicosia, following two teachers in six classes, and (b) in two adult institutions, following two teachers in two classes.

(3) These were assisted by NVivo 9, and included, for example, interactional analyses of selected episodes, preliminary quantitative analysis of questionnaire data, comparisons of discourses and practices in adolescent and adult classes, accounts of the place of Turkish in the wider institutional culture, and discussions of developments in policy, curriculum and the wider social setting over time.

(4) This part was declared an independent state in 1983 but it is still not recognised by the UN. The southern part of the island, inhabited by Greek-Cypriots, constitutes the government-controlled area of the Republic of Cyprus.

(5) The Republic of Cyprus is officially regarded as functioning unaltered in the government-controlled areas, with its northern part being illegally occupied.

(6) For eight of these students, the encounters had resulted from their parents' employment, particularly in the construction industry where there were a lot of Turkish-Cypriots who travelled every day to work. Six others were members of the Maronite community, an officially recognised religious minority in Cyprus, who interacted with Turkish speakers on regular visits to Maronite villages in the northern part of the island. For these students, Turkish had more the character of a bilingual community language.

(7) In contrast, a significant proportion of the adult learners maintained active links with Turkish speakers.

11 Goffman and the Everyday Experience of Surveillance[1]

(co-authored with Louise Eley)

11.1 Introduction

According to the first page of the *Routledge Handbook of Surveillance Studies*, contemporary developments in surveillance have produced 'social changes in the dynamics of power, identity, institutional practice and interpersonal relations on a scale comparable to the changes brought by industrialization, globalization or the historical rise of urbanization' (Lyon *et al.*, 2012: 1). And yet there are empirical uncertainties: '[the] effects [of surveillance] are difficult to isolate and observe, as they are embedded within many normal aspects of daily life' (Lyon *et al.*, 2012: 1; also p. 9). Comparably, Green and Zurawski argue from an anthropological perspective that Surveillance Studies tends to operate with an '*a priori* categorization of what constitutes surveillance', treating 'surveillance as so large, and such a complex set of processes, that it can best be researched and understood through its systems and structures, at the expense of attention to embeddedness in everyday life' (Green & Zurawski, 2015: 31; see also Ball, 2002, 2005, 2009; Ball & Wilson, 2000; Ball *et al.*, 2015).

In sociolinguistics, there is a long tradition of ethnographic work that examines power, ideology and social change in everyday communicative practice. This covers class, ethnicity, sexuality, gender, generation, etc. across a host of sites (including homes, communities, schools, workplaces, clinics, and mass and new media). So in principle, sociolinguistics ought to be able to contribute to the studies of everyday surveillance relations advocated by Lyon, Haggerty, Ball and Green & Zurawski, particularly if surveillance is an interactional relationship between watcher and watched, as many suggest. But somewhat remarkably, there is very little sociolinguistic research on surveillance (see, however, Jones, 2015, 2017; Rampton, 2016, 2017: 11–12).

To understand everyday experiences of being surveilled, the ambient monitoring that everyone engages in as a routine matter of course provides one obvious starting point. This is the kind of 'side-of-the-eye', 'half-an-ear' awareness of other people, objects and events that we rely on wherever we go, and there is a detailed account of how it operates in social situations in Erving Goffman's work on 'unfocused interaction' – the interaction that occurs between people who are physically co-present but engaged in separate activities, focusing on different things. In studies of surveillance, Goffman is sometimes brought into descriptions of the surreptitious practices with which people in subordinate positions transgress, resist or otherwise adjust to rules and regimes that they are unable or unwilling to follow to the letter (e.g. Ball, 2005: 96,102; Cherbonneau & Copes, 2006; Collinson, 1999; Gilliom & Monahan, 2012: 409; Helten & Fischer, 2004: 343; Jacobs & Miller, 1998; Lyon, 2007: 82, 166–167; Marx, 2009: 299; Simon, 2005: 6–8; Smith, 2007: 290, 302, 308). But notions like 'by-standing' and 'civil inattention' – key elements in unfocused interaction – hardly feature. In sociolinguistics, Goffman has had a huge influence, providing concepts that are now accepted as basic to the description of communicative interaction, and he is also a foundational influence in interactional sociolinguistics (Section 2.3 above; Jones, 2016: 37; Schiffrin, 1994: 102ff.). But both here and in adjacent fields of communication research, the overwhelming emphasis has been on what Goffman calls '*focused* interaction', in which people do things together, rather than on people carrying out independent activities in each other's presence.[2]

So in what follows, we first outline Goffman's conception of the 'interaction order', and then within that, 'unfocused interaction', a notion that treats surveillance-like activity as inextricably bound into everyday social life everywhere, regardless of the institutional domain (Jones, 2017: 170) (Section 11.2). In the three sections after that, we focus on scenes from everyday life in Germany in order to bring out the links between unfocused interaction and surveillance commonly understood as 'the focused, systematic and routine attention to personal details for purposes of influence, management, protection or direction' (Lyon, 2007: 14). Section 11.3 examines a video-recording of a woman's brief walk down the street from one shop to another, and it shows how ambient monitoring, a relatively relaxed demeanour and institutional surveillance are closely interwoven, contributing to the normalisation of surveillance. Section 11.4 shifts to two men who engage in the (mildly) illegal practice of posting up stickers, and uses data from participant observation and interviews to bring out differences in their sense of the risks from surveillance, drawing on Goffman to attempt a more systematic account of thought and action at the point of committing an offence under surveillance. This is followed by a brief discussion of the interactions with surveillance technology described in Ole Pütz's (2012) study of airport scanning (Section 11.5). These three empirical analyses are then drawn together in a rudimentary model (Section 11.6), before the final section places our account in a broader context of social change, (in)securitisation and the politics of surveillance (for an extension of this perspective beyond the surveilled to the agents of surveillance, see Heath *et al.*, 2002; Luff *et al.*, 2008; Rampton & Eley, 2018: Appendix; Smith, 2007).

Methodologically, our discussion is offered as an interdisciplinary contribution to opening up the everyday interactional experience of being surveilled (Ball, 2009: 640). In the cumulative process of comparative analysis that informs our (modest) theory building, we draw on different types of data (audio-video recordings, participation observation, interviews) as well as different studies, not just our own. But the only technical vocabulary we use is Goffman's (italicising the first use of terms that are especially significant in our analyses), and for the most part this is treated ethnographically as a framework of 'sensitising constructs', which 'suggest directions along which to look' rather than 'definitive' concepts which 'provide prescriptions of what to see' (Blumer, 1969: 148). In this way, we seek to contribute to ethnographic 'research on the constitution of surveillance relations and processes in everyday life' (Green & Zurawski, 2015: 38).[3]

With this view of the paper's scope and limitations in place, we should now turn to a sketch of the interaction order, within that concentrating on unfocused interaction.

11.2 The Interaction Order and Unfocused Interaction

Goffman's *oeuvre* roams across a plurality of empirical and documentary sources, developing a rather coherent, cumulative career-long project of analytic distillation, focusing on what he came to call the '*interaction order*' (Goffman, 1983). This involves the very basic structural arrangements, forms of attention and ritual sensitivities that arise whenever individuals are physically co-present, and his argument is that this underpins social activity everywhere. The interaction order is certainly always clothed in the kinds of cultural and institutional particularity that ethnographies describe, and these particularities have to be addressed in any empirical analysis of the interaction order. But Goffman insisted that the interaction order is only 'loosely coupled' with institutional systems, roles and relationships, social statuses (age-grade, gender, class, etc.), cultural styles and so forth (what he called 'social structure'; Goffman, 1983: 2) and, as a result, the framework of concepts he developed is unaffected by 'standard [sociological] contrast[s] between village life and city life, between domestic settings and public ones, between intimate, long-standing relations and fleeting impersonal ones' (Goffman, 1983: 2).

The interaction order has a 'body to body starting point', and it comes into operation in 'environments in which two or more individuals are physically in one another's ... presence', whether they are on their own ('*singles*') or in company (in '*withs*') (Goffman, 1983: 2). 'When individuals come into one another's immediate presence,' says Goffman (1971: 135–136), '*territories of the self* bring to the scene a vast filigree of wires which individuals are uniquely equipped to trip over'. These territories cover a variety of preserves – our bodies, our personal space, our possessions, our reputations, the information about us (Goffman, 1971: Ch. 2) – and in one another's presence, we 'become vulnerable [not only] to physical assault, sexual molestation, kidnapping, robbery and obstruction of movement', but also 'through their words and gesticulation to the penetration of our psychic preserves, and to the breaching of the expressive order we expect will be maintained in our presence' (Goffman, 1983: 4). A good deal of co-presence involves *focused interaction* (Figure 11.1) which, prototypically, arises when ratified participants come together 'in a consciously shared, clearly interdependent undertaking, the period of participation itself bracketed with rituals of some kind' (Goffman, 1981: 7). But it also extends to activities in which talk plays a secondary role, like 'card games, service transactions', etc., activities involving an audience and platform format (plays, movies, formal meetings, etc.) (Goffman, 1983: 7), quite large-scale celebratory occasions (Goffman, 1983: 7), and to mediated communication such 'telephonic connection and letter exchange' (Goffman, 1983: 6). In all these settings, participants 'share a joint focus of attention, perceive that they do so, and perceive this perceiving' (Goffman, 1983: 3).

But the interaction order also involves the presence of people (either as singles or withs) who are engaged in adjacent activity within visual range but *beyond* the circle in which one is principally occupied. Goffman calls this *unfocused interaction* (Figure 11.1). When individuals participate in focused and unfocused interaction simultaneously, orienting both to '*ratified participants*' inside particular conversational enclosures and '*bystanders*' within range (who may simply overhear parts of the talk or actively listen in as eavesdroppers; Goffman, 1981: 131ff.), their attention is necessarily divided. As well as being involved in the talk or task that is the main focus for ratified participants, they remain alert to the wider field of

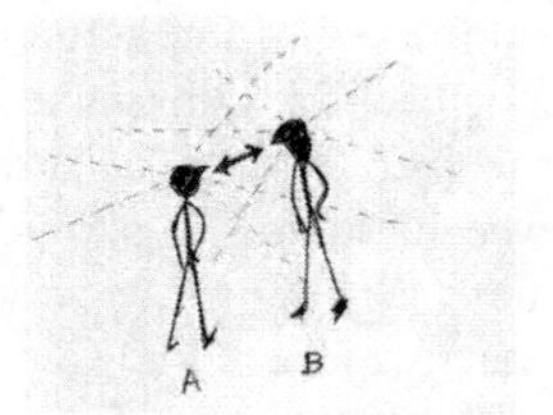

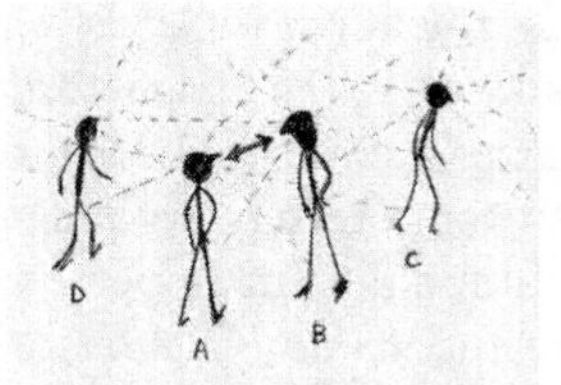

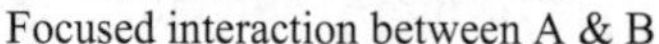
Focused interaction between A & B   Unfocused interaction between C, D & A+B

Key: ↔ : mutually ratified and reciprocated attention
- - - - : ambient awareness

Figure 11.1 Focused and unfocused interaction

'communication in the round' and, particularly in gatherings and public places, they may scan the surroundings out of the corner of their eye, checking that there is nothing nearby to alarm them (Goffman, 1971: Ch. 1). Both within and beyond the project or encounter in which they are principally engaged, people notice but actively *disattend* objects and activities that can be safely ignored (Goffman, 1974: Ch7, 1981: 132), although this distribution of involvement can shift, either gradually or suddenly, so that a person changes from 'placidly attending to easily managed matters at hand' to being 'fully mobilised, alarmed, ready to attack ... or flee' (Goffman, 1971: 282, 1981: 101–104). Within the mutual monitoring environments that constitute unfocused interaction, people also usually design their own behaviour and appearance in ways that display to others that they are not a threat themselves. As well as being able to 'transmit' linguistic signs in talk, people 'exude' information through their *body idiom*, which is open to interpretation by anyone within perceptual range (Goffman, 1970: 5–11, 1963b: 33–35). In addition, 'this kind of controlled alertness to the situation will [often] mean suppressing or concealing many of the capacities and roles the individual might be expected to play in other settings' (Goffman, 1963b: 24–25), and there are a host of *involvement shields* 'behind which individuals can safely do the kinds of things that ordinarily result in negative sanctions' – pieces of furniture, objects, items of clothing, etc. (Goffman, 1963b: 39ff, 1971: 344–345).

As well as observing these *situational proprieties* in their own body idiom, participants usually collaborate in the maintenance of a normative 'communication traffic order' (Goffman, 1963b: 24), and much of the time they do so through *civil inattention*. In civil inattention, 'one gives to another enough visual notice to demonstrate that one appreciates that the other is present ..., while at the next moment withdrawing one's attention from [him/her] so as to express that [s/he] does not constitute a target of special curiosity or design' (Goffman, 1963b: 84). But occasions do arise when civil inattention is abandoned. For a variety of reasons (acquaintanceship, business, etc.), someone may seek to transition from unfocused interaction to a face-to-face encounter, displaying to the person they are approaching that they are not a threat with an *access ritual* like a greeting. Alternatively, some violation of situational propriety may occur – someone steps on a toe, talks too loudly or drops something – and this can instigate either a *remedial ritual*, which involves a variable sequence of interactive moves like 'primes' ('oi!'), explanations, apologies, remedies, appreciations ('thanks') and minimisations ('no problem') or, alternatively, a 'run-in' if for example the source of the infraction pointedly refuses to provide a remedy (Goffman, 1971: Ch. 4, 1967a). There are also 'non-persons' – for example, children, servants and animals – who do not observe situational proprieties and are not accorded civil inattention (Goffman, 1963b: 40, Ch. 5), and there are others in *opening positions*, like police officers, who have 'a built-in license to accost others' (Goffman, 1963b: 129).

In summary, unfocused interaction involves:

(a) perceiving other people's activity from the outside, without being a ratified co-participant in the talk or task they are engaged in, and assuming that they are also aware of you;
(b) styling your appearance and bodily conduct in non-threatening ways, broadly in accordance with the proprieties of the situation;
(c) actively displaying civil inattention and a respect for the boundaries around the joint activity of 'withs' and the territories of the selves of 'singles';
(d) only shifting into a focused encounter with an access ritual that provides reassurance that the approach is non-threatening, or if some unignorable infraction is jeopardising situational proprieties.

There are a lot more subtleties in Goffman's work, but this initial sketch should be sufficient to show that he sees unfocused interaction and the ambient monitoring it entails as an ineradicable aspect of our behaviour in social situations.

How, though, is ambient monitoring in unfocused interaction linked with experiences of surveillance, defined as 'the focused, systematic and routine attention to personal details for purposes of influence, management, protection or direction' (Lyon, 2007: 14). We will explore this in the rest of the paper, and use the resources that Goffman provides to address their connection in everyday experience, beginning with data from Eley's fieldwork in the streets of Frankfurt.

11.3 Walking in a Street and the Normalisation of Surveillance

Eley's doctoral ethnography developed an interactional perspective on the regulation, perception and emplacement of signage in a large public thoroughfare in Frankfurt,[4] and the analysis here focuses on a 3 minute 52 second audio-video recording of a woman leaving one shop, going out into the street in search of another, seeing it and then crossing the road to go into it – all in all, a process that would be hard to beat in terms of day-to-day mundanity (Green & Zurawski, 2015: 40). As such, it is a good test of our ability to document some lived experience of unfocused interaction with Goffman as a guide, and in what follows we will consider the woman's humming and general demeanour, different types of ambient attention, and fleeting experience of the city traffic police, which we recorded with a tiny audio-visual device built into the spectacles that the woman was wearing. Here is a sketch of the background and the main actions recorded on the video.

Background: It's around 3pm on Friday in mid-March. The walker (henceforth 'Inge') is a middle-aged white German woman, who lived for several years in Turkey and speaks Turkish. She lives outside the neighbourhood, but likes to visit it from time to time, when 'I'll run a few errands. I'll go to Her Şey [a kiosk (not its real name)], chat with [the owner]. Buy fruit. The usual. Drink tea' (translated from Eley's conversation in German with Inge about her plans before she set off wearing the video-glasses). But Inge has not been in the neighbourhood for a while, and is looking for Her Şey because 'every time I look for Her Şey, I [can] never find it'. She starts wearing the video-glasses at around 3pm and stops at around 4pm. A video-replay discussion takes place immediately afterwards.[5]

Broad outline of actions:

27.42: Inge starts to leave the Turkish bookshop with her purchase and begins humming softly as she moves to the door. (Inge hummed when walking on other occasions during Eley's fieldwork, including when walking with Eley without the video-glasses);

27.46: turns left onto the pavement and walks along it, humming;

28.28: crosses a side road (without stopping humming);

28.46: briefly interrupts humming to comment on an Indian bakery with papered up windows: 'Oh it's closed or something. Gosh!' (translated from German here and elsewhere in the transcription of Inge's walk). Then resumes;

29.12: moves closer to the left to the shop window and slows down for 4 seconds in front of a display of Turkish books and CDs;

29.26 & 29.37: Inge has been looking across to the opposite side of the main road from time to time (28.52–29.02) and continues to do so later (29.58–30.00; 30.10–30.14), but now she stops and looks across the road for 5 seconds and then again for 8 seconds at a small shop missing a shop front sign displaying its name, with 4 men standing outside (still humming) (Inge during replay: 'there I'm looking for Her Şey'). Then carries on walking (and humming);

30.03: comments looking up at a shop: 'This is new here. Okay?'. Resumes humming;

30.23: approaches a second side road, glances left twice at a small cluster of men (two in city traffic police uniforms), momentarily stopping the humming during the first glance (see below). Crosses the side road (humming again);

30.40: moves to the right of the pavement, and while looking up and down the main road, says: '((*unclear word*)) there seen it';

30.43: crosses the main road (humming until she reaches approximately half-way, resuming when she reaches the pavement);

31.05: slows down as she approaches Her Şey's shop front, which is covered with stickers and posters, and stops humming;

31.09: stops walking for nearly 20 seconds to read a poster stuck to the wall outside, going close up to one (no humming);

31.28: moves along towards the shop door (resuming humming);

31.30: turns right through the door, sees the shop-owner close at hand, and slips straight from humming to a greeting.

There are important clues to Inge's shifts of attention and experience of the surroundings in the humming that she keeps up for most of the walk, stopping at particular moments, and Goffman facilitates three observations.

First, Goffman sees humming as a 'side involvement', one among a number of activities that 'an individual can carry on in an abstracted fashion without threatening or confusing simultaneous maintenance of main involvement. Humming while working, knitting while listening' (Goffman, 1963b: 43, 70; Rampton, 2006: Ch. 3). This fits the video: Inge's main involvement is finding Her Şey, but she drops her humming when she refers out loud to changes that she notices (the shops that have closed and opened since her last visit [28.46; 30.03]), as well as when she stops outside Her Şey to look at a poster (31.09) – in other words, she stops humming when particular things catch or require her closer attention.

Second, whereas full-voiced singing would draw attention, the softness of her humming is consistent with situational propriety and the display of civil inattention. This kind of private orientation to music (and other auditory artefacts) involves an 'inward migration from the gathering': '[w]hile outwardly participating in an activity within a social situation, an individual can allow [their] attention to turn from what [they] and everyone else consider the real or serious world, and give [them]self up for a time to a playlike world in which [they] alone participate' (Goffman, 1963b: 69). Third, Inge's humming suggests that she feels relatively safe in the street, presupposing an environment that does not demand full alertness, where she can 'placidly attend to easily managed matters at hand' (Goffman, 1971: 282). There is, though, one episode relevant to *institutional surveillance* when this situation seems marginally less stable.

As Inge approaches the second side road, a man, who has just crossed it and is walking towards her, briefly turns his head right to look down the side road (30.18, see Figure 11.2), looks ahead again, and then glances back once more (30.19). He passes Inge on the inside of the pavement, and then as she moves closer to the corner with a view down the side road, she also turns her head to look down the side road. A group of three men standing and talking come into view, one of them behind a pedestrian barrier (30.22, see Figure 11.3). Two are in city traffic police uniforms, one with arms folded (behind the barrier), the other with hands held behind his back, while the un-uniformed man has his hands in his pockets. Another pedestrian, who had been walking ahead of Inge and has turned

Figure 11.2 Oncoming pedestrian turning head right to look down side road (circled). (A slightly clearer colour photo can be found online open-access in Eley & Rampton, 2020 (Surveillance & Society 18/2 https://doi.org/10.24908/ss.v18i2.13346).)

Figure 11.3 The scene recorded by the video-glasses at the moment when Inge is turning her head down the side-street and stops humming

Note: The two uniformed men are marked out with the darker oval ring, the un-uniformed man with his hands in his pockets is marked with the lighter one, and the pedestrian glancing back is marked with the circle. (A slightly clearer colour photo can be found online in Eley & Rampton, 2020.)

down the side road, can be seen glancing back in the direction of the group. As the threesome come into view, Inge stops humming for about 2 seconds (30.22–24). She then resumes the tune, turns her head back to the direction she's going (to avoid the bollard ahead, 30.26), but then looks back down the side road once more for a couple of seconds, with the group of three to the left of her vision. After that, she turns her head back in the direction she's going, humming and walking forward across the side road.

So what can we learn from all this about ambient monitoring and experiences of surveillance in unfocused interaction? To answer, we can first focus on the walker, turning to studies of surveillance afterwards.

The video we have described lasts less than four minutes, but it provides quite a rich sociocognitive view of Inge's fluctuating and multi-track attention to the circumstances around her (cf. Goffman, 1974: Ch. 7). Her overall *intention* is to locate and reach Her Şey, and the video captures her actively looking, walking forwards and from time to time *scanning* the opposite side of the road, at one point stopping for over 10 seconds to look more closely (29.26; 29.37). There are also moments of *noticing* when she slows down (29.12; 31.05), stops (31.09) or comments (28.46; 30.03; 30.40) near things that catch her attention and speak to her cultural interests (in Turkish culture, in the poster at the kiosk which she thought was advertising a reading/exhibition, in the changing neighbourhood). For much of the time, she is '*away*' in the tune that she is humming, although she does this in a way that displays respect for the situation (Goffman, 1974: 345). In fact, she passes more than 20 pedestrians coming towards her on the pavement without any problem, and in doing so she employs a '*dissociated vigilance*' that 'provide[s] a running reading of the situation, a constant monitoring of what surrounds ... out of the further corner [of the] eye, leaving the individual [her]self free to focus [her] main attention on the non-emergencies around [her]' (Goffman, 1971: 282). Of course the passers-by also contribute to avoiding collision, mutually monitoring and adjusting their own paths as well (Goffman, 1971: 28; Haddington *et al.*, 2012: ¶40–42, 47; Ryave & Schenkein, 1974).

But beyond the different kinds of (often simultaneous) awareness displayed in Inge's practices, what about her experience of organised institutional surveillance? There is a no-smoking sign on the door of the bookshop that she leaves and, as Jones (2017: 154) notes, this implies that 'someone ... is watching ... to make sure that [customers] do not engage in these prohibited activities'. But in the recording, it appears only very briefly at the edge of the screen – Inge does not appear to pay any attention to this on the video (and does not light up when she gets outside). Nor does she look up at any of the CCTV cameras that she passes.[6] It is most likely that both types of surveillance are just taken for granted, but this is *not quite* the case with the two uniformed employees of the city traffic police she passes, even though their 'opening position' means that they might also be taken for granted. Here it looks as though she is alerted to something non-normal by the two rightward glances of the pedestrian coming towards her, and she appears to pay greater attention to the scene with the traffic police when she glances towards the group for four seconds (30.22–30.26), momentarily stops humming (30.22–30.24), and then looks back for two seconds as she moves past (30.26–30.29). But that is it. The body idiom of the three men suggests nothing untoward (arms folded, hands clasped behind back, hands in pockets); 'as the individual moves, some potential signs for alarm move out of effective range (as their sources move out of relevance)' (Goffman, 1971: 301); and 'the actions of passers-by form a chain of embodied events that signal and help maintain normalcy' (Haddington *et al.*, 2012: ¶35) – the oncoming pedestrian whose sideways glancing Inge copied did not look unduly concerned, and nor does anyone else. All in all, the official surveillance-supported-by-organisations here seems to be inextricably interwoven with the routine practices of unfocused interaction that everyone performs in Inge's vicinity.

If we turn to the literature in surveillance studies, this account of the subjective experience of surveillance is very broadly compatible with the phenomenological approach suggested by Friesen *et al.* (2009) and Ball

(2005: 96–98, following Crossley, 1995, 2001), addressing 'lived space, lived time, lived body, lived human relations' and 'a-thematic consciousness' ('awareness that is not intellectual, interpretive or deciphering') (Friesen *et al.*, 2009: 85, 88). But as an empirical method, the introspectively generated narratives that Friesen *et al.* recommend are unlikely to be able to capture the synchronised interplay of physical movement, built environment, body idiom, gaze and vocalisation recorded in the 10 seconds of video in which Inge oriented to (non-)events with traffic police down the side street. Indeed, more generally, the narratives produced in interviews are likely to have quite serious limitations as sources of insight into the lived experience of surveillance. This is because narratives tend to dwell on what is tellable (and often a little bit more dramatic), thereby missing the mundane unremarkable-ness of surveillance in a scene like the one that Inge experienced during her walk (cf. Green & Zurawski, 2015: 28, 31). And yet it is essential to address this humdrum ordinariness if we are interested in the *normalisation* of surveillance (Lyon *et al.*, 2012: 1). In fact, the combination of Goffman and an audio-video recording like this allows us to spotlight the very practices with which the normality of surveillance is produced and maintained – mid-afternoon on a Friday for Inge.

But of course our account has been closely tuned to the experience of one particular person, a respectable middle-aged white woman. The links we have made to Goffman show that this case is not utterly idiosyncratic, but even so, experiences of surveillance differ considerably, and it is worth now turning to a case study of two people with everyday interests that bring them closer to the borders of legality. In the process, we will develop another angle on how surveillance is experienced, and start build to a model to represent this.

11.4 Posting up Stickers and the Experience of Feeling Surveilled

It is a civil offence in Frankfurt to post up stickers (small pieces of adhesive material carrying text and/or images) in the street, and the local authorities and public transport operators employ cleaners to take them down. Eley's PhD fieldwork included a number of individuals and groups who regularly put up stickers in the neighbourhood she was researching (which also had more CCTV cameras than any other part of the city). While some engaged in stickering for fun, because they liked particular stickers and enjoyed seeing interesting or amusing ones around, others used them in social, political and commercial projects that they were committed to, and their stickers carried messages about welcoming migrants, new musical outlets and so forth (cf. Eley, 2018). In both categories, people said that they liked to have some stickers ready in their pockets whenever they went into the streets. We did not video anyone placing stickers, but we asked about and/or observed the process, and it is worth comparing what two of them told us.

Adnan was in his late 20s, was born in Turkey, came to Germany as a child, now ran a small business, and put up stickers if he liked the political message or found them entertaining. Talking about putting up stickers on trains, he said:

> Yeah because vandalism is anti-social ((laughs)). It's vandalism vis-à-vis the City … There are cameras everywhere … Yeah or ticket inspectors are there. (translated from German)

And he explained how he actually posted them up (Figure 11.4):

> Just like that, put it in your hand … Sticker is here, you hold it so like ((bends fingers inwards to cup hand, traces with other hand the rectangle shape of the sticker)) you take the backing away and ((stretches arm out as if leaning with hand against surface)) … Looks as though it was already there. (translated from German)

In Goffman's terms, Adnan was using his hand as an 'involvement shield', concealing the sticker and disguising his action as a mundane stretch or lean.

James, also in his 20s, was born in the UK but spent a lot of his time growing up abroad. During a stay in Frankfurt he became increasingly involved in a third-sector organisation and remained in the city,

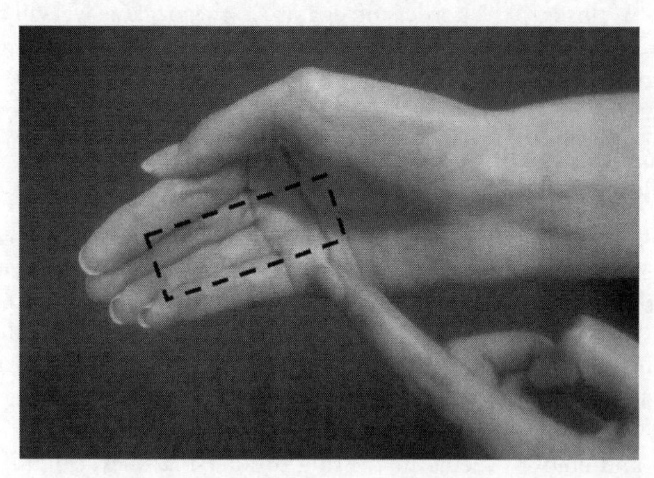

Figure 11.4 Preparing to place a sticker covertly (not demonstrated by Adnan)

supporting himself by working as a waiter. His stickers promoted the work, projects and politics of the organisation, and when we asked him about stickering, he said:

> no I don't care about cameras, a lot of people care about cameras, I don't ... like I don't think anybody is gonna look at a camera twenty-four hours and even if they see somebody sticker something they're like okay, like if you go graffiti something maybe be a bit more wary, but a sticker like yeah it's not much (original language)

And here is Eley's field diary about walking with him from one of his organisation's events to the nearest tram stop:

> James left a trail of stickers along the route that we walked. While he walked, he took the backing from the back of the stickers and placed them on objects along our path, including two bollards, and he left one unstuck on a car. He appeared calm and unconcerned with who may be watching him, not looking around or over his shoulder at all, for example to see if CCTV cameras or any individuals were watching him. He took care and time to place the stickers straight, by holding them at the corners, and then wiped his hand over the top to stick them securely.

There are obvious differences in James's and Adnan's approaches to being surveilled, and Goffman's account of the remedial interchanges that sometimes turn unfocused into focused interaction helps to systematise them. In remedial interchanges, says Goffman, it is important to distinguish between (a) an act, (b) its categorisation or not as an offence, and (c) the interaction following the act in which the moral status of the act and its perpetrator is negotiated (Goffman, 1971: 99, 102, 106). So when, for example, a person does something that appears to breach situational propriety ('the deed'), people in the vicinity are likely to display some concern, and it is how the actor then responds to their display – whether or not s/he appears repentant, convincingly disowns it, etc. – that determines whether the deed is deemed 'inoffensive' and normal order is restored, or whether further sanctions need to be pursued. Both Adnan and James are committed to the act of stickering, but in Adnan's account, bystanders and CCTV watchers would object to the act and initiate an interaction that could lead to sanctions. Adnan's concealment strategy was not only designed to hide the act but also to provide him with a ready denial if held to account ('the sticker was already there'). In contrast, James did not think that anything could happen (no-one would be watching CCTV, and stickering was not serious enough to pursue). But he did imagine other people reacting to his stickers, and this influenced where he placed them: he did not put them up on surfaces belonging to local and migrant-run businesses as 'they're ... in the same bracket as us who are working class. They're the people we wanna get on our side'. So overall, James worried less about being spotted doing something illegal than about creating a bad impression on people that he did not want to alienate. Comparing the two, Adnan's concerns were much more immediate – being seen committing the act and being accused of an offence – and their differences are laid out in Table 11.1.

It is likely that this difference reflects, at least in part, differences in their experiences of racialised insecuritisation. On other occasions, Adnan referred to racial profiling in his encounters with security personnel and police stop-and-searches, and we discuss the wider implications of this in Section 11.7. But staying with the close-up exploration of experiences of surveillance while stickering for the time being, we can bring in Goffman's notion of the *Umwelt* to differentiate Adnan's perspective from James's. The *Umwelt* refers to 'the sphere around the individual within which ... potential sources of alarm are found' (Goffman, 1971: 297), and when stickering, Adnan's sense of *Umwelt* threats was quite pressing. We cannot say for sure whether James's *Umwelt* orientation was closer to Inge's than Adnan's when he was posting up stickers, but if we bring Inge back into the account, we can differentiate experiences of surveillance more clearly.

As Inge walked down the street, there was a 10-second period when the gaze direction of another pedestrian and the sight of a scene in which

Table 11.1 Comparison of how Adnan and James anticipate the act of stickering leading to remedial interchanges

(a)	*Who could observe the act and/or its outcomes, when?* Adnan: CCTV cameras and ticket inspectors – now, during the emplacing. James: Nobody will be looking at the CCTV; later on, local business and car owners, cleaners.
(b)	*What would they think of it?* Adnan: CCTV operators & ticket inspectors – vandalism. James: CCTV operators – too minor to pursue; local car & business owner – a nuisance, requiring time-consuming removal; cleaners – a work task.
(c)	*What actions would they be likely to pursue if they spotted the act?* Adnan: CCTV operators & ticket inspectors – they'd pick you out and intervene, now or later. James: CCTV operators – nothing; locals – scrape off the stickers, and think badly of the project being publicised; cleaners: scrape them off.
(d)	*What are the implications of all this for here-and-now performance of the act?* Adnan: Conceal the act of stickering, and be ready with a disclaimer. James: Ignore the CCTV and carry on stickering as normal; don't post stickers up on local businesses, or use adhesive on local cars; put them on surfaces that cleaners seldom work on.

there were uniformed men drew her attention, but there was no inkling of any untoward event, transgressive act or perpetrator. More generally, other than the cars, oncoming pedestrians and street furnishings that her dissociated vigilance helped her to avoid, there was little sense that Inge was watching out for particular threats or types of people who were likely to draw her into remedial interchanges. This was ambient monitoring in unfocused interaction, running along with a respectfully conducted side-involvement (humming), interspersed with noticings and scannings in search of her destination.

There was much more than dissociated vigilance or being 'away' in the stickering conduct that Adnan described. Rather than operating like Inge with a generalised awareness of whoever happened to be in the vicinity, Adnan was alert to the threat from very particular social types when he posted a sticker up – officials nearby or behind the CCTV – and he engaged in fabrication: 'an intentional effort ... to manage activity so that ... others will be induced to have a false belief about what it is that is going on' (Goffman, 1974: 83). His actions appeared to take a determinate shape that he was able to reflect and report on, and if we combine this with concepts offered by Goffman, we can suggest a general structure for the experience of surveillance that Adnan described:

(i) the experience starts when an individual considers carrying out an act that they know is sometimes regarded as an offence;
(ii) s/he reckons with the *Umwelt*, and imagines co-present observers who are likely to see her/his act as an offence, to view him/her as a suspect, and to initiate particular kinds of remedial sequence (see Table 11.1);
(iii) s/he decides whether to abandon the act or go ahead with it, concentrating on body idiom to conceal it if they opt for the latter;
(iv) the experience ends either when he/she moves out of range of the observers and relaxes, or when the surveillers declare themselves, maybe in uniform or through a public address system, at which point some kind of synchronous focused interaction takes over (an arrest, a remedial interchange, etc.).[7]

As a shorthand for this kind of experience of surveillance, with its heightened but disguised concern with surveilling bystanders, we can refer to Adnan's only-apparently unfocused conduct as 'crypto-focused' interaction under surveillance, distinguishing this from the fluid and multi-track ambient monitoring in unfocused interaction that we saw with Inge on the one hand and, on the other, the kind of focused encounter with officials that Adnan's targeted concealment seeks to evade.

Adnan's conduct broadly matches the accounts of deception that feature most commonly when Goffman is cited in surveillance studies, but we have elaborated it here within a fuller account of unfocused interaction. Indeed, Goffman's framework can also be extended to at least some of the everyday practices that arise when human bodies intersect with surveillant technologies, at 'the surfaces of contact or interfaces between ... lifeforms and webs of information, ... between organs/body parts and entry/projection systems' (Bogard, 1996: 33, cited in Ball, 2005: 94; also Ball, 2005, 2009; Ball & Wilson, 2000; Lyon, 2007: 164; Simon, 2005: 17). This is demonstrated in Ole Pütz's ethnographic study of scanning at an airport security checkpoint, which is briefly discussed in the next section.

11.5 Close-up Interaction with Surveillance Technology

Pütz focuses on the brief but highly standardised process of preparing for an airport security check, stepping through a metal detector scanner, and being patted down by security staff if the scanner raises the alarm (Pütz, 2012: 164). This is a situation in which it is hard for travellers to ignore the fact that they are being actively surveilled as a potential security threat, but Pütz details the ways in which everyone intensifies the effort to act as if nothing untoward is happening. He notes that the closer passengers come to the checkpoint itself, the quieter they become, dropping conversation and turning off their cell phones (Pütz, 2012: 172). Individuals enter the walk-through metal detector one at a time and 'if the scanner detects metallic objects, screeners must identify who raised the alarm and pat this traveller down to locate the source of the alarm on [their] body' (Pütz, 2012: 168). At this point, Pütz brings Goffman into the analysis, and proposes that this patting-down potentially violates the travellers' personal space (cf. 'territories of the self' in Section 11.2). But the screeners and travellers conduct this 'breach of personal space in a way that reduces the social implications of bodily proximity' (Pütz, 2012: 173). The screeners use a hand metal detector ('a lifeless technical object'); they wear gloves so there is no skin to skin contact; and they avoid 'private parts and do ... not linger long on any part of the body' (Pütz, 2012: 173). The travellers who are stopped and patted down 'avert their eyes while being patted down and focus visually on a point in the middle distance. They thus minimise the appearance of [focused] interaction, because eye contact is a clear indicator of [this] ... [But they] do not fully avert the eye or stare dreamily into space; they are able to observe the situation out of the corner of the eye and stay cooperative' (Pütz, 2012: 173).

In Goffman's terms, this seems to be one of those '"blind" transactions in which persons come together to accomplish a joint activity but do not bracket this spate of mutual coordination ritually, that is, do not sustain a social encounter', which would involve 'an exchange of words or other recognition rituals and the ratification of mutual participation in an open state of talk' (Goffman, 1971: 97, also 1963b: 88ff.). Pütz uses the notion of civil inattention (cf. Section 11.2) to explain the participants' conduct at the scanner, and in fact remedial interchanges are also potentially relevant, since at this particular point of the security process, the unstated question motivating the scanning of bodies (and personal possessions) is: 'Do you carry weapons or contraband which is a source of risk?' (Pütz, 2012: 169). This question is in principle potentially offensive to travellers, casting doubt on their character, and this may also contribute to the de-personalising avoidance strategies that Pütz outlines (Pütz, 2012: 175).[8]

This airport scene obviously differs in a number of ways from our characterisation of stickering. The surveillance technologies work differently: CCTV scans the street and picks out individuals, often differentiating them by age, ethnicity and gender as well as activity and appearance, whereas the step-through substance detector at the airport is used on all of the passengers, regardless of social and personal identity. Stickerers vary in their interpretations of potential reactions to their acts of sticker emplacement, whereas in the airport scanner, a standardised interpretation of *Umwelt* risks takes over and governs everyone's behaviour. And their orientations to remedial interchanges are different: the stickerers wanted to avoid them, whereas airport passengers are already drawn into a remedial sequence, positioned as suspects and probed with technologies that investigates whether they are carrying material they should not be carrying. Even so, it looks as though Goffman's account of unfocused interaction, remedial interchanges and the *Umwelt* are relevant to both.

11.6 Surveilled Experiences: A Rudimentary Model

Our discussion of scenes from everyday life has tried to show that Goffman's work provides a multitude of empirical 'entry points' into the (inter-)subjectively lived experience of surveillance, in all its 'ubiquity and relative normalization' (Lyon *et al.*, 2012: 9). Pütz characterises the airport scanning process as a 'non-event' because it does not acknowledge the passenger as an individual (Pütz, 2012: 158), and if we accept this, we can use Goffman to develop the following schematisation of the experiences of surveillance that we have considered. So to begin with, we have:

- *focused* interaction, which we can see, for example, whenever security staff abandon their surveillant position as overhearers/eavesdroppers and engage the (erstwhile) surveilled in a mutually acknowledged encounter such as a remedial interchange (as in stop-and-search). Alternatively, the (formerly) surveilled act up to the cameras (Smith, 2007).

Then we have:

- *unfocused* interaction, exemplified by Inge's ambient awareness, her ease in an *Umwelt* characterised by normal appearances, doing nothing likely to provoke a remedial sequence, displaying only a very fleeting interest in uniformed personnel, taking surveillance for granted for the rest of the time;
- *crypto-focused* interaction under surveillance, involving the appearance of unfocused interaction even though the actor's attention and actions are directed towards co-present observers. This was Adnan, concealing his activity from the CCTV and uniformed personnel that he was now more acutely aware of, and was keen to avoid any remedial engagement with;

and lastly with Pütz:

- *non-focused* interaction under surveillance, involving surveillers and surveilled in a collaborative refusal to initiate a ritually ratified engagement, already finding themselves in a highly standardised remedial interchange, with the surveilled seeking to relinquish the status of suspect as soon as possible.

The lines between these four types of interaction are obviously porous – un-, crypto- and non-focused interaction can swiftly become focused, crypto- can slip back to unfocused, and so forth. And this list certainly is not offered as a comprehensive typology. But it does show that Goffman's framework allows rather a differentiated account of the experience of surveillance, and with recognition of this in place, a number of more general points are in order.

11.7 Implications

Our account of Goffman speaks to at least four issues in the wider discussion of surveillance.

First, it reaches beyond Lyon's (2007: 14) widely cited definition of surveillance as 'the focused, systematic and routine attention to personal details for purposes of influence, management, protection or direction', and connects instead with Green and Zurawski's (2015: 29) interest in surveillance 'as one form or mode of the social, becoming apparent in other activities and practices, something that is created, performed and perceived as such (in all its technical, discursive and interactional modes) – or not'.

Lyon's canonical definition addresses modes of attention, the objects attended to and the purposes guiding this attention, but it skirts over the two-way dynamics of interaction and the relationship between watcher and watched. In contrast, to get closer to the experience of being surveilled, we have brought interactional relations into the account, concentrating on 'unfocused interaction' in Goffman's specialised sense. Unfocused interaction involves: being alert to others beyond the task or encounter that you are focused on, and knowing you are also visible to them; styling your conduct and outward appearance to conform to the proprieties of the situation, restricting intrusive gazes either way with civil inattention; and shifting to direct engagement only if you can display benign intent or there is some un-ignorable infraction. Most if not all these forms of awareness, practices and concerns seem fundamental to sociality, and in the three case studies that we have cited, we have seen how different ways of enacting unfocused interaction contribute to the normalisation of institutional surveillance, as well as to the ways in which sharper experiences of being surveilled are differently configured. In Green and Zurawski's discussion of the ethnography of surveillance, one of the central questions is: can surveillance be approached as a basic 'mode of the social' that is elaborated in different ways in different environments (Green & Zurawski, 2015: 29, 35; Simon, 2005)? Our answer is an unequivocal 'yes'.

Whereas institutionalisation and power stand out in Lyon's definition ('systematic,' 'purposes of management, protection or direction'), a Goffmanian approach to surveillance foregrounds the relations between people along with the activities that connect them. In doing so, it provides more scope to investigate the *emergence* of surveillance in a range of different settings. Obviously, in settings like the airport security checkpoint, the surveillance is very well established and the roles are relatively fixed. But in principle, an approach centred on interactional relations can also cover much less systematic cases that participants themselves might not call 'surveillance' (Green & Zurawski, 2015: 28–29, 34–35) – cases where there is less sophistication in the 'targets' (children or next-door neighbours for example), in the technological supports (e.g. net curtains), in the ideas of who could observe and what is looked for (e.g. late arrivals home), and in the reporting activities (reprimands, gossip, etc.). With Goffman, we can address the question of what 'counts' as surveillance in the context of people's actual experiences. His work on unfocused interaction provides a foundational framework for grasping the vital details of the particular ways in which people enact vigilance to outsiders, to the surroundings, to situational propriety and body idiom in particular environments. And how people feel about any particular relationship between watcher and watched – whether it is sensed as oppressive, intrusive, necessary, acceptable, normal or nothing of note – is subject to the kinds of variation we have described.

Second, building on Adnan's account of racial profiling, Goffman provides a path into the everyday experiences of what Bigo (2008) calls the 'banopticon', the politically cultivated suspicion and surveillance of migrants and minorities that has intensified since 9/11 in many parts of the West (and elsewhere) (see Chapter 9). The experiences and enactments of surveillance that we have considered are themselves influenced and informed by prior knowledge, experience and discourses in society, and in Mangual Figueroa's (2020) formulation, regardless of their actions, certain types of people physically '*embody* the breach' that surveillance watches for. As a result, 'what for some people are practices relatively free of precarity, such as walking down the street, are, for others, sites of constant uncertainty in which at any moment they might be detained, accosted, searched, or even shot by the very agents of state security that promise to keep them safe' (Jones, 2020a: 94–95). It is not difficult to bring these broader characterisations back to the kinds of interactive experience we have described. Goffman (1963a: 70) recognised that 'whether we interact with strangers or intimates, we will find that the fingertips of society have reached bluntly into the contact, even here putting us in our place'. In interactional sociolinguistics, there are well-developed accounts of how circumambient ideologies infuse activity in the here-and-now, explaining how a person's prior knowledge and experience of (in)securitised environments could inform their situated interpretation of the *Umwelt* on hand. And as we have argued, differences in Adnan's and James's experiences of racialised insecuritisation are likely to account (at least in part) for the differences in their perceptions and experiences of surveillance while stickering, as well as in their fleeting in-the-moment anticipations of remedial interchanges.

Following on from this, third, Goffman's recognition that mutual monitoring is a fundamental part of human sociality is also relevant to recent reappraisals of Foucault's emphasis on the mono-directionality and non-mutuality of surveillance (Foucault, 1977: 200),[9] as well as to growing interest in the role of agentive practice in surveillant relationships. So, for example, contemporary technologies like digital phone cameras enable '*sous*veillance', in which subordinates 'watch back' at the surveillers who hold institutional power over them, recording and publicising their conduct (Jones, 2020). Alternatively, in online 'social surveillance' by friends and family on social media, 'each participant is both broadcasting information that is looked at by others and looking at information broadcast by others' (Marwick, 2012: 379). Goffman certainly wrote a great deal about people being the 'object[s] of information', as in Foucault's conception, but his starting assumption was that monitoring is *mutual* even though people's agendas, resources and constraints might be very different. Without this starting assumption, it would be easy to miss, for example, the mutual monitoring practices that contributed to the normalisation of institutional surveillance during Inge's walk in a street, as well as the ways in which security personnel and travellers collaborate in the production of unfocused interaction at the airport scanner. Turning to questions of agency, Haggerty argues that studies of surveillance need to attend more to the activity of the governed: 'while governance inevitably involves efforts to persuade, entice, coerce or cajole subjects to modify their behaviour in particular directions, the targets of governance are understood to be a locus of freedom ... subjects as active agents' (Haggerty, 2006: 40). As Haggerty suggests, some of this agency may be expressed in 'resistance, avoidance or subversion' (Haggerty, 2006: 40), but these terms themselves cover a host of intricate practices, and they overlook a multiplicity of other possibilities, including those we could loosely gloss as 'acceptance', 'cooperation' and 'normalisation'. The subtlety of practices like these does not mean that they are rare – on the contrary, they are very ordinary and all the more consequential because of it.

Finally, remaining with the subtlety of such practices, we can use Goffman's framework to interrogate large-scale generalisations about surveillance, such as the claim that 'technological innovations fundamentally alter the organisation, practice and effects of surveillance relationships' (Simon, 2005: 1), changing 'the dynamics of power, identity, institutional practice and interpersonal relations on a scale comparable to ... industrialization, globalization or the ... rise of urbanization' (Lyon *et al.*, 2012: 1, cited above). If some of the practices and relations that Goffman described in embodied, offline interaction can be found in technologically mediated surveillance, then surveillance before and after technological change can be compared, examining the alteration more closely. All the cases we have discussed involved at least partly embodied interaction, but the concepts we have used are also relevant to surveillance in entirely web-based communication (Jenkins, 2010), such as between peers on social media.[10] Off- and online communication are obviously different, but with Goffman, we can investigate the differences with more specific questions, such as: What semiotic strategies and resources take the place of body idiom in displays of situational propriety in online gatherings? How far and in what ways does digital platform architecture provide new or different resources for concealing negatively sanctionable acts ('involvement shields') and so forth (cf. Westlake, 2008)?

In sum, especially if it is supported by methodological frameworks like interactional sociolinguistics and linguistic ethnography, Goffman's *oeuvre* provides a foundational vocabulary for understanding the dynamic interactional enactment of surveillance and for grasping – empirically – its hugely varying significance in everyday life.

Notes

(1) We are very much indebted to discussion with Emma Mc Cluskey and Constadina Charalambous.

(2) In ethnomethodological and conversation analytic micro-sociology, there is a growing body of work that uses video-recordings to look at how people interact on the move in public places (visiting museums, walking, driving, cycling), but intentional communication remains the central concern, whether this is person-to-person or mediated by material texts or objects (Haddington & Raunioma, 2014; Kendon, 1990; McIlvenny *et al.*, 2014; Mondada, 2009, 2016: 347ff.; but see Haddington *et al.*, 2012; Hindmarsh *et al.*, 2001: 18–19; Liberman, 2013; Ryave & Schenkein, 1974; vom Lehn *et al.*, 2001: 203–207). In sociolinguistics, there is also a body of research that examines public signage in 'linguistic landscapes', and this now extends beyond the analysis of verbal and visual text to a view of how people interact around signs, moving through space (Scollon & Scollon, 2003). This is certainly one significant source of nascent sociolinguistic interest in surveillance (Eley, 2018; Jones, 2017; Kitis & Milani, 2015; Stroud & Jegels, 2014), but even so, the potential significance of Goffman's account of *un*focused interaction for understanding surveillance remains largely unexplored.

(3) We recognise that surveillance takes many forms (Green & Zurawski, 2015: 29; Haggerty, 2006; Walby, 2005: 158) and at least two dimensions of surveillance fall outside our concerns here: 'dataveillance' and the administrative design and management of information about individuals (Lyon, 2007: 23; Simon, 2005: 4; van Dijck, 2013a), and the surveillance that is pervasive in focused interactional encounters with bureaucracy (cf. Ball *et al.*, 2015). Some observations about these can be found in Rampton and Eley (2018: notes 28 & 31).

(4) Eley (2018); see also Blommaert (2013a), Jones (2017), Scollon and Scollon (2003), Stroud and Jegels (2014).

(5) Eley was not in audio contact with Inge during the walk, and did not follow her.

(6) Judging from Eley's photographs of the street, there are at least three CCTV cameras that she walks past.
(7) There is another possibility: the surveilled address the surveillers, turning them into an audience – see Smith (2007: 293–294, 299).
(8) Rampton and Eley (2018: § 5) elaborate the possibilities in more detail.
(9) Foucault's account of surveillance focused on the 'panopticon'. Although it was never built, the panopticon was a prison designed in such a way that the inmates would know that everything they did could be watched by unseen guards, without ever knowing when this was actually happening (Foucault, 1977: 195–228). In the panopticon, the one watches the many and the inmate 'is seen, but he does not see; he is the object of information, never a subject in communication' (Foucault, 1977: 200).
(10) For example, in their investigations of US teenagers' concerns about social surveillance, Marwick and boyd argue that social media present people with entirely new experiences of exposure because of online 'context collapse'. *Off*-line, they suggest, 'different social contexts are typically socially or temporally bounded, making the expected social role quite obvious' (Marwick, 2012: 386), but 'social media technologies collapse multiple audiences into single contexts' (boyd & Marwick, 2011; Marwick & boyd, 2010: 114). There is, though, a serious challenge to this notion of context collapse in Goffman's civil inattention, deriving as it does from our ability to divide attention and handle the co-presence of a lot of different people as a matter of routine, managing a main involvement with ratified participants at the same time as disattending – but remaining alert to – others in the vicinity, known and unknown.

Afterword

Jan Blommaert and the Uses of Sociolinguistics: Critical, Political, Personal

On 7 January 2021, shortly before I finally submitted this book to Multilingual Matters, my friend Jan Blommaert died aged 59, after a 10-month battle with cancer. He was an extraordinary person and a brilliant academic – warm, hospitable, humorous and hugely energising. Jan was also the founding editor of the *Encounters* book series, but maybe most relevant here, he was profoundly committed to – indeed lived – a programme of sociolinguistics that he often traced to the writings of Dell Hymes, who figured prominently in Part I.[1] A number of this programme's core elements were spelled out in the introduction to Hymes' ground-breaking 1969 collection, *Reinventing Anthropology*, a 'book ... for people for whom "the way things are" is not reason enough for the ways things are, who find fundamental questions pertinent and in need of personal answer' (Hymes, 1969: 7). For this tribute to the value and vitality that Jan brought to sociolinguistics – a value and vitality that stretched beyond theory and method to community activism and academic working practices – I have borrowed from the title of Hymes' introduction, 'The use of anthropology: Critical, political, personal'. And, as well as citing some of Jan's own words, I also draw on the reflections of others,[2] evidencing the vigour, clarity and coherence with which he articulated a practice and purpose for work on language in society.

* * *

Jan's colleague, Sjaak Kroon, has summarised very well some of the facts of Jan's working life, moving into his contribution and style of working:

> Jan Blommaert was born in Dendermonde, Belgium in 1961 and grew up in Brussels. He got his doctorate in African Philology and History at Ghent University in 1989 where he also was a Professor of African Linguistics and Sociolinguistics from 1997 to 2005, after a period as

Research Director for the International Pragmatics Association in Antwerp. Then he moved to the Institute of Education, University of London as a Professor and chair of Languages in Education. In 2007 he was appointed Professor of Language, Culture and Globalization at the Department of Culture Studies, School of Humanities and Digital Sciences at Tilburg University where he in 2008 became the Director of Babylon, Center for the Study of Superdiversity. In addition, he held fellowships and visiting professorships at Gerhard-Mercator University Duisburg, University of Pretoria, University of Chicago, University of Jyväskylä, Beijing Language and Culture University, Hellenic American University, and the University of the Western Cape ...

Between 2005 and 2010 Jan wrote three books that I once heard him refer to as a trilogy: *Discourse* (2005), *Grassroots Literacy* (2008) and *The Sociolinguistics of Globalization* (2010a). These books fundamentally changed our field from a sociolinguistics of stability into a sociolinguistics of mobility, dealing with all the complexities that processes of globalisation and superdiversity bring to language, culture and society. In recent years, Jan added a new perspective to his work: the online offline nexus. Titles like *Durkheim and the Internet* (2018a) and *Online with Garfinkel* (2019) bear witness of this new focus in which he used contemporary sociolinguistic insights to develop a new sociological imagination, exploring how we construct meaning and operate in online spaces, and what the implications of this are for offline social practice. This online turn was coproduced with many colleagues and PhD students who as of 2016 produced doctoral dissertations on a variety of topics related to online offline practices.

Over the course of his career, Jan introduced or dealt with concepts like discourse, voice, repertoire, ideology, scale, indexicality, superdiversity, chronotopicity, interaction, accent, supervernacular, ethnographic linguistic landscaping, grassroots literacy, genre, intertextuality, framing, multimodality, the online offline nexus – to name a few – and added to their development but always left the opportunity for others to engage, to contribute, accept, or reject his proposals. (Kroon, 2021)

The opportunity for others to engage, contribute, accept or reject. In Jan's own retrospection, 'discussion and brainstorm were my favourite activities; they were in the most literal sense the ludic, fun, pleasure dimensions of academic life' (Blommaert, 2020). And talking to him was often unforgettable, both in- and outside university environments: 'it was only one sentence, but it made all of my observations suddenly fall into place' (Ico Maly, 2021a); 'none of his stuff was boring. He had a way of making things sound crisp. Debatable. And transferable' (Tom van Hout, 2021); 'while in the workshop, things would happen extraordinarily fast and you'd look back and realise their productivity' (Jim Collins, 2021); 'you told him a story and he turned it into theory …. Everything he said was so quotable' (Panayiota Charalambous, 2021; Paty Paliokosta, 2021); 'I will never forget the moment when he broke the frame of teaching, with humour and high performance … There were simply layers upon layers to be learnt from that moment' (Cathy Kell, 2021); 'every single, however brief, interaction with Jan felt like a profoundly transforming and learning experience. The trajectory was always of the following kind: at first, I would resist, be mystified, and in some disbelief vis-à-vis his idea … only to subsequently find it as one of the most powerful treatments of the subject' (Alexandra Georgakopoulou, 2 June 2021); 'all of us got on the train back to London. A climate of intellectual debate but also of humor and camaraderie was immediately established, [Jan contributing] substantially with two qualities – intellectual vivacity and an ability to have a good time with colleagues' (Anna De Fina, 2021); 'brainstorming with Jan was one of the great privileges of working with him, and it often took place in the least obvious of times and spaces. During walks and drives, while waiting for trains' (Piia Varis, 2021):

> For five years we commuted from Belgium to Tilburg. 'Merxem, 8: 15h' he would text me the night before. After picking him up, we discussed our analyses, shared our incomprehension about the state of our country and the world, criticised the assumptions in journalists' questions and the ubiquitous dilettantism in the public sphere. We discussed unwritten books, research projects and individual ideas. We planned our dream program. We expressed our frustrations, but above all we roared with laughter at regular intervals. There was always the commitment, the drive, and the dedication. There was also the confirmation of his erudition – at times it seemed as if Jan had read everything.[3] That, too, was the duty of the academic.[4] (Maly, 2021a)

These accounts point to Jan's erasure of the lines between scholarship and living, operating with a reflexive habitus that Sirpa Leppänen also experienced in Jyväskylä: 'His extensive reading, combined with his extraordinary ability to crystallize complex concepts and theorizations and to show their relevance to the empirical study of language and communication, … opened up new ways for us to do research – to live a researcher's life. He himself was an embodiment of such a life' (Leppänen, 2021). And in Jan's own formulation, what 'still persuades people to choose a career in research' is 'the freedom to unthink what is taken to be true, self-evident and well-known and to re-search it, literally, as in "search again". It is the *freedom of dissidence* – a thing we often hide, in our institutionalised discourses, behind the phrase "critical thinking".

I see dissidence as a duty in research, and as one of its most attractive aspects' (Blommaert, 2020).

This dissidence was infinitely more than just a quest for novelty. It was grounded in a deep knowledge of classical social science and linguistics: 'to understand what linguists do today, we need to historize it, look back in time and understand where it comes from. Jan writes: "Historicizing epistemologies and methodologies is a pre-requisite for critique. If we wish to improve particular kinds of analysis, it is essential that we remember where the tools for such an analysis come from, in what kind of épistème they are grounded, and what kind of ideological load they carry" (2013b: 6)' (Ana Deumert, 2021). It was disciplined by an exceptionally 'keen capacity for the observation of minute linguistic and interactional phenomena' (De Fina, 2021). And it was driven by the conviction (which he attributed to Hymes) that 'no social cause is served by poor work. Critical commitment demands a never-ending attention to theoretical and methodological improvement. If we believe that languages and their speakers should be equal, we have to understand their actual inequalities precisely and in detail' (Blommaert, 2009a: 242, 2010b: 686). But, he insisted,

> when you set your research program, ... [m]ake sure it includes an acute eye for change within your field. That means that you will have to rebrand yourself like five, six times in your career, like I had to learn about social media very late in my career ... [We] need to speak to reality. Well, reality changes. The bastard changes all the time; society refuses to sit still. Well, we have to adjust to that and incorporate it in our research. (Blommaert & Van Der Aa, 2020: 6)

Combining erudition, analytic acuity and an ingrained sense that 'science can never be submissive, never be a matter of "following a procedure" or "framework"' (Blommaert, 2020), Jan had a charisma that propelled him into 'celebrity culture in academia'. In the end, though, he stepped back from this experience, speaking critically of an emerging system in which

> rockstar headliners bring ... their greatest hits in front of an audience of poorly paid struggling academics who spent their personal holiday budgets purchasing a ticket for such events. Little truly valuable intellectual work is going on there ... this new culture took away and delegitimized a previous culture, one of collegial dialogue, collaboration, slowness, time to think, to reflect and to doubt, periods of invisibility and absence from public stages – because one was doing some serious bit of research, for instance. (Blommaert, 2020)

Quite rightly, he recognised his capacity to inspire, which was something that I often experienced myself, that I repeatedly saw with doctoral students at our linguistic ethnography summer school, and that others have amply affirmed: 'little did I know then that his answer would change my life forever' (Maly, 2021a); 'for me as for so many others, encountering Jan was truly a life-changing experience' (Moore, 2021). 'I remember reading this seminal work for the first time and being blown away ... The book literally changed my academic trajectory' (Christian Chun, 2021); he 'pushed me to be a better version of myself. He spoke highly of his colleagues and PhD students. And drove them to excel' (Van Hout, 2021); 'I remember Jan telling us about Stakhanovism, which means: doing more than is expected from you – and indeed, being ambitious and raising the bar continuously; that is one of the first life lessons Jan taught me' (Annelies Verdoolaege, 2021); he 'showed me – then a young academic at the beginning of her professional career – what academia and scholarship could be, the futures that were possible and our own responsibility in making them happen' (Deumert, 2021). But instead of seeing this ability as a personal trait of the kind one might (pseudo-)modestly disclaim, Jan saw inspiration as an essential element in academic practice. Inspiration, he said,

> is the force that suddenly opens areas and directions of thought, shows the embryo of an idea, offers a particular formulation capable of replacing most others, and so forth. Inspiration is about *thinking*, it is the force that kickstarts thinking and that takes us towards the key element of intellectual life: *ideas* .... [I]n our own practices, we should perhaps also try, consciously and intentionally, to inspire others. I mean by that: we should not offer others our own doctrines and orthodoxies. We should offer them our ideas – even if they are rough on the edges, unfinished and half-substantiated – and explain how such ideas might fertilize – not replace – what is already there. I have quite consistently tried to inspire others, and to transmit to them the importance I attached to inspiration as a *habitus* in work and in life. (Blommaert, 2020)

Inspiration as academic practice had an essential corollary: 'creating communities of academics from all corners of life' (Najma Al Zidjaly, 2021), going 'to great lengths to make you feel like you belonged in academia' (Van Hout, 2021). 'One thing remained constant, wherever Jan went, or whoever you talked to about him; he was generous and set up a system of democratic knowledge sharing wherever he went' (Van der Aa, 2021). He used his 'preternatural gift for communication to foment scholarly collaboration on a global scale, building sustainable networks that brought together researchers from around the world to work on shared problems' (Moore, 2021). 'He always kept in touch with people with whom he had common interests through a stream of initiatives that were aimed at creating networks of collaboration and debate. Jan always was a team player and a proponent of collective initiatives' (De Fina, 2021). I can think of at least five such initiatives (with names) that I have participated in, and they have had a major impact on the direction and tenor of my work.[5] But the democratic knowledge sharing with people from all corners – what he and Van der Aa called 'epistemic solidarity' (Van der Aa & Blommaert, 2015[6]) – extended further, well beyond the academy.

'In my life', he wrote in one of his last publications,

> whenever I doubted the importance of what I was doing academically (and that happened very frequently, believe me), the answer was given by my activism. And the answer was: because THEY need it, these activists, trade union people but also school teachers. I gave lectures all through my life to non-academic audiences ranging from trade unions to individuals and organizations across the social spectrum, and I was everywhere. I was literally everywhere. I also wrote fifteen small books in Dutch for which I never got any academic recognition of course, but they were vulgarizing small books that were used in trade unions, in-service language programs and so on. So the activists were also my audience and THEY told me my academic work was valuable. They told me to continue; they told me to do more; they asked me questions that then became like priorities in research for me. (Blommaert & Van der Aa, 2020: 6)

In consequence, in March 2020,

> when he broke the news that he was ill, he was immediately overwhelmed by the many messages he received on his Facebook, Academia page, Twitter, and email. In Belgium ... hundreds of ex-students, civil society workers, activists, journalists, politicians, and unionists would thank him for his many contributions to society in Facebook posts on his wall. He was not only personally overwhelmed by it all or thankful, he saw it as proof that '*his publication strategy worked*'. A strategy he coined 'knowledge activism' and focused on open publishing and giving back knowledge to other academics and society in general. (Maly, 2021b: 1)

Knowledge activism, of course, generated conflict:

> The Dutch version of *Debating Diversity – Het Belgische Migrantendebat* (Blommaert & Verschueren, 1992) ... was not only self- published because no publisher wanted it, it was also politically explosive. This counter-hegemonic voice came with a price tag .... the rector [tried] to silence him and Verschueren, and journalists, politicians and even academic colleagues tried to denigrate them. This was not a one-time occurrence. Later when Verschueren and he published a new book on antiracism

> (*Antiracisme* Blommaert & Verschueren, 1994), authors from the same publishing house pushed their publisher to withdrew it from the stores. Throughout his life he has received 'tons of shit' to quote him. (Maly, 2021b: 2)

But he was not intimidated, and his knowledge activist critique also covered the counter-productive and anti-democratic structures of academic production.

So, for example, in the course of our language and superdiversity collaboration, we submitted an unsuccessful application to the EU's Horizon 2020 funding programme, spending hundreds of hours and several international trips worth several thousand Euros in preparing the bid. Jan delivered the home truth:

> After submitting, we heard that a total of 147 applications had been received by the EU. And that the EU will eventually grant 2 – *two* – projects. In a rough calculation, this means that the chance of success in this funding line is 1.3%; it also means that 98.7% of the applications – 145 of them, to be accurate – will be rejected .... The paradox is clear: by going along with the stampede of competitive external funding acquisition, *almost all* universities across the EU will *lose* not just money, but extremely valuable research time for their staff. Little academic improvement will be made, and little progress in science, if doing actual research is replaced by writing grant proposals with an almost-zero chance of success. And as long as academics and academic units are told that success or failure in getting EU funding (with success rates such as the one mentioned here known in advance) is a criterium for determining their academic quality, gross injustice will be committed. People will be judged inadequate, mediocre or simply poor academics because they failed to get the benchmark funding – awarded, as we saw, on grounds that have little to do with academic quality assessments of applications. (Blommaert, 2016)

Much more generally, early 'experiences in African universities made me very much aware of the existence of several academic worlds, not the idealized one "academic community" sometimes invoked as a trope',[7] and 'inequality became the central theme in my work *and academic practice* from the first moment I embarked on it' (Blommaert, 2020, emphasis added):

> I disliked and dislike – intensely – the development of academic industrial culture that I was witness to throughout my career, with almost-totalized individualization of academic work and performance measurement, with constant inter-individual competition driving young and vulnerable colleagues to extreme and dangerous levels of stress and investment in work rather than life, and with managers emphasizing – without any burden of

evidence – that the 'single-authored journal paper' (published, evidently, behind a huge paywall) is the pinnacle of academic performance and the gold standard for measuring the 'quality' of an individual researcher. (Blommaert, 2020)

Where there was institutional flexibility, Jan could work very productively with university managers (and at the University of the Western Cape, he 'worked in very close concert with ... the most inspiring and energizing team of academic leaders I had ever met'; Blommaert, 2020). He 'tirelessly discussed with his colleagues not only the work itself but also *how we do the work* as academics ... [M]any a younger scholar, myself included, [is] indebted to him for valuable lessons on how to be an academic in neoliberal academia and the ways in which resistance is not, after all, futile' (Varis, 2021). And maybe Jan's clearest intervention in the practicalities of scholarship was in academic publishing, an industry which in general, he argued, 'has become a disgrace and is an obstacle to science, not a facilitator (let alone an indispensable actor)' (Varis, 2021). Here he embraced open source publication, 'opening up the closed system of academic publishing to professionals and students ... who cannot afford to buy them' (De Fina, 2021), to 'scholars from the Global South who can't afford the commercial versions of my work' (Blommaert, 2020), and to people active in civil society (Maly, 2021a). He co-founded *Tilburg Papers in Culture Studies*[8] and *Diggit*[9] (an online magazine providing an alternative platform for information exchange and debate on digital culture, globalisation and the arts), and he posted prolifically in blogs,[10] tweets, videos and on Facebook. On academia.edu,[11] his papers have over a quarter of a million views (an astonishing figure),[12] and 'you could always find his books first as "working paper" previews somewhere for free, often to the annoyance of his publishers' (Van der Aa, 2021). At the same time, these practical interventions developed in continuous dialogue with theory and analysis, in which he opened 'a new frontier for the analysis of political discourse with his ... reflections on communication in the post-digital world' (De Fina, 2021), generating 'new insights into notions of communities, user identities, and genres' online (Georgakopoulou, 2021).

In sharp contrast to Hymes' work, which Jan deemed generally 'tough reading' (Blommaert, 2010b: 685), Jan's writing was 'always didactic in nature[, taking] the reader, viewer, or student by the hand' (Maly, 2021a), even though it sought to 'give them a glimpse of what lies beyond, of the open terrain for which my writings offered no road map, but which my writings could help them to detect as open for exploration' (Blommaert, 2020). '"Write to be read" and "write a paper you'd like to read yourself" were pieces of advice Jan gave to all of his younger colleagues' (Varis,

2021). But despite this difference, Hymes' writing breached the traditional front- and back-stage boundary in academic work very much like Jan's, and it brought the practices, people and institutions producing analysis into the spotlight alongside the objects being studied, articulating a reflexive methodological programme that embraced intellectual inheritance and practical organisation alongside theory and empirical description (Blommaert, 2009a; Rampton, 2009a). In this way, both scholars innovated with channels of publication, Blommaert exploring the affordances of the internet, Hymes setting up *Language in Society*, sociolinguistics' first journal. Like Blommaert, Hymes' writing questioned university structures and deferential science, asking whether the future of the graduate department in anthropology would 'prove to have been chrysalis or coffin' (Hymes, 1969: 7), declaring that '[p]roductive scholars know that problems lead where they will and that relevance commonly leads across disciplinary boundaries. Yet many an insecure academic compensates for [their] own lack or loss of intellectual [potency] by making it difficult or impossible for students and junior colleagues to benefit from theirs' (Hymes, 1969: 44–45). And Jan's undergraduate teaching achieved something parallel to what Hymes said could be '[t]he greatest contribution of anthropology departments[: T]o send into the world many lawyers, historians, activists, workers for various institutions and agencies, well training in anthropological work' (Hymes, 1969: 57). 'From day one, [Jan] gave me and my former fellow classmates at Ghent University glasses through which to look at the world around us ... Glasses which we still carry with us, and that allow us see the world, its people and their interactions in a totally different way .... [S]ending us to do ethnographic fieldwork in the most intercultural areas of Ghent, we came back with a box full of data gathered that, as [he] had intended, completely altered our relationship with space, place and identity' (Fie Velghe, 2021).

But it is obviously a driving commitment to the development of ethnographic sociolinguistics that connects Blommaert to Hymes most closely, integrating the productivity of two brilliant and innovative minds in a distinctive, powerful and sustainable intellectual programme. As Maly (2021b: 3) notes, Jan 'always started from the idea that language is the architecture of society. Language, according to him, is always socially loaded. It has a history of use, and is used in society. It is not only the stuff that makes us social, it also is socially and politically consequential for humans'. Throughout his career, Jan took the details of linguistic practice as the point of departure for acute analyses that demonstrated how, for example, 'the combination of linguistics and ethnography' can produce a 'layered, multi-scalar and empirically grounded understanding of ideology [that] is perhaps one of the most sophisticated ones in current social science' (Blommaert & Rampton, 2011a: 11). The depth and range of his reading made him a compelling advocate of sociolinguistics for people in other disciplines (as in publications like *Durkheim and the Internet*, strap-lined *On Sociolinguistics and the Sociological Imagination* (2018a)). And again, this was something that Jan could tie to Hymes' *oeuvre*: 'This is how I prefer to remember him and to use Hymes' legacy: as a framework that enables the incorporation of a vast field of social-scientific angles, tools and instruments. Hymesian sociolinguistics' (Blommaert, 2010b: 694).

A fortiori, however, the strands in Jan's practice cohere as the enactment of an approach to ethnography that he associated with Hymes. He scorned the idea that ethnography was just fieldwork-plus-descriptions-of-'context', and actually saw Hymes' writing as 'a victim of such reductions' (Blommaert, 2009c: 260). Instead, ethnography is 'a general programmatic *perspective* on social reality and how real subjects, in real conditions of everyday life, possessed by real interests, make sense of reality' (Blommaert, 2018b: ix, original emphasis). And as well as 'including ontology and an epistemology', Hymesian ethnography is 'a democratic science', a counter-hegemonic politics of knowledge (Blommaert, 2009c: 260–261 *et passim*; Blommaert & Dong, 2020: 12; Hymes, 1980b, 1996). Indeed, beyond the elements of ethnography that people can develop through study and practise, beyond its programmatic features, ethnography – at its most reflexive – seemed in Jan's case a deeply ingrained, personal disposition. 'He preached that theory always flows from specifics, that case studies aren't simply illustrations but are the raw material which allows for theorising' because he was 'an ethnographer *at heart*' (Philip Seargeant, 2021, emphasis added). He wrote about globalisation because he lived it every day,[13] and not even the most pressing personal circumstances could stop the productivity of his participant-observation. For about a year late on in his career, he experienced burnout, 'but hearing Jan talk about how it blindsided him and made him feel utterly incompetent and vulnerable was an eye-opener ... Jan talked about lying fallow, taking back control, slowing down science, and saying no to reproductive, gap-filling research ... He normalized vulnerability and fallow time in the interest of science' (van Hout, 2021). Many of the quotations in the text here draw on what Jan wrote after his diagnosis with terminal cancer, and for many, this 'was an important sign to other scholars, that one does not become a better academic by hiding the difficult sides to life' (Martha Karrebæk, 2021).[14]

* * *

Critical, political, personal. Like all of us, Jan was unique, and his exceptional productivity was founded in the particularity of his marriage to Pika Colpaert, who 'is the reason why I have been able to work the way I have, ... the management who did almost all the administrative and organizational work necessary for my development' (van Schijndel, 2020). In that respect, as sociolinguists we can only thank our good fortune that language in society was the focus for so much of Jan and Pika's extraordinary endeavour. But even though Jan was the exponent *sans pareil* and few can hope to match his brilliance, his originality and his mobilising power across teaching, research *and* activism, he affirms sociolinguistics as a programme with pedigree, purposes and practices that he encourages – or rather, works to inspire – a great many others to join, as best they can. For some, Jan's life stands for

> the academic as public intellectual. The academic who is more than an employee in a diploma factory, but an academic who imagines himself or herself as a cornerstone of democracy. An academic who sees their research, their teaching position and social demonstration as their task, one that should be taken on with care and commitment ... It is high time for academics to examine the structures that curtail that social role, so that we can once again take up the role of public intellectual to the fullest. (Maly, 2021a)

For others,

> still more than a teacher, I think, Jan was a writer. He told me once that he tried every day to devote some of his time to writing, early in the morning before day-to-day business caught him, late at night, or in time stolen from so many holidays. I think it is in writing that Jan found his main *raison d'être*, the final fulfillment of wanting to share his – as he himself said in an interview, often unfinished – thoughts and ideas and challenge his readers, students and colleagues alike, to discuss, complete, reject or elaborate on them, ultimately leading to a multitude of collective (open-access) authorships. (Kroon, 2021)

Plainly, the lines of uptake and engagement are open and unsettled, but wherever the reverberations, for me as for others, Jan stands as the shining contemporary validation of sociolinguistics.

Notes

(1) Rather than speaking of Hymes as a person, it was with what Hymes *wrote* that Jan aligned. He recognised the problems and conflicts associated with Hymes (Blommaert, 2009a: 242), but he insisted that few 'have left an oeuvre of such complexity and richness; this oeuvre deserves profound exploration and examination.

There is a danger, given the animosities that ... surround Hymes, that this ... will be neglected. We would not do ourselves good service if this would happen' (Blommaert, 2009a: 242). This is also the position I take.

(2) Most of these were either offered at Jan's funeral on 16 January 2021, at the Memorial Event for Jan Blommaert on 6 February 2021 coordinated by Karel Arnaut, Jenny-Louise Van der Aa and Piia Varis, or published in *Diggit*, the digital magazine set up by Jan, Ico Maly, Sjaak Kroon and others at Tilburg University.

(3) 'I read massively all through my life. And while part of that reading was "just" reading, another part was *studying*. Most of my career, I was involved in some kind of study, collecting and selecting writings from which I wanted to draw advanced insights, useful for the research projects I was engaged in. I studied, for instance (and the list is not complete), structuralism, existentialism, phenomenology, arcane things such as the works of Rudy Botha on Chomsky and the Functional Grammar attempts of Simon Dik, Talmy Givon and M.A.K. Halliday; but also the entire oeuvre (or, at least, most of what I could get) of Michel Foucault, Carlo Ginzburg, Bakhtin, Freud, Durkheim, Simmel, Parsons, Eric Hobsbawm, E.P. Thompson, Pierre Bourdieu, Charles Goodwin, Dell Hymes, Michael Silverstein, Erving Goffman, Aaron Cicourel, Harold Garfinkel, Anne Rawls, Fernand Braudel, J.K. Galbraith, Immanuel Wallerstein, Arjun Appadurai and several others. I studied Marx and Marxism in its very diverse varieties, Rational Choice, Macchiavelli, Darwin, G.H. Mead's work and influence, Dewey, Paolo Freire, Ngugi wa Thiong'o, Okot p'Bitek, Walter Rodney, Issa Shivji and quite a bit of African political theory from the 1950, 1960s and 1970s. In order to understand a lot of that, I had to study the works of Mao Zedong and the history of the Cultural Revolution in China. And so on, and so forth' (Blommaert, 2020).

'Most practitioners of sociolinguistics are reasonably competent at the analysis of language; very, very few have brought to their work the deep knowledge of social theory – from Durkheim and Marx to new and emerging work – that Jan possessed, and was constantly expanding, thanks to his wide reading and insatiable curiosity' (Moore, 2021).

(4) 'I grew up and studied in the welfare-state educational system of Belgium, and given the modest socio-economic status of my family, I would probably never have received higher education in other, fee-paying systems. I'm very much a product of a big and structural collective effort performed by people who did not know me – taxpayers – and regardless of who I was. I am a product of a democratic society. I remained extremely conscious of that fact throughout my adult life, and my political stance as a professional academic has consistently been that I, along with the science I produce, am a *resource for society*, and *should give back to society* what society has invested in me' (Blommaert, 2020).

(5) Language, Power and Identity 1999–2004; the Ethnography, Language & Communication doctoral training programme (2007–); the International Consortium on Language & Superdiversity 2009–2017; Multilingualism in Society, based at the University of the Western Cape; and the *Encounters* series in which this book is published (2004–2019).

(6) Van der Aa and Blommaert (2015).

(7) As David Parkin (14 February 2021) notes, it is important 'to highlight Jan' s early work on Swahili in Tanzania because ... it provided a foundation for many of the later accomplishments outside Africa for which he is even better known globally ... His brilliant sociolinguistic analysis of *ujamaa* ("African socialism") as

humanitarian philosophy fitted the political views which informed much if not most of his subsequent work'.

(8) See https://www.tilburguniversity.edu/research/institutes-and-research-groups/babylon/tpcs.

(9) See https://www.diggitmagazine.com/.

(10) See https://alternative-democracy-research.org/.

(11) See https://tilburguniversity.academia.edu/JanBlommaert.

(12) As of 24 February 2021, his writing has over 36,000 citations and an h-index of 75 (*Harzing's Publish or Perish* – an app with a name that Jan would recognise but inveigh against!).

(13) Seeing a Belgian write about cricket might make me raise my English eyebrows, but only for a moment until I read: 'One evening recently, I found myself in my local Antwerp night shop along with three other people: the Indian owner, a man from Pakistan and one from Sri Lanka. In a matter of seconds, I got involved in an intense discussion on the 2019 Cricket World Cup' (Blommaert, 2019; https://www.diggitmagazine.com/column/cricket).

(14) As several people noted at his memorial event, 'you could share dark moments' with Jan (Charalambous, 2021); he 'was not afraid of supporting others when they went through difficult moments in time' (Karrebæk, 2021).

Bibliography

Aarsæther, F. (2010) The use of multiethnic youth language in Oslo. In P. Quist and B.A. Svendsen (eds) *Multilingual Urban Scandinavia: New Linguistic Practices* (pp. 111–126). Bristol: Multilingual Matters.

Abrams, F. (1991) Accents and dialects still unmentionable subjects. *Times Educational Supplement*, 14 June.

Abreu, A., Grinevich, V., Hughes, A. and Kitson, M. (2009) *Knowledge Exchange between Academics and the Business, Public and Third Sectors*. Cambridge: UK Innovation Research Centre.

Adamides, C. (2014) Negative perceptions of foreign actors: An integral part of conflict perpetuating routines. In M. Kontos, N. Panayiotides, H. Alexandrou and S.-C. Theodoulou (eds) *Great Power Politics in Cyprus: Foreign Interventions and Domestic Perceptions* (pp. 197–222). Newcastle upon Tyne: Cambridge Scholars Publishing.

Adi, H. and Sherwood, M. (1995) *The 1945 Manchester Pan-African Congress Revisited*. London: New Beacon Books.

Agha, A. (2004) Registers of language. In A. Duranti (ed.) *A Companion to Linguistic Anthropology* (pp. 3–45). Oxford: Blackwell.

Agha, A. (2005) Voice, footing, enregisterment. *Journal of Linguistic Anthropology* 15 (1), 38–59.

Agha, A. (2007) *Language and Social Structure*. Cambridge: Cambridge University Press.

Agha, A. and Wortham, S. (eds) (2005) *Discourse across Speech Events*. Special issue of *Journal of Linguistic Anthropology* 15 (1).

Ahearn, L. (2012) *Living Language: An Introduction to Linguistic Anthropology*. Malden, MA: Wiley-Blackwell.

Alim, S. (2009) Creating 'an empire within an empire': Critical hip hop language pedagogies and the role of sociolinguistics. In S. Alim, A. Ibrahim and A. Pennycook (eds) *Global Linguistic Flows: Hip Hop Cultures, Youth Identities and the Politics of Language* (pp. 213–230). London: Routledge.

Alim, S., Ibrahim, A. and Pennycook, A. (eds) (2009) *Global Linguistic Flows: Hip Hop Cultures, Youth Identities and the Politics of Language*. London: Routledge.

Allen, W. (2004) Teaching languages and cultures in a post-9/11 world: A personal reflection. *Modern Languages Journal* 88, 285–289.

Al Zidjaly, N. (2021) Contribution to Memorial Event for Jan Blommaert, 6 February.

Anderson, B. (1983) *Imagined Communities*. London: Verso.

Androutsopoulos, J. (2001) *From the Streets to the Screens and Back Again: On the Mediated Diffusion of Ethnolectal Patterns in Contemporary German*. LAUD Linguistic Agency No. A522 (pp. 1–24).

Androutsopoulos, J. (2007) Bilingualism in the mass media and on the internet. In M. Heller (ed.) *Bilingualism: A Social Approach* (pp. 207–232). Basingstoke: Palgrave.

Androutsopoulos, J. (2009) Ideologising ethnolectal German. In S. Johnson and T. Milani (eds) *Language Ideologies and Media Discourse* (pp. 182–204). London: Continuum.

Androutsopoulos, J. (ed.) (2014) *Mediatization and Sociolinguistic Change*. Berlin: de Gruyter.

Androutsopoulos, J. and Georgakopoulou, A. (eds) (2003) *Discourse Constructions of Youth Identities*. Amsterdam: John Benjamins.

APPG (All Party Parliamentary Group on Social Integration) (2017a) *Interim Report*. London: APPG. See http://d3n8a8pro7vhmx.cloudfront.net/themes/570513f1b504f500db000001/attachments/original/1483958173/TC0012_AAPG_Interim_Report_Screen.pdf?1483958173.

APPG (All Party Parliamentary Group on Social Integration) (2017b) *Integration not Demonisation*. London: APPG. See http://d3n8a8pro7vhmx.cloudfront.net/themes/570513f1b504f500db000001/attachments/original/1504379228/TC0016_AAPG_Integration_not_Demonisation_Report.pdf?1504379228.

APPG (Joint All Party Parliamentary Groups) (2019) *Visa Problems for African Visitors to the UK*.

Aradau, C. (2004) Security and the democratic scene: Desecuritization and emancipation. *Journal of International Relations and Development* 7 (4), 388–413.

Arnaut, K. (2012) Super-diversity: Elements of an emerging perspective. *Diversities* 14 (2), 1–16.

Arnaut, K., Blommaert, J., Rampton, B. and Spotti, M. (eds) (2016) *Language and Superdiversity*. London: Routledge.

Arnaut, K., Karrebæk, M.S., Spotti, M. and Blommaert, J. (eds) (2017) *Engaging Superdiversity: Recombining Spaces, Times and Language Practices*. Bristol: Multilingual Matters.

Auer, P. (1988) A conversation analytic approach to codeswitching and transfer. In M. Heller (ed.) *Codeswitching: Anthropological and Sociolinguistic Perspectives* (pp. 187–213). Berlin: Mouton de Gruyter.

Auer, P. (2003) 'Crossing' the language border into Turkish? Uses of Turkish by non-Turks in Germany. In L. Mondada and S. Pekarek-Doehler (eds) *Plurilinguisme – Mehrsprachigkeit – Plurilingualism: Festschrift for Georges Lüdi* (pp. 73–97). Tübingen: Francke.

Auer, P. (2006) Sociolinguistic crossing. In K. Brown (ed.) *Encyclopedia of Language and Linguistics, Vol. 11* (2nd edn) (pp. 490–492). Amsterdam: Elsevier.

Auer, P. (2007a) Introduction. In *Style and Social Identities: Alternative Approaches to Linguistic Heterogeneity* (pp. 1–24). Berlin: Mouton de Gruyter.

Auer, P. (ed.) (2007b) *Style and Social Identities: Alternative Approaches to Linguistic Heterogeneity*. Berlin: Mouton de Gruyter.

Auer, P. and Dirim, I. (2003) Sociocultural orientation, urban youth styles and the spontaneous acquisition of Turkish by non-Turkish adolescents in Germany. In J. Androutsopoulos and A. Georgakopoulou (eds) *Discourse Constructions of Youth Identities* (pp. 223–246). Amsterdam: John Benjamins.

Auer, P. and Roberts, C. (2011a) Introduction to special issue in honour of John Gumperz. Special issue of *Text & Talk* 31 (4), 381–393.

Auer, P. and Roberts, C. (eds) (2011b) *In Honour of John Gumperz*. Special issue of *Text & Talk* 31 (4), 375–502.

Back, L. (1995/2003) X amount of Sat Siri Akal!: Apache Indian, reggae music and intermezzo culture. In R. Harris and B. Rampton (eds) *The Language Ethnicity and Race Reader* (pp. 328–345). London: Routledge.

Back, L. (1996) *New Ethnicities and Urban Culture*. London: UCL Press.

Bakhtin, M. (1981) *The Dialogic Imagination*. Austin, TX: University of Texas Press.

Bakhtin, M. (1984) *Problems in Dostoevsky's Poetics*. Minneapolis, MN: University of Minnesota Press.

Bakhtin, M. (1986) The problem of speech genres. In *Speech Genres and Other Late Essays* (pp. 60–102). Austin, TX: University of Texas Press.

Ball, K. (2002) Elements of surveillance: A new framework and future directions. *Information, Communication and Society* 5 (4), 573–590.

Ball, K. (2005) Organisation, surveillance and the body: Towards a politics of resistance. *Organization* 12 (1), 89–108.

Ball, K. (2009) Exposure: Exploring the subject of surveillance. *Information, Communication and Society* 12 (5), 639–657.

Ball, K. and Wilson, D. (2000) Power, control and computer-based performance monitoring: Repertoires, resistance and subjectivities. *Organisation Studies* 21 (3), 539–565.

Ball, K., Haggerty, K. and Lyon, K. (eds) (2012) *Routledge Handbook of Surveillance Studies*. London: Routledge.

Ball, K., Chanoto, A., Daniel, E., Dibb, E., Meadows, M. and Spiller, K. (2015) *The Private Security State? Surveillance, Consumer Data and the War on Terror.* Frederiksberg: CBS Press.

Ball, S.J., Maguire, M. and Braun, A. (2012) *How Schools Do Policy: Policy Enactments in Secondary Schools*. London: Routledge.

Balzacq, T. (ed.) (2011) *Securitisation Theory: How Security Problems Emerge and Dissolve*. London: Routledge.

Barrett, R. (1997) The 'homo-genius' speech community. In A. Livia and K. Hall (eds) *Queerly Phrased* (pp. 181–201). Oxford: Oxford University Press.

Barton, D. (1994) *Literacy: An Introduction to the Ecology of Written Language*. Oxford: Blackwell.

Barton, D., Hamilton, M. and Ivanic, R. (2000) *Situated Literacies: Reading and Writing in Context*. London: Routledge.

Basaran, T., Bigo, D., Guittet, E.-P. and Walker, R. (eds) (2017) *International Political Sociology*. London: Routledge.

Bauman, G. (1996) *Contesting Culture: Discourses of Identity in Multi-ethnic London*. Cambridge: Cambridge University Press.

Bauman, R. (2001) Genre. In A. Duranti (ed.) *Key Terms in Language and Culture*. Oxford: Blackwell.

Bauman, R. and Briggs, C. (1990) Poetics and performance as critical perspectives on language and social life. *Annual Review of Anthropology* 19, 59–88.

Bauman, Z. and Lyon, D. (2013) *Liquid Surveillance*. Cambridge: Polity Press.

Bauman, Z., Bigo, D., Esteves, P., Guild, E., Jabri, V., Lyon, D. and Walker, E. (2014) After Snowden: Rethinking the impact of surveillance. *International Political Sociology* 8, 121–144.

Becker, H.S. (1971) Footnote. In M. Wax, S. Diamond and F. Gearing (eds) *Anthropological Perspectives on Education* (pp. 3–27). New York: Basic Books.

Beebe, L. (1977) The influence of the listener on code-switching. *Language Learning* 27, 331–339.

Beebe, L. (1985) Input: Choosing the right stuff. In S. Gass and C. Madden (eds) *Input in Second Language Acquisition* (pp. 104–144). Rowley, MA: Newbury House.

Beebe, L. and Zuengler, J. (1983) Accommodation theory: An explanation for style shifting in second language dialects. In N. Wolfson and E. Judd (eds) *Sociolinguistics and Language Acquisition* (pp. 195–213). Rowley, MA: Newbury House.

Bell, A. (1999) Styling the other to define the self: A study in New Zealand identity-making. *Journal of Sociolinguistics* 3 (4), 523–541.

Bernstein, B. (1996) Pedagogising knowledge: Studies in recontextualising. In B. Bernstein (ed.) *Pedagogy, Symbolic Control and Identity* (pp. 54–81). London: Taylor & Francis.

Bezemer, J. (2015) Partnerships in research: Doing linguistic ethnography with and for practitioners. In J. Snell, S. Shaw and F. Copland (eds) *Linguistic Ethnography* (pp. 207–224). London: Palgrave Macmillan.

Bierback, C. and Birken-Silverman, G. (2007) Names and identities, or: How to be a hip young Italian migrant in Germany. In P. Auer (ed.) *Style and Social Identities: Alternative Approaches to Linguistic Heterogeneity* (pp. 121–154). Berlin: Mouton de Gruyter

Bigo, D. (2002) Security and immigration: Toward a critique of the governmentality of unease. *Alternatives: Global, Local, Political* 27 (1), 63–92.

Bigo, D. (2006) Globalised (in)security: The field and the Ban-opticon. In N. Sakai and J. Solomon (eds) *Translation, Biopolitics, Colonial Difference.* Hong Kong: Hong Kong University Press.

Bigo, D. (2008) Globalized (in)security: The field and the ban-opticon. In D. Bigo and A. Tsoukala (eds) *Terror, Insecurity and Liberty: Illiberal Practices of Liberal Regimes after 9/11* (pp. 10–49). London: Routledge.

Bigo, D. (2014) Afterword. In M. Maguire, C. Frois and N. Zurawski (eds) *The Anthropology of Security* (pp. 189–205). London: Pluto Press.

Bigo, D. (2016) International political sociology: Rethinking the international through dynamics of power. In T. Basaran, D. Bigo, E.-P. Guittet and R. Walker (eds) *International Political Sociology* (pp. 24–48). London: Routledge.

Bigo, D. (2019) Beyond national security, the emergence of a digital reasons of state(s) led by transnational guilds of sensitive information: The case of the Five Eyes Plus network. In B. Wagner, M. Kettemann and K. Vieth (eds) *Research Handbook on Human Rights and Digital Technology.* (pp. 33–52) Edward Elgar Publishing Limited.

Bigo, D. and McCluskey, E. (2018) What is a PARIS approach to (in)securitization? Political anthropological research for international sociology. In A. Gheciu and W.C. Wohlforth (eds) *The Oxford Handbook of International Security* (pp. 116–132). Oxford: Oxford University Press.

Bijvoet, E. and Fraurud, K. (2010) 'Rinkeby Swedish' in the mind of the beholder: Studying listener perceptions of language variation in multilingual Stockholm. In P. Quist and B.A. Svendsen (eds) *Multilingual Urban Scandinavia: New Linguistic Practices* (pp. 170–188). Bristol: Multilingual Matters.

Blackledge, A. (2005) *Discourse and Power in a Multilingual World.* Amsterdam: John Benjamins.

Blom, J.P. and Gumperz, J. (1972) Social meaning in linguistic structure: Codeswitching in Norway. In J. Gumperz and D. Hymes (eds) *Directions in Sociolinguistics* (pp. 407–434). Oxford: Blackwell.

Blommaert, J. (2001) Context is/as critique. *Critique of Anthropology* 21 (1), 13–32.

Blommaert, J. (2004) Rights in places: Comments on linguistic rights and wrongs. In D. Patrick and J. Freeland (eds) *Language Rights and Language Survival* (pp. 55–65). Manchester: St Jerome.

Blommaert, J. (2005) *Discourse: A Critical Introduction.* Cambridge: Cambridge University Press.

Blommaert, J. (2007) On scope and depth in linguistic ethnography. *Journal of Sociolinguistics* 11 (5), 682–688.

Blommaert, J. (2008) *Grassroots Literacy*. London: Routledge.
Blommaert, J. (2009a) On Hymes: Introduction. In special issue of *Text & Talk* 29 (3), 241–243.
Blommaert, J. (2009b) Language, asylum and the national order. *Current Anthropology* 50 (4), 415–425.
Blommaert, J. (2009c) Ethnography and democracy: Hymes' political theory of language. In special issue of *Text & Talk* 29 (3), 257–276.
Blommaert, J. (2010a) *The Sociolinguistics of Globalization*. Cambridge: Cambridge University Press.
Blommaert, J. (2010b) Dell H. Hymes (1927–2009). *Journal of Sociolinguistics* 14 (5), 682–686.
Blommaert, J. (2012) Chronicles of complexity: Ethnography, superdiversity and linguistic landscapes. *Tilburg Papers in Culture Studies* No. 29. See http://www.tilburguniversity.edu/research/institutes-and-research-groups/babylon/tpcs/.
Blommaert, J. (2013a) *Ethnography, Superdiversity and Linguistic Landscapes: Chronicles of Complexity*. Bristol: Multilingual Matters.
Blommaert, J. (2013b) From fieldnotes to grammar: Artefactual ideologies of language and the micromethodology of linguistics. *Tilburg Papers in Culture Studies* No. 84. See https://www.tilburguniversity.edu/research/institutes-and-research-groups/babylon/tpcs.
Blommaert, J. (2016) Rationalising the unreasonable: There are no good academics in the EU. *Working Papers in Urban Language & Literacies* No. 184; see https://www.academia.edu/19954607.
Blommaert, J. (2018a) *Durkheim and the Internet*. London: Bloomsbury. (Also available as *Working Papers in Urban Languages & Literacies* No. 204. See https://www.academia.edu/30719475.)
Blommaert, J. (2018b) *Dialogues with Ethnography: Notes on Classics, and How I Read Them*. Bristol: Multilingual Matters. (Also available as *Tilburg Papers in Culture Studies* No. 138. See https://www.academia.edu/19342202/.)
Blommaert, J. (2019) Interested in globalization? Watch cricket. *Diggit Magazine*, 25 June. See https://www.diggitmagazine.com/column/cricket.
Blommaert, J. (2019). Online with Garfinkel: Essays on social action in the online-offline nexus. *Tilburg Papers in Culture Studies* No. 229.
Blommaert, J. (2020) Looking back: What was important? *Ctrl + Alt + Dem*, 20 April. See https://alternative-democracy-research.org/.
Blommaert, J. (n.d.) Genre. MS.
Blommaert, J. and Backus, A. (2011) Repertoires revisited: 'Knowing language' in super-diversity. *Working Papers in Urban Language and Literacies* No. 67. See www.academia.edu.
Blommaert, J. and Bulcaen, C. (2000) Critical discourse analysis. *Annual Review of Anthropology* 29, 447–466.
Blommaert, J. and Dong, J. (2020) *Ethnographic Fieldwork: A Beginner's Guide* (2nd edn). Bristol: Multilingual Matters.
Blommaert, J. and Rampton, B. (2011a) Language and superdiversity. *Diversities* 13 (2), 1–21.
Blommaert, J. and Rampton, B. (2011b) Language and superdiversity: A position paper. *Working Papers in Urban Language and Literacies* No.70. See www.academia.edu.
Blommaert, J. and Van der Aa, J.-L. (2020) Jan Blommaert on education: Teaching, research and activism. *Working Papers in Urban Language and Literacies* No. 278. See https://www.academia.edu/44725342.

Blommaert, J. and Verschueren, J. (1992) *Het Belgische Migrantendebat.* Antwerp: International Pragmatics Association (IPrA). See https://www.researchgate.net/publication/338671165_Het_Belgische_Migrantendebat.

Blommaert, J. and Verschueren, J. (1994) *Antiracisme.* Antwerp: Hadewijch.

Blommaert, J. and Verschueren, J. (1998) *Debating Diversity: Analysing the Discourse of Tolerance.* London: Routledge.

Blommaert, J., Collins, J. and Slembrouck, S. (2005) Spaces of multilingualism. *Language & Communication* 25, 197–216.

Blommaert, J., with Szabla, M., Maly, I., Procházka, O., Lu Ying and Li Kunming (2019) Online with Garfinkel. *Tilburg Papers in Culture Studies* No. 229. See https://www.tilburguniversity.edu/sites/default/files/download/TPCS_229-Blommaert.pdf.

Bloor, M. (1997) Addressing social problems through qualitative research. In D. Silverman (ed.) *Qualitative Research: Theory, Method and Practice* (pp. 221–238). London: Sage.

Blumer, H. (1969) *Symbolic Interaction.* Berkeley, CA: University of California Press.

Bock, Z. and Mheta, G. (eds) (2014) *Language, Society and Communication.* Pretoria: Van Schaik.

Bogard, W. (1996) *The Simulation of Surveillance: Hypercontrol in Telematic Societies.* Cambridge: Cambridge University Press.

Borba, R. (2015) How an individual becomes a subject: Discourse, interaction and subjectification at a Brazilian gender identity clinic. *Working Papers in Urban Language and Literacies* No. 163. See www.academia.edu.

Bourdieu, P. (1977) *Outline of a Theory of Practice.* Cambridge: Cambridge University Press.

Bourdieu, P. (1991) *Language and Symbolic Power.* Oxford: Polity Press.

Bourdieu, P. (2014) *On the State.* Cambridge: Polity Press.

boyd, d. and Marwick, A. (2011) Social privacy in networked publics: Teens' attitudes, practices and strategies. See https://www.danah.org/papers/2011/SocialPrivacyPLSC-Draft.pdf.

Bradley, H. (1996) *Fractured Identities: Changing Patterns of Inequality.* Cambridge: Polity Press.

Bremer, K., Roberts, C., Vasseur, M.-T., Simonot, M. and Broeder, P. (1996) *Achieving Understanding: Discourse in Intercultural Encounters.* London: Longman.

Briggs, C. (1997) Notes on a 'confession': On the construction of gender, sexuality, and violence in an infanticide case. *Pragmatics* 7, 519–546.

Briggs, C. (2005) Communicability, racial discourse, and disease. *Annual Review of Anthropology* 34, 269–291.

Britain, D. (ed.) (2007) *Language in the British Isles* (revised 2nd edn). Cambridge: Cambridge University Press.

British Academy (2013) *Lost for Words.* London: British Academy.

Brumfit, C. (1984) *Communicative Methodology in Language Teaching.* Cambridge: Cambridge University Press.

Bryant, R. (2004) *Imagining the Modern: The Cultures of Nationalism in Cyprus.* London and New York: I.B. Tauris.

Bryers, D., Winstanley, B. and Cooke, M. (2013) Whose integration? *Working Papers in Urban Language and Literacies* No. 106.

Bryers, D., Winstanley, B. and Cooke, M. (2014) The power of discussion. In D. Mallows (ed.) *Language Issues in Migration and Integration: Perspectives from Teachers and Learners* (pp. 35–54). London: British Council.

Bucholtz, M. (1999a) 'Why be normal?': Language and identity practices in a community of nerd girls. *Language in Society* 28 (2), 203–223.

Bucholtz, M. (1999b) You da man: Narrating the racial other in the production of white masculinity. *Journal of Sociolinguistics* 3 (4), 443–460.

Bucholtz, M. (2011) *White Kids: Language, Race, and Styles of Youth Identity*. Cambridge: Cambridge University Press.

Bucholtz, M. and Hall, K. (2008) All of the above: New coalitions in sociocultural linguistics. *Journal of Sociolinguistics* 12 (4), 401–431.

Bucholtz, M. and Hall, K. (eds) (2011) *Sociolinguistics and Linguistic Anthropology: Strengthening the Connections*. Special issue of *Journal of Sociolinguistics* 12 (4), 401–545.

Burawoy, M. (1998) The extended case method. *Sociological Theory* 16 (1), 4–33.

Burawoy, M. and von Holdt, K. (2012) *Conversations with Bourdieu: The Johannesburg Moment*. Johannesburg: Wits University Press.

Burgess, T. (2002) Writing, English teachers and the new professionalism. In T. Burgess, C. Fox and J. Goody (eds) *When the Hurly Burly's Done: What's Worth Fighting for?* Sheffield: National Association for the Teaching of English.

Busch, B. (2016a) Methodology in biographical approaches in applied linguistics. *Working Papers in Urban Language and Literacies* No. 187. See www.academia.edu.

Busch, B. (2016b) Heteroglossia of survival: To have one's voice heard, to develop a voice worth hearing. *Working Papers in Urban Language and Literacies* No. 188. See www.academia.edu.

Byram, M. (1995) Intercultural competence and mobility in multinational context: A European view. In M. Tickoo (ed.) *Language and Culture in Multilingual Societies* (pp. 21–36). Singapore: SEAMEO Regional Language Centre.

Byram, M., Nichols, A. and Stevens, D. (eds) (2001) *Developing Intercultural Competence in Practice*. Clevedon: Multilingual Matters.

Cameron, D. (2015) *Extremism*. Speech, 20 July. See https://www.gov.uk/government/speeches/extremism-pm-speech.

Candlin, C. and Candlin, S. (2003) Health communication: A problematic site for applied linguistic research. *Annual Review of Applied Linguistics* 23, 134–154.

Canefe, N. (2002) Refugees or enemies? The legacy of population displacements in contemporary Turkish Cypriot society. *South European Society and Politics* 7 (3), 1–28.

Cantle Commission (2002) *Challenging Local Communities to Change Oldham*. Coventry: Institute of Community Cohesion.

Carmichael, S. and Hamilton, C.V. (1967) *Black Power*. Harmondsworth: Penguin.

Carter, N. (2015) *Transcript. The Future of the British Army: How the British Army Must Change to Serve Britain in a Volatile World*. London: Royal Institute of International Affairs.

Carter, R. (1988) Some pawns for Kingman: Language education and English teaching. In P. Grunwell (ed.) *Applied Linguistics in Society 3* (pp. 51–66). British Studies in Applied Linguistics. London: CILT.

Carter, R. (1990) Introduction. In *Knowledge about Language*. London: Hodder & Stoughton.

Carter, R. (1992) LINC: The final chapter? *BAAL Newsletter* 42, 16–20.

Chambers, C. (1995) *Sociolinguistic Theory*. Oxford: Blackwell.

Charalambous, C. (2009) Learning the language of 'The Other': A linguistic ethnography of Turkish-language classes in a Greek-Cypriot school. Unpublished PhD thesis, King's College London.

Charalambous, C. (2012) 'Republica De Kubros': Transgression and collusion in Greek-Cypriot adolescents' classroom 'silly-talk'. *Linguistics and Education* 23, 334–349.

Charalambous, C. (2013) The burden of emotions in language teaching: Renegotiating a troubled past in the language classroom. *Language and Intercultural Communication Journal* 13 (3), 310–220.

Charalambous, C. (2014) 'Whether you see them as friends or enemies you need to know their language': Turkish-language learning in a Greek Cypriot school. In V. Lytra (ed.) *When Greeks and Turks Meet: Interdisciplinary Perspectives on the Relationship Since 1923* (pp. 141–162). London: Ashgate.

Charalambous, C. and Rampton, B. (2012) Other-language learning and intercultural communication in contexts of conflict. In J. Jackson (ed.) *The Routledge Handbook of Language and Intercultural Communication* (pp. 195–210). London: Routledge.

Charalambous, C., Zembylas, M. and Charalambous, P. (2013) Doing 'Leftist propaganda' or working towards peace? Moving Greek-Cypriot peace education struggles beyond local political complexities. *Journal of Peace Education* 10 (1), 67–87.

Charalambous, C., Charalambous, P., Khan, K. and Rampton, B. (2015) Sociolinguistics and security. *Working Papers in Urban Language and Literacies* No. 177. At www.academia.edu

Charalambous, C., Charalambous, P., Khan, K. and Rampton, B. (2018) Security and language policy. In J. Tollefson and M. Pérez-Milans (eds) *The Oxford Handbook of Language Policy and Planning* (pp. 633–653). Oxford: Oxford University Press.

Charalambous, C., Charalambous, P. and Rampton, B. (2021) International Relations, sociolinguistics and the 'everyday': A linguistic ethnography of peace-building through language education. *Peacebuilding*. doi:10.1080/21647259.2021.1895604

Charalambous, P. (2010) Literature education as social practice. Unpublished PhD dissertation, King's College London.

Charalambous, P. (2017) Sociolinguistics and security: A bibliography. *Working Papers in Urban Language and Literacies* No. 213. See https://www.academia.edu/33687581/ and www.kcl.ac.uk/liep.

Charalambous, P. (2021) Contribution to Memorial Event for Jan Blommaert, 6 February.

Charalambous, P., Charalambous, C. and Zembylas, M. (2016) Troubling translanguaging: Language ideologies, superdiversity and interethnic conflict. In J. Jaspers and L. Madsen (eds) *Sociolinguistic in a Languagised World*. Special issue of *Applied Linguistic Review* 7 (3). (Also available as *Working Papers in Urban Language and Literacies* No. 190. See www.academia.edu.)

Charalambous, P., Charalambous, C. and Rampton, B. (2017) De-securitizing Turkish: Teaching the language of a former enemy, and intercultural language education *Applied Linguistics* 38 (6), 800–823. (Earlier draft available as *Working Paper in Urban Language and Literacies* No. 137.)

Chatterton, M. and Goddard, J. (2000) The response of higher education institutions to regional needs. *European Journal of Education* 35 (4), 475–495.

Cheney-Lippold, J. (2011) A new algorithmic identity: Soft biopolitics and the modulation of control. *Theory, Culture and Society* 28 (6), 164–181.

Cherbonneau, M. and Copes, H. (2006) 'Drive it like you stole it': Auto theft and the illusion of normalcy. *British Journal of Criminology* 46, 193–211.

Cheshire, J., Fox, S., Kerswill, P. and Torgersen, E. (2008) Ethnicity, friendship network and social practices as the motor of dialect change: Linguistic innovation in London. In U. Ammon and K. Mattheier (eds) *Sociolinguistica: International Yearbook of European Sociolinguistics* (pp. 1–23). Tübingen: Max Niemeyer Verlag.

Christou, M. (2007) The language of patriotism: Sacred history and dangerous memories. *British Journal of Sociology of Education* 28 (6), 709–722.

Chun, E. (2009) Ideologies of legitimate mockery: Margaret Cho's revoicings of mock Asian. In A. Reyes and A. Lo (eds) *Beyond Yellow English: Towards a Linguistic Anthropology of Asian Pacific America* (pp. 261–287). Oxford: Oxford University Press.

Chun, C. (2021) My tribute to Jan Blommaert. *Diggit Magazine*, 7 January. See www.diggitmagazine.com.

Cicourel, A. (1992) The interpenetration of communicative contexts: Examples from medical discourse. In A. Duranti and C. Goodwin (eds) *Rethinking Context* (pp. 291–310). Cambridge: Cambridge University Press.

Cicourel, A.V. (1993) Aspects of structural and processual theories of knowledge. In C. Calhoun, E. LiPuma and M. Postone (eds) *Bourdieu: Critical Perspectives* (pp. 89–115). Oxford: Polity Press.

Cicourel, A (2007) A personal retrospective view of ecological validity. *Text & Talk* 27 (5/6), 735–752.

Clark, J.T. (2010) *Negotiating Elite Talk: Language, Race, Class and Identity among African American High-Schoolers.* Manchester: St Jerome.

Clemente, I. (2013) Conversation analysis and anthropology. In J. Sidnell and T. Stivers (eds) *Handbook of Conversation Analysis and Anthropology* (pp. 688–700). Oxford and New York: Blackwell-Wiley.

Cohen, I. (1987) Structuration theory. In A. Giddens and J. Turner (eds) *Social Theory Today* (pp. 273–308). Oxford: Polity Press.

Cohen, P. (1987) Perversions of inheritance: Studies in the making of multiracist Britain. In P. Cohen and H. Bains (eds) *Multiracist Britain* (pp. 9–120). Basingstoke: Macmillan.

Collins, J. (2011) Indexicalities of language contact in an era of globalisation: Engaging with John Gumperz's legacy. *Text & Talk* 31, pp. 407–428.

Collins, J. (2021) Contribution to Memorial Event for Jan Blommaert, 6 February.

Collinson, D. (1999) 'Surviving the rigs': Safety and surveillance on North Sea oil installations. *Organisation Studies* 20 (4), 579–600.

Cooke, M. (2015) Brokering Britain: The teaching of ESOL citizenship. Unpublished PhD dissertation, King's College London.

Cooke, M. and Peutrell, R. (eds) (2019) *Brokering Britain, Educating Citizens: Exploring ESOL and Citizenship.* Bristol: Multilingual Matters.

Cooke, M. and Simpson, J. (2008) *ESOL: A Critical Guide.* Oxford: Oxford University Press.

Cooke, M. and Simpson, J. (2012) Discourses about linguistic diversity. In M. Martin-Jones, A. Blackledge and A. Creese (eds) *The Routledge Handbook of Multilingualism* (pp. 116–130). London: Routledge.

Cooke, M., Bryers, D. and Winstanley, B. (2014). In D. Mallows (ed) Language Issues in migration and integration: perspectives from teachers and learners (pp. 19–35). London: The British Council.

Cooke, M., Bryers, D. and Winstanley, B. (2018) 'Our languages': Sociolinguistics in multilingual participatory ESOL. *Working Papers in Urban Language and Literacies* No. 234. See www.academia.edu.

Council of Europe (2001) *Common European Framework of Reference for Languages: Learning, Teaching, Assessment.* Cambridge: Cambridge University Press.

Council of Europe (2007) *Guide for the Development of Language Education Policies in Europe: From Linguistic Diversity to Plurilingual Education.* Strasbourg: Council of Europe.

Coupland, N. (1995) Pronunciation and the rich points of culture. In J. Windsor-Lewis (ed.) *Studies in English and General Phonetics: In Honour of J.D. O'Connor* (pp. 310–319). London: Routledge.

Coupland, N. (2001) Dialect stylisation in radio talk. *Language in Society* 30, 345–375.

Coupland, N. (2007a) *Style*. Cambridge: Cambridge University Press.

Coupland, N. (2007b) Aneurin Bevin, class wars and the styling of political antagonism. In P. Auer (ed.) *Style and Social Identities: Alternative Approaches to Linguistic Heterogeneity* (pp. 213–246). Berlin: Mouton de Gruyter.

Coupland, N. (2009) Dialect style, social class and metacultural performance: The pantomime dame. In N. Coupland and A. Jaworski (eds) *The New Sociolinguistics Reader* (pp. 311–325). Basingstoke: Palgrave.

Coupland, N. and Jaworski, A. (ed.) (2009) *The New Sociolinguistics Reader*. Basingstoke: Palgrave Macmillan.

Coupland, N., Sarangi, S. and Candlin, C. (eds) (2001) *Sociolinguistics and Social Theory*. London: Longman.

Cox, B. (1990) *Cox on Cox: An English Curriculum for the 1990s*. London: Hodder & Stoughton.

Crossley, N. (1995) Body techniques, agency and intercorporeality: On Goffman's *Relations in Public*. *Sociology* 29 (1), 133–149.

Crossley, N. (2001) Merleau-Ponty, the elusive body and carnal sociology. *Body & Society* 1 (1), 43–63.

Crystal, D. (2010) *The Cambridge Encyclopedia of Language* (3rd edn). Cambridge: Cambridge University Press.

Cutler, A. (1999) Yorkville Crossing. White teens, hip hop, and African American English. *Journal of Sociolinguistics* 3 (4), 428–442.

De Fina, A. (2007) Style and stylisation in the construction of identities in a card-playing club. In P. Auer (ed.) *Style and Social Identities: Alternative Approaches to Linguistic Heterogeneity* (pp. 57–84). Berlin: Mouton de Gruyter.

De Fina, A. (2021) Jan Blommaert, the trail blazer. *Diggit Magazine*, 7 January. See www.diggitmagazine.com.

De Genova, N.P. (2002) Migrant 'illegality' and deportability in everyday life. *Annual Review of Anthropology* 31, 419–447.

Deleuze, G. (1992) Postscript on the societies of control. *October* 59, 3–7.

Depperman, A. (2007) Playing with the voice of the other: Stylised *Kanaksprak* in conversations among German adolescents. In P. Auer (ed.) *Style and Social Identities: Alternative Approaches to Linguistic Heterogeneity* (pp. 325–360). Berlin: Mouton de Gruyter.

DES (Department of Education and Science) (1967) *Children and their Primary Schools* (Plowden Report). London: HMSO.

DES (Department for Education and Science) (1975) *A Language for Life* (Bullock Report). London: HMSO.

DES (Department of Education and Science) (1981) *West Indian Children in our Schools: Interim Report of the Committee of Inquiry into the Education of Children from Ethnic Minority Groups* (A. Rampton Report). London: HMSO.

Deumert, A. (2021) Semiotic future: Celebrating Jan Blommaert's radical scholarship. *Diggit Magazine*, 11 January. See www.diggitmagazine.com.

DfE (Department for Education) (1995) *Ethnic Monitoring of School Pupils: A Consultation Paper*. London: DfE.

Dickerson, L.J. (1975) The learner's interlanguage as a system of variable rules. *TESOL Quarterly* 9, 401–407.

Doran, M. (2004) Negotiating between 'Bourge' and 'Racaille': Verlan as youth identity practice in suburban Paris. In A. Pavlenko and A. Blackledge (eds) *Negotiation of Identities in Multilingual Contexts* (pp. 93–124). Clevedon: Multilingual Matters.

Dorling, D. and Tomlinson, S. (2019) *Rule Britannia: Brexit and the End of Empire.* London: Biteback.

Doughty, C. and Williams, J. (eds) (1998) *Focus on Form in Classroom Second Language Acquisition.* Cambridge: Cambridge University Press.

Douglas Fir Group (2016) A transdisciplinary framework for SLA in a multilingual world. *The Modern Language Journal* 100 (S1), 19–47. doi:10.1111/modl.12301

Dover, C. (2007) Everyday talk: Investigating media consumption and identity amongst schoolchildren. *Participations* 4 (1). See www.participations.org.

Drew, P. and Heritage, J. (1992) Analyzing talk at work: An introduction. In *Talk at Work* (pp. 3–65). Cambridge: Cambridge University Press.

Duchêne, A., Moyer, M. and Roberts, C. (eds) (2013) *Language, Migration and Social Inequalities: A Critical Sociolinguistic Perspective on Institutions and Work.* Bristol: Multilingual Matters.

Duff, P. (2012) Second language socialization. In A. Duranti, E. Ochs and B. Schieffelin (eds) *The Handbook of Language Socialization* (pp. 564–586). Oxford: Wiley–Blackwell.

Dummett, A. (1973) *A Portrait of English Racism.* Harmondsworth: Penguin.

Dummett, A. (1984) *A Portrait of English Racism* (2nd edn). London: CARAF.

Duranti, A. (1997) *Linguistic Anthropology.* Cambridge: Cambridge University Press.

Duranti, A. (ed.) (2001a) *Key Terms in Language and Culture.* Oxford: Blackwell.

Duranti, A. (2003) Language as culture in US anthropology. *Current Anthropology* 44, 323–347.

Duranti, A. (2009) Introduction. In *Linguistic Anthropology: A Reader* (2nd edn) (pp. 91–59). Oxford: Wiley-Blackwell.

Duranti, A., Ochs, E. and Schieffelin, B. (eds) (2012) *The Handbook of Language Socialization.* Oxford: Wiley-Blackwell.

Eade, J. (ed.) (1997) *Living the Global City.* London: Routledge.

Eckert, P. (2000) *Linguistic Variation as Social Practice.* Oxford: Blackwell.

Eckert, P. (2008) Variation and the indexical field. *Journal of Sociolinguistics* 12 (4), 453–476.

Eckert, P. (2012) Three waves of variation study: The emergence of meaning in the study of variation. *Annual Review of Anthropology* 41, 87–100.

EfA (2016) *Annual Report 2015–16.* London: Education Funding Agency. At https://www.gov.uk/government/organisations/charity-commission

Eggar, T. (1991) Correct use of English is essential. *Times Educational Supplement,* 28 June.

Eley, L. (2018) Linguistic landscape: An interactional perspective. Unpublished PhD dissertation, King's College London.

Eley, L. and Rampton, B. (2020) Everyday surveillance, Goffman and unfocused interaction. *Surveillance & Society* 20 (2), 199–215.

Ellis, R. (1994) *The Study of Second Language Acquisition.* Oxford: Oxford University Press.

Erickson, F. (1986) Qualitative methods in research on teaching. In M. Wittrock (ed.) *Handbook of Research on Teaching* (3rd edn) (pp. 119–161). New York: Macmillan. Also available at https://www.researchgate.net/publication/31640397_Qualitative_methods_in_research_on_teaching

Erickson, F. (2001) Co-membership and wiggle room: Some implications of the study of talk for the development of social theory. In N. Coupland, S. Sarangi and C. Candlin (eds) *Sociolinguistics and Social Theory* (pp. 152–181). London: Longman.

Erickson, F. (2004) *Talk and Social Theory*. Oxford: Polity Press.

Erickson, F. (2011) From speech as 'situated' to speech as 'situating': Insights from John Gumperz on the practical conduct of talk as social action. *Text & Talk* 31, 395–406.

Erickson, F. and Shultz, J. (1982) *The Counselor as Gatekeeper*. New York: Academic Press.

Eyal, N. (2014) *Hooked: How to Build Habit-forming Products*. See www.hookmodel.com.

Fairclough, N. (1989) *Language and Power*. London: Longman.

Fairclough, N. (1992) *Discourse and Social Change*. Cambridge: Polity Press.

Fanshawe, S. and Sriskandarajah, C. (2011) *'You Can't Put Me in a Box': Super-diversity and the End of Identity Politics in Britain*. London: IPPR.

Ferguson, C. (1959) Diglossia. *Word* 15, 325–340.

Footitt, H. and Kelly, M. (eds) (2012) *Languages at War: Policies and Practices of Language Contacts in Conflict*. Basingstoke: Palgrave.

Forster, E.M. (1924/1973) *A Passage to India*. Harmondsworth: Penguin Modern Classics.

Fortier, A.-M. (2008) *Multicultural Horizons: Diversity and the Limits of a Civil Nation*. Abingdon: Routledge.

Foucault, M. (1971) Orders of discourse. *Social Science Information* 10 (2), 7–30.

Foucault, M. (1972) *The Archaeology of Knowledge*. London: Tavistock.

Foucault, M. (1977) *Discipline and Punish*. Harmondsworth: Penguin.

Foucault, M. (1978/2003) Governmentality. In P. Rabinow and N. Rose (eds) *The Essential Foucault: Selections from Essential Works of Foucault 1954–(1984)* (pp. 229–245). New York: New Press.

Foucault, M. (1980/2003) Questions of method. In P. Rabinow and N. Rose (eds) *The Essential Foucault: Selections from Essential Works of Foucault 1954–(1984)* (pp. 246–258). New York: New Press.

Foucault, M. (1984/2003) Polemics, politics and problematisations: An interview with Michel Foucault. In P. Rabinow and N. Rose (eds) *The Essential Foucault: Selections from Essential Works of Foucault 1954–(1984)* (pp. 18–24). New York: New Press.

Foucault, M. (2003) What is enlightenment? In P. Rabinow and N. Rose (eds) *The Essential Foucault: Selections from Essential Works of Foucault 1954–(1984)* (pp. 43–57). New York: New Press.

Fraser, N. (1995) From redistribution to recognition? Dilemmas of justice in a 'post-socialist' age. *New Left Review* 212, 68–93.

Fraser, N. (2003) From discipline to flexibilisation? Rereading Foucault in the shadow of globalisation. *Constellations* 10 (2), 160–171.

Fraurud, K. and Boyd, S. (2006) The native–nonnative speaker distinction and the diversity of linguistic profiles of young people in Swedish multilingual urban contexts. In F. Hinskens (ed.) *Language Variation: European Perspectives* (pp. 53–69). Philadelphia, PA and Amsterdam: John Benjamins.

Freeman, S. and Heller, M. (eds) (1987) *Medical Discourse*. Special Issue of *Text* 7 (1).

Freire, P. (1970) *Pedagogy of the Oppressed*. Harmondsworth: Penguin.

Friesen, N., Feenberg, A. and Smith, G. (2009) Phenomenology and surveillance studies: Returning to the things themselves. *The Information Society* 25, 84–90.

Gal, S. (2006) Contradictions of standard language in Europe: Implications for the study of practices and publics. *Social Anthropology* 14 (2), 163–181.

Gallo, S. (2014) The effects of gendered immigration enforcement on middle childhood and schooling. *AERJ* 51 (3), 473–504.

Gallo, S. and Link, H. (2015) 'Diles la verdad': Deportation policies, politicised funds of knowledge, and schooling in middle childhood. *Harvard Educational Review* 85 (3), 357–382.

Geertz, C. (1973) *The Interpretation of Cultures*. London: Hutchinson.

Georgakopoulou, A. (2008) 'On MSN with buff boys': Self- and other-identity claims in the context of small stories. *Journal of Sociolinguistics* 12 (5), 597–626.

Georgakopoulou, A. (2014) Girlpower or girl (in) trouble?: Identities and discourses in the (new) media engagements of adolescents' school-based in interaction. In J. Androutsopoulos (ed.) *Mediatization and Sociolinguistic Change* (pp. 217–244). Berlin: de Gruyter.

Georgakopoulou, A. (2021) Contribution to Memorial Event for Jan Blommaert, 6 February.

Gibbons, M., Limoges, C., Nowotny, H., Schwartzman, S., Scott, P. and Trow, M. (1994) *The New Production of Knowledge: The Dynamics of Science and Research in Contemporary Societies*. London: Sage.

Gibbons, S. (2017) *English and its Teachers: A History of Policy, Pedagogy and Practice*. London: Routledge.

Giddens, A. (1976) *New Rules of Sociological Method*. London: Hutchinson.

Gillborn, D. and Gipps, C. (1996) *Recent Research on the Achievement of Ethnic Minority Pupils*. London: OFSTED.

Gillespie, M. (1995) *Television, Ethnicity and Cultural Change*. London: Routledge.

Gilliom, J. and Monahan, T. (2012) Everyday resistance. In K. Ball, K. Haggerty and D. Lyon (eds) *Routledge Handbook of Surveillance Studies* (pp. 405–411). London: Routledge.

Gilroy, P. (1987) *There Ain't No Black in the Union Jack*. London: Hutchinson.

Gilroy, P. (2006) Multiculture in times of war: An inaugural lecture given at the London School of Economics. *Critical Quarterly* 48 (4), 27–45.

Gilroy, P. and Lawrence, E. (1988) Two-tone Britain: White and Black youth and the politics of anti-racism. In P. Cohen and H. Bains (eds) *Multiracist Britain* (pp. 121–155). Basingstoke: Macmillan.

Goddard, J. and Puukka, J. (2008) The engagement of higher education institutions in regional development: An overview of the opportunities and challenges. *Higher Education Management and Policy* 20 (2), 11–41.

Goffman, E. (1959) *The Presentation of Self in Everyday Life*. Harmondsworth: Penguin.

Goffman, E. (1961) *Asylums*. Harmondsworth: Penguin.

Goffman, E. (1963a) *Stigma*. Harmondsworth: Penguin.

Goffman, E. (1963b) *Behaviour in Public Places*. New York: Free Press.

Goffman, E. (1964) The neglected situation. *American Anthropologist* 66 (6), 133–136.

Goffman, E. (1967a) *Interaction Ritual*. Harmondsworth: Penguin.

Goffman, E. (1967b) The nature of deference and demeanour. In *Interactional Ritual* (pp. 47–95). Harmondsworth: Penguin.

Goffman, E. (1970) *Strategic Interaction*. Oxford: Blackwell.

Goffman, E. (1971) *Relations in Public*. London: Allen Lane.

Goffman, E. (1974) *Frame Analysis*. Boston, MA: Northeastern University Press.

Goffman, E. (1981) *Forms of Talk*. Philadelphia, PA: Pennsylvania University Press.

Goffman, E. (1983) The interaction order. *American Sociological Review* 48, 1–17.

Goldstein, D.M. (2010) Toward a critical anthropology of security. *Current Anthropology* 51 (4), 487–517.

Goodwin, C. (2000) Action and embodiment within situated human interaction. *Journal of Pragmatics* 32, 1489–1522.
Goodwin, M. (2006) *The Hidden Life of Girls: Games of Stance, Status and Exclusion*. Oxford: Blackwell.
Gready, P. and Robins, S. (2014) From transitional to transformative justice: A new agenda for practice. *International Journal of Transitional Justice* 8 (3), 339–361.
Green, J. and Bloome, D. (1997) Ethnography and ethnographers of and in education: A situated perspective. In J. Flood, S. Brice Heath and D. Lapp (eds) *Handbook of Research on Teaching Literacy through the Communicative and Visual Arts* (pp. 181–202). New York: Macmillan.
Green, N. and Zurawski, N. (2015) Surveillance and ethnography: Researching surveillance as everyday life. *Surveillance & Society* 13 (1), 27–43.
Gumperz, J. (1972) Introduction. In J. Gumperz and D. Hymes (eds) *Directions in Sociolinguistics: The Ethnography of Communication* (pp. 1–25). Oxford: Blackwell.
Gumperz, J. (1979/1990) Interview with John Gumperz. In J. Twitchin (ed.) *Crosstalk: An Introduction to Cross-cultural Communication* (pp. 46–55). London: BBC. (Also available in R. Harris and B. Rampton (eds) (2003) *The Language, Ethnicity and Race Reader* (pp. 267–275). London: Routledge.)
Gumperz, J. (1982) *Discourse Strategies*. Cambridge: Cambridge University Press.
Gumperz, J. (1996) The linguistic and cultural relativity of inference. In J. Gumperz and S. Levinson (eds) *Rethinking Linguistic Relativity* (pp. 374–406). Cambridge: Cambridge University Press.
Gumperz, J. (1999) On interactional sociolinguistic method. In S. Sarangi and C. Roberts (eds) *Talk, Work and Institutional Order* (pp. 453–471). Berlin: Mouton.
Gumperz, J. (ed.) (1982) *Language and Social Identity*. Cambridge: Cambridge University Press.
Gumperz, J. and Berenz, N. (1993) Transcribing conversational exchanges. In J. Edwards and M. Lampert (eds) *Talking Language* (pp. 91–122). Hillsdale, NJ: Lawrence Erlbaum.
Gumperz, J. and Cook-Gumperz, J. (2005) Language standardisation and the complexities of communicative practice. In S. McKinnon and S. Silverman (eds) *Complexities: Beyond Nature and Nurture* (pp. 268–286). Chicago, IL: Chicago University Press.
Gumperz, J. and Cook-Gumperz, J. (2008) Studying language, culture and society: Sociolinguistics or linguistic anthropology? *Journal of Sociolinguistics* 12, 532–545.
Gumperz, J. and Hernández-Chavez, E. (1972) Bilingualism, bidialectalism, and classroom interaction. In C. Cazden, V. John and D. Hymes (eds) *Functions of Language in the Classroom* (pp. 84–110). Columbia: Teachers College Press.
Gumperz, J. and Hymes, D. (eds) (1972) *Directions in Sociolinguistics: The Ethnography of Communication*. Oxford: Blackwell.
Gumperz, J., Jupp, T. and Roberts, C. (1979) *Crosstalk*. Southall: BBC/National Centre for Industrial Language Training.
Haarstad, H. and Fløysand, A. (2007) Globalisation and the power of rescaled narratives: A case of opposition to mining in Tambogrande, Peru. *Political Geography* 26, 289–308.
Hacking, I. (2004) Between Michel Foucault and Erving Goffman: Between discourse in the abstract and face-to-face interaction. *Economy and Society* 33 (3), 277–302.
Haddington, P. and Raunioma, M. (2014) Interaction between road users: Offering space in traffic. *Space and Culture* 17 (2), 176–190.

Haddington, P., Frogell, S., Grubert, A. *et al.* (2012) Civil inattention in public places: Normalising unusual events through mobile and embodied practices. *Forum: Qualitative Social Research* 13 (3), 7.

Hadjipieris, I. and Kabatas, O. (2015) *Joint Dictionary of Greek Cypriot and Turkish Dialect*. Nicosia: Lithographica.

Haggerty, K. (2006) Tear down the walls: On demolishing the panopticon. In D. Lyon (ed.) *Theorising Surveillance: The Panopticon and Beyond* (pp. 23–45). Cullompton: Willan.

Haggerty, K.D. and Ericson, R.V. (2000) The surveillant assemblage. *British Journal of Sociology* 51 (4), 605–622.

Hall, K. (1995) Lip service on the fantasy lines. In K. Hall and M. Bucholtz (eds) *Gender Articulated* (pp. 183–216). London: Routledge.

Hall, S. (1980) Encoding/decoding. In S. Hall, D. Hobson, A. Lowe and P. Willis (eds) *Culture, Media, Language* (pp. 128–138). London: Unwin Hyman.

Hall, S. (1988) New ethnicities. *ICA Documents* 7, 27–31. Reprinted in J. Donald and A. Rattansi (eds) (1992) *'Race', Culture and Difference* (pp. 252–259). London: Sage.

Hall, S. (2006) Transcript from Ethnicities Workshop organised by ESRC Identities and Social Action Programme, London School of Economics, 21 June. Unpublished.

Hammersley, M. (1999) *What's Wrong with Ethnography?* London: Routledge.

Hammersley, M. (2007) Reflections on linguistic ethnography. *Journal of Sociolinguistics* 11 (5), 689–695.

Hanks, W. (1987) Discourse genres as a theory of practice. *American Ethnologist* 14 (4), 668–692.

Hanks, W. (1996) *Language and Communicative Practices*. Boulder, CO: Westview Press.

Hanks, W. (2005) Pierre Bourdieu and the practices of language. *Annual Review of Anthropology* 34, 67–83.

Hannerz, U. (1990) Cosmopolitans and locals in world culture. *Theory, Culture and Society* 7, 237–251.

Harris, R. (1997) Romantic bilingualism? Time for a change. In C. Leung and C. Cable (eds) *English as an Additional Language: Changing Perspectives* (pp. 28–39). Watford: NALDIC.

Harris, R. (2006) *New Ethnicities and Language Use*. Basingstoke: Palgrave.

Harris, R. (2008) Multilingualism, community and diaspora. King's College London. MS.

Harris, R. and Lefstein, A. (2011) *Urban Classroom Culture: Realities, Dilemmas, Responses*. London: Centre for Language Discourse and Communication, King's College London. See https://www.kcl.ac.uk/ecs/research/ucc/ucculture.

Harris, R. and Rampton, B. (2002) Creole metaphors in cultural analysis: On the limits and possibilities of (socio-)linguistics. *Critique of Anthropology* 22 (1), 31–51.

Harris, R. and Rampton, B. (eds) (2003) *The Language, Ethnicity and Race Reader*. London: Routledge.

Heath, C., Luff, P. and Sanchez Svensson, M. (2002) Overseeing organisations: Configuring action and its environment. *British Journal of Sociology* 53 (2), 181–201.

Heath, S.-B. (1983) *Ways with Words*. Cambridge: Cambridge University Press.

Hebdige, D. (1979) *Subculture: The Meaning of Style*. London: Methuen.

Hebdige, D. (1987) *Cut 'n' Mix: Culture, Identity and Caribbean Music*. London: Comedia.

Heller, M. (2007a) The future of 'bilingualism'. In *Bilingualism: A Social Approach* (pp. 340–345). Basingstoke: Palgrave.

Heller, M. (ed.) (2007b) *Bilingualism: A Social Approach*. Basingstoke: Palgrave.
Heller, M. and Martin-Jones, M. (eds) (2001) *Voices of Authority: Education and Linguistic Difference*. Westport, CT: Ablex.
Heller, M. and McIlhinny, B. (2017) *Language, Capitalism, Colonialism*. Toronto: University of Toronto Press.
Helten, F. and Fischer, B. (2004) Reactive attention: Video surveillance in Berlin shopping malls. *Surveillance & Society* 2 (2/3), 323–345.
Heritage, J. (1997) Conversation analysis and institutional talk: Analysing data. In D. Silverman (ed.) *Qualitative Research: Theory, Method, Practice* (pp. 161–182). London: Sage.
Hewitt, R. (1986) *White Talk, Black Talk*. Cambridge: Cambridge University Press.
Hewitt, R. (1989) Creole in the classroom: Political grammars and educational vocabularies. In R. Grillo (ed.) *Social Anthropology and the Politics of Language* (pp. 126–144). London: Routledge.
Hewitt, R. (1992/2003) Language, youth and the destabilisation of ethnicity. In R. Harris and B. Rampton (eds) *The Language Ethnicity and Race Reader* (pp. 188–198). London: Routledge.
Hill, J. (1999) Styling locally, styling globally: What does it mean? *Journal of Sociolinguistics* 3 (4), 542–556.
Hill, J. (2001) Mock Spanish, covert racism and the (leaky) boundary between public and private spheres. In S. Gal and K. Woolard (eds) *Language and Publics: The Making of Authority* (pp. 83–102). Manchester: St Jerome Press.
Hill, J. (2004) On where stereotypes come from so that kids can recruit them. *Pragmatics* 14 (2/3), 193–198.
Hill, J. (2005) Intertextuality as source and evidence for indirect indexical meanings. *Journal of Linguistic Anthropology* 15 (1), 95–112.
Hill, J. (2008) *The Everyday Language of White Racism*. Oxford: Wiley-Blackwell.
Hindmarsh, J., Heath, C., Vom Lehn, D. *et al.* (2001) Interaction as a public phenomenon. Stockholm: CID, Centre for User Oriented IT Design.
HM Government (2015) *Prevent Duty Guidance: For Higher Education Institutions in England and Wales*. London: HMSO.
Hodges, A. (2011) *The 'War on Terror' Narrative*. Oxford: Oxford University Press.
Hodges, A. (ed.) (2013) *Discourses of War and Peace*. Oxford: Oxford University Press.
Holmes, J. (2001) *Introduction to Sociolinguistics*. London: Longman.
Holmes, S. (2015) Promoting multilingual creativity: Key principles from successful project. *Working Papers in Urban Language and Literacies* No. 182.
Holmes, S. (2017) Lusondoners: An account of Lusophone-inflected superdiversity in a south London school. PhD thesis, King's College London, Department of Education, Communication and Society.
Howatt, A. (1984) *A History of English Language Teaching*. Oxford: Oxford University Press.
Hudson, R. (1996) *Sociolinguistics*. Cambridge: Cambridge University Press.
Huysmans, J. (2006) *The Politics of Insecurity*. Abingdon: Routledge.
Huysmans, J. (2009) Conclusion: Insecurity and the everyday. In P. Noxolo and J. Huysmans (eds) *Community, Citizenship, and the 'War on Terror': Security and Insecurity* (pp. 197–207). Basingstoke: Palgrave Macmillan.
Huysmans, J. (2011) What's in an act: On security speech acts and little security nothings. *Security Dialogue* 42 (4–5), 371–383.
Huysmans, J. (2014) *Security Unbound: Enacting Democratic Limits*. London: Routledge.

Hymes, D. (1969) The use of anthropology: Critical, political, personal. In *Reinventing Anthropology* (pp. 3–82). New York: Pantheon Books.
Hymes, D. (1972a) On communicative competence. In J. Pride and J. Holmes (eds) *Sociolinguistics* (pp. 269–293). Harmondsworth: Penguin.
Hymes, D. (1972b) Models of the interaction of language and social life. In J. Gumperz and D. Hymes (eds) *Directions in Sociolinguistics: The Ethnography of Communication* (pp. 35–71). Oxford: Blackwell.
Hymes, D. (1975/1996) Report from an underdeveloped country: Toward linguistic competence in the United States. In *Ethnography; Linguistics, Narrative Inequality: Toward an Understanding of Voice* (pp. 63–106). London: Taylor & Francis.
Hymes, D. (1977) *Foundations in Sociolinguistics: An Ethnographic Approach*. London: Tavistock.
Hymes, D. (1978/1996) What is ethnography? In *Ethnography, Linguistics, Narrative Inequality* (pp. 3–17). London: Taylor & Francis. See https://www.academia.edu/36884832/.
Hymes, D. (1980a) Ethnographic monitoring. In *Language in Education: Ethnolinguistic Essays* (pp. 104–118). Washington, DC: CAL. See https://files.eric.ed.gov/fulltext/ED198745.pdf.
Hymes, D. (1980b) *Language in Education: Ethnolinguistic Essays*. Washington, DC: Centre for Applied Linguistics.
Hymes, D. (1983) *Essays in the History of Linguistic Anthropology*. Amsterdam: John Benjamins.
Hymes, D. (1996) *Ethnography; Linguistics, Narrative Inequality: Toward an Understanding of Voice*. London: Taylor & Francis.
Hymes, D. (1997) History and development of sociolinguistics. In C. Bratt-Paulston and R. Tucker (eds) *The Early Days of Sociolinguistics* (pp. 121–130). Dallas, TX: Summer Institute of Linguistics.
Iedema, R. and Carroll, K. (2011) The clinalyst: Institutionalising reflexivity and flexible systematisation in health care organisations. *Journal for Organizational Change Management* 24 (2), 175–190.
Irvine, J. (2001) 'Style' as distinctiveness: The culture and ideology of linguistic differentiation. In P. Eckert and J. Rickford (eds) *Style and Sociolinguistic Variation* (pp. 21–43). Cambridge: Cambridge University Press.
Isin, E. (2008) Theorising acts of citizenship. In E. Isin and G. Nielsen (eds) *Acts of Citizenship* (pp. 15–43). London: Zed Books.
Jacobs, B. and Miller, J. (1998) Crack dealing, gender, and arrest avoidance. *Social Problems* 45 (4), 550–569.
Jacquemet, M. (2005a) The registration interview: Restricting refugees' narrative performances. In M. Baynham and A. De Fina (eds) *Dislocations/Relocations: Narratives of Displacement* (pp. 197–220). Manchester: St Jerome.
Jacquemet, M. (2005b) Transidiomatic practices: Language and power in the age of globalisation. *Language & Communication* 25, 257–277.
Jacquemet, M. (2011) Cross-talk 2.0: Asylum and communicative breakdowns. *Text & Talk* 31 (4), 475–498.
Jaffe, A. (2007) Minority language movements. In M. Heller (ed.) *Bilingualism: A Social Approach* (pp. 50–70). London: Palgrave Macmillan.
Jaspers, J. (2005) Linguistic sabotage in a context of monolingualism and standardization. *Language & Communication* 25 (3), 279–298. (Earlier version available in *Working Papers in Urban Language and Literacies* No. 28. See www.academia.edu.)

Jaspers, J. (2008) Problematizing ethnolects: Naming linguistic practices in an Antwerp secondary school. *International Journal of Bilingualism* 12, 85–103.

Jaspers, J. (2017) The transformative limits of translanguaging. *Working Papers in Urban Language and Literacies* No. 226.

Jenkins, R. (2010) The 21st century interaction order. In M. Jacobsen (ed.) *The Contemporary Goffman* (pp. 257–274). London: Routledge.

Jessop, B. (2007) From micro-powers to governmentality: Foucault's work on statehood, state formation, statecraft and state power. *Political Geography* 26 (1), 34–40.

Johnstone, B. and Danielson, A. (2006) Mobility, indexicality and the enregisterment of 'Pittsburghese'. *Journal of English Linguistics* 34 (2), 77–104.

Jones, R. (2015) Surveillance. In A. Georgakopoulou and T. Spilioti (eds) *The Routledge Handbook of Language and Digital Communication* (pp. 408–411). London: Routledge.

Jones, R. (2016) *Spoken Discourse*. London: Bloomsbury.

Jones, R. (2017) Surveillant landscapes. *Linguistic Landscapes* 3 (2), 150–187.

Jones, R. (2020a) Accounting for surveillance. *Journal of Sociolinguistics* 24, 89–95.

Jones, R. (2020b) Discourse analysis and digital surveillance. In A. De Fina and A. Georgakopoulou (eds) *Cambridge Handbook of Discourse Studies* (pp. 708–731). Cambridge: Cambridge University Press.

Jones, S. (1988) *Black Culture, White Youth*. Basingstoke: Macmillan.

Jørgensen, N. (2008a) Introduction: Poly-lingual languaging around and among children and adolescents. *International Journal of Multilingualism* 5 (3), 161–176.

Jørgensen, N. (ed.) (2008b) *Polylingual Languaging Around and Among Children and Adolescents*. Special issue of *International Journal of Multilingualism* 5 (3).

Joseph, J. and Taylor, T. (eds) (1990) *Ideologies of Language*. London: Routledge.

Karoulla-Vrikki, D. (2004) Language and ethnicity in Cyprus under the British: A linkage of heightened salience. *International Journal of the Sociology of Language* 168, 19–36.

Karrebæk, M. (2021) Contribution to Memorial Event for Jan Blommaert, 6 February.

Karrebæk, M. and Ghandchi, N. (2015) 'Pure' Farsi and political sensitivities: Language and ideologies in Farsi complementary language classrooms in Denmark. *Journal of Sociolinguistics* 19 (1), 62–90.

Karyolemou, M. (2003) 'Keep your language and I will keep mine': Politics, language, and the construction of identities in Cyprus. In D. Nelson and M. Dedaic-Nelson (eds) *At War with Words* (pp. 359–384). Berlin and New York: Mouton de Gruyter.

Keim, I. (2007) Sociocultural identity, communicative style, and their change over time: A case study of a group of German-Turkish girls in Mannheim/Germany. In P. Auer (ed.) *Style and Social Identities: Alternative Approaches to Linguistic Heterogeneity* (pp. 155–186). Berlin: Mouton de Gruyter.

Kell, C. (2015) Ariadne's thread: Literacy, scale and meaning making across space and time. In C. Stroud and M. Prinsloo (eds) *Language, Literacy and Diversity: Moving Words* (pp. 72–91). London: Routledge. (Also available as *Working Papers in Urban Language and Literacies* No. 118 (2013).)

Kell, C. (2021) Tribute to Jan Blommaert. Email circulated 11 January.

Kendon, A. (1990) *Conducting Interaction: Patterns of Behaviour in Focused Encounters*. Cambridge: Cambridge University Press.

Khan, K. (2014) Citizenship, securitization and suspicion in UK ESOL policy. *Working Papers in Urban Language and Literacies* No. 130. See www.academia.edu.

Khan, K. (2015) 'Suspect communities' and multilingual solutions for intelligence and armed conflict. University of Leicester. MS.

Khan, K. (2017) Citizenship, securitization and suspicion in UK ESOL policy. In K. Arnaut, M.S. Karrebæk, M. Spotti and J. Blommaert (eds) *Engaging Superdiversity: Recombining Spaces, Times and Language Practices* (pp. 303–320). Bristol: Multilingual Matters. (Also available as *Working Papers in Urban Language and Literacies* No. 130. See www.academia.edu.)

Khan, K. (2020) Preparing the milk and honey: Between ethnography and academia as a racially minoritized academic. *Applied Linguistics Review* 11 (2), 207–231.

Khan, K. and Blackledge, A. (2015) 'They look into our lips': Negotiation of the citizenship ceremony as authoritative discourse. *Journal of Language and Politics* 14 (3), 382–405.

Kiesling, S. (2004) Dude. *American Speech* 79 (3), 281–305.

Kiesling, S. (2005) Variation, stance and style. *English World-Wide* 26 (1), 1–42.

Kitis, D. and Milani, T. (2015) The performativity of the body: Turbulent spaces in Greece. *Linguistic Landscapes* 1 (3), 268–290.

Kizilyürek, N. and Gautier-Kizilyürek, S. (2004) The politics of identity in the Turkish Cypriot community and the language question. *International Journal of the Sociology of Language* 168, 37–54.

Koole, T. (2007) Review of Ben Rampton (2006) Language in Late Modernity: Interaction in an urban school. *Journal of Pragmatics* 39 (4), 778–780.

Kotsinas, U.-B. (1988) Immigrant children's Swedish – a new variety? *Journal of Multilingual and Multicultural Development* 9 (1–2), 129–140.

Kotthoff, H. (2007) The humorous stylisation of 'new' women and men and conservative others. In P. Auer (ed.) *Style and Social Identities: Alternative Approaches to Linguistic Heterogeneity* (pp. 445–476). Berlin: Mouton de Gruyter.

Kramsch, C. (2009) *The Multilingual Subject*. Oxford: Oxford University Press.

Kroon, S. (2021) In memory of Jan Blommaert. *Diggit Magazine*, 8 January. See www.diggitmagazine.com.

Labov, W. (1972) *Sociolinguistic Patterns*. Philadelphia, PA: University of Pennsylvania Press.

Larsen, J., Urry, J. and Axhausen, K. (2008) Coordinating face-to-face meetings in mobile network societies. *Information, Communication and Society* 11 (5), 640–658.

Lave, J. and Wenger, E. (1991) *Situated Learning: Legitimate Peripheral Participation*. Cambridge: Cambridge University Press.

Lefstein, A. and Snell, J. (2011) Professional vision and the politics of teacher learning. *Teaching and Teacher Education* 27, 505–514.

Lefstein, A. and Snell, J. (2014) *Better than Best Practice*. London: Routledge.

Leonardsson, H. and Rudd, G. (2015) The 'local turn' in peacebuilding: A literature review of effective and emancipatory local peacebuilding. *Third World Quarterly* 36 (5), 825–839.

LePage, R. (1988) Some premises concerning the standardisation of languages, with special reference to Caribbean Creole English. *International Journal of the Sociology of Language* 71, 25–36.

LePage, R. and Tabouret-Keller, A. (1985) *Acts of Identity*. Cambridge: Cambridge University Press.

Leppänen, S. (2021) Contribution to Memorial Event for Jan Blommaert, 6 February.

Leung, C., Harris, R. and Rampton, B. (1997) The idealised native speaker, reified ethnicities and classroom realities. *TESOL Quarterly* 31 (3), 543–560. (Also available as *Working Papers in Urban Language and Literacies* No. 2.)

Levinson, S. (1996) Relativity in spatial conception and description. In J. Gumperz and S. Levinson (eds) *Rethinking Linguistic Relativity* (pp. 177–202). Cambridge: Cambridge University Press.

Liberman, K. (2013) The local orderliness of crossing Kincaid. In K. Liberman (ed.) *More Studies in Ethnomethodology*. Albany, NY: SUNY Press.
Liberty (2018) *The Border Controls Dividing Our Communities: A Guide to the Hostile Environment*. London: Liberty.
Liddicoat, A. (2008) Language planning and questions of national security: An overview of planning approaches. *Current Issues in Language Planning* 9 (2), 129–153.
LINC (1992) *Language in the National Curriculum: Materials for Professional Development*. Nottingham: Nottingham University English Department.
Lippi-Green, R. (1997) *English with an Accent*. London: Routledge.
Luff, P., Heath, C. and Sanchez Svensson, M. (2008) Discriminating conduct: Deploying systems to support awareness in organizations. *International Journal of Human-Computer Interaction* 24 (4), 410–436.
Lyon, D. (2006) (ed.) *Theorising Surveillance: The Panopticon and Beyond*. Cullompton: Willan.
Lyon, D. (2007) *Surveillance Studies: An Overview*. Cambridge: Polity Press.
Lyon, D., Haggerty, K. and Ball, K. (2012) Introducing surveillance studies. In K. Ball, K. Haggerty and D. Lyon (eds) (2012) *Routledge Handbook of Surveillance Studies* (pp. 1–11). London: Routledge.
Lytra, V. (2007) *Play Frames and Social Identities*. Amsterdam: John Benjamins.
Lytra, V. (2014) Multilingualism, multimodality and media engagement in classroom talk and action. In J. Androutsopoulos (ed.) *Mediatization and Social Change* (pp. 245–268). Berlin: De Gruyter Mouton.
Maalouf Report (2008) *A Rewarding Challenge: How the Multiplicity of Languages Could Strengthen Europe*. Report of the Group of Intellectuals for Intercultural Dialogue, Brussels.
MacDonald, M. and Hunter, D. (2013) Security, population and governmentality: UK counter-terrorism discourse (2007–2011). *Critical Discourse Analysis across Disciplines* 6 (2), 123–140.
Mac Ginty, R. (2014) Everyday peace: Bottom-up and local agency in conflict-affected society. *Security Dialogue* 45 (6), 548–564.
Mac Ginty, R. and Richmond, O. (2013) The local turn in peace building: A critical agenda for peace. *Third World Quarterly* 34 (5), 763–783.
Maegaard, M. (2010) Linguistic practice and stereotypes among Copenhagen adolescents. In P. Quist and B.A. Svendsen (eds) *Multilingual Urban Scandinavia: New Linguistic Practices* (pp. 189–206). Bristol: Multilingual Matters.
Maguire, M., Frois, C. and Zurawski, N. (eds) (2014) *The Anthropology of Security*. London: Pluto Press.
Makoni, S. and Pennycook, A. (eds) (2007) *Disinventing and Reconstituting Languages*. Clevedon: Multilingual Matters.
Malai Madsen, L. (2015) *Fighters, Girls and Other Identities: Sociolinguistics in a Martial Arts Club*. Bristol: Multilingual Matters.
Malai Madsen, L. and Karrebæk, M. (2015) Hip hop, education and polycentricity. In J. Snell, S. Shaw and F. Copland (eds) *Linguistic Ethnography: Interdisciplinary Explorations* (pp. 246–267). Basingstoke: Palgrave Macmillan.
Malcolm, I. (2009) *Towards Inclusion: Protestants and the Irish Language*. Belfast: Blackstaff Press.
Maly, I. (2021a) Tribute to Jan Blommaert as public intellectual. *Diggit Magazine*, 8 January. See www.diggitmagazine.com.
Maly, I. (2021b) Jan Blommaert (1961–2021). *Discourse & Society* 32 (3), 394–398. doi:10.1177/0957926521992689

Mangual Figuero, A. (2020) Embodying the breach: (In)securitisation and ethnographic engagement in the US. *Journal of Sociolinguistics* 24, 96–102.

Martin, D. (2017) ALL migrants should learn English before moving to UK: Verdict of Labour MP ... it's time to ditch failed multiculturalism. Daily Mail, 5 January. See https://www.dailymail.co.uk/news/article-4089544/ALL-migrants-learn-English-moving-UK-Verdict-Labour-MP-s-time-ditch-failed-multiculturalism.html.

Marwick, A. (2012) The public domain: Social surveillance in everyday life. *Surveillance & Society* 9 (4), 378–393.

Marwick, A. and boyd, d. (2010) I tweet honestly, I tweet passionately: Twitter users, context collapse, and the imagined audience. *New Media and Society* 13 (1).

Marx, G. (2009) A tack in the shoe and taking off the shoe. *Surveillance & Society* 6 (3), 294–306.

Maryns, K. (2006) *The Asylum Speaker: Language in the Belgian Asylum Procedure.* Manchester: St Jerome Press.

Matras, Y. and Robertson, A. (2017) Urban multilingualism and the civic university: A dynamic, non-linear model of participatory research. *Social Inclusion* 5 (4), 5–13.

May, T. (2015) A stronger Britain, built on our values. Speech, 23 March. See https: // www.gov.uk/government/speeches/a-stronger-britain-built-on-our-values.

Maybin, J. (2006) *Children's Voices: Talk, Knowledge and Identity.* Basingstoke: Palgrave Macmillan.

Maybin, J. (2017) Textual trajectories: Theoretical roots and institutional consequences. *Text & Talk* 37 (4), 415–435.

McCarty, T. (2011) Introducing ethnography and language policy. In T. McCarty (ed.) *Ethnography and Language Policy* (pp. 1–28). London: Routledge.

Mc Cluskey, E. (2017) Everyday (in)security: A bibliography. *Working Papers in Urban Language and Literacies* No. 214. See www.academia.edu and www.kcl.ac.uk/liep.

Mc Cluskey, E. (2019) *From Righteousness to Far Right: An Anthropological Rethinking of Critical Security Studies.* Montreal: McGill-Queen's University Press.

McDermott, R. (1988) Inarticulateness. In D. Tannen (ed.) *Linguistics in Context: Connecting Observation and Understanding* (pp. 37–68). New Jersey: Ablex.

McIlvenny, P., Broth, M. and Haddington, P. (2014) Moving together: Mobile formations in interaction. *Space and Culture* 17 (2), 104–106.

Mehan, H. (1996) The construction of an LD student: A case study in the politics of representation. In M. Silverstein and G. Urban (eds) *Natural Histories of Discourse* (pp. 253–276). Chicago, IL: University of Chicago Press.

Mercer, N. (1995) *The Guided Construction of Knowledge: Talk Amongst Teachers and Learners.* Clevedon: Multilingual Matters.

Mey, J. (1987) Poet and peasant: A pragmatic comedy in five acts. *Journal of Pragmatics* 11, 281–297.

Mitchell, J.C. (1984) Case studies. In R. Ellen (ed.) *Ethnographic Research: A Guide to General Conduct* (pp. 237–241). London: Academic Press.

Moerman, M. (1974) Accomplishing ethnicity. In R. Turner (ed.) *Ethnomethodology* (pp. 54–68). Harmondsworth: Penguin.

Moerman, M. (1988) *Talking Culture: Ethnography and Conversation Analysis.* Philadelphia, PA: University of Pennsylvania Press.

Møller, J. (2009) Poly-lingual interaction across childhood, youth and adulthood. PhD dissertation, University of Copenhagen.

Mondada, L. (2009) Emergent focused interactions in public places: A systematic analysis of the multimodal achievement of a common interactional space. *Journal of Pragmatics* 41, 1977–1997.

Mondada, L. (2013) The conversation analytic approach to data collection. In J. Sidnell and T. Stivers (eds) *The Handbook of Conversation Analysis* (pp. 32–56). Oxford: Wiley Blackwell.

Mondada, L. (2016) Challenges of multimodality: Language and the body in social interaction. *Journal of Sociolinguistics* 20 (3), 336–366.

Moore, R. (2011) Standardisation, diversity and enlightenment in the contemporary crisis of EU language policy. *Working Papers in Urban Language and Literacies* No. 74.

Moore, R. (2021) Eulogy at Jan Blommaert's Funeral, 16 January.

Mugglestone, L. (1995) *Talking Proper.* Oxford: Clarendon Press.

Nortier, J. and Svendsen, B. (eds) (2015) *Language, Youth and Identity in the 21st Century.* Cambridge: Cambridge University Press.

O'Reilly, C. (1996) The Irish language – litmus test for equality? Competing discourse of identity, parity of esteem and the peace process. *Irish Journal of Sociology* 6, 154–178.

Ortega, L. (2019) SLA and the study of equitable multilingualism. *The Modern Language Journal* 103 (S1), 23–38.

Ortner, S. (1991) Reading America: Preliminary notes on class and culture. In R. Fox (ed.) *Recapturing Anthropology: Working in the Present* (pp. 164–189). Santa Fe, NM: School of American Research Press.

Ortner, S. (2006) *Anthropology and Social Theory: Culture, Power and the Acting Subject.* Durham, NC: Duke University Press.

Özerk, K. (2001) Reciprocal bilingualism as a challenge and opportunity: The case of Cyprus. *International Review of Education* 47 (3–4), 253–265.

Packer, M. and Goicoechea, J. (2000) Sociocultural and constructivist theories of learning: Ontology, not just epistemology. *Educational Psychologist* 35, 227–241.

Paliokosta, P. (2021) Facebook post, 7 January.

Papadakis, Y. (2005) *Echoes from the Dead Zone: Across the Cyprus Divide.* London: IB Tauris.

Papadakis, Y. (2008) Narrative, memory and history education in divided Cyprus: A comparison of schoolbooks on the 'history of Cyprus'. *History & Memory* 20 (2), 128–148.

Papadopoulos, D. and Tsianos, V. (2013) After citizenship: Autonomy of migration, organisational ontology and mobile commons. *Citizenship Studies* 17 (2), 178–196.

Parkin, D. (1977) Emergent and stabilised multilingualism: Polyethnic peer groups in urban Kenya. In H. Giles (ed.) *Language, Ethnicity and Intergroup Relations* (pp. 185–210). New York: Academic Press.

Parkin, D. (2021) Personal communication, 14 February.

Pennycook, A. (2007) *Global Englishes and Transcultural Flows.* London: Routledge.

Pennycook, A. (2016) Mobile times, mobile terms: The trans-super-poly-metro movement. In N. Coupland (eds) *Sociolinguistics: Theoretical Debates* (pp. 201–216). Cambridge: Cambridge University Press.

Pantazis, C. and Pemberton, S. (2009) From the "old" to the "new" suspect community: Examining the impacts of recent UK counter-terrorist legislation. *British Journal of Criminology* 49, 646–666.

Pérez-Milans, M. (2013) *Urban Schools and English Language Education in Late Modern China.* London: Routledge.

Petrovic, J. and Kuntz, A. (2013) Strategies of reframing language policy in the liberal state: A recursive model. *Journal of Language and Politics* 12 (3), 126–146.

Peutrell, R. and Cooke, M. (2019) Afterword: ESOL, citizenship and teacher professionalism. In M. Cooke and R. Peutrell (eds) *Brokering Britain, Educating Citizens: Exploring ESOL and Citizenship* (pp. 227–234). Bristol: Multilingual Matters.

Platt, L. (2008) *Ethnicity and Family: Relationships within and between Ethnic Groups: An Analysis Using the Labour Force Survey*. London: Equality and Human Rights Commission.

Pratt, M.L. (1987) Linguistic utopias. In N. Fabb, D. Attridge, A. Durant and C. MacCabe (eds) *The Linguistics of Writing* (pp. 48–66). Manchester: Manchester University Press.

Preston, D. (1989) *Sociolinguistics and Second Language Acquisition*. Oxford: Blackwell.

Prevignano, C. and di Luzio, A. (2002) A discussion with John Gumperz. In S. Eerdmans, C. Prevignano and P. Thibault (eds) *Language and Interaction: Discussions with John J. Gumperz* (pp. 7–30). Amsterdam: John Benjamins.

Price, D. (2004) *Threatening Anthropology: McCarthyism and the FBI's Surveillance of Activist Anthropologists*. Durham, NC: Duke University Press.

Pujolar, J. (2007) Bilingualism and the nation-state in the post-national era. In M. Heller (ed.) *Bilingualism: A Social Approach* (pp. 71–95). Basingstoke: Palgrave.

Pütz, O. (2012) From non-places to non-events: The airport security checkpoint. *Journal of Contemporary Ethnography* 41 (2), 154–188.

Pyke, K. and Dang, T. (2003) 'FOB' and 'Whitewashed': Identity and internalised racism among second generation Asian Americans. *Qualitative Sociology* 26 (2), 147–172.

Quist, P. (2008) Sociolinguistic approaches to multiethnolect: Language variety and stylistic practice. *International Journal of Bilingualism* 12, 43–61.

Quist, P. and Jørgensen, N. (2007) Crossing – negotiating social boundaries. In P. Auer and Li Wei (eds) *Handbook of Multilingualism and Multilingual Communication* (pp. 371–389). Berlin: Mouton de Gruyter.

Rabinow, P. and Rose, N. (2003) Introduction: Foucault today. In *The Essential Foucault: Selections from Essential Works of Foucault 1954–(1984)* (pp. vii–xxxv). New York: New Press.

Ramdin, R. (1987) *The Making of the Black Working Class in Britain*. Aldershot: Gower.

Rampton, B. (1983) Some flaws in educational discussion in the English of Asian schoolchildren in Britain. *Journal of Multilingual and Multicultural Development* 4 (1), 15–28.

Rampton, B. (1987) Uses of English in a multilingual British peer group. PhD dissertation, University of London.

Rampton, B. (1988) A non-educational view of ESL in Britain. *Journal of Multilingual and Multicultural Development* 9 (6), 503–529.

Rampton, B. (1995/2018) *Crossing: Language and Ethnicity among Adolescents* (3rd edn). London: Routledge.

Rampton, B. (1997) Second language research in late modernity. *Modern Language Journal* 81 (3), 329–333.

Rampton, B. (1998) Language crossing and the redefinition of reality. In P. Auer (ed.) *Codeswitching in Conversation* (pp. 290–320). London: Routledge.

Rampton, B. (1999) Styling the Other: Introduction. Special issue of *Journal of Sociolinguistics* 3 (4), 421–427.

Rampton, B. (2001a) Language crossing, cross-talk and cross-disciplinarity in sociolinguistics. In N. Coupland, S. Sarangi and C. Candlin (eds) *Sociolinguistics and Social Theory* (pp. 261–297). London: Longman.

Rampton, B. (2001b) Crossing. In A. Duranti (ed.) *Key Terms in Language and Culture* (pp. 49–51). Oxford: Blackwell.

Rampton, B. (2006) *Language in Late Modernity: Interaction in an Urban School*. Cambridge: Cambridge University Press.

Rampton, B. (2007a) Linguistic ethnography, interactional sociolinguistics and the study of identities. *Working Papers in Urban Language and Literacies* No. 43.

Rampton, B. (2007b) Neo-Hymesian linguistic ethnography in the United Kingdom. *Journal of Sociolinguistics* 11 (5), 584–607.

Rampton, B. (2009a) Dell Hymes' visions of enquiry. In J. Blommaert (ed.) *On Hymes.* Special issue of *Text & Talk* 29 (3), 359–369.

Rampton, B. (2009b) Interaction ritual and not just artful performance in crossing and stylization. *Language in Society* 38, 149–176.

Rampton, B. (2011a) A neo-Hymesian trajectory in applied linguistics. *Working Papers in Urban Language and Literacies* No. 78.

Rampton, B. (2011b) Style in a second language. *Working Papers in Urban Language and Literacies* No. 65. See www.academia.edu.

Rampton, B. (2011c) From 'multi-ethnic adolescent heteroglossia' to 'contemporary urban vernaculars'. *Language & Communication* 31, 276–294.

Rampton, B. (2013) Styling in a language learned later in life. *The Modern Language Journal* 97 (2), 360–381.

Rampton, B. (2014) An everyday poetics of class and ethnicity in stylisation and crossing. In M. Fludernik and D. Jacob (eds) *Linguistics and Literary Studies: Interfaces, Encounters, Transfers* (pp. 261–268). Berlin: Mouton de Gruyter. (Also available as *Working Papers in Urban Language and Literacies* No. 59. See academia.edu.)

Rampton, B. (2015a) Superdiversity and social class: An interactional perspective. In C. Stroud and M. Prinsloo (eds) *Language, Literacy and Diversity: Moving Words* (pp. 149–165). London: Routledge.

Rampton, B. (2015b) Contemporary urban vernaculars. In J. Nortier and B.A. Svendsen (eds) *Language, Youth and Identity in the 21st Century* (pp. 24–44). Cambridge: Cambridge University Press.

Rampton, B. (2016) Foucault, Gumperz and governmentality: Interaction, power and subjectivity in the twenty-first century. In N. Coupland (ed.) *Sociolinguistics: Theoretical Debates* (pp. 303–328). Cambridge: Cambridge University Press.

Rampton, B. (2017) Interactional sociolinguistics. *Working Papers in Urban Language and Literacies* No. 205. See academia.edu.

Rampton, B. and Charalambous, C. (2012) Crossing. In M. Martin-Jones, A. Blackledge and A. Creese (eds) *The Routledge Handbook of Multilingualism* (pp. 482–498). London: Routledge. (Earlier draft available as *Working Papers in Urban Language and Literacies No. 58*.)

Rampton, B. and Charalambous, C. (2016) Breaking classroom silences: A view from linguistic ethnography. *Language and Intercultural Communication* 16 (1), 4–21. (Earlier draft available as *Working Papers in Urban Language and Literacies* No. 116.)

Rampton, B. and Cooke, M. (2021). Collaboration between universities and third sector organisations in language education. *Working Papers in Urban Language and Literacies* No. 281. See academia.edu.

Rampton, B. and Eley, L. (2018) Goffman and the everyday interactional grounding of surveillance. *Working Papers in Urban Language and Literacies* No. 246. See academia.edu.

Rampton, B. and Harris, R. (2010) Change in urban classroom culture and interaction. In K. Littleton and C. Howe (eds) *Educational Dialogues: Understanding and Promoting Productive Interaction* (pp. 240–264). London: Routledge.

Rampton, B., Harris, R. and Leung, C. (2001) Education in England and speakers of languages other than English. *Working Papers in Urban Language and Literacies* No. 18.

Rampton, B., Harris, R. and Leung, C. (2008) Education and languages other than English in the British Isles. In D. Britain (ed.) *Language in the British Isles* (revised 2nd edn) (pp. 417–435). Cambridge: Cambridge University Press. (Earlier version available as *Working Papers in Urban Language and Literacies* No. 18 (2001).)

Rampton, B., Charalambous, C. and Charalambous, P. (2015a) End-of-project report: Crossing languages and borders – intercultural language education in a conflict-troubled context. *Working Papers in Urban Language and Literacies* No. 178. See academia.edu.

Rampton, B., Arnaut, K., Blommaert, J. and Spotti, M. (2015b) Superdiversity and sociolinguistics. *Working Papers in Urban Language and Literacies* No. 152. See www.academia.edu.

Rampton, B., Maybin, J. and Roberts, C. (2015c) Theory and method in linguistic ethnography. In J. Snell, S. Shaw and F. Copland (eds) *Linguistic Ethnography: Interdisciplinary Explorations* (pp. 14–50). Basingstoke: Palgrave Macmillan. (Version also available as *Working Papers in Urban Language and Literacies* No. 125.)

Rampton, B., Cooke, M. and Holmes, S. (2018a) Promoting linguistic citizenship: Issue, problems and possibilities. *Working Papers in Urban Language and Literacies* No. 233. See academia.edu.

Rampton, B., Cooke, M. and Holmes, S. (2018b) Linguistic citizenship and the questions of transformation and marginality. MS.

Rampton, B., Cooke, M. and Holmes, S. (2020) Education, England and users of languages other than English. *Working Papers in Urban Language & Literacies* No. 275. See academia.edu.

Rehner, K., Mougeon, R. and Nadasdi, R. (2003) The learning of sociolinguistic variation by advanced FSL learners. *Studies in Second Language Acquisition* 25, 127–156.

Reyes, A. and Lo, A. (eds) (2009) *Beyond Yellow English: Towards a Linguistic Anthropology of Asian Pacific America.* Oxford: Oxford University Press.

Richmond, O. and Tellidis, I. (2012) The complex relationship between peacebuilding and terrorism approaches: Towards post-terrorism and a post-liberal peace? *Terrorism and Political Violence* 24, 120–143.

Roberts, C. (2016) Translating global experience into institutional models of competency: Linguistic inequalities in the job interview. In K. Arnaut, J. Blommaert, B. Rampton and M. Spotti (eds) *Language and Superdiversity* (pp. 237–260). London: Routledge.

Roberts, C. and Sarangi, S. (1999) Hybridity in gatekeeping discourse: Issues of practical relevance for the researcher. In S. Sarangi and C. Roberts (eds) *Talk, Work and Institutional Order* (pp. 473–503). Berlin: Mouton.

Roberts, C. and Sarangi, S. (2003) Uptake of discourse research in interprofessional settings: Reporting from medical consultancy. *Applied Linguistics* 24 (3), 338–359.

Roberts, C., Davies, E. and Jupp, T. (1992) *Language and Discrimination.* London: Longman.

Roberts, C., Sarangi, S., Southgate, L., Wakeford, R. and Vass, W. (2000) Oral examinations – equal opportunities, ethnicity and fairness in the MRCGP. *British Medical Journal* 320, 370–374.

Romaine, S. (1984) *The Language of Children and Adolescents.* Oxford: Blackwell.

Rose, N. (1999) *The Power of Freedom.* Cambridge: Cambridge University Press.

Rosen, H. and Burgess, T. (1980) *The Languages and Dialects of London Schoolchildren.* London: Ward Lock.

Roth-Gordon, J. (2009) Conversational sampling, race trafficking and the invocation of the *Gueto* in Brazilian Hip Hop. In S. Alim, A. Ibrahim and A. Pennycook (eds) *Global Linguistic Flows: Hip Hop Cultures, Youth Identities and the Politics of Language* (pp. 63–78). London: Routledge.

Ryave, A. and Schenkein, J. (1974) Notes on the art of walking. In R. Turner (ed.) *Ethnomethodology* (pp. 265–274). Harmondsworth: Penguin.

Santos, B. de S. (2012) Public sphere and epistemologies of the South. *Africa Development* 37 (1), 43–67.

Sapir, E. (1929/1949) The status of linguistics as a science. In D. Mandelbaum (ed.) *Edward Sapir: Selected Writings in Language, Culture and Personality* (pp. 160–166). Berkeley, CA: University of California Press.

Sarangi, S. (2011) Editorial: Contextualising John Gumperz. In P. Auer and C. Roberts (eds) Special issue of *Text & Talk* 31 (4), 375–380.

Sarkar, M. (2009) 'Still reppin por mi gente': The transformative power of language mixing in Quebec Hip Hop. In S. Alim, A. Ibrahim and A. Pennycook (eds) *Global Linguistic Flows: Hip Hop Cultures, Youth Identities and the Politics of Language* (pp. 139–158). London: Routledge.

Sarroub, L. (2005) *All American Yemeni Girls: Being Muslim in a Public School.* Philadelphia, PA: University of Pennsylvania Press.

Savage, M. (2007) The coming crisis of empirical sociology. *Sociology* 41 (5), 885–899.

Savva, H. (1990) The rights of bilingual children. In R. Carter (ed.) *Knowledge about Language* (pp. 248–268). London: Hodder and Stoughton.

Schegloff, E. (1999) Naivete vs sophistication or discipline vs self-indulgence: A rejoinder to Billig. *Discourse & Society* 10, 577–582.

Schegloff, E. (2002) Beginnings in the telephone. In J. Katz and M. Aakhus (eds) *Perpetual Contact* (pp. 284–300). Cambridge: Cambridge University Press.

Schieffelin, B., Woolard, K. and Kroskrity, P. (1998) *Language Ideologies.* Oxford: Oxford University Press.

Schiffrin, D. (1994) *Approaches to Discourse.* Oxford: Blackwell.

Schilling-Estes, N. (1998) Investigating 'self-conscious' speech: The performance register in Okracoke English. *Language in Society* 27, 53–84.

Schmidt, R. (1990) The role of consciousness in second language learning. *Applied Linguistics* 11, 129–158.

Scollon, R. (1998) *Mediated Discourse as Social Interaction: A Study of News Discourse.* London: Longman.

Scollon, R. and Scollon, S. (2003) *Discourses in Place.* London: Routledge.

Scollon, R. and Scollon, S. (2004) *Nexus Analysis: Discourse and the Emerging Internet.* London: Routledge.

Scollon, R and Scollon, S. (2007) Nexus analysis: Refocusing ethnography on action. *Journal of Sociolinguistics* 11 (5), 608–625.

Scott, J. (1998) *Seeing Like a State.* New Haven, CT: Yale University Press.

Seargeant, P. (2021) Jan Blommaert in Bloomsbury: Recollections of Jan's years in London in the mid-noughties. *Diggit Magazine*, 5 January. See www.diggitmagazine.com.

Sebba, M. (1993) *London Jamaican.* London: Longman.

Sebba, M. (2007) Identity and language construction in an online community: The case of 'Ali G'. In P. Auer (ed.) *Style and Social Identities: Alternative Approaches to Linguistic Heterogeneity* (pp. 361–392). Berlin: Mouton de Gruyter.

Sercu, L. (2005) *Foreign Language Teachers and Intercultural Competence: An International Investigation.* Clevedon: Multilingual Matters.

Shackle, C. (1972) *Teach Yourself Punjabi*. London: English Universities Press.

Shankar, S. (2008) *Desiland: Teen Culture, Class, and Success in Silicon Valley*. Durham, NC: Duke University Press.

Sharma, D. (2005) Dialect stabilization and speaker awareness in nonnative varieties of English. *Journal of Sociolinguistics* 9, 194–224.

Sharma, D. (2011) Style repertoire and social change in British Asian English. *Journal of Sociolinguistics* 15 (4), 1–29.

Sharma, D. and Rampton, B. (2015) Lectal focusing in interaction: A new methodology for the study of style variation. *Journal of English Linguistics* 43 (1), 3–35. (Also available as *Working Papers in Urban Language and Literacies* No. 79. See www.academia.edu.)

Sharma, D. and Sankaran, L. (2011) Cognitive and social forces in dialect shift: Gradual change in London Asian Speech. *Language Variation and Change* 23 (3), 399–428.

Shaw, G.B. (1916) Preface to Pygmalion. See http://www.bartleby.com/138/0.html.

Sidnell, J. and Stivers, T. (eds) (2013) *The Handbook of Conversation Analysis*. Oxford: Wiley Blackwell.

Silverman, D. (1998) *Harvey Sacks: Social Science and Conversation Analysis*. Oxford: Polity Press.

Silverstein, M. (1976) Shifters, linguistics categories, and cultural description. In K. Basso and H. Selby (eds) *Meaning in Anthropology* (pp. 11–55). Albuquerque, NM: University of New Mexico Press.

Silverstein, M. (1985) Language and the culture of gender. In E. Mertz and R. Parmentier (eds) *Semiotic Mediation* (pp. 219–259). New York: Academic Press.

Silverstein, M. and Urban, G. (eds) (1996) *Natural Histories of Discourse*. Cambridge: Cambridge University Press.

Simon, B. (2005) The return of panopticism: Supervision, subjection and new surveillance. *Surveillance & Society* 3 (1), 1–20.

Smith, G. (2007) Exploring relations between watchers and watched in control(led) systems: Strategies and tactics. *Surveillance & Society* 4 (4), 280–313.

Snell, J. (2010) From sociolinguistic variation to socially strategic stylization. *Journal of Sociolinguistics* 14, 630–656.

Snell, J., Shaw, S. and Copland, F. (eds) (2015) *Linguistic Ethnography: Interdisciplinary Explorations*. Basingstoke: Palgrave Macmillan.

Spotti, M. (2016) Sociolinguistic shibboleths at the institutional gate: Language, origin and the construction of asylum seekers' identities. In K. Arnaut, J. Blommaert, B. Rampton and M. Spotti (eds) *Language and Superdiversity* (pp. 261–278). London: Routledge.

Stallybrass, P. and White, A. (1996) *The Politics and Poetics of Transgression*. London: Methuen.

Staples, W. (2014) *Everyday Surveillance. Vigilance and Visibility in Postmodern Life* (2nd edn). Plymouth: Rowman & Littleford.

Steer, P. (2014) Why we can't go on like this – language qualifications in the UK. See http://www.cambridgeassessment.org.uk/insights/why-we-cant-go-on-like-this-language-qualifications-in-the-uk/.

Stivers, T. and Sidnell, J. (2013) Introduction. In J. Sidnell and T. Stivers (eds) *The Handbook of Conversation Analysis* (pp. 1–8). Oxford: Wiley Blackwell.

Strathern, M. (ed.) (2000) *Audit Cultures*. London: Routledge.

Street, B. (1984) *Literacy in Theory and Practice*. Cambridge: Cambridge University Press.

Strevens, P. (1977) On defining applied linguistics. In *New Orientations in the Teaching of English* (pp. 37–40). Oxford: Oxford University Press.

Stroud, C. (1999) Portuguese as ideology and politics in Mozambique: Semiotic (re)constructions of a postcolony. In J. Blommaert (ed.) *Language Ideological Debates* (pp. 343–380). Berlin: Mouton de Gruyter.

Stroud, C. (2001) African mother-tongue programmes and the politics of language: Linguistic citizenship versus linguistic human rights. *Journal of Multilingual and Multicultural Development* 22 (4), 339–355.

Stroud, C. (2004) Rinkeby Swedish and semilingualism in language ideological debates: A Bourdieuean perspective. *Journal of Sociolinguistics* 8 (2), 196–214.

Stroud, C. (2008) Bilingualism: Colonialism and post-colonialism. In M. Heller (ed.) *Bilingualism: A Social Approach* (pp. 25–49). Basingstoke: Palgrave.

Stroud, C. (2010) Towards a post-liberal theory of citizenship. In J. Petrovic (ed.) *International Perspectives on Bilingual Education: Policy, Practice and Controversy* (pp. 191–218). New York: Information Age Publishing.

Stroud, C. (2018) Linguistic citizenship. In L. Lim, C. Stroud and L. Wee (eds) *The Multilingual Citizen: Towards a Politics of Language for Agency and Change* (pp. 17–39). Bristol: Multilingual Matters.

Stroud, C. and Heugh, K. (2004) Linguistic human rights and linguistic citizenship. In D. Patrick and J. Freeland (eds) *Language Rights and Language Survival* (pp. 191–218). Manchester: St Jerome.

Stroud, S. and Jegels, D. (2014) Semiotic landscapes and mobile narrations of place: Performing the local. *International Journal of the Sociology of Language* 228, 179–200.

Stubbs, M. (1986) *Educational Linguistics*. Oxford: Blackwell.

Svendsen, B.A. and Quist, P. (2010) Introduction. In P. Quist and B.A. Svendsen (eds) *Multilingual Urban Scandinavia: New Linguistic Practices* (pp. xiii–xxiii). Bristol: Multilingual Matters.

Sweetland, J. (2002) Unexpectedly authentic use of an ethnically-marked dialect. *Journal of Sociolinguistics* 6 (4), 514–537.

Swinglehurst, D. (2015) How linguistic ethnography may enhance our understanding of electronic patient records in health care settings. In J. Snell, S. Shaw and F. Copland (eds) *Linguistic Ethnography: Interdisciplinary Explorations* (pp. 90–109). Basingstoke: Palgrave Macmillan.

Swinglehurst, D., Roberts, C. and Greenhalgh, T. (2011) Opening up the 'black box' of the electronic patient record: A linguistic ethnographic study in general practice. *Communication & Medicine* 8 (1), 3–16.

Talmy, S. (2009) Forever FOB? Resisting and reproducing the other in high school ESL. In A. Reyes and A. Lo (eds) *Beyond Yellow English: Towards a Linguistic Anthropology of Asian Pacific America* (pp. 347–365). Oxford: Oxford University Press.

Tarone, E. (1983) On the variability of interlanguage systems. *Applied Linguistics* 4, 142–163.

Tarone, E. (2000) Frequency effects, noticing and creativity. *Studies in Second Language Acquisition* 24, 287–296.

ten Have, P. (1999) *Doing Conversation Analysis*. London: Sage.

Todorov, T. (1988) Knowledge in social anthropology. *Anthropology Today* 4 (2), 2–5.

Tremlett, A. (2007) Representations of the Roma: Public discourse and local practices. PhD dissertation, King's College London.

Turner, B. (2017) Understanding the repertoire of an L2 English speaker through the total linguistic fact. MA dissertation, King's College London.
Tusting, K. (2010) Eruptions of interruptions: Managing tensions between writing and other tasks in a textualised childcare workplace. In D. Barton and U. Papen (eds) *The Anthropology of Writing: Understanding Textually Mediated Worlds* (pp. 67–89). London: Continuum.
Tusting, K. (2020a) General introduction. In *The Routledge Handbook of Linguistic Ethnography* (pp. 1–10). London: Routledge.
Tusting, K. (ed.) (2020b) *The Routledge Handbook of Linguistic Ethnography*. London: Routledge.
UCU (2015) *The Prevent Duty: A Guide for Branches and Managers*. London: University and College Union.
Uhlmann, A. (2011) Policy implications of Arabic instruction in Israeli Jewish schools. *Human Organization* 70 (1), 97–105.
Urla, J. (1995) Outlaw language. *Pragmatics* 5 (2), 245–261.
Van der Aa, J.-L. (2021) Jan Blommaert's struggle. *Diggit Magazine*, 11 January. See www.diggitmagazine.com.
Van der Aa, J. and Blommaert, J. (2011) Ethnographic monitoring: Hymes' unfinished business in educational research. *Anthropology & Education* 42 (4), 319–334. (Version also available as *Working Papers in Urban Language and Literacies* No. 69.)
Van der Aa, J.-L. and Blommaert, J. (2015) Ethnographic monitoring and the study of complexity. *Working Papers in Urban Language & Literacies* No. 150. At www.academia.edu/.
van Dijck, J. (2013a) *The Culture of Connectivity*. Oxford: Oxford University Press.
van Dijck, J. (2013b) 'You have one identity': Performing the self on Facebook and LinkedIn. *Media, Culture & Society* 35 (2), 199–215.
van Hofwegen, J. and Wolfram, W. (2010) Coming of age in African American English: A longitudinal study. *Journal of Sociolinguistics* 14 (4), 427–455.
van Hout, T. (2021) Farewell, Jan Blommaert. *Diggit Magazine*, 12 January. See www.diggitmagazine.com.
van Lier, L. (2000) From input to affordance: Social-interactive learning from an ecological perspective. In J. Lantolf (ed.) *Sociocultural Theory and Second Language Learning* (pp. 245–260). Oxford: Oxford University Press.
van Schijndel, M. (2020) Jan Blommaert: You have the feeling that you have no grip on your body. That is the definition of cancer. *Univers*, 19 November.
Varenne, H. and McDermott, R. (1998) *Successful Failure*. Boulder, CO: Westview Press.
Varis, P. (2021) Personal communication, 28 February.
Velghe, F. (2021) Eulogy at Jan Blommaert's Funeral, 16 January.
Verdoolaege, A. (2015) Reconciliation discourse. In *The International Encyclopedia of Language and Social Interaction*. John Wiley.
Verdoolaege, A. (2021) Contribution to Memorial Event for Jan Blommaert, 6 February.
Verschueren, J. (1999) *Understanding Pragmatics*. London: Arnold.
Vertovec, S. (2007) Super-diversity and its implications. *Ethnic and Racial Studies* 30 (6), 1024–1054.
vom Lehn, D., Heath, C. and Hindmarsh, J. (2001) Exhibiting interaction: Conduct and collaboration in museums and galleries. *Symbolic Interaction* 24 (2), 189–216.
Vygotsky, L. (1978) *Mind in Society*. Cambridge, MA: Harvard University Press.
Walby, K. (2005) Institutional ethnography and surveillance studies: An outline for inquiry. *Surveillance & Society* 3, 158–172.

Walvin, J. (1987) Black caricature: The roots of racialism. In C. Husband (ed.) *'Race' in Britain: Continuity and Change* (2nd edn) (pp. 59–72). London: Hutchinson.
Weber, J.-J. and Horner, K. (2012) *Multilingualism: A Social Approach*. London: Routledge.
Wellman, B. (2001) Physical place and cyberspace: The rise of personalised networking. *International Journal of Urban and Regional Research* 25 (2), 227–252.
Wells, J. (1982) *Accents of English*. Cambridge: Cambridge University Press.
Westlake, E.J. (2008) Friend me if you Facebook: Generation Y and performative surveillance. *TDR/The Drama Review* 52 (4), 21–40.
Wetherell, M. (1998) Positioning and interpretative repertoires: Conversation analysis and post-structuralism in dialogue. *Discourse & Society* 9, 431–456.
Widdowson, H. (1984) *Explorations in Applied Linguistics* 2. Oxford: Oxford University Press.
Williams, R. (1977) *Marxism and Literature*. Oxford: Oxford University Press.
Willis, P. (1977) *Learning to Labour*. Farnborough: Saxon House.
Willis, P. and Trondman, M. (2000) Manifesto for *Ethnography*. *Ethnography* 1, 5–16.
Woolard, K. (2008) Why *dat* now?: Linguistic-anthropological contributions to the explanation of sociolinguistic icons and change. *Journal of Sociolinguistics* 12, 432– 452.
Woolard, K., Schieffelin, B. and Kroskrity, P. (1998) *Language Ideologies*. Oxford: Oxford University Press.
Young, R. (2009) *Discursive Practice in Language Learning and Teaching*. Oxford: Wiley-Blackwell.
Yuval-Davies, N., Wemyss, G. and Cassidy, K. (2019) *Bordering*. Cambridge: Polity Press.
Zakharia, Z. (2020) Language and (in)securitisation: Observations from educational research and practice in conflict-affected contexts. *Journal of Sociolinguistics* 24, 103–110.
Zembylas, M., Charalambous, C. and Charalambous, P. (2016) *Peace Education in a Conflict-Affected Society: An Ethnographic Journey*. Cambridge: Cambridge University Press.
Zimmerman, D. (1998) Identity, context, interaction. In C. Antaki and S. Widdicombe (eds) *Identities in Talk* (pp. 87–106). London: Sage.

Author Index

Note: The page references with letter n denotes the note numbers.

Subject Index